THE EXISTENCE

OF

EVIL SPIRITS

PROVED;

AND THEIR AGENCY, PARTICULARLY IN RELATION TO THE HUMAN RACE,

EXPLAINED AND ILLUSTRATED.

BY

WALTER SCOTT,

PRESIDENT AND THEOLOGICAL TUTOR OF AIREDALE COLLEGE, BRADFORD, YORKSHIRE.

"Ἵνα μὴ πλεονεκτηθῶμεν ὑπὸ τοῦ Σατανᾶ· οὐ γὰρ αὐτοῦ τὰ νοήματα ἀγνοοῦμεν.—2 Cor. ii. 11.

PREFACE.

THE difficulties connected with the subject of the following Lectures are so numerous and great, that some may be disposed to accuse the author of presumption for attempting to grapple with them, and for acting as if he thought that he could advance anything worthy of public attention on topics which are confessedly abstruse in themselves, and which have already been discussed by men of the greatest ability and learning. His answer to this charge, if it should be urged by any, is, that the subject was mentioned to him as suitable for a Congregational Lecture, it arrested his attention, it was one on which he had frequently thought, and also read, as far as he had enjoyed the opportunity: it appeared to him very important, and intimately connected with the essential doctrines of the Gospel. Though not the key-stone in the beautiful, magnificent arch of Christianity, it occupies, in his estimation, a position of so much importance, that if it were removed, others might be loosened or displaced, and thus the symmetry and strength of the whole would be diminished, even if its safety were not endangered. For the correctness of this assertion an appeal may, with propriety, be made to facts. Very generally it will be found that those who disbelieve the existence of fallen, evil spirits, deny also some of the peculiar doctrines of revelation, and, not unfrequently, almost all of them. Add to this, that Unitarians seem to think that the belief of Satanic influence is a peculiarly vulnerable point in what is called the orthodox faith, and hence it is one which they are constantly assailing; and, therefore, one which those by whom it is believed and deemed of importance, ought to defend. I do not hesitate to say, that there are few truths more clearly stated than this, in the whole volume of inspiration; and that by the same process by which it is explained away, the resurrection of the dead, or the existence of a future state of rewards and punishment, might be disproved.

Since the following Lectures were delivered, and indeed after a great part of them was printed, my attention was directed to a pamphlet, entitled "The Devil," being twelve lectures delivered in London, (I suppose, as the address to the reader is dated, Sept. 1, 1842, in the course of last year,) as one of the most plausible and dangerous publications that has ever issued from the press on the subject to which it relates. But notwithstanding its high pretensions, its flippant style, and confident assertions, it contains nothing new, and nothing but what is examined in the following work. The most extraordinary lecture is the last, in which the author attempts to prove "The Atheism of believing in a being called the Devil." The following is the sum of his arguments—" Creation and Revelation both teach that God is a God of order—God's laws, whether in the world of creation or the world of revelation, are for the production of good—The devil—supposing him to exist—must, in acting, act *through and by means of the laws of God;* and as he acts for the production of evil, he must actually, so to do, make God's laws, appointed by him for good, turn to a quite different purpose, namely, the production of evil, which is an absurdity, which is the first step to the dreadful groundwork of Atheism!" Now, how any man of sense and learning can write in such a strain as the above, or put forth such statements for arguments, is to me a complete mystery. Who does not see, at a single glance, that all that he has advanced would prove—if it could prove anything—that there are no wicked men any more than devils, nay, that there can be no such thing as either sin or misery,—moral or natural evil, in the universe? for both these are caused by perverting the order, and transgressing the laws which God has established; or, as the author of the lectures expresses it, "acting through and by means of the laws which the Creator has enacted." Do we not see men transgressing them every day, and thus involving themselves and others in confusion, and crimes, and misery? What right, then, has any one to maintain that they may not be violated by other creatures, and with similar results? He goes on to assert, that, to allow that the devil can violate the laws which God has established, is representing him as able to work miracles; and as ascribing to him "omnipotence, omniscience, and omnipresence." And then he concludes with a flourish of triumph and self-complacency, and in language which ought to lead him to examine whether, to borrow his own elegant phraseology, he has "subdued the devil in himself," especially in his character of a false accuser—"THESE DEVIL-HOLDERS ARE PRACTICAL ATHEISTS."

It really requires no small degree of patience to be able to read with calmness such false charges and flimsy reasoning as the above, especially when, though advanced for the ten thousandth time, they are paraded as if they were quite original. The writer, however, either must know, or ought to know, that those whose sentiments he caricatures, not only do not ascribe either omniscience, or omnipotence, or or omnipresence, to the devil, but that they have shown that their sentiments do not involve this ascription; nay, that according to their representations, the powers and capacities of Satan must necessarily be limited, and he may be resisted and overcome.

Again, in order to show what he calls "the absurdity of the belief in a being called the devil," and that "there is no necessity for a devil," he quotes Gal. v. 17—20, "The flesh lusteth against the Spirit," &c., "The works of the flesh are manifest, which are, adultery," &c.; and then adds, "Now, may it not be asked with confidence, if the flesh is *capable to produce* all these, what is left for the devil to do?" "Let any one detail a vice or suggestion of Satan which is not a suggestion of the flesh, and then will be time for calling in the aid of a being called the devil." Now, a single reference to undeniable facts, to mention nothing else, will annihilate all this flimsy reasoning in a moment. Notwithstanding all the tendencies and suggestions of the flesh, do not men frequently tempt one another? Are they not thus rendered worse than they would otherwise be? Nay, do not many of them commit crimes, which, but for these external temptations, they would never have perpetrated? Is there no need for the exhortation, "My son, if *sinners entice* thee, consent thou not?" May not Satan, then, also tempt men to crimes, into which, but for him, they would never have fallen? After all that "the flesh is capable of producing," human tempters find enough to do; and so may infernal ones. These extracts are, if I am not mistaken, a fair specimen of the book, and I can scarcely forbear adding, of the ease with which all its reasonings and statements may be exposed.

Perhaps it may be expected that some reasons should be assigned why, when there were eight Lectures delivered, only seven are published. This was done, in compliance with the request of the Committee of the Congregational Library, in order to prevent the volume from being too large. The first lecture was, "On the Origin of Moral Evil." It was merely introductory, and not necessarily connected with the proper subject of the book, and therefore could, without any impropriety, be omitted. The object was to show, that none of the theories which have been advanced, on this mysterious question, are at all satisfactory, and that Dr. Williams's, notwithstanding his piety, learning, and ability, involves a contradiction. Possibly the lecture which has been omitted may, in connexion with a few essays on other subjects, be published at some future time.

May the volume, notwithstanding all its imperfections, contribute, by the blessing of God, something towards the attainment of the laudable objects for the promotion of which the Congregational Lecture was established!

Airedale College,
April 27th, 1843.

PREFACE TO THE THIRD EDITION.

WITH the exception of a few slight corrections, and the addition of two or three foot-notes, this edition is a reprint of the second. The author has not seen any reason to alter, or, in anything of importance, even to modify his views of the subject which are discussed in these Lectures. His earnest prayer is, that God, in the plenitude of his condescension and power, may deign to render this volume, whatever may be its imperfections, subservient to counteracting the influence of the father of lies, and to the promotion of that truth by which Jesus Christ destroys the works of the devil.

W. S.

Airedale College,
    April 12*th,* 1853.

CONTENTS.

LECTURE I.

THE EXISTENCE OF EVIL SPIRITS.

PAGE

IMPORTANCE of testimony—The momentous nature of faith—The attention which it deserves—Simplicity of childhood—Credulity and incredulity contrasted—Which is the more irrational?—Aristotle's assertion that "incredulity is the foundation of all wisdom"—The existence of evil spirits has been denied—Strenuous attempts have been made to disprove it—The importance of the subject—Influence of the Bible on the belief respecting evil spirits—If they do not exist, it has misled most of those who have taken it for their guide—The demons of the heathen—Jesus Christ sanctioned the belief of the existence of evil spirits — Evidence from reason, analogy, and facts—Man the lowest order of rational creatures—There may be many much higher—Spirits do not need material vehicles—Matter may be moulded, probably, into more subtile spiritual forms than that in which it exists in him—There may, therefore, be rational and accountable beings far superior to him—Must be defectible—May have fallen—Sin would necessarily deprave them—They would become tempters of others if permitted—The rich man and his brethren—God may permit them to tempt men—Appeal to facts—Character of the demons of the heathen—An important fact, stated with regard to those who deny the existence of evil spirits—The extensive and long-continued prevalence of a belief in the existence of evil spirits under the Christian dispensation—The conduct of Jesus Christ with respect to this belief—Scriptural evidence examined—2 Pet. ii. 4—Erroneous translation, and application of it refuted—John viii. 44 considered—Applied to Satan—Absurd Unitarian exposition of it refuted—Import of the word $\alpha\rho\chi\eta$, "beginning"—1 John iii. 8 illustrated—Matt. xxv. 41—46 explained—$\sigma\upsilon\nu\tau\epsilon\lambda\epsilon\iota\alpha\ \tau o\upsilon\ \alpha\iota\omega\nu o\varsigma$—Satan and

his angels rational, accountable beings—Mark iv. 15, Matt. xiii. 39
—The interpretation of those who deny the existence of Satan exposed—Acts x. 28, Heb. ii. 14, James iv. 5, 1 Pet. v. 8, 1 John
ii. 8—Ridiculous Unitarian exposition—Jude 9—Meaning and application of the word Satan—Strange and arbitrary application of it by Socinians—Beelzebub—Matt. xii. 26, Luke xxii. 21, Rev. xii. 3, 9, and 20, ii. 10, considered—James ii. 19—The Mosaic account of the Fall considered—Literal, not figurative—Saul and his evil spirit from God, 1 Samuel xvi. 14—Satan tempting David to number Israel—Ahab's prophets and their lying spirit, 1 Kings xxii. 21, Job i. 2, &c.—A history, not an allegory—Psalm cix.—Reasons for dwelling so long on this part of the subject. 1

LECTURE II.

THE CHARACTER, STATE, AND POWERS OF EVIL SPIRITS.

General view of the information from Scripture—Fallen spirits originally holy—Have been rendered what they are by their departure from God—This the doctrine of Scripture, 2 Pet. ii. 4, Jude 6—The elect angels—Man the lowest order of rational beings—Proof of this—There must be many above him Reason and analogy prove this—These reasonings confirmed by Scripture—Exod. xxxiii. 2, 2 Sam. xxiv., Dan. iii. 38, Psalm xxxiv. 7, Gen. xix., Matt. xxviii., Acts v. 19, and xii. 10, Luke ii. 9, Rev. xvi. 1, and xxii. 8, Psalm ciii., 2 Thess. i. 7, Matt. xiii. 39—Heb. i. 7 critically examined—The figurative representation of angels, Isa. vi., Ezek. i. 10—Rev. passim—Fallen angels originally equal to holy angels—Different ranks, or orders, amongst them—They do not live in harmony—How Satan may rule amongst them—Jonathan Edwards's opinion, Appendix D.—Their powers and honours when in heaven—The dreadful influence of sin on those who commit it—A practical view of the origin of sin—The first sin of Satan—1 Tim. iii. 6 considered—Scriptural account of the fall of angels, and its consequences—Satan the ring-leader in their revolt—Their punishment not yet complete—Condition hopeless—Character awfully depraved—Harmony of the deductions of reason and the statements of Scripture respecting fallen angels—They are still accountable for their conduct—Epithets of Satan in Scripture—Their capacities and powers are still great—They can operate on matter—Dr. Watts's theory examined and rejected—Proof from Scripture that they can operate on matter—The limited power of our souls when united to our bodies no proof to the contrary—An objection answered—The rapidity of their motion—They are not omnipresent—Milton—Dwight—They have relation to place—Their knowledge must be extensive—It may increase—Sin does not weaken the intellectual powers—The agency of Satan in the temptations of Job—Satan inflicted his calamities—No miracle performed in inflicting them—Conclusion 80

LECTURE III.

THE AGENCY OF EVIL SPIRITS.

Difficulties of this part of the subject—Proofs that evil spirits have intercourse with this world—The different ways in which Satan has been supposed to carry on his intercourse with men—Witchcraft and sorcery—King James on sorcery—Encycl. Britannica—The possibility of witchcraft in the abstract—Many absurdities and impossibilities in the vulgar stories respecting it—The importance of the subject—Reason for discussing it—Baxter's world of spirits—Plan of the lecture—I. Belief in witchcraft not countenanced by Scripture—Some have studied the arts of magic and witchcraft—Some have pretended, and others believed, that they themselves were adepts in them—Witchcraft amongst the Jews was connected with idolatry—It therefore deserved the punishment of death—Deut. xviii. 10 considered—Ventriloquism—Witchcraft amongst the Jews was treason against Jehovah—This witchcraft quite different in its nature from that of modern times—Probable that the witches and necromancers, &c., of Scripture were all impostors—The magicians of Egypt—Different opinions respecting them—Dr. A. Clarke—Thomas Scott—That they were impostors proved from the terms by which they were designated—Farmer's opinion—The narration of Moses considered—The Egyptians famous for their skill in legerdemain—Some of the miracles examined in detail—Changing the rods into serpents—This feat exceeded by jugglers in the present day—Why Moses' rod was caused to swallow the rods of the magicians—Turning the water into blood—The production of frogs—Reasons why the magicians could not imitate the next miracle—The nature of the miracles in which the magicians succeeded, and in which they failed—Balaam—Various opinions respecting him—Probably not altogether an impostor—No evidence that he had any intercourse with evil spirits—The witch of Endor —Different theories respecting her—Proofs that she was an impostor—Striking instance of the power of imagination—How she might gain all the knowledge which she possessed—Saul did not see Samuel—God did not work a miracle and raise Samuel from the dead—Proof of this—An objection answered—Why the sacred writer uses the term Samuel—The woman did not see an apparition —Conclusion 126

LECTURE IV.

THE AGENCY OF EVIL SPIRITS.

THE NATURE AND MANNER OF THEIR INTERCOURSE WITH THIS WORLD; WITCHCRAFT, DIVINATION, ETC., CONTINUED.

II. Absurdities of the records of witchcraft—The witches of Essex and Suffolk in 1645-6—John Goodwin's children and the witch Glover—The feats of Elizabeth Horner—The circumstances of supposed witches—Poor old deformed persons—Some respectable persons accused—Witchcraft not the real cause of the accusation—The confessions of supposed witches investigated—Were obtained by torture—No credit due to them—How obtained in England—By Hopkins the witch-finder general—III. Many of the most plausible stories of witchcraft proved to be falsehoods—The infamous Edmund Robinson—How detected—The trick of vomiting crooked pins detected—Hopkins detected and exposed—IV. The influence of knowledge, philosophy, and religion, on witchcraft—Spirited conduct of a gentleman of New England—Its effect on the proceedings against witchcraft—The principle applied to ghosts and apparitions—What would even now be the effect of punishing supposed and accused witches—The Sibylline oracles—Different opinions respecting them—Import of the name Sibyl—The number of the Sibyls—The time in which they lived uncertain—An abstract of their history—The fate of the Sibylline books—Prideaux's opinion respecting them rejected—Proofs that they are forgeries—1. Their style and spirit—2. Never noticed in the Scriptures—3. The nature and manner of their supposed inspiration—4. The character of the principal Sibyl—5. They were all females—6. The definiteness of the Sibylline oracles an argument against them—Their language, and allusions also—Their non-inspiration, implied in Romans ii. 2—Imprudence and credulity of some of the Fathers—The Sibylline oracles afford internal evidence of forgery—They must be numbered amongst pious frauds—The heathen oracles—Brief account of them (Appendix L)—The Delphian oracle—The object of this lecture—In what sense these oracles were managed by Satan—Abstractedly possible that they might be the residence of evil spirits—Proofs that they were managed by human craft—1st. The Scriptures favour this sentiment—The god of Ekron—Father Baltus—2nd. No real miracle ever wrought in support of a false religion—Real miracles were performed if the oracles were managed by demons—3rd. The way in which the oracles gave their responses, shows that they were managed by the craft of men—The cave and oracle of Trophonius—Manner of consulting the supposed deity—Fontenelle's reflections—All the managers of oracles used similar arts—This made evident when the temples were demolished—The sealed letters that were sent to the oracle, considered—Trajan—The oracle of Mopsus and the governor of Cilicia—Crœsus and the oracles of Delphi—Dr. Platt's marvellous story—The machinery of oracles—Their origin—Many of the heathen themselves did not believe in them—New oracles established—Alexander and Hephæstion—The Christian fathers suspected the oracles of fraud—Clemens Alexandrinus—Eusebius—The silencing of the oracles—The sentiments of the fathers on this subject—Tertullian — Lactantius — Cyprian — Athanasius — Prudentius—Gregory Nazianzen — Gregory Thaumaturgus — Their testimony estimated—Fathers contrasted with Jesus Christ and his apostles—What credit is due to them as witnesses—In many cases very little—Irenæus and the gift of tongues—The sense in which the oracles were silenced by Jesus Christ—Conclusion 172

LECTURE V.

DEMONIACS, ESPECIALLY THOSE OF THE NEW TESTAMENT.

Farmer's definition of the term demoniac not correct—Another definition—Demoniacs not always under the power of the demons—Farmer's theory plausible, but not defensible—The burden of proof here—The language of Scripture respecting them—The foundation of Farmer's system, that the demons of the heathen were the souls of dead men—Fell's sentiments on the subject—Farmer's hypothesis untenable—The first objects of idolatrous worship—How demon worship was introduced—Farmer's concession fatal to his own theory—If the demons of the heathen were "dead men," there might still be real possessions—The Jews had not the same ideas respecting demons that the heathen had—Farmer's views respecting the sphere of action assigned to spirits not correct—Contrary to the statements of the Bible—The sphere of action assigned to spirits may be very extensive—This world may be a part of it—It does not follow that they can work real miracles—Wollaston's opinions on this subject—The statements of Scripture respecting demoniacs rational—A general view of the most remarkable passages relating to demoniacs, Luke x. 17, Mark xvi. 15, 16, Acts xxviii. 3—6, Luke xi. 14—26—Fell on the term Beelzebub—The Pharisees did not by the term Beelzebub mean the god of Ekron, Luke xi. 19—Acts x. 38 considered—Some instances of ejection of demons particularly examined, Matt. viii. 28, &c.—The fierceness of the demoniac—His confession of the Saviour—The question of the Saviour, and the answer of the demons—Dr. Lardner's hypothesis—Farmer's refutation of it—Farmer's hypothesis, that the insanity was miraculously transferred to the herd, confuted—His strange arguments in support of it—No necessity for Jesus Christ to use the customary phraseology on this occasion—The common belief injurious if there are no real possessions—This maintained by Farmer himself—The Saviour did not conceal offensive truths —It does not follow from real possessions, that fallen spirits can work miracles—The Pythoness, Acts xvi. 16—The permission of possessions consistent with the goodness of God—Why they were so numerous in the time of the Saviour—Nothing irrational in confining possessions chiefly, or wholly, to the age of miracles—We have no right to expect that any will be able to eject demons now— Heaton's account of John Evans, a supposed demoniac—A case of epilepsy—Supposed strange effects of mental adjuration, reason to suspect imposition on the part of the boy, and of some connected with him—No means of distinguishing diseases caused by evil spirits (if they do cause them) from ordinary ones 232

LECTURE VI.

AGENCY OF EVIL SPIRITS.

ON TEMPTATION.—THE SAVIOUR'S TEMPTATION IN THE WILDERNESS.

Introductory remarks—The cause of different hypotheses respecting the Saviour's temptation in the desert—Five theories respecting it —Theory of the temptation by suggestion rejected—Le Clerc's theory of a visionary representation caused by Satan—Two insuperable objections against it—Farmer's theory that the temptation was a Divine vision—His first argument, that Christ was in the wilderness already, and could not be driven thither, answered—His second argument, the *Spirit* often signifies the gifts and influence of the Spirit, answered—The import of the terms employed—It does not support Farmer's theory—Nor does the language employed by Ezekiel and John—The supposed advantages of Farmer's system considered—Satan did not appear in what may be called his own form to the Saviour—No difficulty in conceiving *why* Satan should tempt Christ—Might hope to overcome him—Satan is constantly acting irrationally—Jonathan Edwards' views on this subject— Farmer attaches great importance to the symbolical design of the vision—The symbol not necessary for the Saviour—His scheme will have no beneficial influence on the adversaries of the Gospel— Does not exalt the character of the Saviour—The literal scheme far more instructive and consolatory—Most serious objections to Farmer's system—It represents the Spirit as tempting Christ to sin —The literal translation preferable—Objections to the literal sense answered—Not unsuitable to the policy and sagacity of Satan— Not ill calculated to promote the honour of the Saviour or the benefit of his disciples—Heb. iv. 13 considered—Confirming the literal scheme—Does not ascribe the performance of miracles to Satan—Christ being led into the wilderness, Luke iv. 1—Where, and what was this wilderness—The fasting of the Saviour a remarkable fact—The *time* to be taken literally—The first temptation illustrated—Its nature and strength—The victory of the Redeemer— The second temptation presents the chief difficulty on the literal scheme—How Christ might be conveyed to the top of the temple —Lightfoot's opinion—The design of the second temptation—The lesson taught by it—Objections to the literal scheme—The third temptation illustrated—Its principal difficulty obviated—Lightfoot's opinion—Import and force of the temptation—Lightfoot's explanation—The temptation much more powerful on the literal scheme than on any other—The final defeat of the tempter—The importance and glory of the Saviour's victory 278

LECTURE VII.

THE AGENCY OF EVIL SPIRITS.

THE TEMPTATIONS OF SATAN IN THEIR COMMON OR ORDINARY FORM.

Importance of this part of the subject—Etymology and meaning of the word temptation—Some facts on this subject obvious—1st. That Satan does tempt men—Nothing particularly mysterious in God's permitting him to do so—Gilpin's sentiments on this subject —The statements of the Bible—All systems of idolatry bear the image of Satan—They are all the same in their nature and general features, whatever their form—The corruption of Christianity evidently the work of Satan—The papal idolatry a substitute for heathenism—It concentrates in itself all the deceivableness of unrighteousness—Satan, the patron of the errors which are opposed to the peculiar doctrines of the Gospel—The Gospel ministry the special object of his hatred—Missionaries must expect his most determined opposition—Is there any form of sin to which Satan does not tempt?—Second principle, Satan cannot compel, he can only tempt—When men tempt, they possess some advantages which he does not—Satan's power of spiritual fascination—Gilpin's opinion—Gal. ii. 1 does not prove that Satan possesses this power—Nor 2 Thess. ii. 9—16—Nor Rom. i. 28—The power of spiritual fascination not possessed by Satan—He tempts generally through the instrumentality of his agents—R. Hall's sentiments on this subject—He endeavours to conceal his operations—Avails himself of all advantages by those whom he tempts—And by their circumstances—The vigilance of Satan, 2 Cor. ii. 11, Eph. iv. 26, 28—Blasphemous thoughts suggested by him—Bunyan's experience not singular—Satan can suggest thoughts—How far he can know the thoughts of men—He will act as crafty depraved men do—We have much to fear from evil spirits—Means to be used in order to overcome them—Conclusion—Nature of the subjects to which our attention has been directed 314

APPENDIX.

A. Chrysostom on the rich man and Lazarus 349
B. On the rationality of brutes 349
C. Criticism on Psalm civ. 4 351
D. Of Edwards's opinions respecting Satan before his fall, and the cause of his fall 354
E. Ditto 355
F. Remarkable instances of the power of imagination. 355
G. Simon Magus and the Philippian damsel 357
H. Witchcraft in New England 358
I. Remarkable story of Gassendi 360
K. Credulity and duplicity of the Fathers 360
L. Brief account of Oracles 362
M. The story of Thamus and the great Pan . . . . '. 362
N. Satan, the prince of the power of the air 363
O. Gilpin's Demonologia Sacra 364

THE EXISTENCE OF EVIL SPIRITS PROVED.

LECTURE I.

THE EXISTENCE OF EVIL SPIRITS.

WE are indebted for a large proportion of our knowledge, to the information which we receive from others, that is, to testimony. Deprive the most active observers and acute reasoners of all the information, all the ideas which have been imparted to them in this way, how would their mental stores be diminished, how intellectually poor would they become! How narrow is the sphere of the experience, and personal observation, and original invention, of even those who have been the most restless rangers over the surface, and amongst the various countries of the globe; who have passed through the richest variety of instructive and impressive scenes, or who have thought and experimented for themselves with the greatest energy and success! Hence, faith, or belief, presents to us a very interesting and momentous subject of thought and investigation. What are its foundation, its laws, its legitimate sphere and exercise, its influence and results? At our first entrance on life we are disposed (almost necessitated) to believe everything; to credit, unhesitatingly, the testimony of our senses, of external objects, and of our fellow-men. To infancy and incipient childhood belongs the simplicity of believing "every word;" and no wonder, since the child feels his own ignorance, and the superiority, in knowledge and power, of his instructors; and since the kindness which is generally manifested to him by his parents, leads him to feel as if none clothed in a human form would ever deceive him; and how can he distrust his own senses? He has no idea of a lie, of any reason why it should be uttered, or of any end that can be answered by it. But how is he (or at least how would he be, if the scenes did not gradually unfold themselves to his view,) surprised and mortified to find that he is less or more deceived by almost everything; that false information is frequently given him by his fellow-men, by his very senses, and even by the various phenomena of nature, as he understands them. And hence, in some cases, from the extreme of believing everything, he passes to that of believing almost nothing. The being of a God, of a material universe, the difference between good and evil, between happiness and misery, have all been denied; nay some appear not to have been quite sure of even their own existence. Now, of the two extremes, believing everything, however lamentable may be the weakness, credulity, and folly which it implies, or believing nothing, it may well be questioned which is the more irrational and pernicious. Suppose two persons could be found, one of whom literally credited everything that was told him, and trusted entirely also to the testimony of his senses; and another, who would receive as true only that of which he was assured by his own experience, or which could be proved by abstract reasoning and demonstration; which of the two would be more egregiously deceived, and would embrace the greater errors? which would be more extensively incapacitated to manage the affairs of time, or to prepare for the scenes of eternity? "In history it is better to believe too much than too little,—to believe everything, than to believe nothing,—credulity is more lovely than scepticism."* I am aware it has been asserted by no less an authority than that of Aristotle, that "incredulity is the foundation of all wisdom." And though this cannot by any means be granted, since its incorrectness may be demonstrated from both reason and facts, there is too much ground for the assertion, "that credulity is the foundation of all folly," † at least in its various species. For assuredly there is no kind of folly or absurdity in either theory, belief, or practice, into which credulity has not led. What a contrast is presented betwixt the unbelief of men when they have had the testimony of God, and their readiness to believe almost anything on the testimony of men;—their proneness then to suffer themselves to be duped by the most ridiculous pretences, and to follow wherever the grossest impostor may lead the way. The father of lies has always found numbers ready to swallow and digest the greatest and most contemptible falsehoods that he could invent. What a humbling view of human nature is presented by only a few "sketches of imposture, deception, and credulity!" How often do they elicit from the inmost recesses of the astonished and agonized soul the exclamations—" Lord, what is man? What is truth?" And who can write their history in full, and do justice to its appalling facts? Still, perhaps, the verdict in the case just now supposed would be given, were the subject thoroughly investigated, against scepticism, and in favour of credulity. Some degree of the latter, or at least of *a readiness to believe*, is necessary to the acquisition of knowledge, nay, to the very being of society. Whatever may be in this, we cannot wonder, considering the state of human nature, and the part which men have acted, that the existence of evil spirits, or of fallen angels, should have been denied; and that learning, and mental ability, and extensive investigation, and argu-

---

* Professor E. D. Sanbowen, American Biblical Repository, July, p. 131.
† Sketches of Imposture, &c., p. 1, Family Library, No. 63.

ment, should have been put in requisition to prove that they are the creations of fancy, and the offspring of superstition; and that a belief in them has no foundation either in reason, or in the word of God. It is, therefore, far from being unnecessary for those who entertain the common, and what are called the orthodox opinions on this subject, to assign their reasons for thinking that those malignant and unhappy beings do really, certainly exist.

Now the subject, on the discussion of which we are entering, is obviously one of very great importance. It extends its influence, directly or indirectly, to almost every doctrine and every duty; to the whole sphere of our faith and practice. If it can be proved that there are no such beings as those whom we denominate evil spirits, or devils, then what grossly erroneous sentiments has the Bible led by far the greater part of its most devoted readers and students to form! Into what egregious, and even ludicrous errors has it betrayed them, in their faith, their devotional exercises, and their practice! And that not on subjects to which it alluded only incidentally, or which did not come within the sphere of its revelation and teaching, such as astronomy and geology; but on some involved in the purpose for which it was penned, and intimately connected with the religious faith and practice of the servants of God in all ages. It is not strange, it was naturally to be expected, it was even necessary, that popular language should be used in describing the revolutions of the seasons, the appearances of the heavens and the earth, and the formation and structure of our globe; but where was the necessity for using, on religious subjects, not only popular language, but that which had been dictated by false and superstitious opinions, and which, in various ways, affected the holiness and happiness of those for whose benefit the Bible was written? Surely it might have been expected that here the greatest precision would be employed, that every word, and phrase, and reference, which could sanction and confirm the popular delusion, would be carefully avoided. I have said that the Scriptures have led multitudes of their most devoted and diligent students into this error, if it be one; for, according to some of our opponents, the doctrine of the existence of such beings as we call devils, was altogether unknown amongst the heathen. *Their* demons were quite different in their nature and properties from the evil spirits of the Christian creed. And, surely, *those* who deny the tenet in question, must allow that *they* are a small minority amongst the professed disciples of Jesus Christ, (probably they would glory in this,) and that there have been many believers in it who have devoted all the energy of their minds, and all the time they could command, to the investigation of the subject. Is it honourable to Him who was, by way of eminence, the Teacher who came from God, and who appeared in our nature, who came from heaven to earth, that he might reveal to us, as far as necessary, the scenes of the invisible world, and especially the character of the enemies with which we have to wrestle for the kingdom of heaven and the salvation of our souls, to suppose that he has left this interesting subject so much in the dark, that, as it relates to it, by far the greater number of his followers have wandered from the path of truth; nay, that he very commonly spoke and acted, even when performing his miracles, in such a way as was calculated to mislead, because he sanctioned the vulgar superstition, by employing its phraseology, and appearing to take it for granted that the views of its votaries were correct? Surely not. If there are no fallen angels, who were transformed by their own wilful rebellion and apostasy into demons, then how many unnecessary fears have been excited in the breasts of the most devoted servants of God! To what an extent have their combats with their imaginary spiritual foes, been " beating the air!" How many volumes, and even ponderous tomes of divinity, which have hitherto been considered as amongst the most valuable stores of intellectual and moral wealth, bequeathed to us by the learning, and wisdom, and intellect, and piety of past ages, ought to be consigned to the flames, unless they are preserved as monuments of the folly both of those by whom they were written, and of those for whose sake they were penned! If there are no evil spirits, who labour to the utmost of their opportunities and ability to seduce, and deprave, and destroy men, then, what fears which have hitherto been indulged, may we dismiss from our breasts! We have to wrestle *only* with flesh and blood, and not with anything superior, not "with principalities, and powers, and the rulers of the darkness of this world, and with spiritual wickedness in high places." On the contrary, if these powerful, subtle, malignant beings really exist, if they are the deadly enemies of our souls, and are determined, if it is in their power, to ruin us for ever, then it is our incumbent duty to gain as accurate a knowledge as we possibly can, of their character and devices, that thus we may be prepared for the spiritual warfare, and may "stand in the evil day."

Reason and analogy will lead us to conclude that the truth of the common doctrine respecting evil spirits, or fallen angels, is at the least *possible*, nay even *probable*. Surely none will maintain, even if they deny the existence of angels, that man is the only, or the most noble, rational creature in the universe. He evidently appears to be the connecting link betwixt the irrational and the rational creation; and, therefore, it would seem, the lowest order in the latter. How many ranks there may be above him, exhibiting various forms and degrees of intellectual power and moral excellence, and displaying the riches and wonders of the Divine wisdom and power, who can undertake to say? And surely all who believe in the immateriality of the soul, and that it is more excellent than the body, must allow that many of these beings may be pure spirits. Our senses and experience, it is true, can give us no information how these exist without any connexion with matter; and this I apprehend is the cause of the theories, —of the imaginations, I had almost said, of the *dreams*, (and I would not shrink from using the term, because of the celebrity of some by whom the sentiment has been advocated,) of those who maintain that all created spirits have some kind of airy or ethereal vehicles, or bodies, by means of which they act, and which indeed are necessary to enable them to perform various operations; so that God is the only pure spirit in existence. This opinion, I must think, has no foundation in either reason or Scripture; or rather it is contrary to both. However, this does not affect the doctrine which I am endeavouring to maintain. And even those who deny the existence of spirits, properly so called, who assert that the soul of man is material, or the result of the organization of his body, must still grant that matter may be moulded into far more subtle, refined, ethereal, or what may be called spiritual forms, than that in which it exists in him; and that, therefore, even on this theory, there may be many orders of rational creatures far superior to us; and that they must be, as we are, accountable to God, and may have been placed in a state of probation. Farther, facts and experience lead us to conclude that, like men, they may have fallen from their state of integrity. All creatures, however great their powers, however pure and noble their natures, must be fallible or defectible. Infallibility is obviously one of the incommunicable prerogatives of Jehovah. If then they were fallible, they may have fallen. To grant the former, and yet to deny the latter, involves a contradiction. And sin would certainly, from its very nature and necessary operation, pervert their views and feelings, and render them depraved creatures. And may we not conclude that the depth and malignity of the depravity would, if they were left entirely to themselves, and especially in a situation which excluded them from hope, and led them to view God as having cast them off for ever, be proportional to their former excellence, to the exalted privileges which they enjoyed, and to the folly, the enormity, and the high aggravations of their crime? that the depth of the gulf of perdition into which they sunk, would be in proportion to the height of that elevation of honour and happiness from which they precipitated themselves? Do not facts prove that such is the influence of sin, the result of wilful rebellion against the God of heaven? If so, then these fallen beings would immediately become, as far as they had opportunity, the tempters of others, endeavouring to involve their fellow-creatures in a condition like their own. We are warranted, I apprehend, to assert, that there is not a sinner in the universe, if he is left entirely under the influence of sin, who is not disposed to become a tempter to others, nay, who will not necessarily be so. I may be reminded here, perhaps, of the rich man in hell, who prayed that Lazarus might be sent to warn his brethren, lest they should become his companions in torment. To this it is easy to reply, that it was not the design of the Saviour, in this parable, to teach anything respecting the dispositions of those who are finally lost, but to expose the folly of expecting warnings from the invisible world, and their uselessness to those who remained unconverted under the ordinary means of grace; and that it is not certain that the rich man was influenced by benevolence, even allowing, for the sake of argument, that every statement is to be taken literally; and farther, that he might present such a petition as the one under consideration, on behalf of his own brethren,—we might even allow that there were some remains of selfish natural affection towards them in his breast,—and yet might be, in ways innumerable, and even to the utmost extent of his power, a tempter of others.* How often is it the case in this world, that men who are far from being devoid of love to their relations, are yet, to an awful extent, the seducers

* Appendix A.

of all with whom they are connected! From the principles of reason, then, and the testimony of facts, we are warranted to conclude that these fallen-spirits would be disposed to tempt their fellow-creatures. And it is far from being either irrational or unscriptural to suppose that God would permit them to do so; and exposure to their temptations, may be a part of the trial of men while they are in a state of probation. We have the most indubitable evidence that God permits men to become tempters to one another: and, perhaps, in some cases, in a way and to a degree which are more dangerous than the wiles of evil spirits can be. The temptation with which Eve assailed Adam, was quite as powerful as that by which the serpent overcame *her*. If Satan has some advantages over us which our fellow-men have not, *they* have many which he cannot have; and hence he frequently employs them as his instruments, when he could not otherwise accomplish his purpose. Analogy, therefore, leads us to conclude, that God does allow evil spirits to tempt men, and, in some cases, to prevail against them. These considerations, I hope, may suffice to show that the whole of the orthodox faith, and I must be permitted to add, the doctrine of Scripture, concerning evil spirits, is quite agreeable to the principles of reason, and to the evidence of analogy, experience, and observation. It is not, in reality, more wonderful that there should be fallen malignant spirits than that there should be wicked men; nor that the former should tempt the inhabitants of this world, than that the latter should tempt one another.

To these statements it may be added, that the conduct of men, the atrocious, cruel, abominable, unnatural, and sometimes almost gratuitous crimes which they perpetrate, are just such as we might suppose, were we to reason abstractedly on the subject, they would commit, if the earth be the range of evil spirits. Surely our opponents must allow that the world could scarcely be worse, its wars more infernal and bloody, its systems of slavery more inhuman and subversive of all the principles of justice, its impurities more shocking, its impiety more wanton and outrageous, than they have been, supposing the common belief were correct, and that, to use the expressive language of Scripture, the world has been "lying in the wicked one," and that he had been working in men, and even inducing them to worship him as their god. We know that, according to the testimony of the Saviour, "out of the heart proceed evil thoughts, murders, adulteries, and all manner of wickedness;" that men may be so depraved as to become incarnate devils. But then the question is, whether Satan may not have a large influence in rendering man what he is, whether he may not often put into the heart that which comes out of it. We are informed, that Satan put it into the heart of Judas to betray his Master, and into the heart of Ananias and Sapphira to lie to the Holy Ghost. There have been some sins of such a character, and so circumstanced, that they could scarcely be accounted for in any other way than by allowing the influence of an evil spirit. And to take the very lowest ground, the conduct of men has been of such a complexion, that none can bring an argument from what they have been and done, against the existence of fallen angels, and their being continually and sedulously employed in tempting men to all manner of wickedness; especially when we consider the means which God has employed to render them wise and holy. In this respect, too, facts warrant the belief of the doctrine which we are endeavouring to establish.

It may be observed in passing, that though the demons of the heathen were certainly very different beings, in many respects, from the evil spirits of Scripture, yet a belief has very generally, indeed almost universally, prevailed amongst pagans, of the existence of some malignant, wicked, invisible agents, or evil demons, who felt a pleasure in doing mischief, and injuring men in various ways; and as Dr. Doddridge observes, "many of those deities whom they worshipped were, according to their own mythology, so vicious and malignant, as to resemble devils rather than good angels." We are assured that the ancient eastern nations in general, and amongst the rest, the Chaldeans, admitted the existence of certain evil spirits, clothed in a vehicle of grosser matter;* and in subduing or counteracting these they placed a great part of the efficacy of their religious incantations; and that the Egyptians believed in an "evil principle from which they conceived themselves liable to misfortune, and which they deprecated as an object of terror, under the name of Typhon."† And we find from the accounts of missionaries, that similar notions exist amongst many of the heathen at the present day.‡ They have their malignant, as well as their benevolent deities. Some of them worship the devil and not God, and assign as their reason for doing so, that God is good, and will not injure them, and will even confer benefits on them without solicitation or worship; but that, as the devil is malignant, it is necessary to propitiate him by their sacrifices. For the existence of evil spirits in general, then, and of spirits in particular, we have an argument similar to that which is generally urged for the existence of God,—the common belief of men in every age, and in nearly all parts of the world: I do not say equal in strength, but similar in its nature; and the exceptions in both cases are of such a kind that they only confirm the general rule. I know that some will not admit of this argument for even the existence of the Divine Being; but with all due respect for their piety, learning, and ability, I must decidedly differ from them. I cannot at this time assign my reasons.

It may just be mentioned here, not so much as an argument in support of the doctrine which I am endeavouring to maintain, though I am far from thinking that it is desti-

* Enfield's History of Philosophy, book i. chap. ii. p. 20.
† Ibid. chap. viii. p. 44.
‡ See extracts from the correspondence of the London Missionary Society, June 26, 1844.

tute of weight in this respect, but as an important fact, one which may well cause us to pause, and to examine most carefully every step which we take, every concession which we make, every conclusion to which we come, that those who maintain that evil spirits are the figments of a deluded imagination, very generally deny the peculiar doctrines of the Gospel. If we listen to them, and adopt their modes of interpretation, we must come to the conclusion, with the Sadducees of old, that there are neither angels nor spirits, good or bad; that Jesus Christ, when on earth, was but a man like ourselves, and that he is now only one of the most illustrious of glorified saints in heaven, if they will allow us to know even this much respecting him. For one of their leaders assures us that "we are totally ignorant of the place where he resides, and of the occupation in which he is engaged!!" Strange language! inconceivably strange to be uttered by one who had repeatedly read the assertion of the inspired apostle, that he is "gone into heaven, and is on the right hand of God," and that "he ever liveth to make intercession for us." Would Mr. Belsham say we know not where, or what heaven is? We reply,—it is enough that we are certain, wherever it is, the Saviour is there, and that he himself said to those whose knowledge was so circumscribed, that in this respect the very least in the kingdom of heaven now, are greater than they were at that time, "Whither I go ye know, and the way ye know." And surely we can form pretty clear ideas of what "intercession" means. Farther, we shall find that those who do not believe in the existence of evil spirits maintain that there is no Holy Ghost, as it regards distinct personality; that no atonement has been made for human guilt, and in fact, that it needed none; for according to them, sin is rather a misfortune or imperfection than a crime:—that man can renew his own heart; that Divine influence is neither necessary nor to be expected; and that all the difference between the most holy and the most impious persons on earth, as it regards their prospects for the future, is, that the former shall arrive at heaven sooner than the latter, and by a more direct and pleasant path; while both shall take up in it their last and eternal abode: and that the flames of hell shall prove an effectual purgatory to those who, while they were on earth, had resisted all the influence of truth and of the blood of sprinkling.

Now we care not what may be the number or the nature of the preconceived opinions which we may have to reject, or however strange and contrary to our former belief may be the dogmas which we are required to receive, provided sufficient proof be afforded that the former are prejudices, and that the latter are the doctrines of the word of God. We wish to be prepared to follow truth wherever it may lead, or whatever the sacrifices of long-cherished opinions which it may require us to make. If the peculiar views of Socinianism, in even their lowest forms, those in which they appear to us at present to be most directly opposed to the volume of inspiration, be truth, may God reveal them to us, and enable us to embrace them! We have often felt how congenial they are to certain principles and inclinations of fallen human nature, and what painful sacrifices of feelings and wishes must be made to the authority of Scripture, in order to embrace some tenets of a contrary system—sacrifices so painful that nothing but deference to the testimony and command of God could induce us to make them. It would be, on many accounts, a grateful discovery, if we should find that our sentiments respecting evil spirits have no foundation in the word of God, and that we are mistaken in imagining that myriads of noble and glorious beings have transformed themselves, by their wilful rebellion against their Maker and Sovereign, into the most guilty, depraved, and wretched creatures in the universe; and that they are constantly labouring, with all the craft and energy which their powers and malice can put in requisition, to render the whole human race as criminal and miserable as they are themselves. For how much is there appalling and mysterious in the doctrine! What could induce any man, who possesses either a spark of true benevolence or piety, to embrace it, but sufficient, nay, overwhelming evidence of its truth? And such evidence, we most confidently assert, is furnished by the Bible in great abundance.

It may be noticed here, that if there are no such beings as evil spirits in existence, it is very strange, and not very honourable to the Scriptures, that after their canon had been completed, so that no more communications could be expected from heaven to correct any mistakes into which the disciples of Christ had fallen, after the Saviour himself had appeared on earth as the light of the world, as the great prophet and teacher, and after he had poured out his Spirit on his apostles to lead them into all truth, and after they had imparted to the world all that their Master had given them in charge to teach—it is very strange, that after all, still this dogma of the non-existence of devils should have been almost, if not altogether unknown for nearly eighteen hundred years; and that comparatively very few can find it in the Bible, even now, after all the light which has been thrown on it by new translations and expositions. And it appears from the researches of the most learned men, of those who are best qualified to judge on this subject, that during more than seventeen hundred years, the Christian world, however otherwise divided, had on this point no difference of opinion. Even of the denomination whose leaders have, in our own times, embraced with the greatest warmth the negative side of the controversy, the earlier writers never questioned the existence of evil spirits in general, or of the Evil One, peculiarly so called. Socinus and Crellius, and the other commentators of the Racovian school, received and maintained the doctrine of the devil and his angels, not only without qualification, but apparently without suspecting that any qualification of it was possible. "Paulus, cùm de Christianorum hominum pugnâ loquitur, non obscurè carnem et sanguinem opponit spiritibus malis, quibuscum nobis est luctandum."* I repeat what I have asserted: it is surely very strange, and far from being calculated to exalt our ideas of the volume of inspiration, or to increase our confidence in it, that the doctrine of the non-existence of evil spirits, if it be true, since it is evidently very important in itself, and intimately connected with the most momentous truths of the Christian religion, as well as with the duty, and experience, and vital interests of the disciples of Jesus Christ, should remain utterly unknown for seventeen hundred years; and that the multitudes who were most earnestly desirous to ascertain the real meaning of the word of God, and to take it as the rule of their conduct, should have been led by its language, and by the way in which the Saviour performed his miracles, to embrace a tenet which at last is found to be absurd, and even a gross reflection on the government and character of God; for in this light it is represented by our opponents. Surely we might have expected that, if the opinion in question is false, it would have been clearly and pointedly exposed by the Great Teacher, who regarded not the person of men, but taught the way of God clearly, who came into the world that he might bear witness to the truth, and who reprobated, with peculiar plainness and faithfulness, the erroneous and superstitious opinions of the Jews. We should have thought that he would have exposed it as clearly as he did any of their corruptions of the law of Moses, or of the commandments of God;—especially if, as our opponents assert, the Israelites borrowed their notions respecting demons, both good and bad, from the heathen during the Babylonish captivity. How inconceivably strange, how completely at variance with his uniform conduct, that he should ever sanction such a belief

* Heber's Sermons, p. 70. Crellius, Commentarius, tom. i. p. 90.

by the way in which he cured diseases! especially if, as we are assured was the case, "the most learned and skilful medical practitioners of those times disbelieved, controverted, and disproved those absurd and superstitious ideas;" and that "modern men of science and experience agree with those eminent characters of antiquity, that each and all of those maladies arise from such disorganized state of the system."* What! we cannot help asking with indignation, did our Lord and his apostles sanction by their language and conduct, as our opponents in fact assert was the case, "those absurd and superstitious ideas," from which many medical practitioners of the same age endeavoured to free their contemporaries? No wonder that Socinians "think meanly of Christ," when they deem him capable of acting such a part as this, and of being outdone in zeal for the truth by medical practitioners! Surely the exploding of "absurd and superstitious ideas" is more the province of the physician of souls, than of those whose occupation it is only to heal the body! And therefore the former was a very important part of the Saviour's work. If there were no evil spirits in existence, it appears to me impossible that Jesus Christ could have acted as we know he did when curing diseases, and endeavouring, at the same time, to banish the darkness of superstition and idolatry from the world. How could there possibly ever be a more favourable opportunity to inform and convince men, that what they thought possessions of evil spirits were only epilepsies, or cases of insanity, than when he who made the assertion could have demonstrated its truth by effecting an instantaneous, miraculous cure? Is it possible that, instead of doing so, he should have acted as if they were cases of real possession, addressed the supposed demons, pretended to hold conversations with them, commanded them to come out, and permitted them to

* Russell Scott's Analytical Investigation, or Scriptural Claims of the Devil, p. 309.

THE EXISTENCE OF EVIL SPIRITS. 17

enter into the bodies of animals? How could he have adopted a more effectual way of deceiving both the subjects and the witnesses of his miracles, and sanctioning all their erroneous ideas?

Having made these general observations, we shall proceed to consider more particularly those passages of Scripture which relate to the subject of this lecture; for, as it is a doctrine of revelation, the final appeal must be made to the law and the testimony, and by their decision we must abide. I shall first examine those texts which give us the most direct and copious information; as it is in this way that we shall be best enabled to understand those which are more indirect, or concise and obscure.

The first passage, which, according to this plan, claims our attention, is 2 Peter ii. 4, "For if God spared not the angels that sinned, but cast them down to hell, and delivered them into chains of darkness, to be reserved unto judgment," in connexion with the parallel one in Jude, verse 6, "And the angels which kept not their first estate, but left their own habitation, he hath reserved in everlasting chains under darkness, unto the judgment of the great day." Those who deny the existence of evil spirits maintain that the belief in them is founded chiefly on these two texts. The first of these passages is thus translated by one of the most strenuous deniers of the doctrine in question: "For if God spared not the *messengers* that sinned, but having *tartarized them with chains of darkness*, delivered them, thus reserved, unto judgment."* And then he endeavours to prove that the whole statement refers to the spies, or the messengers who were sent to search the land of Canaan, and to bring back a report to Moses and the Israelites. "They sinned," for when they returned, they laid before the people an evil report. "They were tartarized with chains of darkness," for notwithstanding all that God had done before their eyes, they had not eyes to see, nor hearts

* Inquiry into the Scriptural Meaning of the Word Satan, page 4.

IX. C

to understand, but still erred and fell away in the day of temptation; and from their whole conduct we may infer, that as they justly might be, so they really were judicially blinded in the end; or, as the apostle expresses it, "guarded or reserved under chains of darkness unto judgment, unto which they were at last delivered;" for those men, "even those men that did bring up the evil report upon the land, died by the plague before the Lord." He then labours to prove, that these messengers are the same persons with the false prophets mentioned in the first verse. "But there were false prophets among the people, as among you there shall be false teachers." He then supposes, certainly without any evidence, as far as I can see, (and indeed he does not adduce any,) "that as these messengers or spies were heads and rulers in their respective tribes, so they were of the number of the seventy who were appointed to bear the burden of the people with Moses, and who were once partakers of the same spirit with him, and prophesied." He owns, however, that there is no proof of this, and I must think it altogether improbable. If the spirit of Moses rested on them, it would have induced them to act like Moses; and so have prevented them from bringing up the evil report. And as the seventy were appointed to judge the people, and to hear their daily causes and complaints, it is not at all probable that so many of them would have been sent on so long and dangerous an enterprise which would have rendered it impossible that they could attend to the duties of their station; and Joshua, who is expressly called "the *servant* of Moses, and one of his *young* men," Num. xi. 28, could not be one of the elders and an officer of the people, ver. 16; and yet he was one of the spies. He then attempts to show, with very little success, and by a strained application of the words, that the whole of the description of these false prophets may be applied to the spies; that they might be called *prophets*, that they brought in a heresy, that they denied the Lord who bought them, (he does not say *how*—wicked as they were, they did not deny that Jehovah was the true God,) that " they with feigned words made merchandise of the people." He does not even intimate *how* this was done ; nay, he confesses, in fact, that he cannot tell " how far they hoped to make gain of the people." And it is certain that they did not use " feigned words." Erroneous as their views were, they spoke what they thought. But on the whole of this view of the passage, I beg leave to submit the following remarks :—

1. The application of it to the spies does not suit the connexion, nor the natural train of the apostle Peter's thought. These render it probable, to say the least, that the punishment of the angels that sinned took place before that of the old world, as we know that the latter preceded the overthrow of Sodom and Gomorrah. The writer evidently appears to be observing the order of time, in the exhibition of the three examples of the infliction of judgment. I know it will be objected here, that in the parallel passage in Jude, verses 5—7, this order is not observed, the punishment of the refractory Israelites being placed first. But if we compare the two passages, we shall see that Peter, and not Jude, arranges the instances of the Divine justice in the order in which they occurred. The latter employs, in referring to the Sodomites, a different particle of transition (ὡς) from that which he uses in the other case (τὲ,) and Peter in all the three (καὶ). Besides, in Jude, the destruction of those that believed not *included the punishment of the spies;* these were the first that were destroyed, nay, *the only* persons *who were destroyed*, in the ordinary sense of the word, for not believing that God would drive out the Canaanites, and put the Israelites in possession of Canaan ; since forty years was a sufficiently long period to permit all the others who disbelieved God, and despised the promised land, to die a natural death. And the apostle, after referring to the destruction of the

unbelievers, evidently passes on to detail another instance of the Divine vengeance, which was calculated to show, that those ungodly men, whom he had mentioned in the commencement of his epistle, could not possibly escape. He is not enlarging on one particular case included in the general one which he had just mentioned; and, indeed, there was nothing in the way in which the spies were cut off, to warrant its being called, as it is in Jude, "the judgment of the great day," or to render it more worthy of notice than many other instances of the Divine vengeance recorded in the history of the Israelites; for instance, the earth's opening its mouth, and swallowing up Korah, Dathan, and Abiram, while a fire came out from the Lord, and consumed two hundred and fifty men, who were offering incense and endeavouring to invade the priest's office. This was a much more terrible catastrophe than the death, even by the immediate hand of God, of the ten men who had searched out the land. We might adduce other instances recorded in the history of the Israelites, in which God visited their sin upon them, and swept away, in his anger, from the land of the living, those who believed not and rebelled against him; such as the execution of three thousand by the swords of the Levites for making the golden calf;* and the great plague with which the Lord smote the people at Kibroth-hattaavah. With these the destruction of the spies was not to be compared, as awful demonstrations of the certain and terrible doom of incorrigible sinners. These considerations appear to me to render it altogether improbable, that by the messengers, or angels, the apostle meant the spies; nay, certain that he did not.

2. A critical examination of the passage will lead to the same conclusion. Every tyro in the language knows that "messengers" is the literal, etymological translation of the original term ἄγγελοι, and that, in many cases, it must

* Exodus xxxii. 28.

be so rendered. Still, I must maintain that this is not the correct translation in the text under consideration, and in many others which might easily be adduced, and may be noticed afterwards. It is well known that words very frequently drop their original signification; and in consequence of the changes of customs, and of modes of thought and expression, this is almost forgotten, while they are used in quite a different sense. Almost all appellatives were at first significant, but who deems it necessary on this account, to give their primary import in translating them from one language into another? For instance, who, in rendering the Hebrew and Greek words for men, women, heavens, earth, into English or any other tongue, would think of giving their original meaning, instead of using words which direct the mind of the reader at once to the objects which they were intended to signify? So is it here. The Greek words ἄγγελος and ἄγγελοι were often employed by the Jews as appellatives, to denote a certain order of beings, which no native English word would point out, without a circumlocution; and therefore "messengers" is not, in these cases, a correct, full translation; it is not sufficiently specific; it does not precisely designate the order of beings to which it is applied. The word חיה in Hebrew means literally a living thing; but what should we think of the translator who should render it so in the places in which it signifies quadrupeds as opposed to birds and insects,* or wild animals as opposed to cattle?† For instance, if our translators had rendered the twenty-fifth verse, " And God made the *living creature* of the earth after its kind, and cattle after their kind;" would the rendering have been correct? would it have conveyed the same idea to an English reader that the original does to a person who understands Hebrew? They have properly rendered it "beasts;" that is, wild animals. So is it here; the term "messengers," in the verse under consideration,

* Gen. i. 30.   † Gen. i. 25, ii. 2', &c.

would not convey the same idea to an English reader that ἄγγελοι did to those to whom the apostle wrote. It was, doubtless, applied by them to an order of spiritual beings, the existence of which was generally acknowledged ; when used respecting them, the primitive meaning of the word was dropped, and it became an appellative. There are some passages, in which I should think all must acknowledge the propriety, if not the necessity, of translating ἄγγελοι by "angels," rather than "messengers." For instance, Acts xxiii. 8, "For the Sadducees say there is no resurrection, neither *angel* (ἄγγελον) nor spirit." What idea would this convey to an English reader, if ἄγγελον were translated "messenger?" The Sadducees did not, could not, deny that there were messengers. The reference is here most certainly to one of a certain order of beings, the existence and character of which, and not their being employed as "messengers," the term would suggest to all who heard it. The same remarks may be applied to the following passages:—Verse 9th, "If a spirit or an angel has spoken to him." What definite idea of the belief of the Pharisees would be conveyed by saying, "If a spirit or a *messenger* has spoken to him?" "When the Son of man shall come in his glory, and all the holy angels with him."* "Give me more than twelve legions of angels."† Would "messengers" give a correct idea of the light in which those beings to which it relates, were presented to those who heard the Saviour? "Nor death, nor life, nor angels, (*messengers*,) nor principalities, nor powers."‡ "Know ye not that we shall judge angels?"§ How would it lower and darken the sense to say, "Know ye not that we shall judge messengers?" "Though I speak with the tongues of men and of angels, (*messengers*,||) and have not

---

* Matt. xxv. 31. † Matt. xxvi. 53.
‡ Rom. viii. 38. § 1 Cor. vi. 3.
|| What is meant by the tongues of messengers, especially as opposed to the tongues of men?

charity."* Many other similar passages might be quoted. I must maintain, therefore, that our common translation of this word is preferable to the one proposed.

But much more faulty is his rendering of the word ταρταρώσας, "having *tartarized* them." Why should not this term be translated? It is neither a proper name, nor an appellative; it conveys no idea to an English reader when rendered "tartarized," especially as this is the only place in which it occurs in the Bible. There was no difficulty in translating it. Our best lexicographers, quoting from classical writers, tells us, that it means, "to cast and thrust down into Tartarus;"† that is, into hell, according to their ideas, "the most profound depth or abyss of the nether regions, or a place as much lower than the earth as the earth is than the heavens; a place where the gates are iron, and the ground-pavement brass." The passage literally rendered reads, "He committed, or gave them, bound in chains of darkness, and thrust down into the deepest abyss, reserved unto judgment." It is scarcely a breach of charity to say, that the only conceivable reason why the author of the "Inquiry" did not translate this word was, because he could not do so consistently with his own theory, and without subserving that which he wished to overthrow.

He maintains that the passive participle, τετηρημένους, which is in the perfect tense, can never be made to respect the future; and there is no necessity, according to the translation that has just been given, that it should. The perfect relates to the past as connected with the present. These sinning angels had been reserved from the time in which they sinned, till that in which the apostle wrote, and still the time of their further punishment had not arrived. The participle does not, according to the most natural construction of the verse, refer to the judgment, but to the unhappy creatures, as having been, for a long time before

* 1 Cor. xiii. 1.   † Schleusner and Stephanus in verb.

the apostle wrote, delivered or given up to a doom which had not then been inflicted.* His assertion, that there was not in the apostle's time so much as a tradition concerning angels that sinned, is altogether gratuitous. The contrary is evident from the Scriptures themselves, as we may afterwards prove. Jesus Christ and his apostles evidently spoke of them as forming an article of the belief of those with whom they conversed.

His exposition of the expression, " Cast them down into hell, and delivered them into chains of darkness, (he translates it, " tartarized them with chains of darkness,") is exceedingly lame, forced, and unnatural. It would puzzle an Œdipus to tell what is meant by being "*tartarized with chains.*" He explains it, of a judicial blindness inflicted on them by God, because they did not improve that light which had long shone around them, and believe, after all the miracles which had been wrought before their eyes; " so that, as they justly might be, they really were judicially blinded in the end ; or, as the apostle expresses it, guarded or reserved under chains of darkness unto judgment, to which they were at length delivered," when they " died by the plague before the Lord." Now, great as is the importance which he attaches to a literal translation, and one which will give the etymological meaning of the term in the word ἄγγελοι, he gives no translation at all of ταρταρώσας, one of the most important words in the whole passage under consideration, though, as we have seen, its meaning is very plain, or at least very easily ascertainable, by a reference to classical authors. " Tartarize " is not English ; and it can answer no purpose here, but to conceal the meaning of the Greek word, and darken the whole passage. I must again assert that he could not translate it correctly, and give it its only genuine meaning, without subverting his own theory. Farther, this writer represents the sin of the spies in bringing up an evil report of the

* Griesbach prefers the present participle, τηρουμένους.

promised land, as the effect of their being judicially blinded by God himself. This is their being "tartarized with chains of darkness," a strange and unique way, certainly, of saying that they were judicially blinded. Now if, by their being "judicially blinded," he means that they were given up to the blindness of their own minds, and to the hardness of their hearts, it is plain that they were thus blinded before they were spies, or messengers, or else they would have believed. But if he means that God exerted some direct influence on them to prevent them from understanding and believing, then he makes God the author of their sin, of that very crime for which he punished them. Nay, he represents their unbelief and false report as no sin at all; for how can that be a sin which is produced by an irresistible Divine influence on the mind? If a master should put out the eyes of his slave, because he had not used them as he ought to have done in times past, could that slave be criminal for not seeing when he was deprived of his sight? He might and would still be guilty for his perverse disposition, but not for doing that of which he had been rendered incapable, by a power which he could not resist. Is it not highly dishonourable to the Divine Being to represent him as first blinding the spies, and then punishing them for being blind? That must be a desperate cause which needs such a mode of defence.

Again, there was nothing, as already observed, in the day when the spies were punished, to distinguish it so much from many other days which occurred in the history of the Israelites, as to entitle it to the epithet given to it by Jude, "the great day." On the contrary, some of those days were much greater than it was. But there is a day which was well known to the writers of the New Testament, and designated by them "the *day of the Lord*," and "*that* day," namely, the day of judgment, which there can be no doubt Jude here has in view; borrowing his phraseology, perhaps, from the prophets, who frequently called the time when God inflicted signal punishment publicly and to any great extent, "the day of the Lord," or "the great day of the Lord." The natural, I had almost said the *necessary* meaning of Jude then is, that the angels that sinned were reserved till the day of judgment at the end of time. The Jews, and all the primitive Christians, well knew that there was such a day fixed by God; the former were taught by their Scriptures, that " God would bring every work into judgment, with every secret thing, whether it were good, or whether it were evil; "* a passage which they naturally referred to a future judgment, and which the apostle seems to have had in view when he wrote the passage, " In the day when God shall judge the secrets of men by Jesus Christ, according to my gospel ; "—and that "many of those who slept in the dust of the earth should arise, some to everlasting life, and some to shame and everlasting contempt."† And wherever the apostles went, they explicitly informed, and solemnly assured men, that God had " appointed a day in which he would judge the world in righteousness, by that man whom he had ordained," and that this was just as certain as that Jesus Christ had been raised from the dead. How naturally, then, would they refer the expression of Jude to the day of final inquiry and retribution ! This deserves, unspeakably better than that on which the spies were destroyed, the epithet of " the *great day*."

It is urged by our opponents, that "angels that sinned" would be an instance less adapted to the apostle's argument than that of "messengers that sinned." Surely the truth of the reverse of this assertion must be apparent to' all. No matter how different may be the natures of angels and men, the former are superior to the latter; and therefore the plain and impressive inference is, that if God did not spare those exalted beings, but cast them down to hell, the proud and impure false teachers, whom Jude had in

* Eccles. xii. 14. † Dan. xii. 2.

THE EXISTENCE OF EVIL SPIRITS. 27

view, could by no means escape. If a sovereign does not spare his princes and courtiers when they transgress the laws, surely the common people cannot sin with the hope of impunity.

We may add to all that has been advanced, that if the apostles had had the spies in view in the passages under consideration, they would have designated them in a more definite way; they would have mentioned them more explicitly, as they have "the old world" and the "cities of Sodom and Gomorrah," and "the people that were brought out of the land of Egypt;" they would have referred to them as "the spies who brought up an evil report," and not have used terms which have led ninety-nine out of a hundred of those who have read their writings, to imagine that they referred to angelic beings; while it was left to the ingenuity of those who should live hundreds of years afterward, to stretch their language on the rack of criticism, and elicit from it quite a different meaning from its apparently natural import. It deserves to be noticed, in conclusion, that the word, ἄγγελοι, which our opponents would translate "messengers," is never applied to the spies by the Septuagint, in the account which is given of them in the book of Numbers;* nor is there the least proof that they were ever known by way of eminence or distinction as "*the messengers*," and so that the mind of a hearer or reader would naturally refer to them when the words were used. From all these premises we must draw the conclusion, that by "the angels that sinned and kept not their first estate," the apostles meant those beings who are generally denominated fallen angels, or evil spirits, of whom the devil, whom Jude mentions in a following verse, is the chief; and nothing could be better calculated to produce in the minds of those whom they addressed a firm and operative belief, that those false teachers and

* Chapters xiii. and xiv.

seducers whom the apostles had in view could not possibly escape condign punishment.

The next passage which, according to the plan which has been proposed, claims our attention, is John viii. 44 : " Ye are of your father the devil, and the lusts of your father ye will do ; he was a murderer from the beginning, and abode not in the truth, because there is no truth in him. When he speaketh a lie, he speaketh it of his own, because he is a liar, and the father of it." How exactly does this whole verse apply to Satan, according to the commonly-received opinion respecting him! He was a murderer from the beginning of time, and of the existence of the race of men. He tempted our first parents to commit that sin which involved them and all their descendants in death; for " in Adam all die." He ruined at once both their bodies and their souls. He "abode not in the truth," when he rebelled against his Maker, and thus disregarded the most glorious truths, and resisted their influence. He "abode not in the truth " likewise, did not adhere to it, when he tempted Eve, but deceived her by uttering the grossest and the most slanderous falsehoods; and he did this because " there was no truth in him," no love of truth, no regard to it, no inclination to speak it. The lies which he then spoke were " his own," of his own invention and fabrication, and the result of his own disposition. He brought them out of his own stores of deceit and malice. He is, by way of eminence, " a liar, and the father," the cause, the originator of lying in general ; and to his influence may be traced, in one respect or another, all the lies that ever were uttered, all the liars and deceivers that ever appeared in our world. To all of these the language of the Saviour to the Jews may be applied : " Ye are of your father the devil." Such is the obvious, natural import of this verse, expounded according to the plain meaning of its terms, and in its connexion with other passages of the Bible. Let us now see what the ingenuity and criticisms of our opponents can make of it. There can be no question respecting the etymological meaning of the word διάβολος, that it signifies an accuser, and often a false accuser, a slanderer, an adversary. But though it is used almost forty times in the New Testament, there are not above four or five in which it does not refer either directly or indirectly to a being, who was, evidently, known to those to whom the apostles and evangelists wrote, as the great adversary of God and man, the false accuser, the calumniator, by way of eminence; and not unfrequently there is no reference to the ordinary or etymological meaning of the word; but it is used as a proper name, to indicate an individual wicked spirit. He is represented as tempting Jesus Christ; as sowing tares among the wheat; as doomed by the Judge of all at the last day, together with his angels, to everlasting fire;* as taking away the word out of the heart of a certain class of hearers;† as putting it into the heart of Judas to betray the Saviour;‡ as oppressing men, or bringing them under his power.§ Elymas, the sorcerer, is addressed as a "child of the devil."‖ The Ephesians are exhorted not to give place to the devil;¶ and to take the whole armour of God, that they might "stand against the wiles of the devil."** Jesus Christ became incarnate, "that through death he might destroy him that had the power of death, that is the devil."†† James exhorts all to "resist the devil, and he will flee from them."‡‡ Peter assures us that "our adversary the devil goeth about as a roaring-lion, seeking whom he may devour."§§ John assures us that "he who sinneth is of the devil, because the devil sinneth from the beginning," and that for this purpose the Son of God was manifested, that he might destroy the

---

* Matt. iv. 1, xiii. 39, xxv. 41.   † Luke viii. 12.
‡ John xiii. 2.   § Acts x. 28.   ‖ Acts xii. 10.
¶ Eph. iv. 27.   ** Eph. vi. 11.   †† Heb. ii. 11.
‡‡ James iv. 7.   §§ 1 Pet. v. 8.

works of the devil;"* and that the children of God and the children of the devil manifest themselves by their tempers and conduct. The devil is said to have cast some of the church of Pergamus into Prison.† He is denominated "the old serpent, called the devil and Satan, which deceiveth the whole world."‡ And in the last passage in which he is mentioned, we are informed that he is cast into the lake of fire.§ Now, however the word διάβολος is translated in these passages, whether accuser, or slanderer, or adversary, it is equivalent in most of them to a proper name; it evidently refers to one and the same being, who is also called Satan, and the serpent, and the wicked one, and the tempter; while it is plainly implied that those whom the inspired writers addressed, would know by the very term that was used, whom they had in view.

But according to those who do not believe in the existence of Satan, "by *diabolos* in the passage under consideration, is meant the Jewish sanhedrim, or rulers. They were murderers from the beginning, because they hated and opposed Jesus Christ from the commencement of his ministry; and as he who hateth his brother is a murderer, so they were murderers, because they hated the Saviour. They abode not in the truth, because they denied the Divine mission of the Messiah, and bore false witness against him. When they spoke lies or falsehoods, they spoke them of their own, because they were indulging their false and wicked disposition; and the sanhedrim was the father, the fabricator of all the malicious falsehoods circulated concerning Jesus; the father, the source of all the opposition made to the truth. 'The beginning' here means the beginning of the Saviour's ministry, and the Pharisees were the children of the rulers, or of the sanhedrim, because they had imbibed their spirit and were performing their

---

* 1 John iii. 8.   † Rev. ii. 10.
‡ Rev. xii. 9, xx. 2.   § Rev. xx. 10.

work. They were the dutiful children of these false accusers." Now, surely, this exposition is far from being the most easy and natural one. The language of the Saviour was not, nay, could not be, understood in this sense by those who heard him; nor would this meaning ever have been elicited from his language, had there not been some special end to be answered, some system to which their natural and common import was opposed, to be maintained. There is not a single hint given in the whole New Testament, that the Jewish sanhedrim or rulers were ever personified in the way which is here supposed. Would not all impartial readers conclude, that by ὁ διάβολος here, the Saviour had in view the same διάβολος that tempted him in the wilderness; sowed the tares amongst the wheat; had the everlasting fire prepared for him; put it into the heart of Judas to betray his master; "had the power of death;" (in what sense had the Jewish sanhedrim this power?) and whose works the Son of God was made manifest to destroy? In these and several other passages, the term, I do not scruple to say, cannot be applied to the Jewish sanhedrim or rulers, but to some well-known enemy, not only of Jesus Christ, but also of his people and cause in all ages of the world. This is surely the natural, the only correct, construction of the passage.

Farther, "the devil" in this passage is opposed, not to personified bodies of men, but to individual beings, to Abraham and to God. The Jews claimed to be in one sense the children of the former, and in another the children of the latter. As the terms, "God" and "Abraham," then, are allowed on all hands to designate individuals, is it not reasonable to suppose that the word "devil" must do so likewise?

Again, it is highly probable that there were some, if not several, of the Jewish sanhedrim and rulers present when the Saviour uttered the words under consideration. We are informed that "the *scribes and Pharisees* brought unto him a woman taken in adultery." Of scribes, the expounders of the law, the theological doctors of the Jews, and of Pharisees, the most powerful sect, and the most famed for their supposed sanctity, the sanhedrim would doubtless be composed. Nicodemus was a Pharisee, a ruler of the Jews, and also a member of the sanhedrim.* Indeed, it would appear from the preceding chapter, verse 45, that the sanhedrim was composed of chief priests and Pharisees. To understand the terms, "father" and "devil," then, of the sanhedrim and rulers, would represent our Lord as making some of those whom he addressed their own father. Besides, the sanhedrim was not worse than the Pharisees and the Jews in general were. The former was necessarily composed of the latter. Several of those whom our Saviour was addressing, when he uttered the words in question, were as fit to teach the sanhedrim the arts of lying, slander, and murder, as it was to teach them; and therefore it would have been just as proper to have represented them as being murderers from the beginning, and as abiding not in the truth, and as being the father of lying, as it was to bring these charges against their national council.

It may also be observed, that though the sanhedrim and rulers did oppose the Saviour from an early period of his ministry, they were not the first that opposed, rejected, and even attempted to murder him. We read, that at the very commencement of his public course, before he had arrested the attention of the sanhedrim, before they had opposed him at all, or had formed the idea of taking away his life, he came to his own city, to Nazareth, where he had been brought up; and on account of the offence which he gave them by his preaching, they were filled with wrath, and with one accord seized him, and led him to the

* But according to the opinion which I am opposing, he was included amongst those who are called the devil!

brow of the hill on which their city stood, with an intention to cast him down headlong, and thus to destroy him.* So that the sanhedrim and rulers were not the first who rejected our Lord, and thus slandered his character, or who attempted to take away his life. They were not, therefore, even in the sense in which the expression is interpreted by our opponents, "*murderers from the beginning*" of the Saviour's ministry. The men of Nazareth were murderers in this respect before them. We know that the term "beginning," signifies the commencement of any course, or any train of events, to which it may be applied; and that, therefore, in some places it does mean the commencement of our Saviour's ministry; as when it is said, "Jesus knew from the beginning who believed not and who should betray him."† But there is one event to which the Scriptures direct our attention, which is called, by way of eminence, "the beginning." In the beginning God created the heavens and the earth."‡ ."I was set up from the beginning or ever the earth was."§ "Declaring the end from the beginning."‖ "But from the beginning it was not so."¶ God hath from the beginning chosen you to salvation."** "Thou, Lord, in the beginning, hast laid the foundations of the earth."†† Now, when the word is used absolutely, without anything in the connexion to limit it to any particular subject, it is natural for any one who is acquainted with the phraseology of Scripture, and with its great epochs, to refer the term in question to the beginning of *time*, or, at the least, of that course of it to which any particular passage directs our attention. There can be no reasonable doubt that such is its reference here. The natural meaning is, the devil sinneth from the beginning of the period in which sin has been committed. He is the *ringleader* in the rebellion that has been raised

---

* Luke iv. 28. † John vi. 64. ‡ Gen. i. 1.
§ Prov. viii. 23. ‖ Isa. xlvi. 10. ¶ Matt. xix. 8.
** 2 Thess. ii. 13. †† Heb. i. 10.

against the principles of truth and holiness, and the authority and laws of the Most High; and thus he has been accessory, either directly or indirectly, to the murder of all who have perished. "When he speaketh a lie he speaketh of his own;" he is its "father." Other liars were tempted; but it would appear, as far as we are acquainted with the history of the universe, that he was the first tempter, and that he sinned without temptation; the first sin, the first falsehood, was altogether his own, none participated with him in its guilt and depravity. How correct is the language, how obvious its meaning, how natural and forcible its application, when thus understood! And this interpretation is abundantly confirmed by other references and statements of the Scriptures, particularly by the language of the apostle John, whose words we are considering. "He that committeth sin is of the devil, for the devil sinneth from the *beginning*. For this purpose the Son of God was manifested, that he might destroy the works of the devil."* The apostle is here treating of sin, or unrighteousness in general, which the Son of God was manifested to destroy, and not of slander, or murder; he has in view the general nature, and the very origin or commencement of sin, when he says, that "the devil sinned from the beginning." There can be no doubt that by "the devil" here, he has in view the same depraved being, whom he afterwards calls "the wicked one," of whom Cain was, and whose spirit he manifested when he slew his brother. How could Cain be of the Jewish sanhedrim, which did not exist for thousands of years after him? Rather, they were *of him*. Apply the words to Satan, to the serpent that tempted our first parents, and, doubtless, tempted Cain also, as far as he had opportunity, and then everything is clear and natural. Besides, the Son of God was manifested not merely that he might destroy the works of adversaries, of slanderers, of false accusers, much less of

* 1 John iii. 8.

the Jewish sanhedrim or rulers only; but that he might destroy sin in all its kinds, which are all the works of him who was the first sinner and tempter. Many other passages might easily be quoted in support of the interpretation, that by "the beginning" here, is meant the commencement of the history of this world, or rather the first introduction of sin into the universe. On the whole, then, as it regards the passage under consideration, I hope it will not be deemed inconsistent with modesty, or with a due sense of our liability to err, and of our danger of being prejudiced in favour of our opinions and reasonings, to assert that the term "devil" most certainly refers to the chief of evil spirits, the fallen angels, to which Peter and Jude have directed our attention in the passages which we have already considered; to counteract whose plans, and to destroy whose works, the Son of God was manifested in the flesh.

The next passage to which I shall request attention is Matthew xxv. 41—46, "Then shall the King say to those on his left hand, Depart from me, ye cursed, into everlasting fire prepared for the devil and his angels. These shall go away into everlasting punishment, but the righteous into life eternal." The obvious, natural meaning of this language, as far as relates to the subject under consideration, is, that the punishment to which wicked men are at last to be doomed, was originally prepared for a number of depraved, incorrigibly rebellious beings, over whom one rules as chief, so that they all may be considered as his agents or angels. And it is plainly implied that, like men, they have apostatized from God, that they are still accountable to him, and that there is a day fixed, when the Son of man, the Saviour of the world, shall appear as the judge of the universe, and call them, and all the incorrigibly wicked amongst the human race before his tribunal, and punish them for their crimes. And it is not too much to assert, that if ten thousand competent persons, who had no prepossessions on the subject, no system to maintain, were to read the passage either in the original, or in any faithful translation, this is the conclusion to which they would all come. But what is the explanation given of it, by those who do not believe in the existence of Satan? No one, I am confident, could divine by merely studying the passage, or the similar statements of the word of God, what, according to them, is here meant by the devil and his angels, and by the everlasting fire to which they are condemned. By the aid of highly figurative language, and strong eastern metaphors, and determined verbal criticism, and strained resemblances, the passage is stripped of all its apparent terrors as it regards sinners in general. The devil and his angels are converted into the persecuting Roman civil power and its abettors, or the Roman emperor and its agents. "The *angels* or messengers of *Diabolos*, were those persons who were active in accusing, betraying, and persecuting the Christians." "The *sheep* represent the mildness and innocency of those who befriended the followers of Christ, and who practised towards them the duties of hospitality, kindness, and humanity. The *goats* are emblematical of those Jews who were violent and infuriated in their treatment of those who, amongst their own nation, embraced Christianity." "The *everlasting fire* is the *temporal national calamities*, in which the opponents of the cause of Christ, especially the persecutors of his disciples, were to be involved." "But it being the punishment of human beings, and for a *part* of their conduct only, both the reward and the punishment must be of a temporary nature only. The sheep would be protected and preserved amidst the dreadful havoc, devastation, and unparalleled barbarities of those times; whilst the other two parties, Diabolos and his angels, would miserably suffer during those horrible conflicts."* Such is the interpretation of this solemn and impressive passage, which

---

* Scott's Lectures on the Scriptural Claims of the Devil, pp. 127, 128.

those who deny the existence of Satan are *forced* to devise. I use the word *forced*, for surely nothing but dire necessity, the mother of strange and desperate inventions, could induce any one to think of such an exposition. I have given it at some length in the words of its author, because I think that there is scarcely anything better calculated to convince an unbeliever, or to confirm a doubter, that the existence of evil spirits is indeed a doctrine of the Bible, than to see those who deny it driven to such methods of defending their dogmas, by being obliged to interpret the Scriptures in a way, which would not be tolerated with regard to any other book in the world, that professed to teach articles of faith, and to prescribe rules of duty. For my own part, I do not scruple to assert, that if I could think that the Socinian exposition of this passage is even plausible, I should immediately lose all confidence in the Bible, and question whether any man could have satisfactory evidence that he understood a single sentence it contains.

The passage under consideration is connected with all that precedes it, as far as the commencement of the twenty-fourth chapter; and especially with the question which the disciples, after they had shown Jesus the stones and buildings of the temple, proposed to him, and he had assured them that the time would come in which all those buildings, massy, firm, beautiful, and even sacred as they were, would be completely demolished, so that there should not be one stone left upon another, which should not be thrown down:—" Tell us, when shall these things be : and what shall be the sign of thy coming, and of the end of the world?" After all the criticism which has been expended on the words συντέλεια and αἰὼν, I must agree with those who think that they mean here, as they were used by the disciples, "*the end of the world,*" in the ordinary sense of the terms; and, consequently, that our translation is correct. The disciples were most certainly far from thinking that the temple would be destroyed at the close of the age or dispensation under which they lived, or that their Master would overthrow it when he established the worldly kingdom on which their hearts were set, and of which they were constantly dreaming. They had no idea that the Mosaic economy, with which the temple was intimately connected, would be abolished by Jesus Christ. Even after his resurrection they asked him, "Lord, wilt thou at this time restore the kingdom to Israel?" Nay, after the descent of the Holy Ghost on the day of Pentecost, it required a vision, a revelation from heaven, to convince Peter that the ceremonial law might be dispensed with in the case of Gentile converts; and that he might go into the house of those who were uncircumcised, preach to them the Gospel, and partake of their food. Now, the existence of the temple, and the obligation of the ceremonial law, were intimately connected; many of the rites and services of the latter could be observed only in the former. It is to be observed farther, that the disciples were familiar with the use of the words συντέλεια and αἰών, and even with the formula συντέλεια τοῦ αἰῶνος, as applied by their Master to the end of the world, and to his second coming.* And however their minds might be absorbed in the ideas and hopes of worldly power and greatness, their views and expectations were not, could not be, confined to these; they could not be the principal blessings which they sought and expected from their Master. Peter, speaking in the name of the rest, assigned the confidence that he could bestow on them eternal life, as the great reason of their adherence to him: "Lord, to whom shall we go? Thou hast the words of eternal life."† The least spark of piety would prevent them from resting satisfied with anything that ever Jesus Christ could bestow on them in this mortal state, and lead them to look for future happiness. They knew that they must die. They believed that the earth itself would perish, and that the course of

* Matt. xii. 39, 40, 49. † John vi. 68.

time would come to a close; of both these they were assured by the declarations of their own prophets, especially by the writer of the hundred and second Psalm, ver. 25 ; "Of old hast thou laid the foundations of the earth, and the heavens are the work of thy hands. They shall perish, but thou shalt endure; yea, all of them shall wax old as a garment, and as a vesture shalt thou fold them up, and they shall be changed; but thou art the same, and thy years shall have no end ;" and by the following impressive language of the sublime Isaiah;* "Lift up your eyes to the heavens, and look upon the earth beneath; for the heavens shall vanish away like smoke, and the earth shall wax old as a garment, and they that dwell therein shall die in like manner; but my *salvation* shall be for ever." How could those who read or heard, and believed such declarations, and expected this salvation, confine their hopes and wishes to anything earthly? A future state of rewards and punishments, the resurrection of the dead both of the just and unjust,† the end of time, when God would call all the inhabitants of the world to account for their conduct, were common articles of faith amongst the Jews, with the exception of the infidel Sadducees; and the Saviour had assured his disciples that he would both raise the dead and judge the human race.‡ Taking all these things into account, together with the fact that the disciples had no idea that the ceremonial law would ever be abolished as long as the world stood, or that any could be saved without embracing it, I must think that by the words τῆς συντελείας τοῦ αἰῶνος, the disciples meant the end of time or of the world, in the ordinary sense of the phrase : and that they thought the temple would stand till that important period had arrived; and that our Saviour in his answer kept both their questions in view, and gave them much useful information on both, while he did not satisfy their curiosity, or at that time correct their mistakes respecting

* Chap. ii. 6.   † Acts xxiii. 6; xxiv. 15.   ‡ John v. 22, 28, 29.

the perpetuity of the ceremonial dispensation and the temple; the time was not come when they could bear what he had to say to them on these subjects; and that he employed language which might apply both to his coming in the dispensations of providence, (after he had ascended to his kingdom and glory, and obtained possession of all power in heaven and earth,) to destroy Jerusalem and the temple, and to his coming to judge the world at the last day; and that the great end which he had in view was to rouse his disciples to that watchfulness and diligence in the performance of duty, which would prepare them for his advent, either in the ways which have just been mentioned, or by death in the case of each individual. It is only when the Saviour's answer is viewed in this light, that we can see the propriety of all the language which he uses, and of the warnings and exhortations which he gives, in relation to the disciples who asked the questions, as well as to his people in general. How few of even the former were to live to see his coming to destroy Jerusalem! If this view of the subject is correct, the probability is, that the expression, "But of that day and hour knoweth no man, no, not the angels in heaven, but my Father only," as well as what follows, was intended to apply more particularly to the day of judgment, and the end of time. And there can be no rational doubt, in my opinion, that the exhortations, and appeals, and warnings which follow from the forty-fifth verse to the end of the chapter, were intended to show to all, the vast importance and necessity of being habitually prepared for that which would be the end of time and of the world to them—death; and thus they would be prepared for judgment—for the last, the general, and the most glorious coming of the Son of man. In replying to these questions, the Saviour kept in view, not only the benefit of those who proposed them, but of his disciples in all ages of the world. He intended that what he uttered should be recorded in the volume of inspiration; and what he said to those who heard him, he said to all. In the twenty-fifth chapter, our Lord evidently pursues the same train of thought, and keeps in view the same end. The parables of the ten virgins and of the talents, are both intended to point out the only way in which any can be prepared for his coming either at death or judgment; and the consequences of faithfulness and diligence on the one hand, and of negligence and sloth on the other. After which he very naturally proceeds to give a most striking and instructive view of his last coming, with its signs, and glories, and wonders, and infinitely momentous results, and consequently of the end of the world. And this he does, of necessity, partly in figurative language; for how could even He describe the scenes and events of that great day, in such a way as to be intelligible to men, without availing himself of one of the principal instruments of human thought, and mediums of human intercourse? But the figures are all explained, or at least the key to their explanation is given, by the literal terms which are employed. How natural, nay, how necessary is it, on the universally allowed principle of interpreting Scripture by Scripture, to refer the coming of the Son of man in his glory, and the gathering of all nations before him, to that day to which the writers of the New Testament attach so much importance, and which they represent as in a special manner "the day of the Lord;" evidently meaning by the term "Lord," Jesus Christ; that day which "shall come as a thief in the night, when the heavens shall pass away with a great noise, and the earth and the works that are therein shall be burned up," and the new heavens and the new earth are to be introduced.* When "the Lord himself shall descend from heaven with a shout, with the voice of the archangel, and with the trump of God."† When "the Lord Jesus shall be revealed from heaven

* 2 Peter ii. 18. † 1 Thess. iv. 16.

with his mighty angels, in flaming fire, taking vengeance on them that know not God, and that obey not the Gospel of our Lord Jesus Christ."* When "the trumpet shall sound," and the dead be raised incorruptible, and the living changed, and natural death be swallowed up in victory.† When "all that are in their graves are to hear his voice, and come forth; they that have done good to the resurrection of life, and they that have done evil to the resurrection of damnation."‡ I may well ask, is it possible that our Lord could, in the passage under consideration, have any other day in view than that to which those texts evidently refer? Can the language which he uses, and the events which he describes, possibly apply to any other? Let common sense, sound criticism, and true piety determine.

It is plainly implied, then, that the devil and his angels are rational beings, that they were the subjects of Jehovah's government, and owed obedience to him; else he could have had no right to inflict any evil on them; that they had rebelled against him, or else he would not have visited them with the expressions of his displeasure; and that the punishment here denominated "everlasting fire" was originally provided for them; and that wicked men, having imbibed their spirit, and joined with them in their rebellion, are to be involved in the same condemnation. In accordance with those views, the demons who had possessed the two men whose habitation was amongst the tombs, are represented as exclaiming, "What have we to do with thee, Jesus, thou Son of God? art thou come to torment us before the time?" From this it appears that these wicked spirits knew that there was a time fixed when they would be consigned to greater sufferings than they were then enduring.§ We are told that "the devils [or demons] believe and tremble."‖ Hence they know that

---

* 2 Thess. i. 7. † 1 Cor. xv. 51—54. ‡ John v. 28.
§ Matt. viii. 29. ‖ James ii. 19.

they are doomed to some greater punishment than they at present undergo. And to whom can the term "demons" here refer but to fallen angels? It is unspeakably dishonourable to the inspired apostle to suppose that he would sanction, by such a statement as this, the superstitious ideas of the heathen respecting their demons. And we read, that "the devil that deceived them was cast into the lake of fire and brimstone, where the beast and the false prophet are;"* and this took place at the end of time, "when the dead, small and great, stood before God, and the books were opened, and the dead were judged out of those things which were written in the books." Will any say that "*beast*" and "*false prophet*" here are figurative terms, and therefore "devil" must be so too? This will not help their cause; for the term "devil" would still mean evil spirits collectively, as the beast and the false prophet mean collections of men, who had by their crimes exposed themselves to the wrath of God. Had the passage been as consolatory as it is awful, as flattering to human pride as it is humbling, no other interpretation would ever have been known in the world. The facts that the devil and his angels are spirits, and that the word "fire" cannot be taken literally, do not at all invalidate the reasoning which has been adopted, or militate against the conclusion at which we have arrived. Though I may just observe, that it is taken for granted far too easily and unhesitatingly, that matter, and therefore that material fire, cannot affect spirits. We know by experience that it can affect our spirits most powerfully. It is true that this is in consequence of their being *united* to our bodies; but who has told us, or what proof have we, that this is the only way in which God can cause matter to operate on spirit? I must conclude, then, that this passage is sufficient, were it the only one of the kind in the Bible, to prove the existence of wicked spirits, or at least of other rational creatures, beside

* Rev. xx. 10, 12.

men, that have sinned, and are condemned to eternal banishment from God and happiness.

There are many other passages in which the terms "diabolos," or "devil," and "Satan," (which is synonymous, as we may afterwards prove,) can apply to none but to those evil spirits which are the great adversaries of God and man, and especially to their chief and ringleader. For instance, "These are those by the way-side, where the word is sown; but when they have heard, Satan cometh immediately, and taketh away the word that was sown in their hearts."* This *Satan*, this *enemy*, is here represented as constantly endeavouring to counteract the holy and benevolent purposes of Jesus Christ, and as taking away the word out of the hearts of some hearers, wherever the Gospel is preached. Of what human adversaries, or slanderers, or accusers, can this be asserted? Bad as the world is, there are hundreds and thousands who constantly hear the Gospel, without any of their fellow-men making a single effort, and especially under the influence of a fear "lest they should believe and be saved," to cause them to forget its truth, To act in this way, under the influence of such a motive, is truly diabolical; and that this parable is intended to apply generally to all who in any age or part of the world hear the Gospel, is evident from the whole of its construction, and from the caution given in connexion with it: "Take heed how ye hear." Surely if Jesus Christ had had human adversaries in view, he would have told us so in plain terms, when he explained the figurative language which he had used, as he did with regard to the other parts of the parable. "Those on the rock, are they which have no root in themselves." "Those amongst the thorns, are those who are choked by the cares of the world, and the deceitfulness of riches." Doubtless he would have said, 'Those by the way-side are those who are prevented by carnal and wicked men from remembering

* Mark iv. 15.

what they have heard;' surely he would not have employed a metaphor which has misled thousands of his disciples, and excited unnecessary fear in their breasts, while it has diverted their attention from their real danger. The same observation will apply to the parable of the tares. "The enemy that sowed them is the devil;" and these tares, we are informed, are "the children of the *wicked one;*"* of *him* who is the wicked one by way of eminence; and these are found wherever the children of the kingdom, the genuine disciples of Jesus Christ, who are enlightened and sanctified by his truth and grace, exist. Could it be said that any human slanderers, or accusers, or adversaries, sowed all those tares, produced *all* these children of the wicked one? Who or what then produced those accusers or adversaries? for they too must be numbered amongst the tares. But as Satan first induced men to sin, (sowed his tares even in paradise, when God had planted men "wholly a right seed, altogether a choice vine,") and has ever since been engaged in disseminating error and crime throughout the world, with the strictest propriety may it be said that he has always been sowing tares amongst the wheat, and that wicked men are his children.

I am not ignorant of the different interpretation which has been given of this parable. According to those who deny the existence of Satan, the field is not the world, but the Jewish nation; the end of the world " is the termination of the Jewish economy and the destruction of Jerusalem; and the reapers and the angels are," of course, " the Roman emperor and his soldiers:" though this is not expressly said, and we may hope it was some degree of scruple or modesty that prevented this bold assertion, yet it is necessarily implied; and consequently " the separation of the wheat from the tares, and the preservation of the former, mean the protection and escape of the disciples of Christ when the Jewish nation was destroyed." But I

* Matt. xiii. 39.

should think it would be something more than difficult to show how the reapers, according to this representation, viz. the Roman soldiers, gathered the wheat into the garner, or how they contributed anything to the safety of the Christians. And how could it be said that the field was the world, of which Judea was a very small, or insignificant part? The expression ought to have been, " The field is the land of Palestine." But is this the only place where the Son of man sows the seed of his word, and where the tares are found? And yet the design of the Saviour, evidently, was to show how the progress of his Gospel was to be opposed, and its success impeded, wherever it was preached, and not in one locality only.

Again, Peter informed Cornelius and his friends that Jesus Christ "went about doing good, and healing all that were oppressed by the devil."* Peter here refers to the way in which Jesus Christ dispossessed devils, and healed the diseases which were caused by them. Again we ask the question, what human slanderers, or false accusers, or adversaries, oppressed those who were the subjects of our Saviour's miraculous cures? and we challenge our opponents to give a reply that has even the appearance of being satisfactory or solid.

Another passage, which must not be omitted in this inquiry, is Heb. ii. 14; "That by death he might destroy him who had the power of death, that is, the devil, and deliver them who, through fear of death, were all their lifetime subject to bondage." Surely, if, as R. Scott maintains, the apostle had meant to inform us in this passage, that *sin* is the cause of death, and that Christ by his cross delivers men from sin, he would have said so. The apostles were in the habit of using plain language on this subject. They inform us that Christ "gave himself for our sins, that he might deliver us from this present evil world;"† that "once in the end of the world he appeared to put

---

* Acts x. 38. † Gal. i. 4.

away sin by the sacrifice of himself;"* that "he himself bore our sins in his own body on the tree,"† &c. &c. The language in question, taken in its natural import, certainly directs our attention to a single being, however numerous may be the agents which he employs. It is granted that it is not unusual for the sacred writers to personify sin; but I believe not a single instance can be adduced in which they do so in such a way, or to such a degree, as our opponents suppose is done in this passage. The devil may well be said to have had the power of death, as he by his temptation brought death into the world, and, therefore, in a very important sense, inflicted it on all the human race, and is still only too successfully tempting them to the commission of those crimes, the wages of which is death. Hence he is called "a murderer from the beginning."‡ It is quite futile, it is almost worse than trifling to urge, as Russell Scott does in his lectures, that "the devil cannot be the inflicter of death; since we are assured that it is God who has determined the days of men, who has fixed the number of his months, and the boundary beyond which he cannot pass, Job xiv. 5." This reasoning proves too much, and therefore proves nothing. God alone has the power of life and death in the most extensive sense, and therefore sin, which R. Scott thinks is meant by Diabolos (for he cannot in this instance apply the word to any human agents), cannot slay men or cause their death. What then becomes of his own interpretation? Does it follow that, because God has determined the days of men, they cannot put each other to death? that one of them cannot have the power of death over another? How absurd then to say that the devil cannot, in any sense, have the power of death, because it is God who kills and revives! 1 Sam. ii. 6. He asks, "Did Christ destroy by his death the power of him who is called the devil? Certainly not, since his advocates" (who are his *advocates?* what an un-

* Heb. ix. 26. † 1 Peter i. 24. ‡ John viii. 44.

fair and scornful insinuation!) "maintain that he still exists, and not merely exists, but is as strong, as powerful, active, vigilant, and destructive as ever." Now, as our author maintains that it was sin which Christ died to destroy, may we not on his principles ask, "Is sin destroyed? does it not still exist to a lamentable extent, and is it not in many cases as destructive as ever?" The meaning evidently is, that Christ has vanquished Satan, that in multitudes of instances he has entirely destroyed his power, bruised his head, and delivered thousands of his captives, and set them free from the fear of death: and that he has introduced that Gospel into the world which is sufficient to enable all who embrace it to exclaim, " O death, where is thy sting? O grave, where is thy victory? Thanks be to God, who giveth us the victory through our Lord Jesus Christ." In fact, the Saviour destroys sin, and him that had the power of death, in the *same way* and to the *same extent*, and therefore the objection which we are considering, if it had any force, would militate against the interpretation of our opponents, just as powerfully as it would against ours.

The limits within which these lectures must be confined, will by no means permit the examination of the other passages in which the term Diabolos evidently means the devil, in the ordinary sense of the word. In James iv. 7 we read, "Resist the devil, and he will flee from you." We are told that "the devil here means pride and revenge." How pride and revenge will flee in consequence of being resisted, or opposed and mortified, it is not easy to see. Apply the expression to an evil spirit, the tempter of the people of God to pride and revenge amongst other things, who, if he is resisted, will desist from his attempts, and leave the Christian for a season, as he did Jesus Christ; and then we see its propriety; and besides, if the apostle had meant pride and revenge, and other vices, he would have used the plural number, as he does in other places,

2 Tim. iii. 3, Tit. ii. 3, when he had more than one object in view. But, in fact, there is no authority at all for applying the term, in this place, to vices or passions. Nay, though the word, especially in the plural number, sometimes denotes persons, there is not an instance in the New Testament, or in the Septuagint, in which it can with any fairness or propriety be considered as meaning vices. The natural meaning of the word, as well as the connexion, would always lead us to apply it to persons.

The apostle Peter, 1 Epis. v. 8, thus exhorts those to whom he wrote: "Be sober, be vigilant, because your adversary the devil walketh about seeking whom he may devour." Our opponents maintain that "by the devil here is meant a human calumniator or slanderer," or "those adversaries of the Christians who falsely accused them in the courts of justice, and whom they were to withstand;" and as a part of the proof of this assertion, it is pleaded that our translators have rendered the same word, "false accusers," in 2 Tim. iii. 3, and Titus ii. 3. There is this important difference, however, that in these passages the word is in the plural,—here it is in the singular, and also connected with a word which limits it to an individual. If the apostle had meant their heathen and Jewish adversaries, he would doubtless have used the plural number of both the words, and have said, "your adversaries, false accusers, or slanderers;" but his language would necessarily direct their minds to an individual, and we know of none who made it his business to go about and accuse the Christians. Besides, if the apostle had in view, as our opponents assert, false accusers, against them no watchfulness, or sobriety, or innocence, no humility, or submission, or diligence in the performance of duty, or patience in suffering, would be any protection. They could bring *false* accusations against the humble, and circumspect, and diligent, as easily (in a sense more so) as against the proud, and factious, and slothful. But the vigilance and sobriety of which the apostle speaks, and to which he exhorts, are the best armour of defence, are everything against an adversary who, whatever may be his rage, can prevail only by craft, and by taking his victims by surprise.

On 1 John iii. 8, some remarks have already been made. The interpretation which applies it to the Jewish rulers and Pharisees, though it is confirmed by the important word, *must*, is so strained, I had almost said so contemptible, as to require little farther notice. I would ask any reader of common sense, is it possible that the language employed could suggest this idea to those to whom the apostle wrote? Diabolos here, we are assured, "*must* refer to the opposition which the Jewish rulers and Pharisees made to the Gospel from the time that Christ entered on his ministry. Jesus, however, was manifested that he might destroy this malicious opposition of the Jews, and that his religion might supersede that of Moses." According to this view of the subject, then, the *religion of Moses* was amongst those works of the devil which the Son of God was manifested to destroy! And as to the malicious opposition of the Jews, as far as it was directed against Jesus Christ, it could not have existed had he not made his appearance amongst them; so that instead of destroying that which was in the world, and was ruining the souls of men before his incarnation, he destroyed only that which he was the occasion, however innocently, of calling into exercise. We appeal most confidently to the natural and necessary import of the language which the apostle uses, to the scope and connexion of the passage and its parallels, in support of our position, that the apostle is here speaking of *sin* in general, of all that sin which the Son of God was manifested in human nature to take away, and from which he delivers all his people; from which they are kept, and from which they are to labour to keep themselves. This is the work of the devil, because he *introduced* it into the world, and probably into the *universe*; because he is an

THE EXISTENCE OF EVIL SPIRITS. 51

incorrigible transgressor, and is constantly tempting men to sin in all its various forms.

Those who maintain that there are no evil spirits in existence, find it very difficult, perhaps I should say impossible, to explain on their system the language of Jude, v. 9, "Yet Michael the archangel, when contending with the devil he disputed about the body of Moses," &c. And, therefore, their usual resource is to question the inspiration of the whole epistle; just as they attempt to explode the account of the miraculous conception of the Saviour, by denying the authenticity of other parts of the Bible. R. Scott is obliged to acknowledge that this apostle "adduces a dispute between some superhuman being, whom he calls the archangel Michael (but on what authority we know not), and the devil." This is not the place to prove that the Epistle of Jude is canonical; nor is it necessary. Its authenticity and genuineness have been vindicated by the most able and learned critics; and therefore, notwithstanding the authority and bold assertions of Michaelis, that "we have little reason for placing the Epistle of Jude among the sacred writings; if the ancient church had decided positively in its favour, this would not have convinced me that it is inspired," there is no reason for any rational doubt that this epistle was written by the apostle whose name it bears, and that it is a part of the sacred canon. And the evidence which it affords of the existence of Satan remains unimpaired.

Next to Diabolos, Satan is the word which is most frequently applied in the New Testament to the ringleader of the powers of darkness. It is well kwown that this word comes from the Hebrew שָׂטַן, which signifies to *hate*, to feel and act as a determined enemy to any one, to *oppose*; and it has the same meaning in the Syriac, Chaldee, and Arabic.*
Hence it is nearly synonymous in meaning with the word Diabolos, signifying, like it, an adversary, an accuser, and

* Schleusner in verb.

generally a *false* and *malicious* accuser. And the two terms are evidently used in the Scriptures to designate the same being. The fact that the word is not translated into Greek by the inspired writers of the New Testament, though it easily might have been,—its meaning is quite definite and well known,—and that it generally has the article prefixed to it, shows plainly that it is employed as a proper name, to designate a certain well-known being. It is used about thirty-five times by the apostles and evangelists; and in almost all of them it is either applied to the same individual being, or else there is a reference to him; an intimation that those to whom it is given are acting like him, or in some way subserving his cause. This might easily be shown by the investigation of each passage, did time and space permit. But whether the assertion which has just been made is correct or not, every one may easily ascertain, by examining for himself all the texts where the word occurs. A few of them I shall proceed to consider, after observing that, according to those who deny the existence of evil spirits, " Satan" is always used as a kind of figurative appellative, and signifies almost anything or everything.*
In Romans xvi. 20, it designates " the persecutors of the Roman converts." In 1 Cor. v. 5, it signifies " excommunication!" How could this be an adversary, or indulge any hatred, when it was inflicted out of love, and proved the means of saving the soul of the offender? As well might it be said that a salutary medicine, administered by a kind and skilful physician, is an adversary inspired by hatred. In 1 Cor. vii. 7, it signifies " the violation of the marriage vow!" In 2 Cor. xi. 14, "false apostles!" Paul, however, informs us that the false apostles were the ministers of this Satan, who is often transformed into an angel of light. Is not this an intimation that he is an angel of darkness? Our opponents charge the apostle with the redundancy and impropriety of making these false apostles their own ministers.

* Russell Scott, pp. 84, 104.

THE EXISTENCE OF EVIL SPIRITS. 53

In chap. xii. 7, it means "bodily infirmity." But the apostle informs us that the thorn in the flesh was the *messenger of Satan*, not Satan himself. 1 Thess. ii. 18, "Jews persecuting Paul and Silas." 2 Thess. ii. 9, "the same persons persecuting Paul." (Here it is natural to ask, what signs, and power, and lying wonders did those persecutors of Paul ever exhibit, that the wicked one of whom he was speaking could, with the least appearance of propriety, be said to come after their working?) In 1 Tim. i. 20, "excommunication!" But it was by excommunication, according to the meaning of the passage, that the persons in question were delivered unto Satan; how then could it be Satan himself? In 1 Tim. v. 15, "idolatrous indulgences!" In the history of our Lord's temptations, Satan means in the first, "hunger," though we are informed that it was *after* he was hungry that the tempter came to him: and this tempter is represented as a rational being entering into conversation with him; in the second, "presumption and vanity;" and in the third, "ambition as gratified by regal power and riches," In Matt. xii. 26, and in the parallel passages, it signifies "Beelzebub, the idol god of Ekron," because, according to our opponents, the Jews had adopted the opinions of the heathen respecting demons, and they thought that Beelzebub was the chief of those demons, and they wished to persuade the wondering multitudes that Jesus Christ performed miracles by his assistance. But if this had been the case, would not the Great Prophet of his church, who came to banish error and superstition from the world, have told them that this demon had no existence, and therefore it was impossible that he, or any supposed being like him, could do anything, much less work a miracle? Would not this have afforded the most direct and satisfactory proof of the falsehood and folly of the charge which the Pharisees brought against him? Nay, may we not say with reverence, that it would have been incumbent on him to have acted in this way, and not to have confirmed, both by his miracles and by the way in which he vindicated his character from the foulest and most malicious charges, a grossly erroneous, superstitious, and even idolatrous notion; and one, too, which was connected with many others of a similar kind;—one indeed which was calculated to pervert the whole system of the religious views and feelings of those who adopted it? Would he not have acted like the ancient prophets, and have proclaimed respecting these supposed demons, "Be not afraid of them; for they cannot do evil, neither also is it in them to do good?" Jer. x. 5. Would he not have assured his hearers that they were "feeding on ashes, and that a deceived heart had turned them aside?" Isa. xliv. 20. What! shall we suppose that the servants were more bold and explicit than their Lord, to whom they were indebted for all their knowledge and gifts? for it was "the Spirit of Christ" that was in them, 1 Pet. i. 11. Will it be said, that men would not have believed him, if he had assured them ever so solemnly, that Beelzebub and demons had no existence? But was their disposition to believe to be the measure of his announcements of truth? How then was he to enlighten their minds, and to cure their unbelief? They would not believe that he was the Messiah,—that God was his Father, —or even that he was a good man, and spoke the truth; but did he refrain, on that account, from stating and maintaining his Messiahship, and his relation to God; or from vindicating his own character? And what if *they* had not believed him? All his *disciples would*, in following ages, and would thus have been saved from gross error. But the truth of the matter is, that whatever was the origin of the term Beelzebub, the Jews, in the time of the Saviour, applied it to the chief of those fallen spirits, who, as they believed, for their rebellion against God, were expelled from heaven; a doctrine of which they had many hints given them in their own Scriptures, and which, like many others, is more clearly revealed in the New Testament; and to the truth of which our Lord sets his seal, in the way in which he here exposes the malice, and refutes the charges of his adversaries. How lamentable is it, that any intelligent, able, learned, and estimable men, professing themselves to be disciples of Jesus Christ, should, in their zeal and determination to maintain their own opinions, when the word Satan cannot possibly be applied to a human agent, or to any vice or evil, represent the blessed Redeemer, who came into the world to bear witness to the truth, as acting a part and using language calculated to sanction a most absurd and pernicious error!

Great stress, in this controversy, is attached to the circumstance that our Lord, when reproving Peter, called him Satan; "Get thee behind me, Satan," Matt. xvi. 21. On these words, it is rather flippantly said, "You are not prepared nor disposed to believe, I dare say, that Peter was the devil. If not, you must admit that Satanas has some other meaning attached to it, than that of the devil."* We know that it has. Who ever supposed that Peter was the devil? But our Lord could easily have employed a Greek word, signifying *adversary*. But by using an untranslated Hebrew or Syriac word, which was equivalent to a proper name, he might intend, and many are disposed to think he did intend, to convey the idea that Peter was acting the part of Satan, and abetting the design of the great tempter and adversary. Gesenius, who is second to none in acquaintance with Hebrew and oriental languages in general, and who, moreover, cannot be suspected of being incumbered by the trammels of a superstitious regard to any preconceived opinions, has determined, as the result of his critical inquiries, that הַשָּׂטָן, "Satan, with the article, means *the adversary*, κατ' ἐξοχὴν, by way of eminence, and assumes the nature of a proper name, that is Satan, ὁ διάβολος, the devil, the evil spirit in the later theology of the Jews, who seduces men

* Russell Scott, p. 72.

to evil, 1 Chron. xxi. 1, where alone the article is wanting; compare 2 Sam. xxiv. 1; and accuses and calumniates them before God, Zech. iii. 1, 2; Job i. 7, ii. 2—5; compare Rev. xii. 10."* I quote this passage at length, because that profound and accurate scholar has given it as his opinion, that in those passages of the Old Testament, where our opponents maintain that "the term Satan means a human adversary, a tempter," it designates "the devil, the evil spirit, who, in the later theology of the Jews, seduces men to evil;" and consequently in his opinion, contrary to the repeated assertions of those who believe that there are no evil spirits in existence, the belief in such beings was an article in their creed in the time of our Saviour. And this he evidently took for granted in all his intercourse with them; and both by his discourses and miracles he sanctioned their belief, and conveyed the idea that their views, so far, were correct.

In Luke xxii. 21, we read, "Satan has desired to have thee, that he may sift thee as wheat." Satan, we are told, signifies first the maid-servant, and then the others who charged Peter with being a disciple of Jesus Christ, and thus were the means of inducing him to deny his Master. Not to mention other objections to this interpretation, how could it be said with propriety or truth, that the servants of the high priest had desired to have him and sift him, when they were probably ignorant of his existence, till they saw him in the palace of Caiphas, and could not possibly know, when our Lord uttered these words, that he would enter the hall where they were, and therefore could have no idea of sifting him? But view these words as relating to Satan, a fallen, wicked spirit, who employs men as his instruments to tempt each other, besides tempting them in his own person, and then we see the propriety of the language. He desired an opportunity of tempting any or all the disciples; and when it was

* Gesenius, Lex. in verb.

afforded him, with regard to Peter, in the hall of the high priest, it was immediately embraced.

In Rev. xii. 3, 9, and xx. 2, 10, our opponents, of course, maintain, that the words dragon, devil, Satan, and old serpent, all mean exclusively some human enemies of the Christian religion, or some vices or evils; and by no means any wicked spirits, or invisible superhuman adversaries of the cause of Christ. We know well that the former as well as the latter are amongst the agents and actors in the scenes to which these verses refer. In the description which is given of the great red dragon, chap. xii. 3, the immediate primary reference is to the Roman empire in its pagan state, and to the efforts which it made to destroy the Christian religion; and then under the emblem of a beast rising out of the sea, in its papal state, as supporting the power of Antichrist, and persecuting the saints of the Most High. But I must think, that in both cases, and throughout the whole stage of its existence and operations, it was only the instrument of another power. The dragon is expressly said to be, "that old serpent, called the Devil, and Satan, which deceiveth the whole world." And then, in chap. xx. 2, we are told, that this "dragon, that old serpent, which is the Devil, and Satan, was bound for a thousand years, and cast into the bottomless pit;" and this prophecy relates to a period after the Roman empire, both in its pagan and papal state, had ceased to exist, and, consequently, there is nothing said here of the beast with seven heads and ten horns; of the false prophet; or of their being cast into the bottomless pit. These had been taken and cast in, that is, *had been destroyed already*, and still the old serpent, called the Devil, and Satan, was at large, and ready to deceive the nations of the earth, and excite them against the servants and the cause of God. And hence to secure the millennial glory and the triumph of the saints, he too was to be taken and bound, and prevented from deceiving the nations. And then, after the thousand years, (whatever period of time that may signify,) Satan was loosed out of his prison, and permitted for a season to recommence his work of tempting and deceiving men. And then, verse 20, after the defeat and destruction of the last army that he is permitted to raise on earth against the King of kings and his army, he is taken, observe, *after their destruction*, and as their deceiver, and therefore, certainly, as distinct from all the human agents, and errors, and vices, and temptations that he may employ, and cast into the lake of fire and brimstone, into which the beast and the false prophet had been cast long before, to be confined and punished there for ever and ever. And all this takes place at the end of time, long after the Roman empire, the beast and the false prophet had ceased to exist. The dragon is said to be "the old serpent, the Devil, and Satan." Is there not here a reference to the account which we have of the serpent deceiving Eve, and to the application of the terms devil and Satan in the Scriptures to the great enemy of God and man—to him who existed long before the Roman empire was founded, and was always engaged in deceiving the nations? This being admitted, all the representations of those prophetic visions are natural, the figurative language is easily understood, and conveys correct ideas, and there is no danger of being led into error by it. The contrary is the case, if there are no evil spirits in existence. I would observe likewise, that as the armies which fought against the old dragon and his hosts had an invisible spiritual leader, "they overcame through the blood of the Lamb;"—He whom John saw on the white horse—He whose name was called Faithful and True—He who was clothed in a vesture dipped in blood, and whose name was called the Word of God—represented no ideal or figurative personage; no human agents, or energies, or virtues taken collectively—(I suppose our opponents will grant that we are warranted to infer the existence, the dignity, and glory, and influence of the Lord Jesus Christ, from the emblematical representations which were presented to the mind of the apostle)— is it not equally plain that the opposite army had a leader whose existence, and character, and influence, we may infer from the use of his name in these prophetic visions? Indeed I do not see why the real existence of Jesus Christ might not be explained away by the help of Eastern metaphors, and figurative language, and allegorical personages, and accommodation to prejudices and prevailing opinions, on the same principles on which the existence of Satan is denied, and the doctrine of the Saviour's divinity is exploded. It can be no difficult achievement for those who strip him of his glory as God, to rob him of his existence as man.

In James ii. 19, we read, "Thou believest that there is one God; thou doest well: the demons believe and tremble." In this passage there is evidently a reference to the belief of both Jews and Christians, and that in such a way as to intimate that it was correct, respecting those unhappy beings whom they designated demons, and whose state and character corresponded, according to the ideas which were entertained of them, to those of devils in the modern use of the term. They were evidently thought to be fallen, wicked spirits, trembling for fear of the Divine vengeance. The incidental way in which they are here mentioned, and the purpose for which an allusion is made to them, indicate in the clearest manner, that the apostle believed in the existence of these spirits; and he takes it for granted that no one would dispute the fact to which he refers. Would he have used such language, knowing as he did that the demons of the heathen were only the figments of their vain imaginations, if his views had been similar to those of modern Unitarians? We appeal to common sense and reason for an answer.

If the interpretation which has been given of the passages that have been noticed is correct, we can be at no loss how to understand others, which, taken by themselves, might present some difficulty. The plain natural meaning of the whole narrative, and of the words employed, the assertion of the apostle Paul, 2 Cor. xi. 3, that "the serpent beguiled Eve," the repeated declaration in the book of Revelation, that Satan and the old serpent are identical; all warrant us in maintaining, that the account which is given in the third chapter of Genesis is a real history, and that here we have the first notice of evil spirits, and especially of their ringleader. It is well known that our opponents consider the Mosaic account of the fall a "mere allegory, or moral fable, such as is often met with in other parts of the Old and New Testament, in which certain religious duties and doctrines, with the genuine nature and effects of them, are represented, as it were, to our senses, by a fiction of persons and facts, which had no real existence."* And, very strangely, it is asserted, that the design of this allegory was, "to show that there was no foundation whatever for the doctrine of an evil principle, which was maintained by the Egyptians, Chaldeans, and other heathen nations." "Whether this apologue were intended to designate the placidity of a pastoral, or the activity of an agricultural life, *as the history of Cain and Abel appears to be symbolical of the transition from vegetable to animal sacrifices*, or whether its design was to show that, under the Mosaic dispensation, no evil principle, no malignant being existed, either as the opponent of God, or the enemy of mankind, the reason for employing the serpent for one of the actors in the fable is evident, to render more conspicuous the folly and absurdity of serpent-worship, which had become very prevalent among the heathen nations."†!!! This is certainly strange reasoning, if reasoning it can be called. There are, in my apprehension, few things, with

---

* Dr. Conyers Middleton, cited by R. Scott, p. 12.
† R. Scott's Lectures, p. 18.

the exception of direct, plain assertions, more calculated to prove that the existence of evil spirits is clearly taught in the Scriptures, than to find those who deny it obliged to have recourse to such desperate methods to maintain their sentiments. Not only the history of the fall, but also that of Cain and Abel, because it is not to their taste, must be considered a moral fable, or allegory, and symbolical, forsooth, of the transition from vegetable to animal sacrifices: so Cain is the symbol of vegetable sacrifices, and Abel of animal ones!! If we were disposed to pun or trifle on such a subject, we might say, that, according to this view of the subject, Abel ought to have killed Cain, and not Cain Abel; for, certainly, it is more likely that animals should kill vegetables, than that vegetables should kill animals; and that those who are in the habit of offering animals should murder those who offer vegetables, than the contrary. Surely, if plain, simple narrative have any certain characteristics, if there be any possible way of distinguishing it from allegory, either by the occasion on which it was penned, or by the scope, or by the terms employed, or by the connexion, or by allusions to it in other parts of the volume in which it is found, we are fully warranted to conclude, with the greatest firmness, that the account of Cain and Abel is a history, giving a plain, unvarnished account of a most melancholy event, intimately connected with one which, on some accounts, was still more melancholy. Most assuredly it requires no small degree of ingenuity (of a certain kind) to find in it anything that indicates the transition from vegetable to animal sacrifices. The intention of the writer, and of the Divine Spirit by which he was inspired, evidently was, to give an account of the origin of our species, of the way in which it was brought into its present circumstances, and of an event which occurred after man, by transgressing the command of his Maker, had depraved his own nature, and thus brought sin and death into the world; and in this light it is constantly viewed by the subsequent writers of the Bible : the whole system of their religion is built upon the narration; it is always referred to as a real history, and not as a fiction. It has been asked rather sarcastically, and with an air of triumph, " Will you take the account " (of the fall) " literally ? Then only be consistent with the literal interpretation ; say that there grew a tree whose *fruit* was capable of imparting a knowledge of good and evil ; say that God *walked* in the garden to seek for Adam, and that Adam called to *inform* the Deity of his hiding-place ; say that it was a *serpent* which held the conversation with Eve, and tempted her ; and say that this animal was *cursed by God* above every beast of the field, compelled to crawl upon the ground, and eat the dust."* How easy is it to retort here, and say, Will you take the account *figuratively?* Then only be *consistent* with the *figurative* interpretation ; say that we have a *figurative Adam and Eve, a figurative garden, and tree of knowledge of good and evil, a figurative prohibition, a figurative serpent, and a figurative transgression, and a figurative punishment;* and why not a figurative Deity ? And why not interpret the first and second chapters in the same way, and then we have *a figurative creation*, a figurative heaven and earth, and *vegetables and animals;* and, in short, we have nothing but figures or apologues in the Bible, nay, or in the universe. This is most effectually carrying out the theory of Berkeley, as improved by Hume ; only reducing both the material and the spiritual world to figures and moral fables, instead of ideas and impressions. If this is not handling the word of God deceitfully, (I do not say it is done intentionally), and evincing a determination to make any part of it, any statement that it can possibly contain, bend to a favourite hypothesis, I do not know what can be so. According to this principle of interpretation, we might prove, in one sense, anything from the Scriptures, and, in

* Grundy's Lectures, p. 80.

another, we could prove nothing; for it would be impossible to say whether their language was literal or figurative, or whether they meant what they appeared to say, and what their words would naturally suggest, or something entirely different. But who does not know that it is almost impossible to write the shortest and most simple narration, or even to utter a few sentences in common conversation, without employing some words and phrases which are more or less figurative? Will this warrant us to take the whole as a moral fable or apologue? A little care, and impartiality, and common sense, will enable us to determine at once how far it is figurative, and how far it is to be taken literally; and so is it with regard to the account which we are considering. But we have no objection to understand the history of the fall *literally* as far as language in general can be so taken. We maintain that there was a literal tree, and that the *eating* of its fruit, in disobedience to the command of God, did cause the experimental knowledge of good and evil; of the good which had been lost, and of the evil which had been incurred. What a dreadful, distressing knowledge of this kind, of which he was entirely destitute before, had Adam after he had eaten the forbidden fruit! What is there absurd in believing that the Divine Being assumed a visible form, the appearance of a man, on this occasion, as we know he did afterwards, when he appeared to Abraham and others, and that this form was seen walking in the garden, and that it called to Adam, and that he answered from his hiding-place?

It is very possible, I own, that our opponents may consider all the accounts which we have of God's appearances to the patriarchs as fables or figures; and then this argument, whatever it may be in itself, will avail nothing with them. False principles and theories will for a time render those who put them on as their panoply, invulnerable by all the weapons of truth, when wielded by men. But this can be for only a short time. These weapons will at last be grasped by the hand of Omnipotence, and then they must be irresistible. We have no objection to say that a literal serpent, or the form of a serpent, might be employed in tempting Eve, and that, in order to render manifest the dreadful consequences of sin, and the displeasure of God against it, the serpent might be subjected to some natural evils, and therefore so far cursed. And yet we contend that, in addition to all this, both the narrative itself, and other parts of Scripture, plainly show that it was a fallen spirit, *either actuating a serpent, or assuming its form,* or acting such a part, that on account of the ideas which are generally formed of serpents, and the enmity which subsists betwixt them and the human race, the being who was the tempter and seducer, and on whom the curse, in its most dreadful import, fell, was denominated a serpent. This is the most easy, natural, and, I do not scruple to say, rational interpretation of the narration, and it is abundantly confirmed by other passages of the word of God. There can be no doubt that "the seed of the woman" meant Jesus Christ. *He* was not an allegorical personage. Had he nothing to contend with, but an allegorical enemy? R. Scott asserts that "*it*, referring to the seed or posterity of the woman, would have been more perspicuously rendered in the plural *they*," and that "translating the same word, in the same clause of a verse, both in the *masculine and neuter gender, has not only produced* confusion, but a misconception of the passage." Now, although זרע, seed, may be used as a noun of multitude, and, when it is so, translated by a plural, yet, on account of the singular pronouns הוא and ו, which refer to it, the singular is preferable here, or, rather, it must be in the singular. And accordingly, it is so rendered by the Septuagint, and by translators in general, so far as I have had an opportunity of consulting them. The pronoun, certainly, should have been rendered in both cases by the masculine gender; it is not easy to account for its not being so : " He shall bruise thy head, and thou shalt bruise his heel." But this confirms the sense for which I am contending, that, by the seed of the woman, Jesus Christ is principally meant, and this is abundantly confirmed by other passages of the Bible. It represents him as, by way of eminence, the seed of Abraham, in whom all the nations of the earth were blessed; the seed, or the Son of David, who was to erect a spiritual kingdom on earth, and by means of it to confer the greatest blessings on the children of men. He was emphatically, and in such a way as no other was, the seed of the woman, on account of the means by which his human nature was produced, as described by the angel to the virgin : " The Holy Ghost shall come upon thee, and the power of the Highest shall overshadow thee, therefore also that holy thing which shall be born of thee shall be called the Son of God," Luke i. 35. And thus he was manifested to deliver those who should believe on him from the consequences of their apostasy, and to destroy the works of the devil. " I fear," says the apostle Paul, " lest, as the serpent beguiled Eve, so your minds should be corrupted from the simplicity which is in Christ," 2 Cor. xi. 3. Here we are informed that Eve was beguiled by the craft of a *tempter*, called a *serpent*. The same idea is conveyed by the apostle in 1 Tim. ii. 14; "And Adam was not deceived, but Eve, being deceived, was in the transgression." And if we ask who or what was the serpent that deceived her? we have a definite and satisfactory answer given by those passages which have already been quoted, Rev. xii. 9, and xx. 2—10. He was "the old serpent, called the Devil, and Satan, who deceiveth the whole world," and who is at last to be " cast into the lake of fire and brimstone." We must prefer this definite statement to all Unitarian expositions.

Though the passage presents considerable difficulty, and though the opinion that the evil spirit means melancholy, or enmity, or revenge, or temporary and partial insanity, is plausible, yet I must, taking all things into the account, incline to the opinion of Bishop Heber, that the evil spirit spoken of in 1 Sam. xvi. 14, " is precisely the same, both in name and functions, with the evil spirits of the New Testament."* And this is an evidence that the doctrine of the existence of fallen evil spirits " was not first embraced by the Jews during their abode in Babylon," and that there is not the smallest evidence (I might say, not the least probability) that " they derived it from the Chaldeans, or (still less) from the Persian philosophy and superstition." We are told, in the same verse, that the Spirit of God departed from Saul. This must mean that the Holy Spirit withdrew his influence, and, consequently, Saul lost the gifts, the ability for government, and managing the affairs of his kingdom, which had been imparted to him, when " the Spirit of God came upon him, and he became another man," 1 Sam. x. 6. Does it not follow from this, that the tempers which he afterwards manifested were the effects of the influence of an evil spirit, opposite to the Spirit of God? And, as it came upon him in consequence of the withdrawment of the Divine Spirit, and by the permission of the Divine Being, and also as a judgment, it may, with the greatest propriety, and especially in the Hebrew idiom, according to which God is often said to do that which he permits to be done, and renders subservient to his purposes, be represented as from God. This is the natural interpretation of the passage, and that which best agrees with the general doctrine of the Bible respecting evil spirits.

In 2 Sam. xxiv. 1, we read, " And again the anger of the Lord was kindled against Israel, and he moved David against them to say, Go, number Israel and Judah." In a parallel passage, 2 Chron. xxi. 1, it is said, " And Satan stood up against Israel, and provoked David to number Israel." Those who believe in the existence of evil spirits,

* Heber's Sermons, p. 85.

generally, perhaps universally, maintain that by Satan here is meant the ringleader of those spirits, tempting David, either by himself, or by some of his emissaries. Those who disbelieve their existence, contend that by Satan here must be meant the anger of God, or some human adversary, or both. One of them* says, "This enemy or adversary is here called the anger of Jehovah, and said to be the sole cause of inducing David to persist in numbering the people. It is evident from reading these two accounts, that both these writers intended the same thing by the term Shatan and the anger of Jehovah." " The writer of the book of Samuel speaks of God's being incensed at the Israelites, and as setting David against them, by *suggesting to him* the thought of numbering the people of both his kingdoms." And this is asserted after the writer had said, a few lines before, "It is said, and that not *unnaturally* in the language of that age and country, that an enemy, Shatan, had been the cause of his adopting this *injudicious and detestable measure.*" So then, according to R. Scott, God first suggested to the mind of David an " *injudicious and detestable measure;*" yes, and induced him to persist in it, and then punished him for it! It is only justice, however, to our opponent to remark, that he appears to intimate by the expression, " not unnaturally *in the language of that age and country,*" that the author of the book of Samuel might not be giving a correct account of the matter, but only using the language, and speaking according to the views of that age and country; while both the views and the language may be altogether incorrect, in the estimation of those who deny the existence of angels both good and bad. For there is only too much plausibility, to say the least, in the charge which has sometimes been brought against them, that they allow the penmen of the Scriptures to be inspired, only *when* and *so far* as suits their own purpose. Another writer,† in order to obviate

---

* R. Scott's Lectures, p. 27. † Inquiry into the Word Satan, p. 13.

the difficulty which arises from making God the adversary here, and representing him as moving David to commit the offence for which he was punished so signally, reasons thus : " The Lord did not draw David into a trespass against any *moral law;* and, recollect also, that the judgment inflicted was temporal only. As to the judgment of the great day when God shall judge the quick and the dead, we only know that the Judge of all the earth will certainly do that which is right." Just as if we did not also know that the Judge of the earth will *always* do that which is right, as it regards *temporal* as well as *eternal* judgments! and just as if when anything, whatever be its nature, is commanded or forbidden by God, it did not become morally wrong to transgress his law! The distinction that he makes between moral and positive precepts is, in this case, and for his purpose, altogether frivolous. He and Russell Scott both suppose that the Israelites had before this transgressed some moral precepts, and that God had a quarrel against them on this account; and that he might have a *visible* reason for punishing them, he moved David to commit this sin. It is quite consistent with the representations of Scripture, and with the character of God, to say that he may, as a punishment for their iniquity, leave men to themselves, give them up, as he did the Israelites, Psalm lxxxi. 12, " to their own hearts' lusts," or to the influence of Satan ; but inconsistent with both to say that he himself becomes the tempter. James i. 13 : " Let no man say when he is tempted, I am tempted of God, for God cannot be tempted of evil, neither tempteth he any man." Had David, when James wrote these words, been on the earth, he might, if the views of our opponents could be correct, have pleaded that *he* at least was an exception, as God had tempted *him*, nay, more than tempted him, for he had led him by a secret invincible influence to commit sin ; rather I should say, it is certain that James did not entertain the same views of the passage under consideration as they do, or else he never would have written the important words which I have just quoted. While it is lamentable that Scripture should be so perverted, in order to maintain a favourite dogma, it is satisfactory to those who reject that dogma, to find that it cannot be defended, without doing violence to the word of God.

The author of the "Inquiry into the Word Satan," maintains that, in 1 Chron. xxi. 1, it means a human adversary, some king or nation at war with David, and that this was the temptation to number the people; and that this hostile power is called an adversary, or a Satan, in the same way as Hadad the Edomite is called an adversary to Solomon, 1 Kings xi. 14. But can any reason be assigned why, if this had been the meaning, he did not mention his name, or give us some information respecting him, as he did in the case of Solomon? Is not this the usual method of the sacred historians? Have we any account of David's ever being induced by all his wars, to number the people as he did now, so as to bring upon himself the judgments of God? Was this king or nation prevented by David's numbering the people, from prosecuting his hostile design? The whole tenor of the narration indicates that there was no immediate danger of war, but that there were both time and leisure to go through the whole nation from Dan to Beersheba, and take the number of the subjects. There is no intimation that they were enrolled for war, or for the army. An attempt has indeed been made to deduce an argument for this hypothesis, from the fact that three months of war was amongst the things that were proposed to David by Gad. But surely this will no more prove that David and his people were menaced by a hostile nation, at that time, than that they were threatened by famine or pestilence. On the contrary, it is implied that whichever David selected would be sent by the special interposition of God. It is commonly supposed that the sin of David on this occasion consisted in his not requiring the people to pay the half-shekel, which was commanded to be levied, Exod. iii. 11, whenever the people were numbered. This, however, may be questioned; it does not appear probable. If it had been so, surely Joab, when he was remonstrating with the king, would have suggested the propriety of obeying the law, and thus avoiding the trespass. But the sin appears to have consisted in numbering them at all, without any necessity, and evidently under the influence of vanity, or pride, or mere caprice; and Joab seems to have perceived this, and therefore to have very much disliked the measure. Had there been any necessity, such as that of a threatened war, we cannot see why the king's word should have been abominable to Joab; nor is it probable, that, as his motive would have been innocent, to say the least, he wuold have been so severely punished by God.

It is inferred, that because David's numbering of the people is, in Samuel,* attributed to the anger of God, and in Chronicles to Satan, these must signify the same thing, —that God himself must be the Satan, the adversary, who stood up against Israel. But how absurd is this conclusion! The carrying of the Israelites captive into Babylon, is sometimes, in the prophets, attributed to the anger of God, and sometimes to the king of Babylon. Will any rational being argue or conclude, that therefore the anger of God, and the king of Babylon, are identical? Is it not evident that the meaning is, that because the anger of God was excited by the sins of the Israelites, therefore he gave them into the hand of the king of Babylon? That ambitious monarch was plotting and endeavouring to accomplish the conquest of all around him. God was not the author of that ambition; he merely overruled it, to accomplish his own purposes; and hence, in the way which is described in Ezek. xxi. 21, he rendered the superstition and divination of the king of Babylon the means of directing his steps to Jerusalem. "For the king of Babylon stood at

* 2 Sam. xxiv. 1.

the parting of the way, at the head of the two ways, to use divination: he made his arrows bright, he consulted with images, he looked in the liver. At his right hand was the divination for Jerusalem." And how easy is it, on this plain and scriptural principle, to see the harmony of the two passages which we are considering! Satan was as full of malice against Israel, the chosen people of God, as Nebuchadnezzar was of ambition; all that was necessary, was for God to give him permission to tempt David to number them, and it would soon be done: as in the case of Job, when God said, "All that he has is in thy hand;" how quickly did he go to the full limits of the permission! With the greatest propriety then might it be said in one respect, for a very sufficient reason, that God moved David to say, "Go, number Israel and Judah;" and in another, that Satan stood up against them, and provoked David to number them, just as the trials of Job came from God, because he permitted and directed them, and yet they came from Satan, because he inflicted them; or in the same way as the captivity of the Jews was both from God, and from the king of Babylon and his armies.

On the principles which have been advocated, I must think, that in 1 Kings xxii. 21, it is at least implied that fallen, wicked spirits do tempt men; and that false prophets were, in a special manner, their agents. There is no necessity for supposing that any actual conversation took place between God and the angels, or between him and the lying spirit. But can we suppose that any such scenery would have been presented to the mind of the prophet, or that he would have been inspired by the Holy Spirit to represent, even figuratively, a lying spirit appearing before God, if there were no such spirit in existence? If, as some of our opponents would have us to believe, there are neither angels nor devils, even an allegorical allusion to these spirits would never have been made. Here again the most natural sense of the passage is, that

God had permitted a fallen lying spirit to deceive the prophets of Ahab, or to prompt them to pretend to knowledge which they did not possess. To accommodate here the language of an apostle, " their coming," their mission to Ahab, " was after the working of Satan, with all power, and signs, and lying wonders, and with all deceivableness of unrighteousness, in them that perish, because they received not the love of the truth that they might be saved : and for this cause God shall send them strong delusion, that they should believe a lie."

Those who disbelieve the existence of Satan, very generally, perhaps universally, consider the book of Job as an allegory or fable; and, consequently, they maintain that no arguments can be deduced from it to prove the existence of Satan. One of them has roundly asserted, that "to consider the book of Job in any other light than as an allegory, would be to give up all title to common sense." To this it may be replied, that he who can make such an assertion should give up all title to modesty; for most assuredly men distinguished, not only for common sense, but for learning, ability, and piety, have not only considered, but *attempted*, at least, to prove, that it is not an allegory, whatever dramatic writing there may be in it; and their proofs are not to be neutralized by Mr. Heineken's dictum. It has been well answered to him, "He that can suppose that Job was a fictitious being, and his book a fable, must give up all title as a believer in Divine revelation, and appropriate to himself the title of infidel. That Job was a real and not a fictitious character, may be inferred from the manner in which he is mentioned by the prophet Ezekiel and the apostle James: Ezek. xiv. 14, 'Though these three men, Noah, Daniel, and Job, were in it, they should deliver but their own souls by their righteousness, saith the Lord God.' As Noah and Daniel were real characters, we must conclude the same of Job. If he was not a real intelligent being, why did the inspired prophet class him with Noah and Daniel, and expressly call them three men; and not only so, but repeat the statement thrice, as if to guard against any mistake? To suppose that Job was only an imaginary being, is to suppose that the prophet repeats a positive falsehood and absurdity. 'Behold,' says James, chap. v. 11, 'ye count them happy that endure: ye have heard of the patience of Job, and have seen the end of the Lord, that the Lord is very pitiful and of tender mercy.' But adopt Mr. H.'s opinion, and the language of the apostle would read thus: 'Ye have heard of the patience of a fictitious being, and have seen the end of the Lord, that the Lord is very pitiful and of tender mercy.' But to whom? To a fictitious being."* And the persons to whom this was addressed might well reply, it is easy for a man who possesses any fertility of imagination, to suppose and depict a fictitious patience, in any circumstances, and to any amount. But what is that to us? Ours are real sufferings. We need real patience. Where is the force of the apostle's argument? The writer of a dramatic poem, many hundred years ago, gave, in the luxuriance of an oriental fancy, a very fine picture of patience, in an imaginary personage called Job: be ye therefore patient amidst your real and protracted sufferings. What motives can this present to our minds? What have the figments of imagination to do with the realities of life? To reason, or to pretend to reason, from the conduct of the heroes of the former, to the duty of those who are engaged in the latter, and groaning beneath their burdens, and smarting amidst their ills, is little less than a heartless insult. But this is not the place to prove that the book of Job, as far as facts are concerned, is a real history. This has been done by many, particularly by Bishop Patrick and Dr. J. M. Good, in their introduction to that interesting portion of the sacred records.

But if we were, for the sake of argument, to grant that

* Carlisle on Evil Spirits, p. 109.

the book of Job is an allegory, still it must furnish to all who believe in its inspiration a proof of the existence of evil spirits, and even to those who do not, an evidence that its author thought they existed. "Even the allusions with which we meet in the Scripture, are allusions to real facts, and to real beings. The writers of the Scriptures neither did, nor could, consistently with their inspiration, invent imaginary beings, either for the exercise of their genius, or the amusement of their readers. Such conduct would but ill become those who were commissioned to instruct mankind in things spiritual. If therefore we should grant that the first and second chapters of Job are an allegory, still we should maintain that all its allusions are founded on fact, and that the poetical mention of Satan in such a book would be a proof of his existence. Mankind have invented superstitions enough, without receiving additions to them from those Scriptures which are intended for the destruction of error, and the diffusion of Divine truth."* This reasoning appears to me perfectly correct; as has already been observed, the first two chapters of Job, if we allow that they were written by the inspiration of the Divine Spirit, prove the existence of evil spirits, even supposing them to be a dramatic poem, just as clearly as if we take them for a real history; and if we grant that the book is an eastern fable, as some have called it, still it proves that its author believed in the existence of evil spirits. Does not the parable of the rich man and Lazarus prove that Jesus Christ believed in a future state of rewards and punishments, and also of rich men and beggars, even if it were granted or proved that no such persons as Lazarus and Dives ever existed? And the parable of the king who made a marriage for his son, Matt. xxii., though the Saviour might have, and probably had, no particular king in view, takes it for granted that there are kings, and that they sometimes make marriage feasts for their sons, and act

* Carlisle's Essay, p. 110.

such a part as is there described. Mr. Grundy requires us, if we believe that it is a real history, and that it can prove the existence of evil spirits, to take everything literally. To this we answer, the demand is unreasonable, nay, it even implies an absurdity. Are we to suppose, that, because God asks Satan, "Whence camest thou?" he is not omniscient, and did not know where the archfiend had been? In the parable of Jotham, Judges, ix. 7, are we either to grant that the trees thought and spoke, and made a king over them, or else allow that the author of the parable did not believe in the existence of trees and brambles? So we can, with the greatest consistency, say that there is no necessity for asserting that there was any real discourse between God and Satan, or that the latter actually appeared in heaven amongst the angels, the sons of God; (the true worshippers of God on earth may be meant—though it might be shown that there is not so much absurdity as some take for granted, in supposing that Satan actually appeared amongst the angels;) and yet the history may necessarily imply the existence of a wicked being, called Satan, a malignant accuser and tempter; that he is obliged to give account of himself to God, is under the control of the Divine Being, and can do no mischief but by his permission; and that he is sometimes suffered to tempt and injure the righteous. The existence of Satan is just as much supposed here, as the existence of God, or of men, or of marauders, or of storms and diseases. R. Scott thinks that the term Satan is an appellative, and that it includes the Sabeans and Chaldeans, and the wind, and fire, and the leprosy, all of which are dramatically represented as the enemies of Job. This is ridiculous: it implies a violation of even all dramatic laws, as well as of the principles of truth and nature. Could the robbers, and winds, and fire, and leprosy, be represented as appearing before God *amongst his sons?* as being asked by him whether they had considered his servant Job? as intimating doubts respecting the sincerity of his piety? as moving God against him to destroy him? as daring God to put forth his hand and touch all that he had? as going out from the presence of the Lord and smiting Job with sore boils? How ineffably absurd! Such incongruities and impossibilities would not be tolerated in even a work of imagination, far less in a real history, which there is no doubt the book of Job is. But all the circumstances agree well with the character of such a being as we suppose that Satan is. As he is described in the Bible, there is nothing stated here, but what he could and would do, as far as permission was granted to him. Would even Shakspere have ever feigned such beings as his fairies, and witches, and wizards, had he not known that in the periods to which he referred, they were believed to exist? And had he been writing to correct men's views on religious subjects, and to induce them to look to God alone, as the author of all their mercies, and as the dispenser of all their trials, instead of aiming at gratifying their imaginations, would he, not believing in their existence, have introduced such beings into even dramatic representations? Where was the necessity or the utility of introducing a being like Satan in addition to the Sabeans, and representing him as different from them, if he had no existence, especially if it were a real history? and even if it were a moral fable, it would have been as interesting and instructive without him. Everything proves that the author of this book believed in the existence of a wicked spirit, who, by the permission of God, was the instigator of the plunderers of Job, caused the death of his children, and smote him with a painful and loathsome disease.

In the hundred and ninth Psalm, we have the following language: "Set thou a wicked man over him, and let Satan stand at his right hand." This may be correctly translated, "Let an adversary, or enemy, or accuser, stand at his right hand;" and it is thus rendered by good scholars and critics. Still, the question is, to whom does the psalm relate, and who is meant by this enemy? I must entirely agree with those commentators who maintain that it refers to Judas, and that it is a prophetical description of his sin and punishment. " The sin of Judas was the most immoral and unrighteous action which human malignity ever had the opportunity of perpetrating." "I can discover no reason why this psalm should be supposed to relate to David and his enemies, unless a hypothesis, which has little support either from reason or Scripture, is to be accepted as such. Nothing can be more significant of the treachery and detestable impiety of Judas than the accumulated particulars that are contained in this psalm; and in my apprehension, the force of the prediction is materially impaired by any reference to David, besides his being the chosen organ of this remarkable and graphical prophecy."* The question then is, judging from the history of Judas, did any human adversary act the part which is pointed out in the sixth verse? Did any enemy of this kind either tempt Judas, or punish him, or prove the man of his right hand in the commission of his crime? *He* tempted the chief priests by going and asking, "What will ye give me, and I will deliver him unto you?" Matt. xxvi. 15. Both Luke and John assure us it was Satan or the devil that entered into Judas, and put it into his heart to betray Jesus Christ. I cannot but think, therefore, that Satan, or the chief of the apostate spirits, is the adversary that stood at the right hand of Judas, who first tempted him to betray his Master, and then to put an end to his own miserable existence; and that the common translation gives the true sense. Some say that his own avarice was the only devil or Satan that tempted him. But this could not, with any propriety, be said to enter into him then, as he had been under its influence, it had been his prevailing disposition, for years past, perhaps during his whole life.

* Walford on the Psalms.

If he had no tempter but his own covetous disposition, how easy and natural would it have been to have said so! What end could be answered, but that of obscuring the statement, and misleading the reader, by saying that an adversary or a Satan entered into him, and put it into his heart to betray his Master? Nay, I do not think it too much to assert, that if it could be proved that by the term devil and Satan the sacred writer had his avarice in view, still his meaning and the import of the passage are, that it acted the part of an evil being, known by the name of Satan, to him, and that therefore the existence of evil spirits is here recognized. And is not the same idea conveyed, when the Saviour said, "Have not I chosen you twelve, and one of you is a devil?"

There are several other passages which relate to the subject under consideration, such as the following: "Now is the judgment of this world; now shall the prince of this world be cast out," John xii. 31; "The prince of this world cometh, and hath nothing in me," John xiv. 30; "The prince of the power of the air," Eph. ii. 2; "For we wrestle not against flesh and blood, but against principalities, against powers, against the rulers of the darkness of this world," &c. Eph. vi. 12; "And they had a king over them, who is the angel of the bottomless pit, whose name in the Hebrew tongue is Abaddon, but in the Greek tongue hath his name Apollyon," Rev. ix. 11; and the account of our Lord's temptation in the wilderness; on which it may be expected some remarks should be made. But this is not necessary after what has been advanced, and some of them will come under review afterwards. All who believe in the existence of evil spirits will apply them to Satan; and those who are not convinced by the passages which have been illustrated, will not be convinced by any other.

It may be thought by some that I have dwelt too long on this part of the subject, and paid to the statements and arguments of those who differ from us more attention than they deserve. But the subject is one of very great importance, both on account of the doctrine itself which is at issue, its relation to the duty and experience of the Christian; its connexion with other important doctrines; and the principles of interpretation, by which an attempt is made to prove that it is not found in the Bible; and, as has already been observed, in one respect we should rejoice if our opponents could prove that they are right; and, consequently, that there are no such unhappy and malignant beings as those whom we designate evil spirits in existence, and that therefore the Christian has no such formidable enemies as they are to fear. We own that the tenet in question is what some would call an alarming and gloomy one; and so are many others that are presented to us in the clearest light of truth shed around us both from reason, and faith, and the word of God. And if we wish to be "*of the truth*," according to the expressive language of the Bible, we must bow to its authority, whatever it enjoins; we must embrace it in whatever form it appears; we must follow it wherever it leads; and if we do so, it will all be found salutary; for as it is presented to us, in the word of God, it all belongs, in one respect or another, to that "truth which is in Jesus," by which his disciples are sanctified and eternally saved; to that truth which furnishes the principles of Jehovah's government, is the very basis of his throne, and which, we are assured, he "keepeth for ever," as the invariable associate of his mercy in all its glorious manifestations.

LECTURE II.

THE CHARACTER, STATE, AND POWERS OF EVIL SPIRITS.

Having ascertained, from the statements and intimations of the Bible, that there are such beings as those which are commonly denominated devils or evil spirits, we are naturally led to inquire, in the next place, what kind of beings are they; what was their original condition; how were they brought into their present state; what is the extent of their powers; and what have we to fear from them, as the enemies of our souls? On these subjects, though we have not much direct information in the word of God, yet we are furnished with many important intimations and general principles, by which we may be guided in our reasonings and inquiries, and from which we may derive much useful knowledge.

Scripture and reason unite in assuring us that God, and he alone, existed from eternity; and that to him all creatures owe their being and original characters. He is naturally, immensely, and unchangeably good, in the highest and best sense of the word, and therefore nothing that is, properly speaking, bad, can come from him; for as natural evils work together for the good of his people, (Rom. viii. 28,) so we may conclude that, as sent by him, they are always rendered subservient to some beneficial and holy purpose, and are therefore good. The apostle James gives us a beautiful epitome of both the deductions of reason and the doctrine of the Bible on this important point, chap. i. 17, "Every good gift and every perfect gift is from above, and cometh down from the Father of lights, with whom there is no variableness, neither shadow of turning." "The *Father* of lights," and therefore light in all its kinds, and with all its important properties, is his offspring, a kind of emanation from his very nature, if he operates (*ad extra*, as it is sometimes expressed) at all. We learn then from this important declaration what God is necessarily, naturally, and unchangeably; and what must be the character of all his works. This eternal Fountain of all life and excellence cannot send forth both sweet waters and bitter. The uncreated Sun, or Light of the universe, cannot be the cause of darkness, especially in its worst form, that of moral evil, which is the very blackness of the thickest gloom of hell. Not only is there no *real change* with him, but there is not even the *shadow*, the *appearance* of change. How then can there be such a change as would take place, if this eternal, uncreated light were to become the cause, the parent of darkness? "Do not err, my beloved brethren," exclaims the apostle with a peculiar emphasis, which plainly intimates, that to make God in any sense the author of sin, is a gross fundamental error of the most pernicious influence, alike dishonourable to him and injurious to his creatures; and the truth on this subject is, that "every good gift, and every perfect gift, is from above, and cometh down from the Father of lights." And it is plainly implied, no gifts but what are good; all emanations from him partake of this character. He is the Creator of the ends of the earth,—of the universe, and therefore of evil spirits; but as brought into existence by him, they must have been, in their original state, like all his works, *very good;* and they could be reduced to their present condition, and become what they are as it regards their character, only by their voluntary defection and rebellion. In accordance with these principles and reasonings, the apostle Peter, 2 Ep. ii. 4, informs us that they "sinned," and that as a punishment for their sin, they were "cast down into hell, and delivered into chains of darkness, to be reserved unto judgment." And Jude, verse 6, asserts that these "angels kept not their *first* estate," that, doubtless, in which they were placed by their great Creator, "but left their own habitation," and therefore "are reserved in everlasting chains under darkness unto the judgment of the great day." And in the prospect of this judgment, they are represented as "believing and trembling," James ii. 19, and as exclaiming to the Saviour when he was on earth, "Art thou come to torment us before the time?" Matt. viii. 29; "I adjure thee by God that thou torment me not," Mark v. 7. We may conclude, then, both from the dictates of reason and the statements of the Bible, that evil spirits were created by God in a state of perfect purity and happiness; for this is necessary to constitute the goodness of rational and accountable beings: and that they fell from it by their own wilful transgression and rebellion against God. We have already endeavoured to prove the possibility, and even, taking everything into account, the probability of such an event.

In attempting, then, to form an idea of the present state, character, and powers of fallen spirits, it is natural, and even necessary, to advert to their original condition in all these respects, as they were created by God; and therefore to attend to the information which the Bible gives respecting the holy elect angels. And as it is always delightful and profitable to observe and trace the harmony between reason and revelation, to see how, in many most important cases, the latter confirms the conclusions and conjectures, and enlightens the darkness of the former, we may just glance at what it is rational to conclude are the character and powers of these happy and glorious beings, who kept their first estate.

Now there are several things which seem to indicate that man is the very lowest order of accountable creatures.

We know that in him the rational and irrational natures, with their different capacities and powers, are united. He partakes of the senses and instincts of mere animals, and also of the capacities and powers of celestial spirits. Like the former, he is the subject of sensations, and appetites, and passions; he needs the support of matter, moulded into various kinds of nutriment: with the latter, he is capable of knowing the character, of performing the will of God, and of enjoying him as his portion: and it is almost unnecessary to say, that the rational and immaterial, is unspeakably the more important and excellent part of his frame; and that the body appears to contract the capacities of the soul, to fetter its powers, and to impede them in their operations. How often, in this respect as well as others, when the spirit is willing, and even vigorous, the flesh is weak! Farther, in man we see rationality in the lowest, feeblest form, or state, in which it can possibly exist.* Its principles lie dormant for some time in the breast of the infant. He is at first entirely the creature of instincts, and sensations, and appetites. Then he begins to have some faint perception of reality, and truth, and right, and wrong, and to reason on the facts with which he has gained a slight acquaintance. In a lower state than this, the power of reason cannot exist; here we see, as it were, its very commencement, its first glimmering dawn, connected, in the improvement which is afterwards realized, with its advancement towards the perfect day. But betwixt its most effective development, its highest attainments in man, in his present state, and its absolute perfection, its infinitude in the Divine Being, what a distance, what a chasm exists! Is it then left entirely empty of rational beings? Is it possible that man is at once the lowest and the highest order of them? Would not this be a notion similar to that of those who, in times that are past, imagined, because this world is the

* Appendix B.

only part of the universe to which they had personal access, the inhabitants and productions of which they could examine for themselves, that it alone is inhabited; and that all the stars and planets are only shining points or gems, the sparkling ornaments of the canopy which is stretched over our heads, and that they were all created for the exclusive pleasure, or benefit, of men? And will not this remark apply, at least in some degree, to the opinions of those who deny the existence of angels, either good or bad, for no other reason, that I can conceive, but because they cannot bring them, in any way, beneath the cognizance of their senses? We see a gradation, without any void, or chasm, in vegetable life, from its very lowest to its highest forms, endued, as far as we can conceive, with all its possible sensibilities and beauties; and also in animal life and capacity, from the very dullest insect or shell-fish, to the half-reasoning dog, or beaver, or elephant. Are we not then warranted, by analogy and reason, to think that there will be found, in the universe, a similar gradation, of which man is the commencement, the lowest step, in rational capacities and powers, to an inconceivable height above us in various forms of glorious creatures? And how high may it rise! How extensive may be the capacity, how mighty the powers of many of these orders or ranks, especially of the highest! while still there is, and must be, an infinite distance betwixt them and the Great Infinite Eternal! How delightful, how animating, the hope presented to us by the Gospel, and by the Gospel alone, of one day joining these glorious beings; gaining the most accurate acquaintance with their characters; being numbered amongst their friends; emulating them in their celestial excellences; and uniting with them in their worship and pursuits; and of thus coming, in the most emphatic sense of the term, to an innumerable company of angels; and yet of viewing their glories as only the imperfect reflection of the uncreated effulgence of Jehovah! Alas, that this hope should be forfeited, for anything that earth and sin can afford or promise! How often is the folly of Esau, in its worst form, repeated! For what trifles and low gratifications do men barter their celestial birthright! And are we not warranted to conclude that the lowest order of these spiritual, celestial beings must soar far above us in capacity, power, excellence, and happiness? The meanest of the animal tribe rises, by the very possession of life and feeling, far above the highest order of vegetables. There is something unspeakably more interesting in a capacity to feel, to enjoy, to suffer, to be sensible, in some degree, of its own existence, and of that of other creatures, than in all the forms, and laws, and motions, and affinities, and beauties, of merely organized, but still completely dead matter. There is a great gulf betwixt the former and the latter, which nothing but infinite knowledge can fathom; over which nothing but almighty power can carry. Were we once to allow that mere matter could be rendered capable of sensation, by any division, or composition, or motion, or position, of its particles, without any change in its essential properties, or having united with it, or infused into it, anything of a superior nature, we could not stop here; we must allow that it is capable of thought and reason, of being rendered all that men are; and consequently we must admit all the absurdities connected with this supposition, give up the immateriality of the soul, and allow that there is no essential difference between the most highly gifted philosopher, or the most eminent saint, and the stones or mire of the streets. In like manner, the meanest, the most stupid rational creature, that can reflect on his own existence, and inquire after his Maker,—can distinguish betwixt holiness and sin,—can enjoy the satisfaction of a good, or smart beneath the lashes of a bad conscience,—can rise in its thoughts and desires to heaven, and exult in the smile of Jehovah, or tremble at his frown, —can thus enjoy an infinite good, or suffer an infinite evil,—is unspeakably, I had almost said infinitely, superior to the most sagacious animal, to which the least idea of God, and heaven, and eternity, could never be conveyed by any possible culture, or by all the means that could ever be used. Are we not then warranted by analogy to allow, that as man appears to be the lowest order of rational beings; and at the same time, the link between matter and spirit, rationality and irrationality, or between mere instinct connected with life,—and reason,—that the lowest order of rational spiritual beings, the next link above him in the chain of life and mental power, may be, I had almost said, must be, far superior to him? That as there is an important property in animal life, which there is not in vegetables; and in rational beings, which is not in mere animals; so there may be in pure, spiritual existence, some property or power, or at least a modification of a property or power, which there is not in a compound being like man, that will render the lowest order of the former superior to the highest of the latter, especially while the soul is united to a gross mortal body, and that too, as ours is, deteriorated by sin.

Now these reasonings, or conjectures, if such they must be considered, are abundantly confirmed by the views which the Scriptures give us of good angels in all their ranks and gradations. They are always represented as far superior to us, as possessing powers to which, as it regards their extent, we can make no pretensions, and as able to perform operations which may well fill us with astonishment, and which are far above the reach of our ability. Hence, in Exod. xxxiii. 2, God promises to send an angel before the Israelites, to drive out the seven nations of Canaan. Here an angel is represented as able to subdue all those kings and their armies, or which amounts to the same, to enable the Israelites to obtain the victory over them, and that by some unseen influence or assistance afforded to them in their conflicts, and, as it would appear from some facts which are recorded in the history of the wars of Joshua, by rendering the laws of nature subservient to that purpose. And that God had a created angel in view here, and not the Angel of the Covenant, is evident from the threatening which was connected with the promise; "For I will not go up in the midst of thee;" and from the effect produced on the people; "They mourned, and no man did put on him his ornaments." Again, in 2 Sam. xxiv. and 1 Chron. xxi. we are informed, that an angel was sent to punish the Israelites, and to destroy Jerusalem, and that he smote in one day, from Dan to Beersheba, seventy thousand. It is true this was done by a pestilence, but it seems to be plainly intimated that this plague was inflicted in an extraordinary way, by the ministry of an angel. Or if we were to allow, for the sake of argument, that this was merely a visionary representation to the minds of David and Ornan, for both saw him, still there is a reference to the native power of angels. Again, in Daniel iii. 38, we read, that "God sent an angel and shut the lions' mouths," even when they were hungry and ravening for their prey. From this it follows, that angels can control the instincts and appetites of savage animals, by an influence of which we have no conception. Psalm xxxiv. 7; "The angel of the Lord encampeth round about those who fear him, and delivereth them." Here it is implied that an angel is equal to a host, and can guard the righteous on every side. The angels that came to Lot smote the inhabitants of Sodom with blindness. This they did, it would seem, by exciting some influence either on the air or on the bodies of these unhappy men, without coming into contact with them. When an angel descended from heaven to roll back the stone from the door of the sepulchre on the morning of the Saviour's resurrection, there was a great earthquake, and it seems to be plainly intimated that it was caused by his power. In Acts v. 19, we find that the angel of the Lord opened the prison doors, so that the keeper knew nothing of what was done. In like manner the angel brought Peter out of prison, and caused the iron gate which led into the city to open of its own accord, Acts xii. 10. When the angel of the Lord appeared to the shepherds at the birth of the Saviour, he caused a celestial glory to shine around them, which overwhelmed them with fear. John (Rev. xviii. 1) saw a mighty angel who shone with so much effulgence, that "the earth was lightened with his glory;" and this appearance was doutless intended to indicate the greatness of his mental power and moral excellence. And it was an angel that presented to the mind or imagination of John all the visions of the Apocalypse, Rev. xxii. 8. They are said to "excel in strength," Psalm ciii., and it is evident that the Psalmist has in view chiefly intellectual and moral strength, which qualifies them for the service of God; for "they do his commandments, hearkening unto the voice of his word;" though, as I may afterwards endeavour to show, it does not exclude what is equivalent to physical energy, or power over matter to mould, and influence, and render it subservient to their will. They are also denominated "*mighty* angels," 2 Thess. i. 7, where the apostle has in view an occasion on which there might will be put in requisition, and manifested in the most striking manner; for the great probability is, that they will be employed to effect many of the changes that will take place, and to exhibit many of the wonderful scenes that will be manifested, at the second coming of the Lord Jesus Christ: and we are assured, that at the end of the world, "The reapers are the angels," and that "the angels shall come forth, and shall sever the wicked from amongst the just," Matt. xiii. 39, 49. And it is evident from all the accounts which are given us of them in the Bible, that they excel in wisdom as much as in strength; or rather, as has just now been observed, that their strength is principally the power of wisdom and knowledge: and that in these they are far superior to men is plainly implied in the language of the

Saviour, Matt. xxiv. 36, "But of that day and hour knoweth no man, no, not the angels of heaven, but my Father only." The same fact is evident from Psalm civ. and Heb. i. 7, where we are informed, that God "maketh his angels spirits, and his ministers a flaming fire."*

That angels are far superior to men in activity, knowledge, power, and dignity, is clearly implied in the figurative representations which are given of them in Scripture, particularly in Isa. vi., Ezek. i. and x., and in the book of Revelation, where the cherubim and seraphim and living creatures are described as being full of eyes, to denote their knowledge and wisdom, as having six wings, as not resting day or night, as running to and fro like flames of fire, as being the constant attendants on God, and being permitted to see his glory, and to stand in that presence which no man can see and live. They sustain the highest honours, and realize all the happiness, and discharge the most important offices, of that celestial kingdom, which flesh and blood cannot inherit. And if any should object that the living creatures are not angels, since in the book of Revelation the former are distinguished from the latter, Rev. v. 11, this would not invalidate the argument; for the angels are, in this passage, presented to us as their companions, as equal to them, and as engaged in the same work. The dignity, the powers, of these celestial beings, and their great superiority to men, are also plainly implied in the names and epithets which are given to them in the Scriptures. They are denominated not only angels, or messengers, by way of eminence, but also cherubim and seraphim, thrones, authorities, dominions, principalities, and powers. In addition to all this, they are perfect in holiness; for they are designated by way of eminence, "holy angels," Matt. xxv. And we are sure that their moral purity must be *complete*, without the least imperfection or stain, for they dwell in the immediate blissful

* Appendix C.

presence of God, they are the constant inhabitants of those glorious regions into which nothing that defileth can possibly enter. It is also evident from the statements of the Bible respecting them, that they are *immortal*. Some of them may have been for millions of ages employed in contemplating the glories of God, and in realizing intellectual improvement; and still eternity is before them. In every respect, they are far superior to men.

To these glorious beings, fallen angels originally belonged. It is the dictate of reason, it is plainly implied in the statements of the Bible, that they, as well as men, were created in the image of God, perfect in knowledge, wisdom, purity, and happiness. What was their rank amongst these exalted spirits, we have no means of ascertaining. But, as it evidently follows from the representations of the Scriptures, that there are gradations, as it regards intellect and dignity, amongst the holy angels, so it is probable, that those who fell might belong to several orders of the celestial hierarchy; and consequently that there are subordination and superiority amongst them still—that some excel others in capacity and power, and exercise a degree of authority over those who are inferior; and even that some are worse, more depraved, more impious, and malignant, and impure than others. Whilst the Scriptures, as well as fact, assure us that amongst the fallen sons of men "there is none righteous, no not one;" that all are under the influence of the carnal mind, which "is enmity against God;" yet some even of those who are placed, as far as possible, precisely in the same circumstances, are far more depraved than others; it is reasonable then to suppose that similar gradations in wickedness will exist amongst fallen spirits. Farther, we find that outlaws and robbers, and even systematic murderers, (such as Thugs and slave-dealers,) are obliged to have some kind of government amongst them, to have rulers and laws; and that the boldest and most vigorous, those who are best qualified to be ringleaders in mischief, and to repel the attacks of enemies, or the efforts of those who endeavour to reduce them to order, and maintain the authority of law and government, are invested with rule amongst them. So we may suppose, nay, we may regard it as certain, it is amongst those unhappy beings who are banished from heaven, and are leagued in rebellion against the Sovereign of the universe. The principles of rationality, even when perverted, the influence of sin, to a certain extent the necessity of the case, would lead to this combination which we have supposed. So far, then, we may allow the representation of our great poet to be correct:—

"Devil with devil damned firm concord holds."

We should greatly err, however, were we to imagine that they live together in harmony and love, that all amongst them is peace and concord. No, this would be to transfer, in our imaginations, one of the glories of the celestial regions, one of the sources of their happiness, to the infernal world. Heaven is the region of love and peace; hell of hatred, discord, strife and confusion. Fallen spirits, doubtless, even more than fallen men, "live in malice and envy, hateful and hating one another." All this is consistent, however, with the subordination of which I have spoken, and with their being leagued in rebellion against God, and in their efforts to diffuse sin, confusion, and misery, throughout the universe. One in particular, denominated in Scripture *the devil*, by way of eminence, the old serpent and Satan, the wicked one, appears to be "the king of the bottomless pit," the ringleader and ruler of its wretched inhabitants. To him, partly, perhaps, in consequence of the force that is exerted on them, and partly out of infernal policy, all the hosts of hell submit, and under him they carry on their impious warfare against their Creator and lawful Sovereign. That God should permit them to do this for a long course of ages, and even to realize various degrees of success in their impious warfare against heaven, and in many cases to execute their plans, is not more mysterious or unaccountable, than are numerous facts connected with this lower world. These led a prophet to exclaim, "Wherefore doth the way of the wicked prosper? wherefore are they all happy that deal very treacherously?" Jer. xii. 1. "Behold, these are the ungodly who prosper in the world, they increase in riches," Psa. lxxiii. 12. Indeed, it deserves to be carefully remarked and repeatedly asserted, that there is not a single cavil which has been raised, or objection that has been urged against the scriptural account, and I must add, against what is called the orthodox belief, as held by intelligent Christians, respecting evil spirits, and the part which they act as it regards the human race, which might not be raised and urged, against what we see and feel every day. Now, on account of the subordination of which we have spoken, their ringleader is represented in the Bible as a ruler, a king, amongst these unhappy beings, and they as his angels, his messengers, his agents, Matt. xxv. 41. Under him there may be "thrones, and dominions, princedoms, powers," in hell as well as in heaven. If we suppose that pride was the first, the ruining sin of Satan, his punishment would inflame, would madden his ambition, instead of quenching it. The representation of the poet, here again, perfectly agrees with truth and nature. We might almost imagine that Satan actually exclaimed,

> "To reign is worth ambition, though in hell;
> Better to reign in hell, than serve in heaven."

May not something take place amongst these fallen spirits similar to what we know often occurs amongst men? May not Satan, the tempter of the rest, attach to his part and plans those who were next to him in power and dignity? And may not these influence others, and thus all their ranks and multitudes be induced, be forced, to submit to the prince of hell; especially because his depraved views and dispositions are similar to their own? Notwithstanding all their knowledge and craft, they are all supremely foolish; who can say how far he might impose on them by his "glozing lies," and specious promises, though false as hell? We are fully warranted, then, by the deductions of reason and sound philosophy, in supposing that, according to the intimations of the Bible, there are various orders amongst the fallen spirits, and that all are subordinate to one chief; and that therefore we may consider them as the devil and his angels.*

We are justified, then, in asserting that their powers and honours might be inconceivably great in heaven—that Satan, their ringleader, might be equal to Gabriel or Michael—that

> "High in the midst of all the throng,
> Satan, a tall archangel, sat;"

and that mighty spirits, of various ranks, fell with him. And how great was their fall! Who can say with how much ardour love to God burned in their breasts; how near to his burning, splendid, majestic throne they were able to approach; what smiles of his countenance, what tokens of his regard they realized; what blessings they received from him; with what ecstasy, and in how lofty strains they sang his praises; how glorious was their purity, or what rapturous pleasure filled their breasts? Here again we have *scriptural facts* both for argument and illustration. How amiable and excellent was the character of our first parents when created in the image of God; in that image which includes in it all possible moral excellences; all the principles and graces which the omnipotent influences of the Divine Spirit are necessary to form in the character of believers, and which heaven itself will only complete! What favours did they receive from God! what manifesta-

* Appendix D.

tions of his glory did they witness! what wonder and gratitude and pleasure must have filled their breasts! We can scarcely help imagining that they actually sang,

> " These are thy glorious works, Parent of good
> Almighty; thine this universal frame,
> Thus wondrous fair; thyself how wondrous then!"

What then must have been the case with those who were angels and archangels in heaven! The very fact of their being, in consequence of their rebellion and fall, in such a degraded and wretched state—utterly and for ever banished from heaven and from hope, "reserved in chains under darkness, to the judgment of the great day," implies, that their privileges and glories were something like what we have supposed, on the principle, that, "to whomsoever much is given, of him shall much be required," that "the servant who knew his Lord's will, and did it not, shall be beaten with many stripes," and that in proportion to the nearness to heaven to which any are exalted, must be, if they rebel, the profundity of the depths of hell into which they are cast. What an appalling contrast is presented between their present and their past state and character; one that may well, at times, diffuse deep, awful solemnity through the frames of the blessed angels themselves. How must the hell of these fallen spirits be half formed by the recollection of their former heaven! And how dreadful the power of moral evil, since it thus perverts and destroys the noblest works of God! Is it not probable that one act of wilful, determined rebellion against God, or of trifling with his authority, and transgression of his law, would, by its native influence and necessary operation on all rational creatures, have transformed angels of the highest order into demons; an archangel into the prince of hell; one of the most glorious and happy, into one of the most deformed, and hateful, and wretched beings in existence, ruining him for ever and ever? How evil and bitter a thing is it to depart from the living God! How *destructive* that death into the regions of which those who do so, wander! What then must be the influence of all the sins which every one of us has committed, if we are left under their guilt and power through the ages of eternity! Into what an abyss of depravity and wretchedness must they sink!—it must be a bottomless pit!! The fall of these exalted beings directs our attention to that most difficult question, whether considered naturally or morally, the origin of sin in one of its most mysterious forms. For how, it may well be asked, is it possible that creatures so wise, and holy, and happy, could, and that without being assaulted by any tempter, be dissatisfied with their state, could desire any change, and endeavour to effect one, by acting so foolishly and wickedly? But on this subject we must merely observe, that we know by facts and experience, presented to us, not only in the history, but in the present state of the world, that wise and holy creatures can act foolishly and impiously, and directly contrary to their general views, and inclinations, and habits. A man who can with truth, and in the presence of God exclaim, "Oh how I love thy law! it is my study all the day," has grossly violated that law, and that in cases in which we should have thought his principles and habits would have effectually secured him. And the most plausible theories must be wrong when they are opposed to undoubted fact.

What was the *first sin* which Satan committed, and for which he was banished from heaven, it is of course, as nothing is expressly revealed respecting it, impossible to determine.* The general opinion, and it is, to say the least, as probable as any other, is, that it was pride; and there is one passage of Scripture which seems to favour this sentiment, 1 Tim. iii. 6: "Not *a new convert*, lest being puffed up with pride, he fall into the condemnation

* Appendix E.

of the devil." Some render this "the condemnation of the accuser" or evil speaker. In this way Erasmus, Coverdale, Cranmer, and others translate ὁ διάβολος. But though it often has this meaning, I cannot think that there is here a reference to any human accuser or evil speaker, and to the way in which he would condemn, or cause to be condemned, one who was lifted up with pride. For those who brought the charge against him, in the case supposed, would not be false accusers or slanderers, they would be speaking the truth; and pride is not a sin which would have arrested the attention of the enemies of the Christians, and induced informers to cause them to be condemned and punished by either Jews or heathens. The words ὁ διάβολος most naturally refer to the great accuser of the brethren and slanderer of God and men, and the sin which he committed. Not to urge that the word κρίμα sometimes means crime, or fault, and might, without doing violence to either the text or connexion, be rendered "the crime, or fault of the devil." The most natural interpretation of the passage then is, lest being puffed up with pride, which was the first sin of the devil, the young bishop be condemned as he was. And when we consider the character, the original dignity and circumstances of Satan, as far as we can form any idea of them, ambition, leading him to aspire to be independent of God, if not equal to him, was the sin into which he was most in danger of falling. If he was one of the loftiest spirits in heaven; if he felt working within him a mighty celestial energy of thought and action; if he was invested with authority over inferior spirits, all of which were yet powerful and glorious in their measure, and even in a high degree; if in these circumstances he sinned at all, the probability is, that it would be by forgetting his duty to his Maker, by arrogating to himself independence on God, if not equality to him, and by requiring from inferior spirits that homage and obedience which were due to Jehovah. Hence we find that pride was the spirit which he breathed when he seduced our first parents, the essence of the sin to which he tempted them; " Your eyes shall be opened, and ye shall be as *gods*, knowing good and evil;" equality to God was what he proposed to *them*. And as his design was to ruin them, what would appear to him more likely to accomplish his purpose, than that which ruined himself? In accordance with this, we find that he endeavoured in the same way to overcome the blessed Redeemer. When his other attacks had failed, he proposed all the kingdoms of the world, and all the glory of them; hoping that this might enkindle the flame of ambition in the breast of even the illustrious Messiah.

Whatever was their sin, the apostles Peter and Jude inform us that they *did sin*. " They kept not their *principality*," or their government, as the word is correctly rendered by some; that state of dignity and power and high privilege,—and perhaps of dominion in the case of many of them, over inferior spirits,—in which they were placed by the supreme authority and goodness of the Sovereign Lord of the universe; and which they could preserve only by paying to him the homage to which he had the most sacred claims. They " left their *own habitation*," or residence, or sphere. Perhaps " by their own habitation," heaven in general may be intended. This, while they continued innocent, was their *home*, their Father's house, in which they were created, or as it were born, to which they had constant access, and in which they enjoyed the immediate presence of God. Or, according to some interpreters, the word οἰκητήριον may denote a residence or station assigned to them in some other region of the universe, where they had important duties to perform, still enjoying, however, the presence of the omnipresent Jehovah, and realizing complete felicity; and it is not at all improbable that this may be its meaning. If so, the language of the apostle intimates that they voluntarily, in opposition to the will and command of God, left their office and residence, and neglected and refused to perform their duty. Or if the former interpretation be preferred, then the expression appears to denote they willingly left heaven itself, and preferred the loss of all its glories to submission to God, and the performance of the duties which he required.

In this revolt, it appears from the hints which are given in other passages of Scripture, the being known by the name of Satan, or the devil, was the ringleader. In his mind, enlightened and pure as it was, the idea (unaccountably to us) sprung up of disputing the claims of God, breaking his laws, forming and executing plans directly opposed to his, and finding happiness,—greater than even that of heaven,—in a state of moral and spiritual separation from the eternal Source of all felicity! This project, we may suppose, he communicated to others, presenting it in the most plausible forms; and unhappily he prevailed, and persuaded multitudes of the heavenly hosts to enlist under his standard of rebellion; in consequence of which they left heaven, or left their own office or residence, and were therefore completely and for ever excluded from the realms of happiness. The apostles inform us that they were thrust down into the regions of darkness, and reserved in everlasting chains, (chains that can never be broken, and will never be loosed,) under darkness, to the judgment of the great day. Chains are one means of securing prisoners, and places of confinement, especially dungeons, are usually dark. In allusion to these facts, the fallen angels are said to be reserved in chains under darkness, and wherever they go, in whatever part of the universe they are permitted to range, they are still bound in these chains, they are still surrounded with this darkness, they are still in the prison of eternal justice, they may at any time be seized in a moment, and dragged to the tribunal where their final doom is to be pronounced. The historian of the Roman empire has elegantly and forcibly said, that the whole world was but a spacious prison for those who offended the emperor of Rome; he could reach the objects of his displeasure at any time, or in any place, and drag them to punishment. With much greater propriety may it be said that the *universe* is but a spacious prison to those who have offended the universal Sovereign, and are doomed by him to destruction; and a sense of his displeasure and of their own depravity must involve them in the most dreadful spiritual and moral darkness wherever they go, even if they were permitted to appear in heaven itself. "Darkness is a state obviously suitable for beings to whom the light of heaven was unsatisfactory and odious; and chains are most proper for beings whose proud and wanton wishes were discontented with the glorious liberty of the sons of God. Both also united form a degradation eminently fitted for beings who, at the head of the created universe, were impatiently ambitious of a higher station. Both at the same time, constitute a proper temporary punishment for beings who rebelled against the government of God himself."*

But, however dreadful their state, their punishment is not yet complete; they are reserved to the judgment of the great day, when they are to be called to an account, not only for their original rebellion, but for all their subsequent wickedness; and especially for seducing and ruining men, and tempting them to crimes of every description, and for their opposition to the Son of God, and to the spiritual kingdom which he has erected on earth.

It does not appear that there is the least degree of hope either of their obtaining mercy, or of their being disposed to seek for it by repentance and submission; and perhaps we may say that these two things are inseparably connected, and operate one on the other; and that, in a very important sense, the latter is the cause of the former. Were their

* Dwight, vol. i. p. 357.

wickedness and depravity not of such a character that they will never repent and seek for mercy, and desist from their opposition to God, it is not for us to say what might be the conduct of the Divine Being towards them. We read in Heb. vi. 4, of some who had so sinned amidst the enjoyment of great and peculiar privileges, that it was "impossible to renew them again to repentance," and especially because they had "trampled under foot the Son of God, and had accounted the blood of the covenant wherewith they were sanctified, an unholy thing." Perhaps, then, on account of the circumstances in which the fallen angels sinned, amidst the light, and enjoyments, and privileges of heaven itself, there is the same impossibility of renewing them to repentance—the same reason, essentially, for dooming them to eternal punishment. This impossibility may be not merely a great difficulty, but something connected with the very nature of things, and the wisdom and rectitude of the Divine government. But not to dwell on this, we know, from the very constitution of rational beings, and from the nature and influence of sin, that these fallen spirits must be dreadfully depraved. The very act of rebelling against Jehovah, amidst all their light, and their knowledge of his character, and all their experience of his goodness—the violence they must have done to their own judgment and convictions, before they could indulge any dishonourable ideas of a God of infinite perfection, and dare to trample on his authority and law, must have dreadfully perverted all their views and feelings, and disordered their whole moral frame. The entire failure of their attempt, whatever it was; their complete loss of all self-respect; the condemnation, the reproaches of their own consciences; the workings of the evil passions which they engendered in their own frames; the frowns of the Almighty: the sentence passed on them; the despair which would seize their breasts, and spread its frightful clouds all around; the punishment, however just, that was inflicted on them, would, as it were, madden and infuriate them, and render them desperate and reckless in wickedness, and would thus deprave them, to the utmost extent of their powers and capacities, and fill them, as we know sin has done men, with all unrighteousness, impurity, wickedness, maliciousness, envy, deceit, pride, cruelty, impiety, and hatred of God, Rom. i. 29. If such a description as this will apply to the human race,—is applied to them by an inspired apostle, notwithstanding all the restraints under which they are laid, and all the means which God is using with them to bring them to repentance, (for the apostle proves that there is no difference between Jews and Gentiles—that of both it may be said, "Their throat is an open sepulchre; with their tongues they have used deceit; the poison of asps is under their lips; whose mouth is full of cursing and bitterness; their feet are swift to shed blood,")—what must have been the effect of sin committed by angels in heaven!—what its influence, since they were left without hope, without, as far as we know, any means being employed to stop them in their downward course; but when, on account of the way in which they were forsaken by God, and of the condemnation of their own consciences, and the operation of their depraved and guilty passions, they must have sunk into despair of ever finding mercy, and that *partly*, perhaps *principally*, because they were conscious of being entirely destitute of the least disposition to seek it in any way that could be acceptable to God! It is a generally admitted principle, established by reasoning and verified by facts, that the more excellent anything is in itself, and the more important the purposes to which it can be applied, the worse, the more corrupt and vile (if it is capable of vileness), the more destructive does it become when it is entirely perverted. What would be so injurious to man as the food on which he lives, or the air which he breathes, if its properties were so changed as to become the very reverse of what they are? It is not within the range of possibility that an irrational animal should ever become so hateful and pernicious a being as a thoroughly wicked man. It requires the perversion, the utter depravation of an angel, to make a devil; of an archangel, to produce the prince of the devils. In proportion, therefore, to the height of capacity and power, of dignity and happiness, to which Satan and his associates were raised by the omnipotence and bounty of the Great Creator, must necessarily be the depth of the gulf of depravity and wretchedness into which they precipitated themselves by sin; a gulf out of which they can never rise, and from which we have fearful intimations in the Scriptures that God will never raise them.

It follows, then, that the hints which the Scriptures give us respecting the fall and malignity of evil spirits, their determined opposition to God, their insane attempts to frustrate his plans, and their ceaseless efforts to ruin man, to render him as depraved and wretched as themselves, are perfectly consistent with the deductions of reason, and with the evidence of facts. And this observation will apply to their not being immediately doomed to suffer the full punishment due to their rebellion, but being "reserved to the judgment of the great day," and their being permitted in the mean time to tempt men, and to oppose the plans of God. Both of these are perfectly analogous to what we see and experience of the Divine dispensations in the government of the world. When evil spirits rebelled and incurred the Divine displeasure, they did not cease to be accountable as it regarded their future conduct. Banishment from heaven, and consignment to that condition which is represented in the Scriptures as being "cast down to hell, and delivered into chains of darkness," constituted all the punishment which God saw fit to inflict at that time. It is in vain for us to imagine or conjecture what would have been the case if they had ceased from their opposition to God, and had humbled themselves under his mighty hand; for this we know they have not done, and from the very nature of sin, whenever it pervades the frame of rational creatures, and perverts all their views and feelings, this they never will do. But doubtless their state, had this been the case, and the conduct of God towards them, would have been very different from what they are. Is it not probable that the incorrigibleness of sinners, or the fact that they never will repent of themselves, is one thing that renders an atonement necessary, before God can, consistently with his justice, bestow on them one of the most valuable of all his gifts, viz. the influence of his Spirit, to renovate their hearts and make them partakers of his holiness? Fallen angels, however, whatever be the degree of punishment inflicted on them, and whatever was the design of that infliction, are still responsible for their deeds, and at that great day they will have to give account not only for their original rebellion, but for all their subsequent wickedness. May it not be said, then, that in one sense they are still in a state of probation; that God is trying them in order to manifest to themselves and to the universe all that is in their natures, and thus to demonstrate that it is an unspeakably evil and bitter thing to forsake God and rebel against him? The fact that the result with regard to them is certain, and well known to the Divine Being, is no valid objection against this assertion. He well knew how the Israelites would act in the wilderness, and how men, whether saints or sinners, will conduct themselves in all circumstances. The issue of the trial is just as certain in their case as in that of the fallen angels, and yet this does not render the probation of the former superfluous. Why should it be thought to render unnecessary that of the latter?

But to return from this digression, it follows from what has been advanced, that the character of these fallen spirits must be a compound of craft, subtlety, envy, hatred to God and all his creatures, pride, obstinacy, malignity, and impiety; that they must be morally capable of any act or form of wickedness, which their power and circumstances render it possible for them to perpetrate. In how many lamentable cases do we see men reduced to such a state, and their characters and conduct presenting such a compound, as that which has just been specified! And hence the names or epithets which are given in the Scriptures to these wretched beings, and especially to their ringleader, as the representative of all the rest. He is denominated "the Devil," that is the accuser or slanderer; "Satan," the enemy, and that in the worst sense of the word; "the wicked one;" "Apollyon," and "Abaddon," the destroyer: "the spirit that worketh in the children of disobedience;" "the tempter;" "the old serpent;" "the great dragon." He is represented as the great opponent and determined enemy of the Son of God, who came to destroy his works and deliver his captives; as constantly engaged in tempting and destroying men; as excluded from all hope; and as doomed to spend his eternity in unquenchable fire, which was prepared for him and his angels;—names and representations of fearful, terrible import, and which lead us to conclude that he is the most depraved and wretched being in the universe! How miserable are those who are taken captive by him at his will, and who are to be involved with him in his ruin! Let none think that they are exempt from danger here, because of the moral excellence of their character, and the amiableness of their disposition, if they are forgetting God, if they are destitute of supreme love to him, and of faith in Jesus Christ. Trusting to moral excellence, when confined to the claims of men, valuable and lovely as it may be, is just one of the devices of Satan to ruin immortal souls. It is one of the golden chains with which he binds his captives; or, to change the figure, one of the opiates which he administers to those whom he has lulled to sleep, and whom, perhaps we may say, he would not disturb by urging them, if he could do so, to the commission of gross crimes. How valuable the promise—who would not seek an interest in it? "The God of peace shall bruise Satan under your feet shortly!"

It follows from what has been advanced, especially from the statements of the word of God, that while there are different degrees of intellectual capacity amongst evil spirits, yet the powers of all of them, and especially of their prince, and of the highest orders, must be fearfully great; I say *fearfully*, because they employ them only to do mischief. I can by no means adopt the theory, that if we suppose the abilities of devils to have been originally a little superior to those of a highly-gifted man, and take into the account the way in which they must have been increased by exercise and experience, and the knowledge they have acquired, our estimate may probably be nearly correct. If the premises which have been laid down are valid, the lowest order of them must have originally possessed capacities and powers superior to the greatest of men; while, perhaps, the united intellect of hundreds of mortals would not equal that of the superior ranks, especially of their leader. Probably they may possess a degree of vigour of intellect, of power of acquiring knowledge, of operating on matter, and rendering it subservient to their purposes, of communicating their ideas to one another, and of influencing the minds of men, and therefore of acting the part of tempters, of which we have little conception; and the actions which are ascribed to them in Scripture, and the hints which it contains respecting their influence on men, as well as the views which are given of the powers and actions of good angels, confirm this opinion. And also, we must take into the account their invisibility to human vision, their immortality, their exhaustless vigour and power of action, (for exhaustless it may be deemed when compared to ours,) their long and varied experience, gained in *heaven*, on *earth*, and in *hell;* and then we shall see that they possess vast advantages over us in our spiritual warfare; they must, therefore, prove most dangerous enemies.

I know it has been maintained by some writers, and amongst others by Dr. Watts, in his Philosophical Essays, that spirits have no natural power of operating on matter, and that therefore they cannot influence it at all, unless special, extraordinary ability is imparted to them by God for that purpose. But, notwithstanding the plausible arguments by which they defend this opinion, I must think it incorrect; nor do I see any difficulty in answering, were this the proper occasion, all the objections (and their proofs of their own opinion are chiefly presented in the form of objections) which they urge against the contrary sentiment. It is granted by them that God, the Father of spirits, possesses complete power over matter, to create and annihilate, to mould and influence it as he pleases. Created spirits bear the image, and partake of the nature of God; and this implies some portion, however small, of his power to think and act. We know of only two substances in the universe, matter and spirit. Those who believe that the soul of man belongs to the latter, must allow that in its essence it resembles God, and participates of the properties of his essence. Since he, then, possesses infinite power over matter, must not created spirits be endued with limited power over it, according to the measure of their native ability? How, otherwise, could they bear the image of God, or partake of the properties of his nature? Some, indeed, maintain, that power, knowledge, wisdom, holiness, and benevolence are essentially different, not only in their degree, but in their very nature and properties, in God, from what they are in the creature. But this opinion is not consistent with either the language of Scripture, or the conclusions of reason. The Bible not only informs us that men were *made*, and are *renewed* in the likeness of God, but it exhorts us to study conformity to him, to be "holy as he is holy." It informs us that believers are made " partakers of the Divine nature." And if there were an essential difference betwixt the spirituality of God, and the spirituality of angels, and of the souls of men; betwixt his power, and wisdom, and goodness, and holiness, and happiness, and theirs, (and not merely an infinite superiority in him, as it regards degree, and the manner of their existence,) how could we be said to possess any knowledge of God, or any correct ideas of him at all? He would be, in that case, as much to the wisest Christian, we might say to the wisest angel, as he was to the idolatrous Athenians, an "unknown God." Can this be the case? Both reason and Scripture reply, No. His existence is necessary and underived, and includes all duration and all space; the existence of creatures is contingent, derived, and confined to a portion of duration and of space; but there is a real resemblance betwixt them in nature and properties, so far as *mere existence*, opposed to *non-existence*, is concerned. Again, he knows all things; men and angels know some things; but knowledge, which is an acquaintance with truth or facts, is the same in its nature in both cases. The benevolence of God is infinite, that of men and angels is limited; but its essential property, wishing well to beings that are capable of enjoyment, and feeling satisfaction in their welfare, is the same in each; and similar observations might be made with regard to wisdom, and purity, and happiness. Are we not, then, led to the conclusion that the power of spirits is the same in its nature with that of God, though infinitely less in its degree; and consequently, that as his extends to matter, and includes complete control over it all, in every respect,—so theirs must extend to it likewise, and include ability to move and influence some parts or portion of its various forms, and to render them subservient, to a limited extent, to their purposes? That we cannot form any conception of the way or manner in which this is done, is no argument at all against the truth of what has been advanced. We are utterly ignorant of the way by which our souls can, by a mere volition, move the members of our own bodies; we only know the fact by experience; the mode is just as mysterious as the way in which disembodied spirits may operate on matter can be. That angels have possessed the power in question, and have rendered material substances subservient to many purposes which they wished to effect, is evident from the statements of the Bible; and there is no evidence whatever that any special energy was imparted to them by God on those occasions; or that he exerted his omnipotence when some words were uttered, or signs were given by them. For instance, we are not to suppose, when the angel rolled away the huge stone from the door of the sepulchre on the morning of the Saviour's resurrection, that the Divine Being exerted the energy requisite, and that the action was really done by him, though it appeared to be performed by the heavenly messenger. The narration in this, and in similar instances, leads to the conclusion that the actions were performed by these celestial spirits themselves. And how could it with any propriety be asserted of them, that they "excel in strength," if whole legions of them could not, by any inherent or natural power that they possess, and can exercise when they please, have effected that which a few puny mortals could easily have accomplished? which is certainly implied in the hypothesis which we are opposing; for the latter could have rolled away the stone, and the former could not; nay, would it not follow that all the angelic hosts of heaven could not move a pebble or a feather? Angels must have some means of discerning the forms and appearances of matter, of ascertaining its presence and extent, and some of its properties; or else how could the morning stars have sung, and the sons of God shouted for joy, when the foundations of the earth were laid? And how could they perform the services with which they are frequently charged, since these have a relation to matter? How could they minister to the saints, as we know from the Scriptures they frequently do? And to those who believe in real possessions we may say, unless they have some means and power of operating on matter, how could evil spirits have taken possession of the bodies of men in the time of our Saviour, produced insanity, inflicted various diseases, and tormented and lacerated them in the most shocking manner? How could they have entered into the swine, and caused them to run violently into the sea? In all these cases their influence seems evidently to have been exerted on the bodies of their victims. Surely we cannot suppose or allow that God would have exerted his omnipotence, in order to communicate to them ability which they did not possess naturally, nay, that he would have wrought a miracle, in order to enable these wicked spirits to do mischief, or to give effect to their malicious wishes. This appears to me a far greater difficulty than any with which the contrary opinion is encumbered.

The fact that our spirits cannot operate on matter, or produce any effects or changes in it, with the exception of their own bodies, or through them, as instruments, does not at all militate against the theory which I am endeavouring to support; for, from the extent of their power, when they are united to a portion of matter so intimately as to form one person with it, or to be one constituent part of that person of which matter is the other, so that they cannot think or act, but through its instrumentality, and that a comparatively slight change in some of that matter will deprive them of their power either to think or act, and even of the very consciousness of their existence; and so that they are affected by almost every impression which is made on their bodies, and sometimes in the most powerful manner; we are not warranted to infer what they would be able to effect if that union were dissolved, much less what are the capacities and powers of spirits that have never been united to matter at all. For, is it extravagant or absurd to suppose that, as God intended our souls to exist in a state of union to bodies, not only in this world but in the next, (we know his intention by what he does,) there may be something in their very frame and capacities, to fit them for that union, and to prevent them from ever being perfect without it; while angelic spirits may be so formed, as that they may attain their perfection in a separate state, and, that though it may be an advantage to the former to be united to matter, it would be a disadvantage to the latter? It is only on this hypothesis that we can see how the resurrection, to which the Scriptures attach so much importance, and which they represent as being one of the richest fruits of the death and triumphs of the Saviour, can be a blessing to the saints, or indeed at all desirable; or how angels do not labour under some disadvantages on account of not possessing bodies. But all God's works are perfect in their various kinds, and each of them adapted to the end for which it was created. The circumstance, then, of the influence of our souls being confined to that part of matter to which they are united, does not prove that angels, whether good or bad, have no power over material substances.

The greatest difficulty attendant on this view of the subject, and therefore the principal objection against it, is, that if evil spirits possess the power which is thus attributed to them, they would be constantly inflicting the most terrible evils on men, they would throw the whole natural world into confusion, or, in the words of Dr. Watts, " devils would not content themselves with the mere temptation of souls, but would always be making wretched mischief in this natural world, and overspreading it with calamities and desolations, with plagues and fire, with earthquakes and misery and death, if they had an innate and natural power to move bodies." To this it is sufficient to answer, that we owe our protection, every day and every moment, from evils innumerable, of various kinds, to the presence and power of God. He is the Preserver of men, and whatever may be the malice and energy of these fallen spirits, and whatever their ability to agitate matter, and to render it subservient to their will, he can restrain and control them every moment, give them commands which they cannot, dare not transgress, and say to them, as he does to the waves of the sea, "Hitherto shall you come and no farther." That God possesses and constantly exerts influence which is abundantly equal to all that has now been advanced, is implied in the prayers and thanksgivings which we are constantly presenting to him, and which he requires from all his rational creatures; as well as in the promises and representations of his word. That glorious, sovereign, irresistible authority, which could effectually command evil spirits to leave the bodies of those of whom they had taken possession, to abandon a certain region,—and without the permission of which (and the language employed evidently conveys the idea that permission was all that he gave, or they requested, not the communication of any new power) they could not enter into irrational animals,—can easily give to even devils commands which, notwithstanding all their stubbornness and impiety, they dare not, they cannot transgress. And besides, it is to be taken into the account that the great object of Satan, *that* to the accomplishment of which he bends his most vigorous efforts, is not to injure the bodies of men, or to inflict temporal calamities of any kind, but to ruin their souls, and therefore to lead them into the commission of sin. And moreover, there is a great difference between spirits having no power at all over matter, no, not so much as to move a single particle of it, and being able to control and change the laws of nature, and raise tempests, and produce earthquakes, whenever or to whatever extent they please; or to change portions of it into pestilential miasma, and thus to diffuse disease and death all around. Their power is necessarily limited, and must vary in degree in proportion to their intellectual abilities; all that we suppose them capable of doing, is, to take advantage of the laws of nature,—as men can do, to a certain extent, and render them subservient to some of their purposes. And even in those cases, God can cause the wrath, and malice, and power of devils, as well as of men, "to praise him," and the remainder of them "he can restrain."

In endeavouring to form some idea of the power of fallen spirits, and therefore of their ability to tempt and effect mischief, we must take into the account their *activity*, and the rapidity with which they can move from place to place. We are far from attributing to them omnipotence, or omnipresence, or ubiquity, as some of the opponents of this doctrine, in their attempts to caricature it, and cause it to appear absurd, have been pleased to assert. According to the representations of the word of God, we believe, not that Satan is everywhere present, but that he "*goes* about seeking whom he may devour," that he goes "to and fro in the earth;" not that he is omnipotent, but that he "seeks whom *he may* devour." And whatever may be the number of fallen spirits, we do not think that they literally fill the earth or the air, or that they are constantly present with men, or permitted always to tempt them. Though this fallen, sinful world is infested with them, it does not follow that it is their only range or habitation. This is not implied either in the statements of the Bible, or in the general belief on this subject. If they go about, they must, according to any ideas or conceptions we can form, transport themselves from place to place, and this they may be able to do with inconceivable rapidity—"to fly through nature ere the moment end."* The following well-known passage, in Dan. ix. 3, 20—23, is commonly thought to prove and illustrate this. "And I set my face unto the Lord my God, to seek by prayer, and supplication, and fasting, and sackcloth, and ashes." "And while I was speaking, the man Gabriel, *being caused to fly swiftly*, touched me about

* Milton.

the time of the evening oblation," &c. "At the beginning of thy supplications the commandment came forth, and I am now come to show thee." "From this remarkable story we learn that some time in the day Daniel set himself to seek the Lord by fasting and prayer; that after his prayer was begun, the commandment was given to Gabriel to explain to him the vision and prophecy. In verses 20, 21, we are told that Gabriel came to him while he was speaking; that this was his evening prayer; and that during the time in which he was employed in uttering his prayer, Gabriel came from the supreme heaven to this world. This is a rapidity exceeding all the comprehension of the most active imagination, surpassing beyond any comparison the amazing swiftness of light. Light is several years in coming from such fixed stars as are visible to the eye of man. But there is the best reason to believe that the heaven of heavens is at a much greater distance than those stars; so as not improbably to be a heaven to them as the fixed stars are to us. The poet therefore is justified by this wonderful fact in that forcible expression, 'The speed of gods (angels) time counts not.' No stronger exhibition can be asked or given of the activity (and it may be said, speed or swiftness) of these wonderful beings."* Whatever may be thought of the meaning of this remarkable passage, and of Dr. Dwight's inferences from it, which however appear to be quite legitimate, when we think of the swiftness of light, which is either a material substance, or dependent on the motion or vibration of matter, (and according to the latter theory, its rapidity would appear to be greater than is implied in the former,) and yet is *computed* to move at the rate of 200,000 miles in a second, what must be the rapidity with which angelic spirits can move! Compared with this, matter, in its most subtile and refined forms, is dead and sluggish! What must have been the speed of Gabriel when he was "caused to fly

* Dwight, vol. i. p. 316.

swiftly!" Truly it must far, far exceed all our power of conception; it must be almost as great as that of our thoughts, and must secure a kind of ubiquity. And there is no good reason to suppose that fallen angels have lost this activity, or that they are much inferior in it to good angels.

But here again our subject is involved in difficulty and obscurity, in addition to what naturally belongs to it, by the metaphysical subtleties of the schoolmen, as stated and maintained by Dr. Watts and others. They assert that spirits have no relation to place, that they cannot be said to be in one locality more than in another, and consequently that they do not move from place to place. But with all deference to the abilities and learning and piety of many of these writers, I must be permitted to say, that there is more force in the plain common maxim, or axiom, as it may be called;—for surely it is as self-evident as that it is impossible for a thing to be and not to be at the same time, or that the whole is greater than the parts,—" *Quod nullibi est, non est,*—what exists no where does not exist at all,"—to prove that spirits must have a relation to space or to place, than in all the abstruse reasonings that can be employed to evince the contrary. Heaven must be a place as well as a state, since the celestial bodies of Enoch and Elijah, and the glorified body of the Saviour, are there; and this earth is a place. Can the holy angels then be at one time in heaven paying their homage to the Redeemer, and at another on earth, ministering to the heirs of salvation, without some relation to heaven in the former case, and to earth in the latter,—nay, without being actually on earth in the one, and in heaven in the other? Surely our souls, when united to our bodies, which are always in one place or another, must have a relation to space. This does not imply that they are extended or divisible; why then should this relation be thought to involve either extension or divisibility in disembodied spirits? We grant that the

POWERS OF EVIL SPIRITS.   115

relation of spirits to any locality, and their motion from one to another, present many difficulties and mysteries, But the opposite opinion seems to imply an absurdity, a contradiction, and therefore I cannot hesitate [which to embrace.

Knowledge is power, and it must be so in the case of evil spirits; and when we take into the account their original capacities, the activity of their spiritual frame, the long period of their existence, the various scenes through which they have passed, and the events which they have witnessed, the manifestations of character which they have beheld, the results of their own experience, and of the various methods they have employed to seduce men, of the plans which they devised to counteract the purposes and to destroy the works of God : their knowledge, such as it is, must be varied and great. How far they may possess anything like a desire after knowledge, and make efforts to acquire it ;—whether the representation of Milton may be correct, that some of them reason deep and high, concerning predestination, " fate and free-will, and foreknowledge absolute," is not for us to say; though I can see nothing unreasonable or improbable in it, or inconsistent with their being miserable outcasts from heaven. The disadvantages under which they labour, however, arising from their wretchedness, their depravity, the " chains under darkness," in which they are confined, their banishment from those regions where the most glorious manifestations of the perfection of Jehovah, as well as of the various characters and excellences of created existences, are exhibited, must lay them under immense disadvantages, so that their knowledge is undoubtedly scanty, when compared with that of holy angels, who look into the works of God, and especially into the plan of human redemption, in the light of glory, and amidst all the advantages which it affords.

The last observation suggests the question, whether sin, by its operation on the mind, directly and immediately weakens the faculties of those who are brought under its power, and therefore whether we may suppose that Satan lost any of his intellectual ability, when he rebelled against God : in other words, whether his memory was rendered less retentive, his discernment as it regarded natural objects and truths less acute, his invention less prolific, than they were before he fell. That sin is unfavourable to mental improvement, and that it always perverts the moral judgment and affections, and weakens the moral powers, must, I apprehend, be granted by all. But whether we attend to facts, or to general reasoning on this subject, we shall be led to the conclusion, that it does not enervate the intellectual faculties. I do not know that any reason has been or can be assigned, why the omission of any duty, or the violation of any command, or placing the affections on any wrong object; why the exercise of pride, or selfishness, or envy, or aversion to God, should diminish the retentiveness of the memory, or the quickness of perception, or the ability to compare one object with another and to perceive their agreement or disagreement in scientific investigations, any more than that they should lessen the acuteness of the senses, or the vigour of the body ; there does not appear to be any conceivable way in which they can affect the result in question. We can easily see how, by the influence of the feelings to which sin naturally, nay, necessarily gives rise, or which it calls into operation, such as self-love, fear, desire, and aversion, it will blind the understanding, pervert the taste and the judgment, and disorder all the affections, as far as moral truth and duty are concerned,— how it will produce a dislike to the law which condemns, and aversion to the God who threatens to punish, and who must necessarily disapprove of what has been done ; and how it must destroy the nice, and well-adjusted, and most important balance between reason and conscience on the one hand, and appetite and passion on the other. For instance, we can clearly see how and why Adam, after he had eaten the forbidden fruit, should be averse to hold any intercourse with God, and should wish to hide himself from him: nay, why he should desire a change to take place in the character and requirements of his Maker, which is the very essence of enmity to him; but we cannot see how this should make him forget what he had previously known, or disqualify him for investigating abstract truth, or the natures and properties of matter or spirit. And if we attend to facts, they confirm this reasoning, and the conclusion to which we have come. How often do we find superior mental abilities connected with a most depraved heart and vicious life; almost the powers and acquirements of an angel, with the temper and conduct of a fiend! And if sin had a direct and necessary tendency to weaken and destroy the mental powers, it would follow that the more vicious men were, the more weak and stupid they must become, till at last they would be reduced to the condition of idiots, which is contrary to numerous incontrovertible facts; and on this hypothesis the intellect of Satan must long since have been destroyed. On the contrary, there is no absurdity or even difficulty in supposing that his capacity may have been enlarged, and his powers strengthened, by the knowledge and experience which he has gained, by the efforts which he has made; and thus he may become a more, instead of a less formidable adversary. But still his advances in knowledge and in mental ability must be far inferior to what they would have been, had he continued stedfast in his allegiance to the Most High.

The views which I have been led to form and state of the powers of fallen spirits, necessarily lead me to differ from one, whom on account of his talents, piety, amiableness of character, and the important services he has rendered to the religious world, and to the cause of truth, I, in common with all who know him and can appreciate his worth, must highly esteem. But *amicus Socrates*, &c. Dr. Wardlaw, in his judicious and instructive Essays on the Book of Job, lately published in the Congregational Magazine, maintains that Satan did not produce or cause the fire that burnt up the sheep and the servants of Job, nor the wind from the wilderness that buried his sons and daughters beneath the ruins of the elder brother's house. And I suppose, though he does not assert this, he would maintain that he did not, by any direct agency, smite Job with "sore boils from head to foot," whilst he allows that he might instigate the plundering Sabeans and Chaldeans who carried off the oxen and camels. And the reasons which he assigns for his opinion are, that the common belief on this point invests Satan with a power which can belong only to God; that it represents the prince of darkness as controlling the laws and wielding the elements of nature, causing the thunder to roll and the tempest to rage, in a way that would seem to trench upon the prerogatives of God, and which is inconsistent with the language and appeals of the Scriptures, and especially with the appeals of the book of Job; "Who hath divided a watercourse for the overflowing of the waters, or a way for the lightning of the thunder?" "Canst thou send lightnings, that they may go and say to thee, Here are we?" "The thought," says Dr. W., is to me unsufferable, of any inferior agent actually possessing and exercising such power as this. If you once admit the principle, then when the rolling thunder and the resistless lightning fill your spirits with the sublime emotions of reverential awe; and the shrinking humility of a conscious impotence, and "'tis listening fear, and dumb amazement all,' how distressingly are our minds disturbed, amidst the full and solemn recognition of the might and majesty of the omnipotent God, by the intruding recollection that the immediate agency by which all these tremendous scenes are produced, is or may be, the agency of the prince of darkness. Nor do I feel myself at all satisfied or relieved by being told that the dependent or malignant agent can go no farther than he is permitted. The question still recurs, does the wicked one possess power, even when permitted, such as enables him to perform these wonders, to wield the elements of nature in the thunder and storm?"*

That there is considerable force in the reasoning contained in the passage just quoted, is at once granted. Still, however, I must think that Satan actually did effect, and that by his native power, what is attributed to him in the passage under consideration, and that for the following reasons.

First. The plain natural import of the language, and scope of the passage, lead to this conclusion. "Behold," says God to the tempter, "all that he hath *is in thy power ;* only on himself *put not forth thy hand,*" Job i. 12. And again, "Behold, he is *in thy hand;* but save his life," chap. ii. 6, 7. "So went Satan forth from the presence of the Lord, *and smote Job with sore boils* from the sole of his feet unto the crown." And would it not require as much command over the laws of nature to manage diseases, to inflict the leprosy by a secret, invisible influence, as to raise a storm, or to cause fire to descend from the skies to destroy cattle? The language employed, the representations given, are of such a nature, that every person who reads the account without any preconceived opinions, or any hypothesis to maintain, would infallibly be led to the conclusion that Satan by his own power effected what is here ascribed to him. God is not represented as imparting to him any energy, much less as exerting his omnipotence, to subserve the designs of the tempter, but merely as *permitting* him to exert the ability which he possessed. I know that there are cases in which the language of the Bible, accommodated to the views of men, would, if taken according to the ordinary or general import of the words and phrases which are employed, lead into error; but it remains to be shown that either facts, analogy, or the general tenor of the word

* Congregational Magazine, October, 1840, p. 662.

of God, or the clear statements of any one part of it, render it necessary here to depart from the literal meaning.

· Second. Is there not, to say the least, as great a difficulty in supposing that God would exert his omnipotence, would roll the thunder, and hurl its bolts, and raise the tempest, at the instigation, as it were at the bidding of Satan, and to gratify his impious and malignant desires, as that the mighty fallen spirit, who is represented in the Bible as no mean or contemptible antagonist to the Son of God himself, can influence, to some extent, the laws of nature, or rather take advantage of them to accomplish his purposes? To me the mystery and difficulty appear unspeakably greater in the former case than in the latter. I know it will be said that Jehovah intended not to *gratify* Satan, but to *mortify* him; not to accomplish the wishes of the enemy, but to try his own servant, to cause his graces to be exhibited in the clearest light, and that for the benefit of the church in all ages, and to furnish materials for some of the most instructive pages of the Divine record; and that God might at any time have destroyed the cattle and servants of Job by thunder and lightning, or his children by a whirlwind, and have inflicted on him a noisome disease. This is readily granted. But still, why do these at the instigation of Satan? or why represent them as done by him, if they were effected by God himself?

Thirdly. The comparison of the case with that of an authenticated miracle, contains, as far as I can see, no solid argument in support of Dr. W.'s hypothesis. It is granted that in customary language we speak of the prophet or the apostle as "having done the miracle;" and this language is sometimes, but far from generally, used in Scripture. But there is almost always something, either in the terms employed, or in the accompanying actions or circumstances, which plainly indicate that the power did not reside in the human agent. God, we are informed, "wrought special miracles by the *hands of Paul*." " In the *name of Jesus Christ of Nazareth*, rise up and walk." " Eneas, Jesus Christ maketh thee whole." " But Peter put them all forth, and kneeled down and prayed." " Why marvel ye at this, as though by our own power or holiness we had made this man whole ? " This is only a specimen of the language of the Bible, in the account which is given us of the performance of miracles by human agents. It is generally plainly intimated, and often expressly asserted, that the work was performed by God; that the apostle or prophet did nothing more than merely give notice, by some words which he uttered, or some sign which he gave, that God was about to exert his omnipotence, and control or contravene the laws of nature. I therefore fully agree with Dr. W. that it would be " a flagrant absurdity," to suppose that the power by which the miracle was wrought, "resided, for a time, in the human agent, by transference. It is God by his own power that effects it, interposing at the will and intimation of his messenger. It was not Moses or Aaron that smote the Egyptians ; it was not Peter or Paul that gave sight to the blind," &c. " But persons are represented in Scripture language as doing that which God does either by them, or for them, or at their will." It does not follow, however, from this, that Satan, who is far superior to men in power and skill, may not so far take advantage of the laws of nature as to produce all the phenomena that were exhibited when Job's children, and cattle, and servants were destroyed. I do not say that he wrought a miracle, for we have no intimation that any miracle was performed. We have no reason to think that Satan can work one (though, perhaps, he might effect something which would appear to us miraculous). There is nothing contrary to the established laws of the universe in a tempest arising to such a height as to level houses with the ground, or in cattle being struck dead by lightning, or in a man's being affected by leprosy. It is not strictly correct, however, to say, as Dr. W. does, that God wrought miracles at the *will* of prophets or apostles. It is very evident that they could not perform them whenever they chose, but only when they could exercise the requisite faith; else why could not the disciples cast out a devil on a certain occasion, when they actually made the trial? Indeed, it would seem that God gave those whom he thus honoured, perhaps by enabling them to exercise the required belief, or by some impulse or impression on their mind, a sign or intimation which was sufficient for their guidance, when he was about to perform a miracle on their behalf, and when it was proper for them to request him to do so. Moses, for instance, could not stretch out his rod whenever he pleased, and smite Egypt with plagues, or divide the sea, or cause the water to spring from the rock. In every case he received a command from God. And it is absurd to suppose that the Divine Being would so far place his omnipotence, and wisdom, and honour, at the disposal of the best and holiest of men, as to work a miracle whenever they might wish him thus to interpose. If he had done so, some of them might have brought down fire from heaven on very improper occasions.

But fourthly. As there was no miracle performed, so it is not certain that the elements of nature were wielded so far as to produce thunder and lightning, or a general tempest. Might not the evil spirit produce a fire that would destroy the sheep of Job, and a commotion in the air that would overthrow the house in which his children were feasting, and yet not be able, nay, be utterly unable, to manage the tempest, or to thunder with a voice like God? Men can do something very like both the one and the other. Paltry as are their "imitations of the wonderful phenomena of nature," yet when we think of their destructive warlike engines, of the way in which they can direct even the lightning to one place, and divert it from another, of the degree in which they can render the electric fluid subservient to their purposes, and how they can produce combustion by concentrating the rays of the sun, while yet they are utterly unable to alter or to manage as they please the laws of nature, what absurdity or difficulty is there in supposing that Satan may be so far superior to them in intellect, knowledge, and experience, as to be able so to take advantage of the laws which God has established, and so to render the electric fluid, or some other subtile agent, subservient to his purpose, as to produce flames that would destroy all the sheep of Job, or a commotion of the air which would overthrow a house? How easily could men, by what Dr. W. calls their "paltry imitations," effect both! And even if we were to allow that both were done by real thunder, and lightning, and tempest, is it impossible that these took place according to the ordinary course of things, and changes of the elements; and that all that Satan did was to take advantage of these to effect his purpose? Whatever be in this, it is God alone who has established the laws of nature, who preserves them constantly in operation, who can manage them throughout all their extent, and in all their energy. The mightiest creature can render them subservient to his purpose only so far as God has been pleased to put them beneath his control; and the meanest, the weakest, can do this likewise; and therefore those who think that Satan actually did all that is attributed to him in the Book of Job, can easily tell what to make of the sublime appeals to which reference has been made. If it is asked, "Who hath divided a water-course for the overflowing of waters, or a way for the lightning of thunder?" they answer, *Jehovah only;* though creatures may partially guide waters in their course, when they are divided by God, or the lightnings in their way, when the Almighty sends them. And "when the tempest bursts forth in its impetuous fury, bearing all before it," those who believe in Satanic agency to the extent which has been pointed out, do not find their "minds distressingly disturbed amidst the full and solemn recognition of the might and majesty of the omnipotent God, by the intruding recollection " of the agency of any creature ; for they know that no creature could form the elements and establish the laws by which these majestic phenomena are produced ! it can only avail itself to a limited extent of these laws and elements, when God puts them in operation. Nor do they find it necessary to believe that even Satan could raise a general storm, or cause majestic peals of thunder to sound through the heavens. They can unite intelligently, and with all their hearts, in the sublime language of the Psalmist in the twenty-ninth Psalm; " The voice of the Lord is upon the waters; the God of glory thundereth; the voice of the Lord is powerful; the voice of the Lord is full of majesty," &c.

What a mournfully impressive and interesting subject has come under our review in this lecture ! How wonderful and mysterious are the plans and ways of God ! Which of his works or dispensations can we contemplate, without finding occasion to exclaim, " Who, by searching, can find out God ?" How unsearchable are his judgments ! What a universe is this in which we live ! What scenes must death and eternity unfold ! Let us remember that we must either rise to that state of glory and happiness, of equality with angels, from which Satan and his associates fell; or else sink to that miserable, guilty, and hopeless condition to which they have reduced themselves by sin ; and that they are constantly labouring to prevent the former, and to effect the latter. How necessary is it, then, that we should be interested in Him who was made manifest to destroy the works of the devil ! If we overcome this enemy, it must be through the blood of the Lamb, and by the word of the testimony which he has given us. To form correct ideas, however, of the state, characters, and powers of our deadly foes, will necessarily much assist us in detecting their machinations, and in repelling their attacks.

These ideas are, in fact, a part of the "whole armour of God," which we are commanded to put on, that we may stand in the evil day, "having our loins girt about with truth."

LECTURE III.

THE AGENCY OF EVIL SPIRITS.

THE NATURE AND MANNER OF THEIR INTERCOURSE WITH THIS WORLD; WITCHCRAFT, DIVINATION, ETC.

AFTER considering the character and powers of evil spirits, the next question that naturally presents itself is, to what extent, and in what ways are they permitted to exert themselves to injure the human race, or what are the nature and degree of their intercourse with this world? What may we learn on this subject from the inferences of reason, from well-authenticated facts, and from the principles and statements of the word of God? This topic is confessedly very difficult, especially as, in addition to its own abstruseness, imposture, craft, and wickedness, on the one hand, and ignorance, credulity, weakness, imagination, superstition, and, it may be added, disease, on the other, have all combined their influence to involve it in mystery, and to furnish many melancholy and revolting facts to its history; yet in lectures on evil spirits some notice of it seems required by the subject.

That these fallen spirits have intercourse with this world, that it is a part of their permitted range, that, as they first tempted man to rebel against his Maker, so they are still, as far as they have opportunity, enticing him to wickedness of every kind, and that they have actually succeeded in urging him to the commission of the greatest crimes, are facts plainly stated in many parts of the Scriptures, and as evidently implied in others. The ringleader is called "the god of this world," doubtless because he is the great opponent of the true God, and even his rival for the service and worship of men; "the spirit that worketh in the children of disobedience," "the devil, that deceiveth the nations," and "the prince of the power of the air," &c. It may be inferred then from the various representations of the word of God, that Satan is, to a great degree, the author of the different systems of heathenish superstition and idolatry, with all their egregious falsehoods, shocking caricatures of the truth, abominable impurities, appalling cruelties, and insolent impieties. How characteristic are these of such a being as he is! Lamentably fallen and depraved as men are, yet considering the natural affections which still work in their breasts, the restraints under which they are laid, the means that God has used to reclaim them, the enactments and inflictions of human laws, we can scarcely, at times, refrain from exclaiming, Surely it must require such an influence as the Scriptures attribute to evil spirits, to render men so atrociously, so insanely, so gratuitously and systematically wicked, and wantonly impious as they are! Surely the depravity of human nature can hardly account for all their horrid deeds! The Scriptures indeed assure us that the human heart is deceitful above all things, and desperately wicked; and that out of it proceed evil thoughts, murders, &c., in their most repulsive forms; but we know also, from the representations of the same inspired volume, that it is *this heart*, when under the *influence* of Satan, when he works in it, and suggests most daring, and cruel, and depraved conceptions, that is thus wicked, and productive of evil. Clear and definite views on this subject, then, are obviously necessary, to enable us to understand the Scriptures, to fit us for the performance of duty, to free us from imaginary terrors, and to inspire us with that fear, respecting which the wisest of men exclaims, "Blessed is the man that feareth always!" .

The principal means by which Satan has been supposed

to exert his power, and to carry on his intercourse with this world, are witchcraft, sorcery, divination, necromancy, and enchantment, in their different forms,—false oracles, possessions, and temptations of various kinds. In some of these, such as necromancy and divination, other spirits, or invisible beings, for instance, the souls of those who once inhabited this earth, have been thought to be concerned ; and the efficacy of some of the forms of divination and enchantment have been supposed to result from something like inevitable fate, or pre-established laws, put in requisition by the charms that were employed ; at least there seems to have been an indefinite notion of this kind, operating on the minds of many who have believed in these arts. But perhaps in the case of all who have been acquainted with the Scriptures, these spirits have been thought to be either directly connected with Satan and his angels, or to have been under their control; and therefore it is not necessary to our present purpose to descend to particulars; we may consider all these practices which have just been mentioned, as the supposed result of Satanic agency ; and as witchcraft has been deemed one of its most remarkable forms, it may be proper to consider, more particularly, this "work of the flesh." *

Sorcery is intimately connected with witchcraft. The difference between them is, that in witchcraft, according to the notions which have been entertained of it in comparatively modern times, those who practised it were supposed to have sold themselves to Satan, to have made a kind of agreement with him, (though none have ever shown, as far as I know, how the father of lies could be induced to keep his promise in any one instance, or for a single moment,) that, in consequence of some advantages which he undertook to secure to them, they would be his at death, or after the expiration of a certain period. The sorcerer was supposed to have obtained power over the devil and evil

* Gal. v. 20.

spirits in general, so that he could command them to appear at his pleasure, and execute his orders. He was thought to have acquired this influence by his skill in charms and invocations, or by his acquaintance with some occult sciences, and with the laws of the material and invisible worlds. It was imagined, too, that he was able to soothe or to irritate and put to flight evil spirits by smells and fumigations. In this way Tobias, according to the absurd account which is given of him in the apocryphal book of Tobit, caused the evil spirit to flee into the remotest parts of Egypt, by the smell of the burnt liver of a fish. And Lilly reports, that " one Evans, having raised a spirit at the request of Lord Bothwell and another person, and forgetting a fumigation, the spirit, vexed at the disappointment, pulled him without the circle, and carried him from his house in the Minories, into a field near Battersea crossway." King James, in his Demonologia, has given a very full account of the art of sorcery. " Two principal things," says he, " cannot well in that errand be wanted ; holy water, (whereby the devil mocks the papists,) and some present of a living thing to him. There are also certain days and hours that they observe in that purpose. These things being all ready and prepared, circles are made, *triangular*, *quadrangular*, round, double, or single, according to the form of the apparition they crave, when the conjured spirit appears, which will not be till after many circumstances, long prayers, and much muttering and murmuring of the conjurors, like a papist priest despatching a hunting mass ; how soon, I say, he appears, if they have missed one jot of all their rites, or if any of their feet once flied over the circle, through terror of his fearful apparition, he pays himself at that time in his own hands of that dire debt which they owed him, and otherwise would have delayed much longer to have paid him; I mean he carries them with him body and soul." The author of the article on witchcraft in the Encyclopædia Britannica adds,

"How the conjurors made triangular or quadrangular circles, his majesty has not informed us, nor does he seem to imagine there was any difficulty in the matter. We are therefore led to suppose that he learned his mathematics from the same system as Dr. Sacheverel, who in one of his speeches or sermons made use of the following simile: —'They concur like parallel lines, meeting in one common centre.'"* But if King James's account of the art of sorcery is correct, there was not much difference between it and witchcraft; for the witch had to use some charms or incantations, to secure the attendance of the familiar spirit; and therefore the observations which may be made on one of these arts, will apply to the other.

Now it must be granted, I should suppose, that if once the existence of Satan and his associates, and their intercourse with this world, are proved and believed, and also that they are permitted to tempt men to the commission of crimes of every description, and that they were at one time allowed to take possession of their persons, and inflict on them various diseases and calamities, there seems nothing irrational in the general idea of personal intercourse being carried on betwixt Satan and wicked men, of their entering into some compact, in consequence of which the devil would assist his votaries in effecting their nefarious purposes, that he might both gratify his love of mischief, and bring them effectually under his power, and thus more dreadfully ruin them for ever; and, in order to this, that he should appear to them in a visible form. I cannot see anything absurd in this conclusion; nay, if we were to reason *à priori* on this subject, without any attention to facts, real or supposed, it appears to me, that we should be led to grant that it is very probable, in case permission were granted by God. And when we consider how Satan is allowed to tempt men, and bring them under his spiritual power, it would appear not impossible, to say the least, that he might

* Encyclopædia Britannica, art. Sorcery.

be left so far at liberty as to enter into a compact with them; and probably the rationality of this persuasion, and its apparent accordance with some of the statements of the Bible, as they have been understood, have contributed to the wide prevalence of a belief in witchcraft and sorcery, and their kindred arts. It must be owned, I apprehend, by all who have seriously considered the subject, that it is a difficult one, and that those who believe in the practices in question can adduce many plausible arguments from reason, Scripture, and apparently well-attested facts, in support of their faith, And the assertion, that there never has been any compact between Satan and wicked men, that he never has been permitted to obtain such a power over them, and assist them in such a way, as are implied in witchcraft, would, I must think, be a bold one, and should be supported by most cogent arguments. We cannot wonder, even should we be able to prove that the opinion, after all, is unfounded, that it has been embraced by great, and wise, and good, and philosophic men; and I say this, notwithstanding the assertion of the writer in the Encyclopædia Britannica, "That there ever were witches, is an opinion which cannot for a moment be believed by any thinking man;" and of Mr. James Patterson, in a very good essay on this subject, "That a man of Dr. Robertson's information and abilities could have believed witchcraft possible, is not for a moment to be credited." Men quite equal to Dr. Robertson in both information and abilities have not only thought it possible, but have firmly believed in its actual existence, have argued strenuously and written copiously in support of their faith, and have been as ready to wonder at the infidelity of those who disbelieved it, as the latter can be to express their surprise that any men of learning and sense should think it possible. It is sufficient to mention the names of Luther, Bacon, Judge Hale, Baxter, and Glanville, to whom many others, distinguished for both abilities and information, might easily be added. I have in view in these observations only the general idea of a compact between evil spirits and wicked men. I fully agree with both the writers whom I have quoted above, respecting the absurdity and even impossibility of witchcraft, as it is presented to us in the stories of Satan being raised and laid by spells and incantations, of the nocturnal revels of witches, and the way in which they were conveyed through the air; of their power to assume almost any shape and form at pleasure, and to torment their victims by arts and charms of the most insignificant nature, without ever coming into contact with them. Some of these supposed practices are too ridiculous, I had almost said, for the malice and infernal dignity of Satan. It is truly lamentable and humbling that such a man as Baxter should gravely, and in the most positive manner, have adduced such stories as those to which I allude, as proofs of the existence of God, of spirits, and of a future state of rewards and punishments, and that they should have been believed by men like Luther, Judge Hale, and the Puritan fathers of New England. The details of the effects of believing in witchcraft, and of the charges which have been credited, and the cruel punishments which have been inflicted on the unhappy victims of superstitious credulity, form some of the darkest, blackest pages in the gloomy, revolting history of human absurdity and folly; especially as the crimes and cruelties have been occasioned, in a great degree, by erroneous views of some passages of Scripture. Verily, the worst things are produced by the perversion of the best. Without, then, denying the *possibility* of compacts between evil spirits and wicked men, or positively asserting that it has not in any instance taken place, I must at once avow my firm disbelief in witchcraft, according to the ideas which are entertained of it by most who have faith in its existence. And I shall endeavour to substantiate my views by the following arguments.

But in the present enlightened age, when intellect has

been so effectually aroused and illuminated — when it has already so far advanced in the path of knowledge, and is still rapidly continuing its march—when children can laugh at those stories of ghosts and witches, as well as of hobgoblins and fairies, which caused their ancestors to tremble in even manhood and old age—when, as it has been expressed, " the world is grown too old, and the church too wise, to dream or drivel again about the devils of superstition; these are all gone for ever with the ghosts and hobgoblins of antiquity—science and common sense cast out these imps, and therefore no superstition can bring them back;" * it may, probably, be thought by many, that some special reason, or even apology, may be necessary for requesting the attention of an audience like the present to witchcraft, or any of its kindred arts, or for making them the subject of a public lecture. For it may be said, Who now believes or feels interested in them? or how can the discussion of them be rendered subservient to any useful purpose? To this I answer, that even at the present time, and in our large towns, and I have no doubt in this metropolis, with all their learned and scientific societies, and places of worship, and intelligence, and shrewdness, there are not a few who believe in witchcraft, in some of its forms or degrees. And this faith exists amongst some who are intelligent, enlightened, and pious, and operates in a very injurious way. And even if this were not so, if witchcraft were everywhere treated with all the contempt which it deserves, still it is an interesting subject; its strange, humbling, mortifying, and almost incredible history deserves attention, as one of the most singular developments of human nature; and it must be interesting and useful to all who are engaged in the study of mankind. It shows us of what we are capable, from what evils we have been delivered by the light of experience, reason, learning, and philosophy; and, therefore, what we might have been. And

* Philip's Life of Bunyan, p. 147.

in a special manner, the subject is interesting to Christians, because mistaken views of some passages of the Bible have been the main support, with not a few, of a belief in witchcraft, and have led many pious and excellent persons to abet its absurd and cruel deeds. And it will be one principal object of this lecture to show, that the Scriptures, rightly understood, give no sanction to either the faith or the practices of the believers in witchcraft or sorcery, in any of its kinds, and that the Bible is blameless, however erroneous may have been the views, and culpable the conduct, of many of its well-meaning adherents.

And farther, that it is not unnecessary, even in the present age of knowledge and mental improvement, to reason and write on this subject, is evident, not only from the belief of many uneducated and superstitious persons, and from the proneness of infidels to ridicule the Scriptures, because they are supposed to sanction the belief of witchcraft and apparitions, but also from the fact, that so lately as 1834, Baxter's World of Spirits, and Cotton Mather's Wonders of the Invisible World, have been republished by one who is apparently an educated, sensible, and religious person; and yet who, in a preface, avows his firm belief in witchcraft; and says, that his design in editing the publication, is to expose the folly of those who do not believe in it; for, according to his own language, they "charge pious, grave, and venerable judges with being murderers, and the wisest and best men of former times with being fools and knaves. Those that can bring themselves to such an absurd and ridiculous conclusion, must possess a power which we do not pretend to; they must be able to believe whatever they please, and to disbelieve in opposition to the strongest and most convincing evidence."* Such is the language of a pious and sensible man. And it is well known, that several eminent and excellent ministers in recent times, (and there can be little

* Baxter's World of Spirits, preface, p. 23.

doubt that there are still some such living,) were firm believers in witchcraft, and apparitions of evil spirits and ghosts. This, as well as the circumstances which have been already mentioned, shows that the discussion of the subject is far from being unnecessary. I shall therefore endeavour to show :—

I. That the Scriptures give no countenance to the belief of witchcraft, or that the witchcraft mentioned in them is quite different in its nature from that of the middle and following ages.

II. The stories which are found in the records of witchcraft are of such a character, as to furnish the means of their own refutation.

III. Many of them have been disproved. It has been demonstrated that they may all be traced to craft and knavery on the one hand, and to credulity, weakness, morbid imagination, or disease, on the other.

IV. Witchcraft has always vanished and been discredited in proportion as knowledge, philosophy, and religion have extended their influence.

I. The Bible gives no countenance to the belief of witchcraft. And as one of the most lamentable facts connected with the delusions, cruelties, and wickedness of this art is, that an incorrect translation, and a misapprehension of the import of some texts, have been rendered subservient to a belief in it, and to the vindication of the practices to which it has led, it is more necessary to examine this subject particularly. " Thou shalt not suffer a witch to live," Exod. xxii. 18, is one of the principal passages on which the believers in witchcraft ground their faith, and on which laws and judicial sentences were founded in times that are now happily past, condemning those who were thought to practise it, to suffer death. The word מְכַשֵּׁפָה, which our translators have rendered " witch," and which occurs about ten or eleven times in the Bible, is by Buxtorf translated "*præstigiis utens; præstigiator, maleficus*," " a person who is skilled in legerdemain, a juggler, a poisoner;" by Gesenius, "a magician, a sorcerer," and he derives it from a word which he tells us signifies in Syriac, "to pray, to offer prayer or worship," and, like many other Syriac words pertaining to religious rites, this word in the Hebrew is confined to idol worship. It is by the Septuagint, and also by Josephus, translated φαρμακὸς. This comes from a word which literally signifies medicine or drugs, and then in a secondary sense, poison ; φαρμακὸς, therefore, seems to signify one who mingles and uses drugs for various purposes. Hence some would translate the passage, "Thou shalt not suffer a *poisoner* to live;" and the word in question may be translated "juggler, or magician, or practiser of curious arts." There can be little doubt, however, that the word מְכַשֵּׁף signifies one who pretended to be possessed of supernatural skill and power, and to be able, by his art, and by the use of potent drugs or charms, by his acquaintance with the secrets of nature, or with the aid of spirits of some description, to know and effect what was above the reach of ordinary mortals ; and therefore it means some kind of a magician, or charmer, or pretended dealer with familiar spirits. But then the question is, what were these persons? to what did they profess? and what could they accomplish? While multitudes who have professed these arts have been gross impostors, actuated solely by the love of gain, or by some base motive, there can be little doubt, that there have been several who believed in the power of magic and witchcraft, just as many have in astrology and alchemy, and who have at least *endeavoured* to obtain possession of it for themselves, and have studied and practised the rules which have been prescribed for that purpose. Nay, I apprehend that we may grant that there have been several who have endeavoured to secure intercourse with spirits, and even with Satan himself, in order to gratify their curiosity, or pride, or revenge, or avarice, or to enable them to effect some unlawful purpose; and that some of them have supposed that they were successful, and that they actually could, by their spells, and charms, and incantations, exercise some control over the inhabitants of the invisible world, and cause them to appear at their call, and, to a certain extent, perform their will and gratify their wishes, by inflicting injuries on their fellow-creatures. Without, then, believing that there ever have been such witches as could raise tempests at their pleasure, transport themselves and others from place to place through the air in a moment of time, transform themselves into any shape, and compress all the matter of their bodies into the size of an insect, render themselves invisible, and call Satan or any of his angels to their assistance almost whenever they pleased, we may grant that there have been persons who have been involved in almost all the guilt of these practices, who would have carried them all on had it been in their power. It cannot be doubted that there have been those who have professed magic, witchcraft, and intercourse with the world of spirits, and have undertaken to perform wonders in consequence. The witch of Endor asked Saul whom she should bring up to him, intimating that she could call up any one whom he might name. Simon Magus gave himself out for some great one. Now, whether those who made these professions were altogether impostors, who knew that they had no such power, or skill, or intercourse with spirits of any kind, as that to which they pretended, or whether they were the dupes of their own imaginations, and seriously made the effort to obtain a knowledge of the supposed arts of witchcraft, to render fallen, impure, and wicked spirits subservient to their will, and were so far given up by God to believe a lie, as to suppose they had succeeded,—their crime was very great, and the punishment which the law of Moses denounced on them, however severe, was perfectly just; and especially, because any Israelites who practised these arts adopted them from the heathen, amongst whom they were almost always connected with idolatrous rites and worship. The Gentiles believed in the existence of demons, both benevolent and malignant, whom they thought to be partly spirits of the dead, and, perhaps, partly other spirits, inferior to their gods. Their magicians, and jugglers, and enchanters pretended to have intercourse with these demons, and that it was by their assistance they performed their wonderful works. And, therefore, witches in all their varieties and forms, amongst the Hebrews, symbolized with idolaters, acknowledged the existence and powers of these demons, and consequently, the divinity of their false deities.

Thus their arts and practices were calculated to draw God's chosen people into idolatry, with all its absurdities and abominations. Witchcraft was therefore a virtual denial that Jehovah was the only true God. It was treason against his majesty and government, as the sovereign Legislator and King of the Jews. That this is a correct representation of the matter is evident, from the connexion in which witchcraft and its kindred arts are placed in various passages of the Bible, particularly in Deut. xviii. 9 ; "When thou comest into the land which the Lord thy God giveth thee, thou shalt not learn to do after the abominations of these nations. There shall not be found among you any one that maketh his son or his daughter pass through the fire, or that useth divination, or an observer of times, or an enchanter, or a witch, or a charmer, or a consulter with familiar spirits, or a wizard, or a necromancer. For all who do these things are abomination unto the Lord." Verse 20 : "But the prophet who shall speak a word in my name, which I commanded him not; or who shall speak in the name of *other gods*, even that prophet shall die." It is evident from this passage, that the practisers of witchcraft, and other kindred arts, in all their forms, were chargeable with idolatrous tenets and observances ; and this, doubtless, was one reason why they were considered worthy of death. They spoke in the name of the gods of the heathen, and acted the part of false prophets. If any of them professed to derive their information from God, or from good spirits commissioned by him, they uttered lies in his name. If they endeavoured to obtain their knowledge and power from demons, or any of the spirits of the heathen mythology, they practically substituted those in the place of God, and acknowledged their divinity. If they were entirely impostors, and did not believe in the efficacy of their own arts, but were wilfully deceiving others, their conduct, where religion and the prerogatives of God were concerned, was highly criminal. And, therefore, again I would observe, they merited the punishment awarded to them.

Now the observations which have been made on the word מְכַשֵּׁפָה will apply, to a great extent, to the other terms which are employed in the Hebrew to denote unlawful arts, and those who practise them. For instance, Deut. xviii. 10, just now quoted, where they almost all occur together. קֹסֵם קְסָמִים (Septuagint, μαντευόμενος μαντείαν, a diviner,) is by the Hebrews restricted to false prophets, such as Balaam, to whom it is applied, Josh. xiii. 22. מְעוֹנֵן (Septuagint, κληδονιζόμενος, ominor, an observer of time,) comes from a word which signifies to cover, to gather the clouds, to act covertly, to use covert acts, and it does not at all favour the modern idea of witchcraft. It is not necessary to dwell particularly on the rest. Dr. More, and those who give credit to the power of magic, translate them by English names that imply a great power, as diviner, enchanter, charmer, necromancer, witch, wizard, and consulter with familiar spirits, (though the word that is translated "spirits," is of doubtful signification, and the word "familiar" is added; there is nothing in the Hebrew that corresponds to it). "Those who think all magic to be mere pretence and imposition, translate them astrologers, fortune-tellers, soothsayers, impostors, observers of the flying of birds, conjecturers, consulters with oracles, ventriloquists, Gnostics, and jugglers; and they give as probable reasons for these renderings as are given for the other. But let them be taken which way they may, I do not see that we can attach much importance to them. Names are sometimes taken by impostors themselves, to magnify their own art; and sometimes are given by the credulity of the people, or the ill-will of parties. Time changes them, and makes some better and some worse than their original significations."* With these observations I fully agree.

There are only two more of these words on which it may be desirable to make a few additional remarks, viz., those which are rendered in our translation, "a consulter with familiar spirits,"—Hebrew, אוב בעל (Septuagint, ἐγγαστρίμυθος, ventriloquist.) The word אוב literally means a leathern bottle, or water-skin; and it was used to signify a necromancer, or sorcerer, or conjuror, because, while possessed by the demon, (as he pretended, and as those who believed him thought,) he was inflated and rendered like one of these bottles when full of wine.† There is every reason, however, to think that these pretended dealers with spirits were merely ventriloquists, who possessed the power, as they do now, of speaking out of their stomach or belly, (and an acute observer of a modern ventriloquist says, that every time that he spoke he suffered distension in the epigastric region,) and of so modulating their voice, as to make it appear to come out of the earth, or from any particular object. And amongst the ancients this power of ventriloquism was often misused for the purposes of magic. Ventriloquism seems to be a natural gift or power, depending in a great degree on the conformation of the body, especially of the organs of speech, however it may be perfected by art and practice. There must, I should conceive, be some tendency in the physical constitution, which leads to make the attempt to speak in this peculiar

* Hutchinson on Witchcraft, p. 184.
† Gesenius in loc. Encyclopædia Britannica, Physiology, Ventriloquism.

way, and which secures success in it. Amidst the ignorance, then, which prevailed in past ages, especially in some parts of the world, and particularly as it regarded natural science, when thousands and millions had no idea of the nature of the art of ventriloquism, or even of its existence, what apparent wonders might those who were adepts in it perform! How effectually might they impose on ignorant, gaping multitudes, and even on some who were acute and intelligent! How easily might they make them imagine that voices came from either heaven or earth, and returned answers to the various questions that were proposed! How confident might those who were deceived be that they had heard with their own ears gods or demons speaking out of the ground, or from the clouds! It is difficult to conceive a limit to the deceptions that might thus be practised; and in superstitious ages and nations, those who possessed this art, and used it for the purposes of deception, would naturally connect it with religion, and pretend to intercourse with demons and imaginary deities. In this way they would excite great reverence for themselves, and secure the most ample gains; and consequently it was intimately associated with idolatry and imposture of the worst kind. On this account the Israelites were forbidden to pay any attention to its professors, Isaiah viii. 19: "And when they shall say to you, Seek unto them that have familiar spirits, and unto wizards *that peep and that mutter*," (it is plainly implied, you shall not hearken to them;) "should not a people seek unto their God?" Should not those who know the living and true God seek to him and not to impostors? "For the living to the dead?" That is, Will you inquire for the living of the dead? or, Is it not absurd for the living to apply to the dead? (See Dr. Henderson's note on this passage.) This passage condemns the practice of necromancy and demonology, as both iniquitous and absurd, and as leading to the rejection of the claims and authority of the living and true God. And hence, in Lev. xix. 26, after telling the Israelites, "Ye shall be holy unto me, for I the Lord your God am holy, and have severed you from other people, that you should be mine;" it is added, verse 27, "A man also, or a woman, that hath a familiar spirit, or that is a wizard, shall surely be put to death." That is, dealers with familiar spirits and wizards counteracted the design of God in severing the Israelites from other people; they led them to associate with the Gentiles in their idolatrous rites and practices. And on this account they were to be put to death. The heathen were in the habit of applying to these impostors, especially in the time of danger and difficulty. Isaiah xix. 3, "And the spirit of Egypt shall fail in the midst thereof, and I will destroy the counsel thereof; and they shall seek to the idols, and to the charmers, and to them that have familiar spirits, and to the wizards."* Other passages of similar import might be quoted, all confirmatory of what has been advanced, that witchcraft in all its forms was connected, amongst the heathen, with idolatry, and that was the reason why, by the express command of God, it was punished with death amongst the Jews, since those amongst them who practised it acknowledged the existence and power of the false deities and demons of the Gentiles, and thus enticed God's chosen people to serve other gods.

Now from what has been advanced, I think the following conclusions may legitimately be drawn:—

First. That the law which denounced death on witches, necromancers, &c., under the Mosaic economy, emanated from the theocracy; that the reason of it was found in the peculiar relation in which God stood to the Israelites, and in the character which the practices in question necessarily then assumed. Therefore, if it could be proved that witchcraft in modern times is essentially the same as it was amongst the Jews, it would by no means follow that

* See also Exodus vii. 11; Nahum iii. 4.

it would be right, or at all consistent with the spirit of the religion of Jesus Christ, to punish it with death under the Gospel dispensation; any more than that it would be just to make blasphemy or idolatry capital crimes, because they were so under the theocracy. The Sovereign of the universe has prerogatives which can never be communicated to any earthly governor. Had the Bible been rightly understood, none would ever have been put to death for witchcraft. But,

Secondly. It follows from what has been advanced, (and this will be farther illustrated in the sequel,) that the witches, and necromancers, and magicians of whom we read in the Bible, and even those which then existed amongst the heathen, were quite different from the witches and magicians of the middle and of modern ages. They claim, or others have claimed for them, powers to which the former never pretended. We have no evidence that the Hebrew witches ever professed to be able to command Satan to appear at their pleasure, to control him by certain spells or charms, to render themselves invisible, or to transform themselves or others into the shape of animals, as modern conjurors have done, &c. The existence of the latter by no means follows from that of the former. But,

Thirdly. The great probability, if not the certainty is, that the witches and magicians mentioned in the Bible, and therefore all of a similar character, were either impostors, or else persons who were deceived by their own imaginations, in other words, rank enthusiasts; and that there never were any compacts made with Satan or spirits of any kind, or any supernatural power or knowledge imparted by them to their votaries, whatever the latter might wish, or attempt, or believe, or pretend. There are many intimations given us in Scripture that this was the case. We have already seen that the word which is translated "witches," means, sometimes at least, jugglers or impostors. The Jews were forbidden to entertain any fear of the false gods or idols, or of the astrologers or magicians of the heathen; Jer. x. 2, "Thus saith the Lord, Learn not the way of the heathen, neither be dismayed at the signs of heaven; for the heathen are dismayed at them." Does not this mean, Pay no regard to astrologers, or soothsayers, or augurs; they are all deceivers? The prophet adds, speaking of idols, ver. 5, "Be not afraid of them, for they cannot do evil, neither also is it in them to do good." Now, perhaps the most stupid idolater never imagined that the idol itself, the wood, or the stone, or the metal, which he, or others for him, had moulded into the shape of a man, or of some animal or material object, could do either good or evil. They all had the notion, formed and entertained indeed with different degrees of definiteness, that some deity or spirit either took possession of the idol, or visited it occasionally, or in some way connected himself with it. Hence the importance which was attached, in many cases, to consecration, and the performance of some mystic rites. Now, if the ideas of those who believe in witchcraft, necromancy, and heathen oracles, are correct, infernal malignant spirits might come and take possession of the idols and temples of idolaters, might communicate superhuman knowledge and power to their priests and magicians, and enable them to do both good and evil on an extensive scale; how then could it be said that the false gods of the Gentiles could do neither good nor evil? The apostle Paul informs us, 1 Cor. viii. 4, that "an idol is nothing in the world." But if devils could take possession of idols and their temples, and enter into compact with their worshippers, and inspire them to foretel future events, how could it be said that an idol is nothing? True, it would not be a god; but instead of being nothing, it would be one of the most important objects in the world. To those passages which have been quoted, others of a similar character might be added, such as Isaiah xli. 22—24, xliv. 10—25, and xlvii. 12, 13. And on this principle we may account for all the instances of witchcraft and divination mentioned in Scripture; and therefore to an examination of the chief of them I shall now proceed.

The account of the magicians of Egypt naturally claims our attention in the first place. Now it must be acknowledged, that their history presents considerable difficulty whatever hypothesis may be adopted, and consequently, as might be expected, different explanations of it have been given. Some maintain that in the imitating the first miracle, real serpents were produced by sleight of hand or juggling; others, that they were furnished to the magicians by Satan, or by some demons with whom they were in compact; others, that evil spirits produced the appearance of serpents, by blinding or dazzling the eyes of Pharaoh and his servants, and causing them to think that a real miracle was performed. " How much more rational," says a learned commentator, " is it to suppose, that these magicians had familiar spirits, who could assume all shapes, change the appearances of the subjects on which they operated, or suddenly convey one thing away and substitute another in its place ! Nature has no such power, and art no such influence, as to produce the effects attributed here and in the succeeding chapters to the Egyptian magicians."* But the strangest hypothesis, in my opinion, is that of those who suppose that " while the magicians used their enchantments, expecting assistance of the demons to whom they applied, God himself was pleased to interpose, and to effect a real change of their rods into serpents; and as they could not certainly know how far the power of their demons extended, they would naturally suppose that this was the effect of their enchantments."† With all proper deference to the piety, learning, and good sense of the excellent commentator, who appears to adopt this theory, I must think it is utterly indefensible ; and I cannot see how it is not dishonourable to the Divine Being.

* Clark, Com. in loc.   † Scott in loc.

In the first place, let it be observed, that there is not a single hint given in the narration, or in any part of the Scriptures, that God did thus interpose and exert his power; nothing that in the least implies that this was the case; but on the contrary, all that was done is ascribed to the magicians. "They did also in like manner with their enchantments."

Second. On the hypothesis which we are combating, there was as real and great a miracle wrought by the magicians as by Moses: the creating power of God was exerted in both cases, and the power by which his rod was changed into a serpent, no more resided in him, or was exerted by him, than the power by which theirs were changed resided in them; the omnipotence of Jehovah effected the transformation in both cases. Now, as the point at issue between Moses and the magicians was, whether the Lord was the only true God, to whom all, and amongst others Pharaoh and his servants, should submit, or whether the gods of Egypt were not real deities likewise, and possessed of supernatural power, can we suppose that the Divine Being would work a miracle to support and sanction the grossly erroneous and idolatrous views of those who maintained the latter; and afford them not merely a plausible pretext, but a solid reason to think that, though the God of Moses was stronger than their gods, yet they possessed true divinity as well as he did; and that, though he prevailed against them in this contest, yet in the next, they might prevail against him? I ask again, can we, consistently with anything that God has revealed respecting himself, suppose that he would do this; that he would exert his omnipotent power to sanction, though but for a short time, a gross delusion, producing rebellion against his own authority? I confess, I feel myself utterly incapable, in the absence of anything like proof from the narration in question, or from any other part of the Scriptures, to conceive that this could be the case. And without denying or doubting for a moment the agency of evil spirits, or asserting positively that Satan did not assist the Egyptian magicians in their efforts to rival the miracles of Moses, I have little hesitation in adopting the hypothesis of those who maintain that there was nothing supernatural in what the wise men of Pharaoh did, but that all was effected by sleight of hand; and that gross imposition was practised on the king and his servants. In support of this opinion, I beg leave to offer the following considerations.

First. The language employed by Moses does not by any means imply that evil spirits had any share in effecting the apparent wonders that were wrought by the magicians. There are three words used to designate the actors on this occasion, and two to express the means which they employed, Exodus vii. 11. They are first called wise men, or magi, חֲכָמִים, a word which is generally taken in a good sense, and is far from implying any intercourse with evil spirits, or even the use of any unlawful arts. They are next called sorcerers, מְכַשְּׁפִים, a word which, as we have seen, may be translated jugglers, mixers of potions of various kinds, practisers of secret arts. The third word employed is חַרְטֻמִּים, which our translators have rendered magicians, and the Seventy ἐπαοιδοὶ, enchanters or fascinators by singing or music. The Hebrew is derived from a word which means to cut or grave, and the term in question is rendered by Gesenius, "sacred scribes, skilled in sacred writings or hieroglyphics, a class of Egyptian priests," and by Buxtorf, magi. This term, then, does not at all convey the idea that they had any intercourse with Satan, or that they could exert any supernatural powers. These wise men of Pharaoh are said to have "done so by their enchantments," לַהֲטִים, a word which comes from לָהַט, which signifies "to burn, to flame, and then to wrap up, to cover;" and the term which is used in chap. viii. 7, comes from לָאַט or לָהַט, which signifies "to wrap up, to muffle, to cover." Taylor says, it signifies "to cover, wrap, or muffle up, 2 Sam. xix. 4, what is secret, covered, and concealed from the knowledge of others, Job xv. 11 ; to do a thing secretly, softly, covertly, so as not to be perceived, Judges iv. 21." Hence juggling, sleight of hand trick, or any artifices whereby real appearances are covered, and false ones imposed upon the spectators, Exod. vii. 22. Hence, also, to do a thing gently or softly. The passage then might be translated, " And Pharaoh also called the magi, the conjurors, or the magicians ; and the sacred scribes of Egypt did so with their dexterous arts, or sleight of hand tricks ; " so that there is great force in the observations of Hugh Farmer* on these passages ;· " So far is Moses from ascribing the tricks of the magicians to the invention and power of demons, or to any superior being whatever, that he most expressly refers all that they did or attempted in imitation of himself, to human artifice and imposture. The original words which are translated 'enchantments,' are entirely different from those rendered enchantments in other passages of Scripture, and do not carry in them any reference to sorcery, or magic, or the interposition of any spiritual agents ; they import deception and concealment, and ought to have been rendered secret sleights, or jugglings, and are thus rendered even by those who adopt the common hypothesis with regard to the magicians. These secret sleights or jugglings are expressly referred to the magicians, not to the devil,"—and it may be added much less to God,—" who is not so much as named in the history. Should we therefore be asked how it came to pass, in case the works of the magicians were performed by sleight of hand, that Moses has given no hint thereof ; we answer, he has not contented himself with a hint of this kind, but, at the same time that he ascribes his own miracles to Jehovah, he has, in the most direct terms, resolved everything done in imitation of them, entirely to the fraudulent contrivances of his opposers, to

---

* A learned dissenting minister, whose works will often be quoted.

legerdemain, or sleight of hand, in contradistinction from magical incantations. Moses could not intend to represent their works as real miracles, at the very same time that he was branding them as impostors."* And then Farmer proceeds to give a translation of the original words בְּלַהֲטֵיהֶם and בְּלָטֵיהֶם,† which entirely corresponds with that already given. Now, without altogether concurring in the representation of Farmer, or asserting with him that all the words employed are entirely different from those which in other passages of Scripture are rendered enchantments, and not denying that most of them may be applied at times to enchanters and witches, who pretended to have intercourse with the invisible world, (I am far from thinking that the terms necessarily imply that they ever had this intercourse in reality, or that they could by all the arts which they used render evil spirits subservient to their designs,) still it is certainly the fact, that the terms employed by the sacred writer, whether we attend to their original meaning or their common usage, ascribe the pretended miracles of the Egyptian magicians, not to the power of God or to the influence of evil spirits, but rather to legerdemain, and to the arts and dexterity of impostors.

Second. Though Moses employs the same language in narrating the pretended miracles of the wise men of Egypt as he does in stating his own; though he says, that " they did so with their enchantments; for they cast down their rods, and they became serpents;" this by no means implies that real miracles were performed. For as Farmer well observes, " Nothing is more common than to speak of professed jugglers as doing that which they pretend, and appear to do; and this language never misleads, when we reflect on what kind of men are spoken of, namely, mere impostors on the sight." The language employed signifies nothing more than that they attempted to imitate Moses,

---

* Farmer on Miracles, p. 452.
† Exod. vii. 11, 22; viii. 7, 18.

and succeeded in causing the spectators to imagine that they wrought miracles similar to his. And if we adopt the hypothesis of those who maintain that real serpents were produced, that the magicians cast down their rods, or seemed to do so, and then that, by sleight of hand, serpents which they had prepared on purpose were dexterously substituted for them, (and this appears to me by far the most probable opinion,) we can easily see why Moses says, " They cast down their rods, and they became serpents," or " they were *to* serpents," or "*for* serpents." In both cases there was a real substitution. When Moses cast down his rod, it was by the power of God changed into a serpent; and when the magicians cast down their rods, serpents were dexterously introduced instead of them, so that the spectators thought the former had been changed into the latter. And besides, the expression, " they did so," or "they did in like manner," cannot necessarily imply that their performances equalled his, or that they wrought any miracle at all, for the very same language is used in recording their failure, chap. viii. 18, " And the magicians *did so* with their enchantments to bring forth lice, but they could not;" and even when they to a certain extent succeeded, the language does not imply that their works were equal to his. Thus when Moses had turned all the water into blood, it is said the magicians did so with their enchantments; and when he had covered all the land of Egypt with frogs, it is again said they did so with their enchantments; but how could they possibly turn all the water into blood, or cover all the land with frogs, when this had been done already? All that can be meant is that they produced some humble imitation of the miracles of Moses, which afforded Pharaoh a pretext to ascribe the latter as well as the former to magic, and thus to reject the claims of the God of Israel.

Third. It should be further observed here, that the Egyptians, as well as the Indians and Chaldeans, were famous for their skill in legerdemain and magical arts. They made them their peculiar study, and might therefore be able to effect, by deception, many things that would appear wonderful, and even miraculous. Moreover, they had all the prejudices and wishes of the Egyptians, that is, of all the spectators, in their favour; and, doubtless, they had all necessary time and facilities afforded them for carrying on the deception. It is said, "They did so with their enchantments," or with their arts. They must then have had time allowed them to practise these arts, to go through all their ceremonies, and to use all the means which they would maintain were necessary to secure success. There can be little doubt that their practices in this respect were similar to those of the pretended magicians and sorcerers of modern times, who are very far from ever undertaking to operate instantaneously, or in any place or circumstances. They must always have time to prepare.

Fourth. If we examine in detail their pretended miracles, we shall not find in them anything which might not be effected by legerdemain; especially in such circumstances as those of the Egyptian magicians. The feat which presents the greatest difficulty, and which appears, both in itself and on account of the way in which it is narrated, to exhibit the nearest resemblance to the real miracles of Moses, is that of the change of their rods into serpents. But really, when we recollect that they could easily procure tame serpents, (for it is well known that they can be tamed,) or those whose stings had previously been extracted, prepared for the purpose, there could be no great difficulty for those who were skilled in legerdemain, and who would have all necessary facilities afforded them, while Moses would not be allowed to expose their arts, or to put them to any such test as he might wish to employ,— to convey the rods away, and to substitute serpents in their place. Feats equally wonderful, or even more so, are frequently performed with serpents, as well as in other ways, by Indian jugglers to this day. Nay, some more difficult are exhibited by professors of legerdemain, or natural magic, in our own country. Surely it would be more easy for them to cause the Egyptians to suppose that they changed their rods into serpents, than for jugglers amongst us to cause spectators to imagine that they can eat or spit fire, or swallow knives or swords, or change an egg into a beautiful bird, singing most delightfully, and again transform it into an egg, or that they can stand the discharge of a musket loaded with ball, without being injured. I must maintain that some of these things require much greater skill and dexterity, than would be requisite to enable the Egyptian magicians to substitute a serpent for a rod, in such a way that ignorant and credulous spectators would think that the latter had been changed into the former.*

Moses's rod, we are informed, swallowed up those of the magicians. Moses would not have been permitted, had he made the attempt, to expose their arts, and to prove that they effected all their seeming wonders by sleight of hand; and as God was pleased to permit them to succeed so far as to substitute serpents for their rods, the best, the only way of exposing them was, to cause the serpent which had been produced from the rod of Moses to swallow up theirs. As the spectators thought, whatever were the real facts of the case, that the magicians had produced serpents as well as Moses, this would be to them a proof, and one which they could easily understand, that the God of Israel was far superior to their gods, and that he would at last destroy them, and punish their worshippers.

The next miracle which the magicians attempted to imitate, was the turning of all the water in the land of Egypt, whether in the Nile, or in the streams, or ponds,

---

* While these lectures were being delivered, a professor of natural magic to the King of Prussia performed, in London, feats more wonderful than any achieved by the Egyptian magicians.

or even in vessels of any kind, into blood. And how did the magicians imitate or rival this? Did they wait till the water had been restored to its natural state, and then change it all again into blood, as Moses had done? No; they doubtless got a small quantity of that which the Egyptians procured by digging, and operated on it, or substituted one quantity of it for another, in such a way as to cause the spectators to imagine that they produced a change in it similar to that which had been effected by the power of the God of Israel. Surely it was no difficult matter for dexterous jugglers to do this.

The third and last miracle which they attempted with some degree of success to imitate, was that of producing frogs. These reptiles had been suddenly generated in such swarms, when, at the command of God, Aaron stretched out his rod, that they soon filled the whole land of Egypt; and it is plain that they were not removed till after the magicians had performed their feats; they were utterly unable to destroy the frogs, however they might profess to bring them. The probability then is, that a comparatively small space was cleared, and then, in a short time, caused to swarm with these reptiles, produced, as the jugglers pretended, by their arts. A matter of no great difficulty surely, when they were crawling all around, and intruding themselves into every place.

In their attempts to mimic the next miracle, the magicians utterly failed; and when we examine its nature and circumstances, it is not difficult to discover the cause of their failure. In the two former miracles, they had notice of what was expected of them, and time to make preparation. The plague of lice was inflicted without any warning being given, and consequently the magicians were taken by surprise. And it deserves to be noticed, that those parasites which were the infliction of the fourth plague, from their smallness, and from the circumstance of their being found only on the bodies of men and animals, and therefore on the magicians themselves, were not easily managed by legerdemain, and could not with facility be removed from one place to another, so as to impose on the spectators. No wonder then that, though the jugglers succeeded in their imitations in the former cases, they utterly failed in this, and were obliged, in order to save their credit, to confess, "This is the finger of God," or "of a god," as some render it; for it is not at all probable that they intended to acknowledge that the God of Israel was the true God, but merely that the miracle had been performed by some god, whose influence was superior to that of magic, and that therefore their failure was not at all wonderful or disgraceful.

Whether the magicians attempted to oppose Moses in the next two plagues, we are not informed. Warning was given of the plague of flies. But when these insects were swarming everywhere, and, probably, being still produced almost every hour in countless myriads, it is difficult to see how the jugglers could find an opportunity of counterfeiting it; and perhaps as it was in some respects similar to the last in which they failed, they retired from the contest. And the imitation of the murrain on the cattle, would be still more beyond the reach of their legerdemain. How, when almost all the cattle of the Egyptians were affected, and a contagious disease raging amongst them, so that fresh victims were constantly falling under its power, could the magicians so far impose on the credulity of the king and his servants, as to make them believe that they sent a murrain likewise? Had they inflicted it on the cattle of the Israelites, this would have answered some purpose; it would have shown that their gods were as powerful as the God of Israel. And if they could change rods into serpents, as some would have us to think was the case, surely they might have affected cattle with disease. I know it will be said that both on this occasion, and when they were unable to produce lice and flies, they were restrained by

THE AGENCY OF EVIL SPIRITS. 155

the power of God. But where is the evidence of this? There is not a single intimation given that this was the case, and we cannot accept assertions for arguments. The whole history certainly indicates that whatever the magicians did, they effected by their own art, and that it was because this art failed them, not because they were forsaken by evil spirits, or laid under any restraint by God, that they could imitate Moses, and impose on the Egyptians, no longer. At last they were completely baffled and put to shame. Their folly was made apparent to all. The plague of the boils affected them as much as it did the rest of the Egyptians, and reduced them to such a state, that they at once were ashamed, afraid, and unable to appear before Moses; and hence we are told, chap. ix. 11, that "the magicians could not stand before Moses, because of the boils; for the boils were upon the magicians and upon all the Egyptians." And thus it was demonstrated that the former were impostors, that they had been grossly imposing on all who believed them, that Moses had wrought genuine miracles, and that the God of Israel was the true God, the Author of the laws of nature, and the Creator of the universe, and Pharaoh and his subjects were left utterly inexcusable in persisting in their rebellion against him. The plagues, comparatively light and gentle at first, became more and more severe, as the conduct of the king of Egypt and of his servants became more and more inexcusable, till the country was almost destroyed; and then at last the death of the firstborn in every house, in one night, and by a similar disease, according to the prediction of Moses, affected for a time the most hardened, not excepting even Pharaoh himself, subdued the most obstinate, and rendered them willing even to purchase the departure of God's chosen people by loading them with wealth of every description. I hope it appears, then, from the critical investigation of the meaning of the terms which Moses employs, from general considerations, and from a particular examination of the miracles which were performed, and which the magicians endeavoured to imitate, that there is no reason to think that they wrought anything supernatural, or that they had intercourse with evil spirits, any farther than they were tempted and stimulated by them, as wicked men and impostors generally are. It deserves particular notice that the miracles which the Egyptians counterfeited, were precisely those in the imitation of which persons who were skilled in the arts of juggling were most likely to be successful; that they failed in those which were obviously most difficult of imitation; and that when at last Moses was commissioned to work such as it was impossible for any art, any skill in legerdemain, to counterfeit, they were utterly baffled, and were forced to retire from the contest. And when God arose in his might, thundered in the heavens, and poured forth tempests of hail and fire; when he spake, and swarms of locusts infested the land, and destroyed the remainder of its produce which the hail had left; (to have imitated this miracle the magicians must have brought similar swarms after the former were removed;) when he covered the whole land with darkness as gloomy as if the sun had been blotted out from the heavens, and when by the sword of the destroying angel, or by the pestilence which walketh in darkness, he laid the firstborn in every family dead at once; when he thus stretched out his mighty arm in a way which no power or art of man could, even in the humblest degree, imitate, the magicians entirely desisted from all attempts to counterfeit the wonders of Jehovah's omnipotence. In other words, the history agrees exactly with the hypothesis of their being gross impostors and jugglers, and not with the supposition that they were assisted by any Satanic agency.

The history of Balaam, Num. xxii., &c., is the next which claims our attention in examining the records of witchcraft, so far as they are presented to us in the Bible. The information which is given us respecting him is very scanty, so that it is difficult to determine what he was. Some think that he was originally a true prophet, and even a really pious man, but that he apostatised and endeavoured to unite the study and practice of divination, or magic, with the influence and inspiration of the Spirit of God.* Others, that he was never anything more than a soothsayer, or magician, but that God was pleased to employ him to deliver a true prophecy, and to bless his chosen tribes. The latter opinion appears to me by far the more probable of the two. He is indeed called a prophet, 2 Peter ii. 16. But he may be so designated merely on account of his pretensions, and the ideas which were entertained respecting him. It is not said that he was a true prophet; nor can it be inferred that he was so, because he was employed in one instance, to deliver messages from God and to foretel some future events; for we find, Jer. xxviii., that Hananiah is called a prophet, though he was an impostor. Be that as it may, his history affords no evidence that he had any real intercourse with Satan, so as to be enabled to utter predictions, and to perform anything like miracles. Nothing that is related respecting him, gives any colour to the modern ideas of witchcraft. He is called in Joshua xiii. 22, a soothsayer, from a word which signifies to divine, to practise divination, and which is applied generally to false prophets. The primary idea, according to Gesenius, is that of cutting up, and then it is transferred to divination, so that there is probably a reference to the method of divining by cutting up animals, and observing their entrails; a practice to which many heathen nations, and amongst others the Chaldeans, Greeks, and Romans, were much addicted. It is said, Num. xxiv. 1, that "Balaam went not, as at other times, to seek *enchantments.*" The word which is rendered enchantments, נְחָשִׁים, comes from one which signifies to utter a low hissing sound like that of a serpent, to whisper; and it is applied especially to the

* Watson, Institutes, vol. ix. p. 271.

whispering or muttering of sorcerers, (Gesenius;) and then it signifies to practise sorcery, enchantment, or divinations, and likewise to augur, to forebode; and the word in question, derived from this root, means both divinations and omens. According to Taylor, the verb signifies to observe with great attention and accuracy, in order to make a discovery; to make curious observations about omens, &c. The same word signifies also a serpent. Hence, some suppose that when it refers to divination or augury, it means to divine or take the auguries by means of serpents. On the whole, it seems that Balaam was a famous professor of divination or augury, or both, that he was skilled in all their arts, that he professed both to know future events, and to be able to exert supernatural power for both good and evil; and that being a man of great abilities and sagacity, and perhaps of considerable rank, he had gained a high reputation as an augur and magician; so that the general belief respecting him was, as it is expressed by Balak, that those whom he blessed, were blessed, and those whom he cursed, were cursed, It was a very common opinion amongst the heathen, that their priests, and augurs, and diviners, had a power to curse and bless efficaciously on certain occasions, and hence in war they were employed to curse their enemies, and to devote them to destruction.* Balaam, it appears, had gained a high reputation for the possession of a power of this kind, and doubtless accompanied the exercise of it with various mystical incantations, and with the observation of omens and auspices; and this will explain the reason why he said to Balak, " Stand by thy burnt-offering, and I will go; peradventure the Lord will come to meet me," Num. xxiii. 2; and "he went to a high place." And again, when Balak had brought him to the top of Pisgah, he said, " Stand by thy burnt-offering, while I meet the Lord yonder." And then, chap. xxiv. 1, we are told that " when Balaam saw that it pleased the Lord to bless

* Dr. A. Clarke, in loc.

Israel, he went not, as at other times, to seek enchantments." This seems to intimate that he had gone to seek those enchantments, to use his magical arts and ceremonies, and to consult his auguries and omens, in the attempts which he had made at the request of Balak to curse Israel; for it is evident that he wished to be able to curse them, and came with the intention to do so if it were in his power. The probability is, that he was not altogether an impostor, to whatever degree he might endeavour to render craft and deceit available to the accomplishment of his purposes; but that he thought there was in his mystic arts and observances a real power, derived perhaps from some of the laws of nature, or the influence of fate, to cause good to those whom he blessed, and evil to those whom he cursed, in connexion with his magical incantations; and hence he evidently hoped that he might be able, by the use of them, to induce God to permit him to curse the Israelites. Hence he once and again offered the perfect or mystic number of sacrifices, and boasted of what he had done. Whatever he was, or had been, he possessed some knowledge of the God of Israel, and this appears to have been the case with Balak likewise; for there is no reason to suppose that this knowledge was entirely lost in Moab and Midian; the contrary is evident; and hence Balaam calls him Jehovah, acknowledges his authority, and professes a desire to please him, when the princes of Balak came to him for the first time. But he was evidently endeavouring to serve both God and mammon, and to connect the arts of divination and witchcraft with what knowledge he had of the Creator and Governor of the universe, and to render even the Divine authority and influence subservient to his own unhallowed purposes. And yet, profane and wicked as he was, he durst not act directly contrary to the express command of God, or dare his vengeance; and therefore he once and again made the declaration, " What the Lord telleth me, I must speak; if Balak would give me his house full of silver and gold, I cannot go beyond the word of the Lord my God, to do less or more." In short, if we take into the account the ignorance of the times in which he lived, the general prevalence of the belief in omens, and magic, and enchantments, the abilities, and experience, and craft which Balaam no doubt possessed, and the high credit which some who were evidently and confessedly impostors have attained amongst the ignorant and credulous, the strange discoveries which they have been supposed to make, and the lying wonders which they have been believed to perform—so that in the estimation of many they have almost rivalled Balaam, and applications have been made to them not dissimilar to those which were made to him—and if we connect with all these, the meaning of the words which are employed to designate his arts and achievements, there is no reason to think that he carried on any intercourse with fallen spirits, or that he exercised anything like witchcraft. The erroneous ideas, therefore, that have been entertained on that subject, and the cruel practices to which they have led, are not at all sanctioned by the history of Balaam. "All that is deducible from his story is, that by artifice he attempted to deceive the credulous ; or, being himself addicted to superstition, that he acted consistently with such folly,"* or rather, perhaps, that both craft and credulity (for they are by no means incompatible) were united in his character, and contributed to enable him to deceive others.

The history of the witch of Endor, 1 Sam. xxviii., next presents itself to our notice. Saul, by his repeated, wilful transgressions of the express commands of God; by his rebellion, manifested in such forms, that it was as bad as the sin of witchcraft perpetrated in favour of idolatry ; by his envious, malignant, and impious persecution of David, though known and acknowledged by him to be the Lord's anointed, had reduced himself to the most deplorable

* Patterson on Witchcraft.

situation. The determined and deadly enemies of his person and kingdom had assembled in vast numbers; so that though he was evidently a man of great natural courage and resolution, as he demonstrated by his conduct in the most hopeless situation, "he was afraid, and his heart trembled," and his whole army participated in his fears. In this extremity he betook himself to God,—not as a humble penitent, to solicit the pardon of his sins, prepared to accept of the punishment of his iniquity, and to wait on the Lord, even if he should hide himself from him,—no, but to make an experiment, whether he could obtain from God the information and assistance he needed, but determined, if he could not succeed with heaven, to have recourse to hell.* Accordingly, when, as he was regarding iniquity in his heart, God would not hear him, would not answer him, "neither by Urim, nor by prophets," he betook himself to a reputed witch. This he did, though he well knew the utter unlawfulness of this practice in all its forms, and that it was most offensive to the God of heaven; nay, though he had himself, a short time before, in a fit of selfish or ostentatious devotion, "put away those that had familiar spirits, and the wizards, out of the land;" perhaps wishing either to pacify his conscience, and to appease the offended majesty of heaven, or to be able to say, "Come and see my zeal for the Lord of hosts; I am as religious as David, though God has rejected me and chosen him." In answer to Saul's inquiries, and in obedience to his commands, his servants told him, "Behold, there is a woman that hath a familiar spirit at Endor;" and to her he immediately applied. Now the question is, was this woman a witch in the ordinary sense of the word? Had she any intercourse with evil spirits? Did they bring up Samuel for her, or personate him, so that she thought he was brought up from the dead, or from the invisible

---

* "Flectere si nequeo superos, Acheronta movebo."

Virg. Æn. vii. 312.

world? Or did God work a miracle, and cause Samuel to appear? Or was she an impostor? Did she deceive Saul by her crafty, false pretences? I am strongly inclined to believe, nay, I have little doubt, that the latter hypothesis is correct, and that it will enable us to account for all the particulars of the narration.

On the word אוב, *ôb*, translated "familiar spirits," some observations have already been made. It has been shown, that it might be translated, a ventriloquist, and that it seems most naturally to signify one who, by ventriloquism, acts the part of a necromancer. As far then as the original word is concerned, the probability is, that she had no power over evil spirits, but that she was a base deceiver, or a miserable enthusiast, or both. And that she was to a great extent an impostor, surely all must grant. For what did she undertake and profess? When Saul said to her, "Divine for me by the familiar spirit, and bring me him up whom I shall name unto thee," her answer was, "Whom shall I bring up unto thee?" Now, was not this equivalent to a profession that she could bring up any one whom he might name, and, consequently, that she had power over all the regions of the dead; and that she could at her pleasure, and by the efficacy of her charms, either raise bodies from the grave, or bring spirits from the invisible world? It would be mere trifling to expose the absurdity of such pretensions, and to prove that she was so far a gross impostor, and claimed a power which belongs exclusively to God. To raise the dead is the work of Omnipotence. Jesus Christ has, and always had, "the keys of hades and of death;" their gates "he opens, and none can shut; he shuts, and none can open;" and who can suppose that he would entrust them for a moment to a witch, and to an evil spirit, even if they had power to bear and turn them? So far, then, her pretences were as false as they were impious. And if it be said, but Satan, or her familiar spirit, might appear in the form of the person whom she was requested to bring up, and speak and act in his name; we reply, this is not asserted or even implied in the narrative. She might assert that she saw persons ascending out of the ground, describe their appearance, pretend to talk with them, and by the art of ventriloquism cause those for whom she was divining to believe that they talked with her and she with them, while nothing of the kind took place in reality. Nay, if her imagination was warm and morbid, her judgment weak, and her health unsound; if she was the subject of mental aberration, and of a superstitious belief in the power of charms, she might when practising her incantations actually believe that spirits had appeared at her command, that she saw what had no existence, and heard what was never uttered. Imagination has performed far greater wonders, and caused far grosser delusions, than are implied in what has now been supposed.*

And if we examine the narrative, I apprehend we shall find nothing in it for which we may not account on the supposition that she was an impostor, who practised her art, and made high pretences, for the sake of admiration and gain, to what she did not possess. Let it be observed, that she was a professed necromancer or sorceress, and consequently was skilled in all the arts of deception connected with that profession, that Saul went to her by night, that probably she or some one connected with her was a ventriloquist, and that in the case of Saul she had all the advantages of darkness to aid her in the work of deception, that she might be well acquainted with Samuel, and therefore might easily give such a description of what she pretended she beheld, as would cause Saul, firm believer as he evidently was in the art of necromancy, to think that she actually saw the prophet. She had doubtless heard of the declarations and prophecies of Samuel, that God had rejected Saul, and had given the kingdom to another, and

---

* In Scott's Demonology, p. 13, is recorded a striking instance of the power of imagination.—See Appendix F.

that David had actually been anointed by the command of God, and was to be the successor of Saul; that unhappy king himself knew all these facts; indeed, they were matters of public notoriety. Moreover, it was easy for the witch to see that his time was come; that the storms of the Divine vengeance were gathering thick around him; and that as he was forsaken by God, there was no hope of his escape; for a general belief of all this, and, consequently, of the prophetic character of Samuel, is by no means irreconcileable with her pretensions to witchcraft. She probably knew likewise the strength of the Philistines' army and the comparative weakness of that of Saul; and she saw his trepidation and gloomy forebodings—how could he avoid these, when he knew that God had cast him off? Doubtless, then, the despair which caused him to faint when he heard, as he supposed, the declaration of Samuel, "The Lord shall deliver Israel with thee into the hand of the Philistines," was secretly working in his breast before, and would manifest itself in his countenance, and in all his actions. She might easily therefore predict the event of the battle; and a regard to her credit, for her statements were heard by the servants of Saul, and probably by others, would induce her to foretel what she thought would come to pass. And to carry on the deception, and to maintain her own pretensions, it was necessary to do this in the name of Samuel, and therefore to cause the king to believe that the prophet spoke to him in the name of God. It is perhaps commonly supposed that Saul heard Samuel speaking to him, or, at least, that he thought he heard him; but this is by no means certain; as he did not at first see Samuel, but believed he was there from the description which the woman gave of his appearance, so he might never hear any voice himself; the supposed enchantress might state to the king what she pretended the prophet said. I know it is maintained by some, that though Saul did not see any one at first, he did afterwards; since it is said that he "*perceived* it was Samuel, and he bowed himself to the earth." But the word which is rendered "perceived," יֵדַע, *yadang*, by no means implies that he saw him, but merely that he learned, or thought from the description which the woman gave, that he was there, and then he would naturally, looking on him as a messenger from the invisible world, and even from God, bow himself to the earth. Indeed, I cannot but think that the natural inference from the whole of the narration is, that Saul never saw anything, but that he trusted entirely to the reports of the woman. If Samuel was actually raised from the dead, or sent from heaven, by the power of God, according to the belief of some, or if Satan, or any of his angels, personated him by assuming his form, why did not Saul see it at once? What was to render it visible to him afterwards? So far, then, as it is absurd to suppose that any evil spirit could either raise Samuel from the dead, or bring his spirit from the invisible world, so there is no evidence from the history that any familiar spirit personated Samuel. We may account for everything from the craft of the sorceress, and from the necessity under which she was laid of speaking in the name of Samuel, and of employing such language as it might be supposed he would have used, had he been present.

But there is another hypothesis, which on account of its plausibility, in some respects, the way in which it enables those who adopt it to explain one part of the narrative, and the talents, piety, and learning of some by whom it has been adopted, must be noticed here. It has recently been stated and defended with great clearness and force, by one to whom, on account of his ability, learning, and piety, as much deference is due as ever can be given to human authority. The hypothesis is this; that whatever the woman might be, however unable she was to accomplish what she undertook, God was pleased to interpose on this occasion, and either to raise Samuel from the dead, or to send his Spirit from heaven, in order to assume the form which he wore when on earth, to reprove and reproach Saul, and to foretel his death and that of his sons, together with the defeat of the Israelitish army. And they urge in support of this hypothesis, that "the woman was evidently surprised and terrified at what she saw, that something took place which she did not expect, and that she immediately recognised Saul, and, after answering his question respecting the form of the apparition, left the king and the resuscitated prophet to continue the solemn interview."* It is further urged that the appearance of Samuel is a simple historical fact, as much so as any other recorded in the Bible, and that no less than five times it is expressly stated by the inspired writer that it was Samuel. It is farther pleaded, and with perfect propriety, that it is the Spirit of God who is here speaking, and not any other person; so that it is in effect the Holy Ghost who says that it was Samuel that appeared, and who spoke and prophesied; "so that the passage is not introduced as containing an account given by some uninspired person, but as a continuation of the sacred history, and perfectly tallies with the preceding and following context. The rejection of its obvious import can be effected only at the hazard of unsettling the entire basis of the divinely inspired narrative."† Such arguments as those just now quoted, connected with such an assertion as that which follows them, and that from so eminent a biblical scholar and critic, may well make any one pause, before he ventures to maintain a contrary hypothesis, and may, perhaps, in the estimation of some, expose him to the charge of temerity for making the attempt. And I must own that some of the arguments are so powerful, and the difficulties of the whole subject so great, as to cause me to hesitate, and after all to embrace and advocate a contrary opinion with some diffidence. Still on the whole I must embrace and advocate it,

* Henderson on Inspiration, p. 167.   † Ibid. 169.

as being that which is attended with the fewest difficulties, and as being most accordant with the sacred narrative, and with the general doctrines and principles of the Scriptures.

I know well that it is not for us to limit the Holy One of Israel; and that we are seldom in greater danger of erring than when, uninstructed by facts and the declarations of the Bible, we undertake to say either what God can, or must, or cannot do. "Who hath prescribed to him his way, or who shall say to him, Thou hast wrought iniquity?" Still, I find it difficult to conceive that the Divine Being, after having refused to answer Saul by either "dreams, or Urim, or prophets," that is, in any lawful or prescribed way, should, when he had recourse to unlawful arts, to a practice which was forbidden under pain of death, have wrought a miracle to give him an answer and to gratify his curiosity. I know it is said this was done to punish him. But the addition which this made to the punishment which was hanging over him was so slight, that it is not easy to see how it was consistent with the character of God to work a great miracle in order to secure its infliction. Besides, Saul was in such a state of suspense and perplexity, that it is questionable whether he would not deliberately have chosen, in order to be delivered from it, to know the worst; so that in fact he was gratified, rather than punished. Samuel is thought, by those who maintain the opinion in question, to have been resuscitated. How much is implied in this? He had not been very long dead; probably his body was not entirely decayed. Is it supposed or asserted, then, that it was actually restored to life, and brought beneath the ground from Ramah to Endor, and caused there to ascend, according to the representation of the witch, out of the earth? But must not this have been done, in order to present the appearances which were said to be exhibited, and even to work the miracle which is supposed to have been performed? If Samuel had been commissioned to foretel the death of Saul, is it not much more likely that his spirit would have been sent from heaven in a human form? And therefore it would have appeared to come from the skies, and not to rise out of the ground, in a way calculated to confirm the sorceress, and all who were present, in their belief of the efficacy of her enchantments and spells, or to beget faith in them if it did not previously exist. It is indeed said that one end to be answered by the event was, "a more complete exposure of gross superstition and imposture." Now I can scarcely conceive of anything less calculated to answer this end, or more likely to cause all who witnessed this transaction, or who heard of it, to believe in the efficacy of witchcraft. There is no intimation given by the historian that the supposed miracle was wrought by a Divine power, or that anything which the woman did not expect took place; at least nothing more transpired *than what she undertook to effect*, when she said, "*Whom shall I bring up to thee?*" All that we read is, that Saul applied to the witch; she promised to bring up to him whomsoever he should specify; he named Samuel; the sorceress betook herself to her divinations, and, according to her, Samuel appeared. This, in my apprehension, would have done more, supposing the prophet was really brought from the invisible world, to secure belief in the art of necromancy, than anything, or than all things, that had occurred since the beginning of the world. If the woman had no faith in her spells before, this was enough to cause her to believe in them afterwards; and to think, if she viewed the appearance of Samuel as a miracle, that her incantations had power in heaven as well as in hell. I must own, that if I believed that Samuel was really raised from the dead, or brought from heaven, on the occasion in question, I do not know how I could avoid a belief in the efficacy of necromancy. I cannot see how it could be consistent with the character of the Divine Being, or in unison with anything which, as far as we know, he has ever done, to work a miracle, so closely and apparently connected with the spells of witchcraft, and yet to give no intimation that he had interposed.

It is argued that something took place which the woman did not expect; that she was surprised and terrified when she saw Samuel, and that she manifested this by her crying out, and by being enabled immediately to recognise Saul. It is not said, however, that she was terrified, but merely that she "cried out." This she might very naturally do, in order to aid the deception which she was carrying on, and to cause the king to believe that she saw something supernatural. And how the sight of Samuel, supposing that he did appear, could enable the woman to know Saul, I cannot conceive. For she exclaimed, "Why hast thou deceived me? for thou art Saul," before the supposed Samuel had uttered a single word. She did not receive her information from him. If the association of ideas led to the discovery, why had not the name of Samuel the same influence? She might know him before, and yet to gain the greater credit to the influence of her art, she might pretend to have gained the knowledge by her charms; or when she uttered her loud cry, Saul, who was a believer in witchcraft, might have been surprised and terrified, and thus led unawares to do something which would enable her to recognise him. The querulous complaint, "Why hast thou disquieted me to bring me up?" accords better with the witch personating Samuel than with the dignity of a messenger from the invisible world.

The most powerful argument, and the only one of any importance, for the actual appearance of the prophet, and the greatest difficulty connected with the opposite opinion, is that the sacred writer repeatedly uses the word "Samuel," and represents him as present, and as speaking. Here we have a choice of difficulties, and I must think that those which are connected with the hypothesis that Samuel was raised from the dead, are far greater than those which are presented by supposing that the sacred writer narrates what occurred according to the profession of the sorceress, and the belief of those who were present. It must be allowed by all that the inspired penmen do sometimes use popular and not philosophical language; in other words, relate things as they appeared, and as they were believed to be, and not according to their reality. Instances in abundance, in illustration of this position, are given by defenders of the modern system of geology.

There are some who think that Samuel was neither raised from the dead, nor sent from heaven, but that a vision or spectre was presented to Saul, or to the woman, caused perhaps by the ministry of an angel, and that Samuel was then personated, and a conversation with the king was carried on in his name. This interpretation is liable to many of the objections that have been urged against the one which has just been examined. And neither those who adopt it, nor those who think that a spirit was raised by the incantation of the woman, can attach much importance to the principal objection which lies against the hypothesis which I have endeavoured to defend, namely, that the sacred writer repeatedly says that it was Samuel himself who appeared. For if it was merely a vision presented to the imagination of Saul, still it could not in strict propriety of language, but only by way of accommodation, be said that Samuel appeared, and that Samuel spoke, when his body was in the grave, and his soul in heaven, and when it was either an angel that spoke, or else all was an illusion of the imagination. On the whole, the great probability, to say the least, is that there was no appearance either of any evil spirit, or of an angel, or of Samuel, on this occasion, but that all was managed by the art of the sorceress.*

Let it be observed, that whatever may be thought re-

* See Appendix G.

specting witchcraft as implying a compact with Satan, doubtless all are in league with him who are in an impenitent state, all who are trifling with the authority of God, all who have not intelligently, cordially, and without any reserve, submitted to the authority of Jesus Christ, and that this will as certainly ruin their souls for ever as if, according to the ideas of some respecting witches, they had entered into a verbal contract with the prince of darkness, and had sealed it with their blood. All who are not turned to God are under the power of Satan, so far that he will certainly ruin them for ever if they are not delivered; and this deliverance can be effected only by the power of the Saviour, and by a cordial reception of the Gospel. Jesus Christ has solemnly declared, " He that is not with me is against me," and, it is plainly implied, is so against me as to be one of the associates of my great adversary. To have Christ formed in the heart as the hope of glory, is the only security against the craft and influence of Satan; in this way may we all be secured! Amen.

LECTURE IV.

THE AGENCY OF EVIL SPIRITS.

THE NATURE AND MANNER OF THEIR INTERCOURSE WITH THIS WORLD;
WITCHCRAFT, DIVINATION, ETC.—CONTINUED.

VERY few remarks must suffice on the other particulars which were proposed to be considered, in order to expose the folly and absurdity of pretensions to witchcraft. I proceed to show,

II. That the stories with which the records of this practice abound, are of such a character that they are not entitled to any credit; nay, they furnish the means of their own refutation; and yet the whole system is intimately connected with them. Many of these stories attribute to Satan and his agents, and to their spells and enchantments, some things which are absurd and ridiculous, others which are evidently above the power of any creatures; nay, which are impossible in their very nature. In proof of these assertions, we may take almost any of the cases which are recorded by Baxter or Mather, or any of the most respectable believers in this art. Only a few instances can be given, from which, however, we may judge of the rest: "Ex uno disce omnes."

"The hanging of a great number of witches, in Suffolk and Essex, by the discovery of one Hopkins, in 1645 and 1646, is famously known. Mr. Calamy went with the judges in the circuit, to hear their confessions, and to see that there was no fraud or wrong done them. I spake with many understanding, pious, and credible persons that lived in the counties, and some that went to them in the prisons, and heard their sad confessions; amongst the rest, an old reading parson, named Lewis, not far from Framlingham, was one that was hanged, who confessed that he had two imps; that one of them was always putting him on doing mischief; and he being near the sea, it moved him to send it to sink the ship; and he consented, and saw the ship sink before him. One penitent woman said, that her mother lying sick, and she looking to her, something like a mole ran into the bed to her, which she being startled at, her mother bade her not fear it, but gave it to her, and said, 'Keep this in a pot by the fire, and thou shalt never want.' She did as she was bid. Shortly after, a poor boy (seemingly) came in, and asked leave to sit and warm him by the fire; and when he was gone, she found money under the stool; and afterwards oft did so again; and at last he laid hold of her, and that she made no other compact with the devil, but that his imps sucked her blood." Such is the account given by Baxter. It is not necessary to dwell on the absurdities and puerilities implied in this account. That an imp had power to sink a ship at any time;—what ships would ever be safe for a moment if this were the case? —and yet, that it could not do this without the consent of the wizard. That the devil, or some one of his imps, should be transformed into a mole, and be in this form kept for days, or months, or years in a pot; and that he should have power to inveigle men or women into what would have the force of a compact with him, by his imps sucking their blood, apparently without their knowledge or consent;—were this practicable, who could be safe? who might not find himself in compact with Satan the next hour? And the whole evidence which is presented to us, to induce us to believe all this, is a hearsay story, which was never generally known till forty or fifty years after the death of all who were concerned in it, and when it could not be scrutinized. It has been well observed, that " men of too easy belief venture to publish hearsay stories. None trouble themselves to confute them, or if they do, the confutation is, frequently, seen but by few, and may soon be lost, when the history may continue; as it is very likely Mr. Baxter's book upon so acceptable a subject may have a tenth impression, when this obscure dialogue will be forgotten. Thus fabulous histories get credit, and poison the generations after them."* It deserves to be noticed, that the correctness and importance of the closing remark of the above quotation are strikingly exemplified by the fate of the book from which it is taken, when compared with that of Baxter. I should suppose that the readers of the latter, compared with those of the former, may be more than ten to one.

The story of John Goodwin's† bewitched children is well known to all who are conversant in the history of witchcraft. On account of its length it must be omitted, but the following are some of the feats of the witch Glover, and her familiar. " The tongues of the children would be drawn down their throats, and then pulled down their chins to a prodigious length; their mouths were forced open to such a wideness that their jaws went out of joint, and anon clapped together again with the force of a spring lock; and the like would happen to their shoulder-blades, and their elbows, and their hand-wrists, and several of their joints. They made piteous outcries that they were cut with knives, and struck with blows, and the plain prints of the wounds were seen on them. Their necks would be broken, so that their neck-bone would seem dissolved unto them who felt it; yet on a sudden it would become so stiff that there was no stirring of their heads." And all this was effected by the following means. " The woman's house being searched, several images, or puppets, or babies, made of rags, and stuffed with goat's hair, were thence produced, and the vile woman confessed, that her

---

* Hutchinson on Witchcraft, p. 81.   † Of Boston in America.

way to torment the objects of her malice was by wetting of her finger with her spittle, and streaking of these little images. . . . . . One of the images being brought unto her into the court, she oddly and swiftly started up, and snatched it into her hand; but she had no sooner snatched it, but one of the children fell into fits before the whole assembly." Verily, these images were almost as wonderful and potent as Aaron's rod. To give credit to this story, we are required to believe that the imp of the witch could inflict wounds with a knife, invisibly, and heal them in a moment; (for nothing but the 'scars of the wounds were seen;) that it could dislocate joints, even the joints of the neck, and keep them in this state for a considerable time, so that they could be examined by others, nay, "*dissolve* the neck-bone," and yet preserve life, and restore them to their natural state.* And all these miracles (for such they are) were effected by the rubbing of certain insignificant dolls. If this is not absurd and ridiculous, what can be so?

But more monstrous things than even these must be swallowed and digested, if we would be consistent believers in witchcraft. In the trial of Elizabeth Horner, before the Lord Chief Justice Holt, at Exeter, 1696, three children of William Bovet were thought to have been bewitched by her, whereof one was dead. It was deposed that another had her hands inverted, and yet from her hands and feet she would spring five feet high. The children said, "Bess Horner's head would come off from her body, and go into their bellies." The mother of the children deposed, that one of them walked on a smooth plastered wall till her feet were nine feet high, her head standing off from it. Now, this was said, and *sworn* in open court, by those who averred that they saw and felt what they deposed; so that

---

* Baxter's Wonders of the Invisible World, p. 132. Baxter says of this story,—" It comes with such convincing evidence, that he must be a very obstinate Sadducee that will not believe it!"

these gross absurdities and impossibilities are just as well attested as any stories of witchcraft can be. Verily, if it were possible to bring human testimony altogether into discredit, so that we should be justified in not believing it in any case, the history of witchcraft would have this effect. But how different are the miracles which are recorded in the Bible, in their nature, and how infinitely superior in their evidence! What a contrast betwixt the dignity and sobriety of the one, and the wildness, and extravagance, and puerility of the other!

And I do not see how those who believe in witchcraft can with any propriety avoid giving credit to such absurdities as the following. That a witch transformed herself in a moment into a greyhound, and a boy into another, and then changed both into their natural shape again; and then by shaking a bridle over the head of the boy, she changed him into a horse, took by force a boy, who had called her a witch, before her, and carried him away to a witches' feast.* It is true, this imposture was detected; but the account of the boy was just as credible as most charges of witchcraft have been, which have caused numbers of unfortunate beings to be put to death.

Now, in addition to the inherent absurdity and impossibilities of many of the cases of reputed witchcraft, we must take into the account the condition and circumstances of reputed witches, the way in which evidence against them was obtained, the character of their accusers, and the prejudices which operated against the accused, on account of the almost universal belief in witchcraft in all its extravagances. What were the condition and circumstances of reputed witches? They were commonly poor persons, who were destitute of the means of defending themselves; and in addition to this, often old and deformed creatures, whose very appearance operating on the fancies and feelings of those who believed in spells and incantations, was

* Scott's Demonology, p. 242.

enough to cause them to imagine what never existed, disposed as they were to associate witchcraft with a wrinkled, forbidding countenance, or haggard form. It is true, charges of being in league with Satan have been brought against some who were respectable in both rank and character. This was the case with the Duchess of Gloucester, who was accused of consulting witches concerning the mode of effecting the death of her husband's nephew, Henry VI. Several of her accomplices in the supposed witchcraft were put to death or died in prison. The charge of sorcery was also brought by Richard III. against the queen dowager, Jane Shore, and the queen's husband, and Morton, Archbishop of Canterbury.* Many other instances of a similar nature might easily be found. But in most of them witchcraft was only the ostensible cause of their condemnation. "It was chosen only as a charge easily made, and difficult to be refuted or repelled," in order to effect the purposes of tyranny or bigotry. In other cases, when the witchcraft-phobia (if the expression may be allowed) had raged for a considerable time against the poor and aged, as soon as it extended its attacks to the rich it was presently checked and cured.† In other cases, the supposed witches were evidently under the influence of a disordered frame and imagination, or of partial insanity, and perhaps in this condition they really thought that they entered into a league with Satan, or endeavoured to do so.‡ Doubtless some of them, actuated by malice and a wish to injure others, employed certain spells and charms, which they thought would be effectual to accomplish their malignant purpose: such as making images of wax, and melting them gradually before a fire, hoping to cause the object of their revenge to waste away at the same time; or pricking certain figures with pins, in order to torment the objects of their spite; (these were

* Scott's Demonology, p. 104. † See Appendix H.
‡ See Appendix I.

certainly, in one sense, in compact with the devil, and under his power;) and when such things were practised, in many instances, and by numbers of persons, it would have been strange indeed if no misfortunes had befallen some against whom the spells were directed; and a few coincidences of this kind would be sufficient to cause the ignorant, the credulous, and the superstitious to believe in the efficacy of these arts, and in the power of those who used them.

But the believers in witchcraft plead that many have confessed the crimes with which they were charged, and have owned that they had entered into a compact with Satan, and have related particularly how it was made, and what power was conferred on them in consequence. But how were those confessions obtained? and in what circumstances were they made? Let the following extract from Scott, quoting from Monstrelet, answer the question. After giving an account of some persons who were accused of being in compact with Satan, and of repairing, under cloud of night, by the power of the devil to some solitary spot, amid woods and deserts, where the devil appeared to them in a human form, save that his visage was never perfectly visible, and read to the assembly a book of his ordinances, informing them how he would be obeyed, distributed money amongst them, &c., he proceeds to state, "On accusations of access to such acts of madness, several creditable people of the town of Arras were seized and imprisoned, along with some foolish women, and persons of little consequence. They were so *horribly tortured*, that some of them admitted the truth of all the accusations, and said besides, that they had seen and recognised in their nocturnal assemblies many persons of rank, prelates, lords, and governors of bailliages and cities, being such names as the examinators had suggested to the persons examined, while they constrained them, by torture, to impeach the persons to whom they belonged. Several of those who had been thus informed against were arrested, thrown into prison, and tortured for so long a time, that they also were obliged to confess what was charged against them. After this, those of mean condition were executed, and inhumanly burnt, while the richer and more powerful of the accused ransomed themselves by sums of money, to avoid the punishment and the shame attending it."—He adds, " It ought not to be concealed that the whole accusation was a stratagem of wicked men for their own covetous purposes, and in order by those false accusations and forced confessions to destroy the life, fame, and fortune of wealthy persons."* Now I ask, in the name of justice, reason, and even common sense, what importance can be attached to confessions obtained by such horrible means as these, and by such iniquitous, and cruel, and deeply prejudiced examiners? Persons may be forced by torture to confess anything, however absurd, that can be laid to their charge; for not only may the pain be so great, that, in order to be delivered from it, they will assert whatever is dictated to them, but they may be deprived of the use of their rational faculties, and be reduced to such a state, that they are, if not actually insane, yet deprived of self-command, and therefore no dependence can be placed on their statements. It should be observed, that these confessions were obtained by Romish inquisitors, persecuting the poor Waldenses, and actuated partly by avarice, and partly by hatred of the Protestant religion. And as they at once forced, and heard, and reported the confessions, to what credit are they entitled? One of the inquisitors, Pierre de Lancre,† was so foolish as to believe, or so depraved as to pretend to believe, that the constancy with which the sufferers at first bore their tortures, and refused to confess, was owing to this, that Satan supplied them with strength to endure their sufferings, and that when

* Scott on Demonology, p. 196.
† Scott, p. 201.

these were so increased that he could support them no longer, he endeavoured, by mere force, to prevent them from confessing and exposing him, by some material obstruction in their throats; and that when, in one of the nocturnal meetings of the witches and fiends, he was accused of not accomplishing his promise, and of not granting to them and to their relations the protection he had promised, the arch-fiend vindicated himself by assuring them that he had been engaged in a law-suit with the Almighty, which he had gained with costs, and that six score of infant children were to be delivered up to him, in name of damages; and the witches were directed to procure the victims accordingly."* I ask again,. what credit is due to such confessions as these, wrested from unhappy wretches by insupportable tortures? and these are only specimens of what might be adduced in great abundance. And even in England, when the use of torture was not allowed, methods were adopted to torment the accused into a confession of their guilt. In 1593, the children of a Mr. Throgmorton thought fit to accuse two poor old persons, a man and his wife of the name of Samuel, and their daughter, of bewitching them. One of the children happened to see, when she was not very well, the old woman in a black knitted cap, and therefore fancied that she had bewitched her. The other children joined in the charge, and pretended that they were all bewitched; and the result was, that the poor old wretch was partly wheedled and partly worried into something like a confession, or to utter words which were construed to be one, and they were all put to death, though the father and the daughter never could be induced to confess, and died protesting their innocence.

The infamous Hopkins, " the witch-finder general," as he was called, in order to obtain confessions adopted the following method. "He kept the poor wretches waking,

* Scott.

in order to prevent them from having encouragement from the devil, and doubtless to put infirm, terrified, overwatched persons in the next stage to madness; and, for the same purpose, they were dragged about by their keepers, till extreme weariness and the pain of blistered feet might form additional inducements to confession."

"Having taken the suspected witch, she is placed in the middle of a room upon a stool, or table, cross-legged, or in some other uneasy posture; to which if she submits not, she is bound with cords, where she is watched and kept without meat or sleep for twenty-four hours, for they say that they shall, within that time, see her imp come and suck. A little hole was also made in the door, for the imps to come in at, and lest they should enter in some other shape, they who watch are enjoined to be constantly sweeping the room, and if they see any spiders or flies, to kill them, and if they cannot kill them, they may be sure that they are imps."* Strange that those imps, which have power to sink a ship, (according to the believers in witchcraft,) and to do many other miraculous feats, should not be able to enter a room without a little hole being made in the door for them, and should be obliged to render themselves visible in one form or another, even in that of spiders or flies, if they can do no better, so as to expose themselves to the danger of detection. How astonishing that such a man as Baxter should found his belief of the reality of witchcraft on such evidence as this; and also gravely adduce such stories as proofs of the existence of spirits, and of the truth of religion! Lord, what is man! "Verily, every man in his best estate is," in every respect, "altogether vanity."

III. Many of the most plausible stories of witchcraft have been disproved; it has been shown that they all may be traced to craft and knavery on the one hand, or to credulity, weakness, or disease on the other. Dr. Hutchinson

* Scott, p. 250; Hutchinson.

gives an account of seven detections of supposed witchcraft, which were quite as well attested and as plausible as any of those which are adduced by Baxter, or Mather, or any believers in compacts with Satan, or in the power of spells or enchantments. I shall abridge one of them, from which a judgment may be formed of the rest.

"On the 10th of February, 1633, Edmund Robinson, son of Edmund Robinson, of Pendle, eleven years of age, deposed on oath before two of his majesty's justices of the peace, by whom he was examined, respecting the great meeting of witches at Pendle, that whilst he was gathering bullets he saw two greyhounds, the one black and the other brown, running over the field towards him. He thought them to belong to a person whom he knew; when they came near him they fawned on him, and in the mean time a hare rising very near him, he thought he would have some sport with them, but he found they would not run after her. Being angry at this, he tied them to a bush and beat them, when to his surprise, instead of the black greyhound, the wife of a neighbour whom he knew started up, and instead of the brown one, a little boy whom he knew not. Being terrified at this, he attempted to run away, but the woman prevented him, and offered him a shilling not to tell of what he had seen. This he refused to promise, and even called her a witch. Being angry at this, she pulled something like a bridle out of her pocket, which she threw over the head of the little boy who had at first appeared in the form of the brown greyhound, and he became a horse. Then immediately the woman mounted the horse, seized Robinson, and took him before her to a new house about a quarter of a mile off, where there were collected about sixty persons, roasting meat before a good fire. A young woman, whom he knew, offered him some of the meat, and also some drink, which he refused to take, saying it was naught. Soon after this, some of the company going into a barn, he followed them, where he saw six of them kneeling and pulling six ropes which were fastened to the top of the barn; soon after he saw smoking flesh, lumps of butter and milk, as it were, flying from the said ropes, and falling into basons which were placed under the ropes. After these had done, six others took their places, and went through the same process. All the while they made such ugly faces, that the boy was frightened and ran away. Two of the witches ran after him, and would have caught him, had not two horsemen luckily come up at the time; but he knew one of them to be one Soind's wife. And that after this he saw this same Soind's wife sitting on a cross piece of wood in his father's chimney; and that when he called her to come down, she immediately vanished out of his sight. After this he met with a boy with whom he quarrelled and fought; but finding the boy too much for him, he looked down and saw that his antagonist had a cloven foot, which so terrified him that he gave up the contest. After stating on oath several wonderful things of the same kind, he named and accused as witches nineteen persons whom he knew, and one more as he believed, as having been present at this famous meeting of witches. His statement, especially as it regarded the plight in which he was found after his combat with the cloven-footed boy, was confirmed by his father, who stated that he found him crying most pitifully, and so affrighted and distracted, that he knew neither his father, nor where he was; and that he continued in this state a quarter of an hour before he came to himself. These informations, as given on oath, were signed by the two justices who heard them and took the depositions. In consequence, the nineteen persons against whom he gave the information were all either committed to prison, or bound over to appear at the next assizes. The boy and his father being poor, went about from church to church, that the boy might discover and point out the witches, who were at the meeting to which he was carried by the witch that appeared at first in the form of a black greyhound; as he said there were a great many present whom he should know if he saw them. Amongst others, he was brought into Kildwick church, where a Mr. Webster was preaching, and set on a stool to look all around to see if there were any witches there. After the service, Mr. Webster went into the house where he was, wishing to examine him in private; but two men who were with him would not allow this. He then asked the boy to tell him truly whether some one did not tell him to say all these things about himself, and those whom he accused of witchcraft; but the two men would not suffer the boy to answer, and they said, moreover, that the boy had already been examined before two justices of the peace, and they had never asked him such a question.

"At the following assizes at Lancaster, seventeen were found guilty by the jury; but, happily, the judge was not satisfied with the evidence against them, in consequence of which they were reprieved; and his majesty and the council being informed of the matter by the judge, the Bishop of Chester was appointed to examine the accused, and to certify what he thought respecting them. This he did; and, in consequence, four of them, Margaret Johnson, Frances Dickenson, Mary Spenser, and Hargrave's wife, were sent for up to London, and committed to the Fleet. Great sums of money were gotten by showing them. They were examined by his majesty's physicians and surgeons, and afterwards by his majesty and the council. These all were persuaded that the supposed witches were not guilty, but that the boy had been suborned to accuse them falsely. He and his father were then parted from one another, and put in separate prisons.' Soon after this, the boy confessed that he was taught and encouraged by his father and some others to forge the stories which he had told, and to bring all the above charges against his neighbours; and it appeared that envy, revenge, and the hope of gain, had induced the prompters of the boy to act the base part which has been detailed." And yet, on such evidence as that which this crafty, depraved boy gave, seventeen innocent persons were in danger of losing their lives; and had all been as credulous, or stupid and careless, as his majesty's two justices before whom the boy was first brought, would have been executed. And how deplorable and mournful is the fact, that on no better evidence of guilt than was exhibited in this case, hundreds of innocent men and women have been tortured most cruelly, and then put to an ignominious death! Poor human nature! how low hast thou fallen! what a spectacle dost thou exhibit to the universe! What cause have all who partake of thee to be humble and cautious in all their belief, and in all their actions! Solomon informs us, that in his time he "saw under the sun the place of judgment, that iniquity was there." But perhaps we are warranted to affirm, that he never beheld such enormities perpetrated at the seat and in the name of justice, as those which the records of witchcraft present. But how evident is it that the witchcraft condemned under the Mosaic law, was quite different from that to which our attention has been directed! No such scenes were ever known amongst either Jews or heathens, as those which a superstitious belief in witchcraft, and a false interpretation of a few passages of Scripture, have caused to be exhibited in countries professedly Christian, and in which, most unhappily and unaccountably, wise and good men have sometimes been the principal actors.

"Vomiting crooked pins and nails was one of the practices of those who pretended to be bewitched, and one of the evidences which was thought conclusive against the accused. This practice was detected and exposed in a trial before Lord Chief Justice North, when it was pretended that a woman vomited them in great quantities, and of such a form that they differed from the crooked pins usually produced on such occasions, and could not be concealed in the mouth. But it was proved that this woman in her convulsive fits, which preceded her vomiting, sunk her head on her breast, so as to take up the pins, which she had concealed in her stomacher. The man whom she had accused was of course acquitted. A frightful old hag, who was present, distinguished herself so much by her benedictions on the judge, that he asked the cause of the peculiar interest which she felt in the acquittal. 'Twenty years ago,' said the poor woman, 'they would have hanged me for a witch, but they could not; and now, but for your lordship, they would have murdered my innocent son.'"*

Hopkins, the witch-finder general, who went through the whole country, charging twenty shillings a town, and his board and lodging, and expenses of travelling, for discovering witches, (which he professed to do by stripping them naked, and thrusting pins into different parts of their bodies, to discover the witch's mark, and by such-like sagacious methods,) was at last exposed and proved to be an infamous impostor. "And the popular indignation was so excited against him, that some gentlemen seized him, and put him to his own favourite experiment of swimming;"† and, perhaps, for anything that appears, drowned him; at any rate, the country was freed from him; and as was the case in other instances, with the witch-finder and accuser, the witches disappeared also. One anecdote, recorded by Scott, deserves to be told, both because it exposes the baseness of Hopkins, and substantiates an assertion which has already been made, that torture often deprives of the use of reason, so that no importance can be attached to any confessions which it elicits. "A miserable old woman had fallen into the hands of the miscreant Hopkins, near Hoxne, a village in Suffolk, and had confessed all the usual enormities, after being without food or rest for a sufficient time. Her imp, she said, was called Nan. A gentleman in the neighbourhood, whose

* Scott, p. 260. † Ibid. p. 252.

widow survived to authenticate the story, was so indignant, that he went to the house, took the woman out of such inhuman hands, dismissed the witch-finders, and after due food and rest, the poor woman could recollect nothing of all the confessions she had made, but that she gave a favourite pullet the name of Nan." The name of this gentleman ought to have been recorded. It deserves a niche in the temple of fame, better than many that are found there. It is refreshing to find some oases in the desert, some verdant spots rich with the verdure and fruits of wisdom, virtue, and piety, amid the extensive frightful wilderness of human depravity. But I must proceed to observe shortly, in the

IVth place. Witchcraft has always been discredited, and has disappeared, in proportion as knowledge, philosophy, and religion have extended their influence. Ignorance of the laws, and of the causes of the various phenomena of nature in general, as well as of the human frame in particular, must have operated in a twofold way in favour of a belief in witchcraft. It would enable those who had obtained a more extensive knowledge of those laws and causes than others, to do things, to exhibit feats, which the ignorant would deem marvellous or supernatural; and it would dispose the latter to believe the pretences of impostors, and both incapacitate and indispose to detect them. How easily could any one who is well acquainted with the principles and facts of chemistry, electricity, and galvanism, and is able to experiment dexterously in those sciences, have astonished those who lived in the ages when witchcraft, in all its absurdities and impossibilities, was believed! Some who, at that time, excelled in the knowledge of the works and laws of nature, were on that very account accused of witchcraft, such as Zoroaster, Pythagoras, Roger Bacon, Albertus Magnus, Ripley, and others. During those ages, too, sound accurate learning was in a low state; biblical criticism, especially, was almost totally neglected. And hence some passages of Scripture, improperly translated, or misunderstood, were perverted, and rendered a foundation for faith in witchcraft; while men's general belief and ideas of the existence of spirits, and of their intercourse with our world, were perverted by superstition to subserve its purposes. Now, this being the case, it might be expected that even when learning, both secular and sacred, did revive, and knowledge was increased, and arts and sciences were successfully studied, it would require some time to correct men's erroneous ideas, to change their habits of thought and action, and to counteract and alter the customs of society. Hence we cannot wonder that the belief in witchcraft remained, and produced its dreadful effects, even after the Reformation and the revival of letters and science; especially since this belief in the art, and the notions that had prevailed respecting it, were, in many cases, found convenient for gratifying avarice and revenge, for crushing a political adversary, or bringing into discredit and punishing supposed heretics. Even the sun cannot all at once, when he diffuses his genial rays in the spring, banish the cold, and hush the storms of winter: he must, to accomplish this, exert his influence, day after day, and even week after week; nor can he produce the warmth and splendour of noon when he first rises in the east. So it was with the sun of science, and learning, and religion; it was only by degrees, and after having for some time exerted its influence, that it could banish the darkness of error and superstition, and create a moral and intellectual spring. But the general important fact is certain, whatever exceptions may be produced, that in proportion as knowledge and learning prevailed, the belief in witchcraft was weakened, and its practices vanished. Writers on this subject have shown, that from the time that the Royal Society was formed in England, in 1662, and the French Academy of Sciences about twenty years after, and the secrets of nature were explored and revealed, and its laws to a great extent ascertained by the experimental philosophers, prosecutions for witchcraft were discouraged, those who were brought to trial were acquitted, and sometimes their accusers punished. Several writers appeared, who exposed the practices of witch-finders and their accomplices who pretended to be bewitched; and magistrates and judges were found who opposed their authority to the craft, and folly, and wickedness of witchery in general. Even in New England, mournful as was the tragedy that was acted there, it is evident, that the piety and good sense of the descendants of the Puritan Fathers rendered the scene less gloomy than it otherwise would have been. Had it not been for these, instead of sixteen months, and nineteen executions, the witchcraft mania might have continued for years, and sacrificed hundreds of victims. It is not necessary to enlarge: the fact is certain, and I appeal for the correctness of the assertion to the history of the world, that witchcraft, in the popular sense of the word, cannot bear the light of truth; and that in proportion as knowledge in general, and an acquaintance with the laws of nature in particular, and with the doctrines and statements of Scripture on this subject, prevail, witchcraft has disappeared; and that the belief of it now, in the sense in which it has been exposed, lingers, with comparatively few exceptions, only amongst the ignorant and uneducated class of society, and in the dark places of the earth. This is surely an evidence that it vanishes before the light of reason, science, and religion; that it is not founded on fact, but is supported only by ignorance, superstition, craft, and wickedness. One thing more deserves to be noticed, that prosecutions and punishments for witchcraft have always augmented the number of accusations, and of supposed witches; because they have confirmed and called into exercise the popular belief and feelings on the subject, and encouraged accusers and informers. But whenever the prosecutions were discouraged, and the promoters of them baffled, and especially when they were punished, witchcraft has soon disappeared; the devil and all his imps, and all the charms that were employed to secure their aid, have vanished, to return no more. In New England, when a sensible and spirited gentleman of Boston was accused of witchcraft, at Andover, he sent a writ to bring an action against the accusers, for a thousand pounds damages. This soon put an end to the proceedings against witches at that place. And generally, throughout the whole country, when those who could not prove their charges against the supposed witches were subjected to actions for damages, the accusations were soon at an end. And this has been the case universally whenever this method has been tried. It is an infallible cure for witchcraft and sorcery in all their kinds. In a word, let only the superstitious belief in witchcraft, and prosecutions for it, be banished from any country on the face of the earth, and witches will either not exist at all, or be found perfectly harmless. And I would apply a similar principle to ghosts and apparitions. None, I am persuaded, will ever see them or be troubled with them, but those whose credulity, disordered frames, and superstitious fears, or hopes and *wishes*, give them an imaginary existence. In proportion as intelligence, accurate learning, sound philosophy, and scriptural religion prevail in the world, witches, and imps, and apparitions, to whose appearances and operations the darkness of ignorance and superstition is more necessary than even the gloom and witching hour of midnight, will certainly disappear from our earth; and an enlightened understanding, and a rational scriptural faith, will discern and admire the realities and wonders of both the natural and spiritual world; and this will be as useful and elevating as the belief in witchcraft has been degrading and pernicious. On the other hand, I have no doubt that even now, in our enlightened age and country, and even in this metropolis, with all its learned societies, and colleges, and places of worship, if supposed witches (for some such are still to be found,) were punished, and their accusers encouraged, they would soon be found in as great numbers as ever, and scenes as disgraceful and revolting as have ever been presented in any of the eras of witchcraft, would again be exhibited to the world.

THE SIBYLLINE ORACLES.

Though the controversy respecting the Sibylline oracles does not come, properly speaking, within the plan of these lectures, since few persons will say that those which are extant at the present time were dictated by Satan, any farther than, if they can be proved to be forgeries, they may be attributed to him as the father of lies, yet it may be proper to notice them, as they are intimately connected with some of the topics under discussion, and as they are reckoned by those who believe in them amongst the oracles of the heathen, and are considered by them as affording an unanswerable proof of the truth of the Christian religion; whilst others regard them as one means by which evil spirits have perverted the truth, and opposed the cause of God.

The Sibyls, whom we have now in view, were supposed, and are still deemed by some persons, to have been real prophetesses, inspired by the Spirit of God, and sent to reprove the heathen for their sins, and especially for their idolatry, to call them to repentance, and to foretel the coming of Jesus Christ; in short, that they were to the Gentiles what the Jewish prophets were to the Jews, and that they were raised up in different parts and ages, and wandered from place to place, uttering their predictions, and exhorting all to repent.

The epithet or name Sibyl comes from two Greek words, Σιὸς, the Doric for Θεὸς, and βουλὴ, counsel; and it signifies one who makes known the counsel of God, or a prophetess.

As it regards the number of them, the learned are not agreed. Some maintain that there was but one. Lactantius, Varus, and Floyer, think that there were ten; the Persian or Chaldean, the Libyan, the Delphian, the Cimmerian, in Italy, the Erythrean, who is believed to have foretold the destruction of Troy, the Samian, the Cumanian, (who is reported to have brought nine books to Tarquinius Priscus, of which she burnt all but three, because he would not give her the price which she asked for them,) the Hellespontine, the Phrygian, and the Alburnian. And it is thought that some Sibyls had different names, as the Babylonian is called Erythræa.

The time in which they lived, according to those who believe in their inspiration, is not certain. It is not necessary to give the different opinions that are entertained on this point. Some of them are supposed to have been contemporary with the judges of Israel. The Delphian is thought to be the most ancient of them, and to have furnished Homer with some of his verses.

The Sibylline oracles were destroyed in the conflagration of the Roman capitol in the time of Sylla, about eighty-three years before Christ; and to repair the loss which was thought to have been sustained, commissioners were immediately sent to every part of Greece, to collect whatever could be found of the inspired writings of the Sibyls. What eventually became of these is uncertain. The only question with which we are concerned at present is, whether these Sibylline oracles which are now extant are genuine and Divinely inspired, or not. Some learned men have maintained that they are; amongst others Sir John Floyer, who published a translation of them in 1713, strenuously vindicates their authenticity and Divine inspiration, but in my opinion without any success. The general opinion of those who are best qualified to judge, is, that the famous Roman collection of the Sibylline oracles were all political forgeries and engines, and that those which are now extant were forged in the second century, by some Christian, who wished thus to subserve the cause of truth, though by acting contrary to its spirit, and to the maxim of the apostle, "not to do evil that good may come."

The following appears to me to be the truth of the matter respecting them. For ages before the coming of Christ, the Jews had been dispersed, by various means, amongst almost all nations; thus both furnishing a striking fulfilment of the prophecy which their own legislator had, in the name of God, uttered respecting them, and accomplishing the purpose of Jehovah in selecting them from the other nations of the earth, that they might be his witnesses that he alone was God, and that the deities of the heathen were vanity and lies. They, of course, carried copies of their sacred writings with them wherever they went, and doubtless stated, in conversation with their heathen neighbours, their views and hopes respecting the Messiah. By this means the predictions of the Jewish seers would be known to the pretended prophets and prophetesses of the Gentiles, who might well be struck with their sublimity and beauty, and therefore incorporate some parts of them with their own effusions. Some of these ideas and descriptions might be found amongst those Sibylline oracles which the Romans first procured, and kept for political purposes in the capitol. When, after these were burnt with that edifice, the Romans sent ambassadors into various countries to procure others, the value of these oracles would naturally be raised, and their fame diffused, and abundance of them would soon be produced. As a proof of this, more than two thousand volumes of them were burnt by Augustus and Tiberius.

But besides the copy of these which were left, which was deposited in the capitol, there were also copies in private hands, and from one of these Virgil might easily get the sentiments which he has introduced into his celebrated fourth Eclogue, as the prophecy of the Cumæan Sibyl; and also some things, which are found in those which are now extant, might be taken from the oracles which were collected by the Romans, and which were all finally destroyed by the emperor Honorius, about four hundred years after Christ, because a prophecy which was found in them, respecting the Christian religion, utterly failed of its accomplishment. The prediction was, that Peter had established the cause of Jesus of Nazareth by magic, and that it was to last only three hundred and sixty-five years; that at the end of this term it was to vanish from the world. These three hundred and sixty-five years terminated in A.D. 398, and hence these oracles were convicted of falsehood, and destroyed. Stilicho, in consequence of the decree of Honorius, committed them all to the flames, and entirely demolished the temple of Apollo, in which they had been deposited. Prideaux thinks, that in addition to the knowledge of the Jewish Scriptures and of the expected Messiah, which would infallibly be diffused amongst the heathen in the way which has just been stated, the demons that presided in these oracles might be forced, before they finally left them, which he supposed they were obliged to do before the advent of our Saviour, to utter true prophecies respecting him, and the affairs of his kingdom, as Balaam was forced to foretel the rising of a star out of Jacob, and Caiaphas the death of a Saviour. This, I must confess, for reasons which I may afterwards assign, appears to me altogether improbable. The circumstances of both the false prophet and of the Jewish high priest, were quite different from those of the heathen Sibyls, especially the connexion of the former with the chosen race, and with the production of those Scriptures which are the oracles of the living God. I must then adopt the opinion of those who maintain that the Sibylline oracles which are now extant, were the forgery of some injudicious professor of Christianity in the second century, who might avail himself of the remains of those which before existed, and make to them such additions as he thought would answer his purposes; and therefore I must entirely dissent from the opinion of Sir John Floyer, and his party, who maintain that the Sibyls were prophetesses, and their oracles the dictates of the Spirit of God. I do so for the following reasons.

First. The style, the sentiments, the spirit, and the whole character of these oracles are so different from those of the Holy Scriptures, that it is difficult to conceive how the same Divine influence which dictated the latter could have produced the former. What a contrast between David, or Isaiah, or Jeremiah, and the best of the Sibyls, after all their borrowing from the Bible, as it regards plainness, sublimity, pathos, spirituality, and piety! Read the 23rd or 103rd Psalms, or any of the pages of the evangelical, or of the weeping prophet, and then peruse such effusions as the following, not carefully selected, but almost the first that occurs at the opening of the book:—"No more torment thy mind, do not trouble thy heart, thou that art begotten of God, abounding in all riches, the flower desired of God alone, the glorious light, the pleasant offspring, the desirable plant. O Judea! thou beloved and beautiful city, inspired with hymns, the impure Grecian king shall not revel through the Persian country any more, having a mind like to Bacchus for his justice; but thy illustrious inhabitants shall honour thee, and shall employ themselves in holy and learned songs, and all sorts of sacrifices, and prayers for the honour of God; and for their small afflictions, whosoever has borne much labour and misery, they shall enjoy more and pleasant good things who are righteous; but the wicked, who use their wicked tongues against heaven, shall cease from their calumnies which they spoke amongst themselves, and shall hide themselves till the world is changed." * I can as easily conceive that the lucubrations of the dullest and most trifling intellect

* Floyer, p. 127.

that ever felt the *cacoëthes scribendi* flowed from the genius of Demosthenes, or Plato, or Milton, as that these and similar effusions were dictated by the same holy and heavenly Spirit which rapt Ezekiel in prophetic vision, and touched the lips of Isaiah, and warmed his heart with a live coal from the heavenly altar, and filled the breast of David with the devout emotions which induced him to exclaim, "Bless the Lord, O my soul, and all that is within me bless his holy name." But to do justice to this subject, and fully to exhibit the difference between the two productions, it would be necessary to compare one of the books of the Sibyls with one of the prophets; or rather the whole of the productions of the former with those of the latter.

Secondly. If the Sibyls had been inspired prophetesses, as some would have us to believe, why was no notice taken of them by either Jesus Christ or his apostles? especially as, in their time, they were generally known. When preaching or writing to the Jews, the apostles constantly appealed to their own Scriptures, and quoted the prophecies which they contained respecting the Messiah and his kingdom. Would they not have pursued a similar course when addressing the Gentiles, if there had been amongst them any writings which had been produced by the inspiration of the Spirit of God, and that with a view to foretel the advent of the Great Deliverer, the Desire of all nations, and containing many clear predictions and statements of his character and work? We can scarcely conceive it possible that they would not have availed themselves of this source of argument and illustration, this means of facilitating the performance of the work in which their whole hearts were engaged. Nay, would not this have been necessary for the attainment of the end for which those writings were given to the world, if they had been Divinely inspired? This argument appears to me quite decisive of the point in question. I know it has been said, on the authority of Clemens Alexandrinus, who lived in the second century, that Paul, in his preaching to the Gentiles, frequently referred to these oracles. But the bare assertion of Clemens, (and it is only too evident that the writers of that period were far from being sufficiently careful, as it regarded either their arguments, their belief, or their statements,) without any proof, is quite insufficient to counterbalance the evidence of the contrary, from the fact that Paul never so much as alludes to them in his epistles, which were epitomes of his preaching to the Gentiles.

Thirdly. The manner in which those supposed prophetesses were inspired, was quite different from that in which the prophets of the Jews received their communications from heaven. Though the Sibyls were not shut up in caves like the Sibyl of Virgil, or the priestesses of the temple, but wandered from place to place, yet they were thrown, during the time of their inspiration, into a kind of enthusiastic delirium or fury, and deprived, it would seem, to a great degree, of the use of their natural faculties. It was quite otherwise with true prophets; they heard the voice of God, or had clear and vivid visions presented to their minds, or distinct ideas conveyed to their understandings, while they had the full use of their natural powers, and could think and speak, and utter their predictions, in a calm, and connected, and dignified manner. " The spirit of the prophets was subject to the prophets." This was far from being the case with the Sibyls; witness the language of one of them in the commencement of the second book :—" God caused my verses to cease for some time, as I entreated him; but a pleasant voice speaking Divine words, *my whole body is struck and convulsed, and I know not what I say.*"* And again, " Thou heavenly Author of thunder art happy, and hast the cherubim under thy throne;" (is it not plain that the writer of this was acquainted with the Jewish Scriptures?) " I pray thee spare

* Floyer, p. 21.

me a little who always speak the truth ; for I am weary in my mind. But why does my heart palpitate again ? Why is my mind struck as with a whip, forced to declare from within a prophecy unto all men ?"* And again, " These things I prophesied to the world concerning God's wrath, when I was inspired with a fury, and left great Babylon and Syria." Again, "I am tormented, I who am the sister of Isis, when an unhappy prophecy comes into my mind, though it be a Divine song of oracles."† Other passages of a similar nature might be quoted, all of which show that the Sibyl was a heathen priestess, and not a prophetess of the living God. Surely the eternal Spirit, the Spirit of love, and power, and of a sound mind, will always be consistent with himself, whenever he inspires mortals to make known the counsels of heaven. I may be reminded here of the language of Jeremiah, chap. xx. 9, " Then I said, I will not make mention of him, nor speak any more in his name. But his word was as a burning fire shut up in my bones, and I was weary with forbearing, and I could not stay." But how different is this from the fury and force of which the Sibyl speaks ! Jeremiah felt on this occasion unwilling to prophesy, on account of the persecution to which his message exposed him; and the operations of his conscience, and his sense of the importance of the truths which he had to deliver, and consequently his uneasiness when he was silent, were the " fire shut up in his bones," and which rendered him " weary with forbearing."

Fourthly. The abominable wickedness and gross impurity of which the principal Sibyl had been guilty, accord-

---

* Floyer, p. 32. This language reminds us of Virgil and his Cumæan Sibyl, rather than of David or Isaiah:—

"At Phœbi nondum patiens immanis in antro
Bacchatur vates, magnum si pectore possit
Excussisse deum; tanto magis ille fatigat
Os rabidum, fera corda domans, fingitque premendo."
Æn. vi. 77.

† Floyer, p. 81.

ing to her own confession, nay, in which she was living at the time when she prophesied, render it very improbable that God would have endowed her with the Spirit of inspiration, or employed her to be his messenger to the world. I know the history of Balaam is adduced as a sufficient answer to this objection. I have already shown that it will not apply; that there is an essential difference between the two cases. Amongst the Jews, "holy men of God spake as they were moved by the Holy Ghost;" it is surely very improbable that it would have been otherwise amongst the Gentiles, had God been pleased to raise up any prophetesses to them.

Fifthly. It may just be noticed that the Sibyls were all women; there was not a man amongst them. Now, though there were some prophetesses amongst the Israelites, as Deborah, and Huldah, and others, yet the generality of those who were employed to publish the counsels of heaven, and all who were commissioned to commit the volume of inspiration to writing, were males. This, especially as combined with some other things which might be mentioned, as it regards the character of the Sibyls, renders their claim to inspiration altogether improbable.

Sixthly. The fact that some of the Sibylline predictions are much clearer and more definite than any that were delivered by even Isaiah himself, or any of the Jewish prophets, is a powerful argument against their inspiration; whilst their language and allusions, in several places, are proofs that these parts of them, at least, were forgeries, committed after the New Testament had been penned. Where is there anything in the Old Testament like the following? " I will sing heartily of the great and celebrated Son of the immortal God, to whom the Supreme Father gave the possession of a throne before he was born; and taking flesh, he became of two natures." " He was washed in the stream of the river Jordan." " He is the first God of the first fire, and his Son begotten of a dove, the Spirit which appeared like a dove with white wings." "O land of Sodom! thou crownedst him with a crown of thorns, and didst mix bitter gall for the greater abuse." "Oh, the happy wood on which God was extended," &c. Surely it is very unlikely that clearer revelations would have been made to the Gentiles, concerning whom we read that "God suffered them to walk in their own ways," than to that peculiar people whose distinguishing privilege it was that to them were committed the oracles of God; the apostle certainly means to *them only.* Indeed, it may well be said, that the oracles in question are either so dark, and enigmatical, and indefinite in their expressions, that they cannot be understood, and are capable of being applied to almost anything; or else they are so plain and definite, that they excite a suspicion of having been taken from history, and generally received doctrines. We do not find in them that happy, and wise, and, I had almost said, Divine medium, betwixt literal statements, or unmeaning generality and mysticism, which characterizes the Scripture prophecies; and which, while it does not enable men to become prophets, yet renders it evident, when the prediction is explained by the event, that everything, in all its minutiæ, was known to the Divine Spirit, by whom the sacred writers were inspired.

Seventhly. The passage which has just been quoted from the epistle to the Romans, that to the Jews were committed the oracles of God, and that this was the great advantage, the chief privilege which they had, furnishes another argument against the Divine inspiration of the Sibyls. If these effusions were dictated by the Holy Spirit, and were intended to answer, to a certain extent, the same end that the communications of the Israelitish prophets were, how could such an assertion be with propriety made, when oracles, in some respects plainer, were given to the Gentiles, and prophetesses were raised up to them in constant succession till the very coming of Christ? And if God had given them a commission to deliver such messages, would he not have enabled them to produce credentials like those of Moses, and Elijah, and Samuel? I know it is said, that these oracles afford a proof of the truth of the Christian religion, and that they prepared the Gentiles to receive it. Any support that they can yield to the Gospel, is just like that which a bundle of reeds could have given to the temple of Solomon, in addition to all its massy pillars of hewn stone and cedar wood; and I should more than question whether a single heathen was induced by those productions to embrace the cause of the Saviour. The fathers, most assuredly, rather injured than served the interest of the truth, by their appeals to the oracles of the Sibyls. I know that, in the estimation of some, the fact that Justin Martyr, and several others of the ancient writers of the Christian church, quoted those books, is the great argument for their genuineness. But it is well known that Justin, whatever were his excellences in other respects, was exceedingly credulous, and that he and the fathers, as they are generally called, were far from always adopting the best methods of defending the cause to which they were so warmly attached.* A most striking contrast, in this respect, as well as others, is presented betwixt them and the apostles, for which we can account only by allowing the inspiration of the latter, while the former were left to their own unassisted powers. In addition to what has been stated, it may be observed, that in these books there is a reference to the doctrine of a millennium, or of Christ's reigning on earth a thousand years. This, according to Prideaux,† proves that they could not have been written till after the second century, when this doctrine was first introduced by Papias, bishop of Hierapolis, in Phrygia. Those who believe in the inspiration of the Sibyls may reply, that these passages contain a prophecy. This answer, however, can have no weight with those who think that the doctrine in question is anti-scrip-

* See Appendix K.   † Book ix. p. 617.

tural. These books also contain a list of all the Roman emperors, from Julius Cæsar to Antoninus Pius, given in such a manner as proves that they contain a history rather than a prediction; for why should the enumeration stop here, if the author was a prophetess? And in the same book the pretended Sibyl tells us, that she was "wife to one of the sons of Noah, and that she was with him in the ark during the deluge; and many other particulars of the same nature are found in them, all savouring of fiction and imposture. All these things put together, prove that a great part of these books, instead of containing a true collection of the oracles received for Sibylline among the heathen before the time of Christ, is nothing more than the invention and imposture of the compiler."* On the whole, these books must be numbered amongst those pious frauds by which some of the mistaken advocates of Christianity endeavoured to propagate and defend it. Though these were not employed to any great extent till the third century, nor publicly avowed, perhaps, till the fourth, yet, as even in the apostle's time, " the mystery of iniquity, whose coming was after the working of Satan, with all power, and signs, and lying wonders," (and amongst the latter, these supposed wonderful oracles must be reckoned,) " was working," we may be certain that it had developed itself in the second century to a degree sufficient to produce the oracles in question, and which, whatever might be the design of their author, have much more effectually subserved the cause of Satan than that of the God of truth.

THE HEATHEN ORACLES.

The much-famed heathen oracles must not be omitted in considering the agency of Satan, and the means which he has adopted to oppose the cause of God, and to deceive and ruin the souls of men. Of all the devices which he has ever employed for these purposes, one of the most

* Prideaux, book iv. p. 627.

THE AGENCY OF EVIL SPIRITS. 203

successful has been to invest, as far as he was able, error with the form, and to array it in the beauties of truth; to imitate all the methods which God has adopted to demonstrate the divinity of the true religion; and thus to transform himself into an angel of light. If God has raised up *true*, Satan has raised up *lying* prophets. If God has commissioned his servants to work real miracles, Satan has employed his to exhibit counterfeit ones. If to the Jews were committed the oracles of God, to the heathen were committed the pretended oracles of Delphos and Dodona, and many others. If the intrinsic excellence and the purifying tendency of the doctrines of the Gospel, and the beauties of holiness adorning the character of those who have been commissioned to publish them, are amongst the means which God has employed to recommend his truth, the servants of Satan have been transformed as the ministers of righteousness, and have pretended deep concern for the happiness of those to whom they have delivered their message. And it has been thought, and is maintained at the present day by some, that his giving answers by the oracles to which our attention is now to be directed, has been amongst the principal means by which he has carried on his intercourse with our fallen, sinful world.*

The most famous of the ancient oracles, as all know, was that of Apollo at Delphos, where he was worshipped under the name of the Pythian, an appellation derived, according to some, from the serpent Python, which he was supposed to have killed, or according to others, from a Greek word (πυθέσθαι) which signifies to inquire, because people came thither to inquire of him. Historians give the following account of the origin of that oracle. "There was a cavity upon Parnassus, from whence an exhalation arose, which made the goats skip and dance about, and intoxicated the brain of those who inhaled it. A shepherd was anxious to know the cause of these effects, and in order to satisfy his

* See Appendix L.

curiosity, he went and stood so near the cavity that he inhaled the vapour, and was immediately seized with a violent agitation of body, and a strange elevation of mind (we may suppose something like what is produced by a dose of opium), and pronounced words, which, though he did not understand them himself, were significant of the future. Others made the same experiment, and with the same success." The ignorant and superstitious people of that age and country,—who had forsaken and forgotten the living and the true God, the glorious Creator, but who deified almost every creature, imagining that there was something Divine in the exhalation, that it proceeded from some divinity, or was under his control,—at first placed a tripod over it, and appointed a priestess to inhale the vapour, and to deliver oracles, while under its influence; and in process of time, a city arose around the supposed sacred spot, and a magnificent temple was built, and so enriched with the offerings of superstition, and the exactions and avarice of a crafty priesthood, that compared with it, the temple at Jerusalem, dedicated to the true God, was probably poor even when its treasures were most abundant. This oracle at last threw all the others into the shade.

Now what we have to determine, if we can, respecting these oracles, is simply this: were their temples the resort of evil spirits, or merely of priests and priestesses, and their assistants? Did the answers that were returned to those who came to inquire of them, emanate, at least, partly, and at times, from the knowledge and power of the former, or from the craft and management of the latter? I must own, that after giving to this difficult and yet interesting subject all the attention of which I am capable, and reading pretty extensively on it, I must adopt the opinion of those who think that the great probability is, that they were entirely the result of human depravity and fraud, and that evil spirits had no more share in them than they have generally in tempting men to sin.

In one respect, indeed, all who believe in the existence of Satan, and that he is the god of this world, and the spirit that worketh in the children of disobedience, will at once allow that they were his device, and that by them he carried on his work of deceiving and ruining the human race. And surely none who allow that he can exert any influence, either on matter or on the minds of men, will find any difficulty in allowing that, were we to reason abstractedly on the subject, and attend merely to some isolated facts, or at least reported facts, we should be led to conclude that the probability is, that evil spirits did, at times at least, inspire the priests and priestesses, and deliver the oracles of heathenism. For what means, we might ask, could be better adapted to carry on their great design of robbing God of his glory, and of the allegiance and homage of his rational creatures, and involving them in the thickest darkness, and sinking them into all the abominations and cruelties of idolatry, and thus, in the most insolent and malignant manner, insulting God, and degrading human nature? And when we attend to the history of these oracles, and consider the horrid crimes, the human sacrifices, the gross, nameless impurities to which they were rendered subservient, nay which in some cases they seem to have originated, there appears at least some plausibility in the arguments of those who maintain that men could never have been induced to act so wickedly, so unnaturally, had they not had irresistible evidence, that there was something superhuman in the oracles by which these cruelties were enjoined, and that in practising these crimes, they were obeying their supposed divinities. Nor can I see much force in the argument against this, taken from the fact that these oracles frebuently uttered lies, and deceived those who trusted to them; for surely all will allow that, as evil spirits have no certain knowledge of the thoughts of men, or of the events of the future, they might therefore be deceived themselves. On the same principle we may account for their inability to give definite answers on various occasions, when the inquiry was respecting futurity. Nor can it be thought strange, that Satan should flatter the rich and great, and assist and encourage them in their plans and deeds of oppression, and robbery, and blood. Suppose the oracle of Delphos did Philippise, according to the charge which Demosthenes brought against it, and another oracle did sanction Augustus, in the gratification of his passions, by taking to his bed the pregnant wife of another; this is only, it may be said, what might be expected from those impure spirits who delight in sin in all its forms. But after having made these concessions, on what grounds, it may be asked, is it maintained that none of those oracles were managed, or their answers given, by the direct influence of Satan, but solely by the craft of men?

In the first place, I should attach considerable importance to the fact, that the Scriptures give no sanction to the theory that these oracles were managed by Satan or his angels, in any other way than by their spiritual influence in tempting men to iniquity of every kind. The inspired writers, as we have already seen, represent the heathen priests, and prophets, and diviners, and necromancers, as impostors and liars; but never, as far as I can find, as being in league with Satan, so as to obtain from him the knowledge of the future, or of distant objects and events, and to be able to utter prophecies, or to tell what men were doing in secret in a distant part of the world; or to be able to divine their thoughts, or to tell, as Elisha the prophet could do, by Divine inspiration, what they were doing in their bed-chambers, as it is pretended the oracle of Delphos did in the case of Crœsus; and the god of Heliopolis in the case of Trajan.

The answerer of Fontenelle, Father Baltus, the Jesuit, maintains that we have at least one instance of a heathen oracle recorded in the Scriptures, in 2 Kings i. 2. Ahaziah "sent messengers, and said unto them, Go, inquire of Baalzebub, the god of Ekron, whether I shall recover of this disease." But there is no mention made here of any oracle, or any intimation given that the god of Ekron could foretell future events. That the heathen had their idols and their imaginary gods, whom they consulted on various occasions, we all know. But this is quite different from having an oracle like that of Delphos or Dodona, where their gods were supposed to work miracles and foretell things to come. God, by the prophet Isaiah, xli. 22, challenges all the heathen deities to "show what shall happen," to "show the things that are to come hereafter, that we may know that ye are gods: yea, do good or do evil, that we may be dismayed and behold it together." But if there was at this very time, when Isaiah uttered those words, an oracle at Delphos, under the superintendence of a powerful fallen spirit, foretelling the future, and revealing the unknown and the distant; working miracles in fact, by shaking, as was pretended, the superb temple to its very foundations, whenever he came to inspire the priestess, and to enable her to utter her predictions, (the true prophets had not generally such visible credentials as these to attest their missions,) and inflicting punishments on those who disputed his power or profaned his temple,—if this had been really the case, how easy would it have been for idolaters to reply, "Here is a god that can foretell the future, that can secure the greatest benefits to his worshippers, and cause those who despise him to smart for their folly!" The prophet Isaiah never imagined, evidently, that any idolaters could with the least plausibility return such an answer, or urge such a plea as this. If these oracles were really the resort of evil spirits, who could utter predictions and perform supernatural actions, they presented by far the most imposing form of heathenism, compared with which idols did not deserve to be named. Why then did the inspired prophet expend all his eloquence on the latter, and make no allusion whatever to the former? which would just be acting as if a disputant were to exhaust all his resources in refuting one of the weakest arguments of his opponent, and entirely omit the most forcible; an art, it must be confessed, with which disputants are not unacquainted. All would see at once what was the reason, and all would draw the obvious inference; especially if there was, as Father Baltus would have us to believe, at Ekron, in Palestine, and on the very borders of the land of Israel, an oracle like that of Delphos, uttering prophecies, and deceiving its votaries by the inspiration of the devil; surely Isaiah would have exposed it, and assured those who heard his prophecy, or might read his book, that all this was the work of Satan, and one of the worst forms of idolatry. On this part of the subject it would be easy to enlarge; but I must rest satisfied with stating, that I cannot find the existence of these oracles recognised in the Bible, any farther than they are included amongst the false gods and prophets of the heathen; though considerable portions of it were written to expose idolatry in all its forms.

Secondly. I would observe, (and this observation, perhaps, includes the reason why Satan was not allowed to avail himself of these oracles, in the way in which some suppose he was, by actually inspiring their agents, and vending his lies through their instrumentality,) we have no evidence that God has ever permitted any *real* miracle to be performed, or even wonder to be exhibited, or true prophecy to be uttered, in support of any false religions, much less of idolatry, the worst, or rather a concentration of them all. It is evident from the principles laid down in the Scriptures, that if this had been done, idolatry would have been, to say the least, excusable. "If I had not done amongst them the works which none other man did," says Jesus Christ, "they had not had sin; but now have they no cloak for their sin." The heathen would certainly have had a cloak for their sin, if Æsculapius at his oracle had cured diseases, if the god of the oracle of Claros had, as is reported of him, known the thoughts of men's hearts, and "needed not that any one should testify of man; for he knew what was in man," according to the assertion of an evangelist respecting Jesus Christ.

Thirdly. If we consider the way in which oracles were delivered, and the prodigies which were thought to attend them were exhibited, we shall find everything to correspond with the hypothesis, that all was accomplished by the craft of men, and not by the agency of Satan. If the latter had been the case, if evil spirits had been permitted really to take up their abode at Delphos, or at the cave of Trophonius, for instance, why, at the former, should answers have been given at first only once a year, and afterwards only once a month? and why should there have been so many unfortunate days specified, in which it was unlawful to consult the oracle at all? And why should the Pythia have been required to fast three days, and to prepare herself by purifications and sacrifices, and other ceremonies? And why should she have been thrown into a frenzy before she prophesied? while, after all, the words which she uttered were almost inarticulate? Surely Satan, had he been permitted, could have managed things better than all this. And why should there have been any necessity for prophets to collect her ravings, and for poets to turn them into verse? And why should it have been requisite for those who went to consult the oracle of Trophonius, to pass through all the following ceremonies and preparatives? They were first to spend some days in attending to expiations of all kinds, and presenting various sacrifices; and then they could not descend into the cave till the auspices taken by inspecting the entrails of the victims that were slaughtered, were favourable, according to the report of the priests; that is, *till their own time came,* and all their preparations were complete: and then two children, of the age of twelve or thirteen years, must rub all the body with oil. Then they were conducted to the source of a river, and made to drink of two kinds of water; that of Lethe, or forgetfulness, which effaced from the mind all profane and worldly thoughts with which it had been occupied; and that of Mnemosyne, which had the virtue, according to their representations, to enable those who partook of it to recollect all that they might see or hear in the sacred cave. (Oh that we could procure a copious draught of such waters whenever we read the Bible, or hear the words of truth and wisdom!) Then they were led to the statue of Trophonius, where they presented their prayers; when they were clothed with a linen tunic, and adorned with certain sacred fillets or bandages, and thus they were prepared to go to the oracle.

This was situated in a mountain in an enclosure of white stone, on which obelisks of brass were raised. In this enclosure was a cavern of the figure of an oven, cut out by the hand of man, into which those who came to consult the oracle descended, not by steps, but by small ladders. When they had made this descent, they found another small cavern, with a very narrow entrance. There they lay down on the ground, and were required to take in each hand a composition of honey, which they must by no means quit. They then put their feet into the entrance of the small cavern, into which they immediately felt themselves drawn with great violence.

Then commenced their supposed intercourse with the god. The future was said to be revealed to them, but in different ways; to some by what they saw, to others by what they heard. They left the cavern in the same way as they entered it, being drawn out by their feet. Immediately the attendants, or the ministers of the reputed god, placed them on the chair of Mnemosyne, and asked them questions respecting what they had seen and heard. "From thence," says Fontenelle, "they were led away, all confounded and deprived of their senses, which they recovered by degrees, and then they began to laugh," (I suppose he means at their own folly and the craft of the priests;) "for till this time, the grandeur of the mysteries, and the divinity with which they had been pervaded, must have effectually prevented them from laughing." It seems to me that they ought not to have waited so long before they commenced their laughter.

Pausanias relates that there had been only one man who entered the cave of Trophonius, and who never returned, and this was *a spy*, who was sent thither by Demetrius, to see if there were any treasures in the sacred place worth plundering. The body of the unhappy person was afterwards found at a distance from the place; but it had not been thrown out *by the sacred entrance* of the cave.

"How many reflections present themselves," says Fontenelle, "on all these transactions! What fine opportunities had the priests, during all these sacrifices, which they demanded of all who entered the cave, to examine whether the individual was a proper person to be admitted into the cavern, and to see and hear the mysteries; for assuredly Trophonius selected his favourites, and did not receive all who applied! How would all those ablutions and expiations, and nocturnal journeys, and passages through narrow and dark caverns, fill the mind with superstitious fears and terrors! How many machines were they able to employ, amidst the darkness which pervaded the cave! The history of the spy teaches us that there was no safety in these recesses for those who did not go thither with good intentions; and that besides the sacred entrance, which was generally known, there was another secret one for the use of the priests. Who can doubt that, when those who entered the cave were drawn by the feet into the small cavern, cords were employed? All was profound darkness, and they were prevented from using *their hands*, because they must *grasp the composition of honey*, which they must by *no means lose*. The caverns might be full of perfumes and odours which would affect the brain, and deprive of the power of thought and feeling, and the waters of Lethe and Mnemosyne might be prepared to produce the same effect; to say nothing of the spectacles and noises which were calculated to operate in the same way. And at last, when those who had consulted the supposed divinity came out of the cave in this confused and disordered state, they related what they had seen and heard to the priests only, who well knew how to mould all so as to answer their own purpose."*

Now, in connexion with all the oracles, some means of a similar kind were employed, to give the priests and the managers of them time to form their plans, to draw from those who came to consult them the information that was necessary to enable them to return an answer craftily adapted to the circumstances of the case, and to mould it into such a shape, that whatever might be the event, they would be safe. We grant it may be said that evil spirits might require all these preparations, in order to impress the minds of those who applied to the oracle with an idea of their sacredness, or because they would even mimic the way in which the true God was worshipped; or, that although Satan sometimes assisted the priests and the priestesses, yet at other times he left them to themselves, and then they needed all their apparatus, and all their craft, to deceive those who applied to them. This is possible. But we are considering now what were the facts of the case. And I would ask, is it probable that if devils had been permitted to manage these oracles, by inspiring the priestesses, and producing dreams, and making impressions on the senses, and employing all their experience and knowledge to form conjectures respecting the future or the distant, &c., that all this apparatus would have been necessary for them? and that they would ever, and that at the time when they seemed to possess the greatest power, have

* Fontenelle, p. 92.

limited their communications to their devotees to once in the year, and afterwards have extended them no farther, as the utmost stretch of their liberality, than to once a month, and that they would have been so fastidious in the choice of days? And why could not the Pythia prophesy till she was intoxicated by the vapour? I must repeat the observation, that if Satan had been permitted to manage those oracles, he would have acted in another, and a superior style. All must allow that much was done by the craft of men, that all the ceremonies and apparatus were as well calculated as they could be to aid them in their work of deception. And I must think that nothing was ever done or exhibited, no answers were ever given, but what may be accounted for in this way. When the temples were explored and demolished, there were traces and evidences in abundance of the works and schemes of men; nothing to indicate that any supernatural influence had ever been exerted.

"The thousands of frauds and impostures," says Rollin, "which had been detected at Delphos, had not opened men's eyes, nor in the least diminished the credit of those oracles." It is a maxim in philosophy, not to admit, for any effect or event, more causes than are necessary to produce it. If the fraud and depravity of men, and the spiritual influence of Satan, are amply sufficient to account for all the effects connected with these oracles, and we are sure that these causes were at work, in all their forms and power, why seek for another cause, which was altogether unnecessary to produce the effect?

Great importance has been attached by those who maintain that, at the least, some of the oracular responses were dictated by evil spirits, to the answers that were returned to the sealed letters which were sent to them, and returned unopened. Trajan, at the request of his friends, applied to the god of Heliopolis, to know whether he should be successful in his expedition against the Parthians. The emperor, who had not much faith in oracles, wished to try the skill of the god, and, therefore, sent him a sealed letter, which was to be answered without being opened. There was *nothing* in the letter, and a blank was returned with it in reply; and this is considered by some an evidence that Satan must have informed the priests of the fact. But is this supposition at all necessary? We are informed that the friends and courtiers of Trajan had a high opinion of oracles, and that in order to induce him to apply to them, they related to him the wonderful predictions which they had uttered. Now, as it is well known that the managers of some of these oracles had their agents and friends in almost every place, (the false prophet Alexander, who had established his oracle at Pontus, had his correspondents at Rome, who informed him of the most secret affairs of those who applied to him,) is it at all impossible or improbable that some of them might be amongst the servants of Trajan, and that they might know how he intended to try the oracle, and give information to the priests? And might not the managers of the oracle have some way of opening these letters, and sealing them again so dexterously, that no one could discover what had been done? The letters were required to be *left in the temple all night, on the altar of the god, to which, of course, the priests had access.* A much more effectual way of trying the god would have been to require an answer, without sending the letter.

In reality, I can see no difficulty whatever in managing this matter. The credulity of Trajan, the ease with which he was satisfied, appears to me the most wonderful part of the whole business, much more marvellous than anything which was effected by the oracle. Plutarch informs us that the governor of Cilicia, who was addicted to the opinions of the Epicureans, and consequently had not much faith in oracles, sent one of his servants to Mopsus, with a sealed letter, to which he requested that, without its being opened, an answer might be returned in a dream.

The servant slept in a temple, and saw, in a dream, a fine-looking man, who appeared to him and pronounced the word "black." The servant returned this answer to his master. It excited the ridicule of the Epicureans at court. But the governor was astonished, and on opening his own letter, and showing them that he had inquired whether he should sacrifice a white or a black ox, they, too, were astonished, and, according to Father Baltus, were completely silenced. Now as it was necessary that the letter should be carried into the temple, and left there during the night in which the servant had the dream, where would be the great difficulty of dexterously opening it and sealing it again? And then, it is very well known, that if one can have access to a person when he is asleep, there is not much difficulty in producing such a dream as it may be wished he should have; at least, this can be done in some cases. And is it all likely that servants would be proof against the address, the arts, and the bribery of the priests? And, as Fontenelle has well observed, "If a demon gave the answer, where was the necessity of its being *forty days* out of the hands of the governor?" And we may add, why was not the governor himself favoured with the dream? in every case it was necessary that those letters should be sent to the temple, and left there for some time. We can see how this was necessary for the priests, but not how it was so for the demons.

The famous story which occurs in the history of Crœsus presents, it must be owned, considerable difficulties. In order to put to the test the knowledge and fidelity of the oracle of Delphos, Crœsus required it to tell what he was doing at a certain time, which he specified: and in order to try the god to the utmost, the king resolved to be occupied in the most unlikely way possible. Accordingly, he shut himself up in a convenient place, and cooked a tortoise and a lamb in a brazen vessel; a very unlikely employment, it must be owned, for a king. The oracle, however, specified his employment most correctly. Now I do not undertake to say exactly how this might be done, on the supposition that evil spirits had no share in these responses. The information which we have respecting it is very scanty, and is given by those who were evidently believers in the divinity of oracles, and were disposed to make the most of fortunate occurrences or remarkable coincidences; and it would be wonderful if, at this distance of time, we could detect everything that was accomplished by the fraud of those practised deceivers. Many things equally strange and unaccountable are found connected with the second sight, with the experience of those who believe in dreams and apparitions, and even in their almanacs, and their foretelling the state of the weather. Suppose that we cannot tell how the priests of Delphos obtained their information of what Crœsus was doing; this one unaccountable fact is a slender foundation for the faith of those who believe that these oracles were managed by Satan. In the words of Rollin already quoted, " Thousands of frauds and impostures had been detected at Delphos;" and these are so many thousands of proofs that the oracles were managed, and their answers given, by the fraud of men; and we have only to place in opposition to these, two or three dubious indications that they were under the superintendence of devils. Which shall we believe? Which hypothesis is the more probable of the two, and supported by the best arguments? But it is intimated in the story that Crœsus was not cooking the tortoise himself, but only ordering it to be cooked. So then, some of his servants knew what he was doing, and some time must elapse before the answer of the oracle could be brought back. If then the priests had some of these servants in their pay and interest, there would be no great difficulty in managing this affair. There have been kings and politicians, who by means of their spies in every part of the country, and almost of the world, have obtained intelligence of what was being transacted in distant parts, almost, if not altogether, as surprising as that which is supposed in this case. The story which is related by Dr. Plot in his Natural History of Oxfordshire, and inserted in the Encyclopædia Britannica, under the article *Spectre*, contains feats much more wonderful than the answer of the oracle to Crœsus. The commissioners of the commonwealth thought they had ocular and sensible demonstration, that the house was haunted by a host of demons, and consequently refused to remain in it any longer. Many believed, for a long time, that no human power could effect what was there exhibited. And had the fraud not been discovered, and the means by which all the apparent wonders were performed explained, it might have been quoted to this day as an indubitable proof of Satanic interference in the affairs of this world.

But the subject is almost boundless. It has been proved by Van Dale, Fontenelle, and others, that all the oracles had the machinery of deception in their temples and in their vicinity, and that the very places where they were situated were favourable to the tricks of their managers. At Delphos almost all the inhabitants of the city were, in one way or another, connected with the oracle, or under its influence; and they were therefore ready to assist the priests. This furnishes a satisfactory answer to the objection of Father Baltus, who asks, "How is it that the priests were able to get their machinery constructed and repaired without artificers and workmen of various kinds? and how could silence be imposed on all these?" We answer, With the greatest ease. Fear on the one hand, and interest on the other, would be quite sufficient to restrain their tongues, and even to influence their views and thoughts. They would not be disposed to think, (as, alas, their ideas of their divinities were far from being very exalted!) that for anything they knew, these machines might be necessary for their gods, to enable them to carry on their operations. There is no difficulty whatever in accounting for the origin of those oracles, (we have already seen how the most famous of them all, that of Delphos, commenced,) without attributing them in the first instance either to Satanic influence in inspiring the priestesses, or to designed fraud on the part of those who first pronounced them sacred. We have only to recollect the erroneous and grovelling ideas of the Gentiles respecting their gods, and their propensity to deify almost everything, and to fancy spirits in every cave, or mountain, or stream, or grove, and to attribute to their influence every uncommon appearance. There were always some amongst the heathen philosophers and princes who did not believe in these oracles. Fontenelle maintains that the Cynics, the Peripatetics, and the Epicureans, despised and ridiculed them; and he brings forward an instance of Œnomaus, a Cynic, diverting himself and others, and rallying Apollo in grand style on account of the oracle which he delivered to Crœsus, "That if he passed the river Halys, he should overturn a great empire." Father Baltus puts in requisition all his learning and ingenuity, which certainly were by no means small, to prove that Fontenelle was mistaken, and that none but a few Cynics and Epicureans disbelieved and despised them; but without success. The fact is certain, that many of the heathen accounted them cheats, and not a few who professed to believe in them, did so out of policy. Instances are produced by Fontenelle and Van Dale, in which the priestesses and priests were corrupted by bribes, or overawed by power, to deliver as the oracles of the gods that which had been suggested to them. The fraud was in some cases discovered, and the culprit punished. But as the proofs of intercourse with the supposed divinity depended very much on the assertions and fidelity of these deceivers, what dependence can be placed on them?

New oracles were established at different places, which soon became almost as popular as the old ones. Alexander was astonished that he could so soon and so easily transform his friend Hephæstion into a divinity, and that his oracle succeeded so well; and he was delighted to find, that he could not only rise to the rank of a god himself, but that he could make gods. And if we grant to Father Baltus that Satan might come and take possession of these new oracles, as he had done of the old ones, and endeavour to render them subservient to his purpose, (it remains, however, to be proved that he did so in either the one case or the other,) still we have in those facts an historical account of the way in which oracles were founded by the art and influence of men, without any direct assistance from evil spirits. There are not a few instances which might easily be produced, in which the priests and prophets who conducted those oracles were obliged to confess that they had imposed on those who came to consult them, and to expose all their apparatus and machinery to the world. The Christian fathers themselves, disposed as they were to believe that these oracles were managed by Satan, and that they were silenced at the birth of Christ, had their suspicions on this point. Clemens Alexandrinus, after referring to the most celebrated oracles and necromancers, says, "All these things are only extravagant impostures, and pure tromperies, like games at dice. The goats which have been employed for the purposes of divination, and the ravens which have been taught to return answers, what are they but the instruments or associates of those charlatans who deceive the world?" And Eusebius, in his fourth book "De Preparatione Evangelicâ," assigns, as Fontenelle expresses it, the best reasons in the world for believing that the oracles were nothing but the work of impostors. And if we should grant to Father Baltus that he produced there the opinions of others, and what might be said in defence of them, still it is evident, by the way in which they are stated, that he thought these arguments not destitute of weight. And there is great reason to fear that Fontenelle is correct, when he insinuates that he was influenced too much by his mistaken zeal for the honour of the Christian religion. This remark directs our attention to a very interesting question: When did these oracles lose their credit? and by what means were they silenced? and what regard is due to the opinion and testimony of the Christian fathers on this subject, when they maintain that both these were effected by the coming of the Saviour, and often by the mention of his name, by the very presence of one of his followers, or even by the sign of the cross? This is a copious and interesting subject, and one too on which it is impossible to enlarge in a part only of a single lecture.

There can be no doubt, however, of the fact, that the oracles began to be despised, and to fall into decay, before the birth of the Saviour; and that some of them, and even that of Delphos, existed, and were consulted, and pretended to give answers, long after that important event. This Father Baltus himself is obliged to grant; and he maintains, and indeed proves, that neither Eusebius, nor Tertullian, nor Athanasius, nor Lactantius, asserts that the oracles ceased all at once, but only that they were silenced by the spread of the Gospel, and by the name and cross of Christ. Sir Thomas Browne reckons the opinion, that oracles were silenced all at once at the birth of Christ, amongst vulgar errors. And it is evident from history, that they had not entirely ceased in the reign of Julian, almost four hundred years after the advent of the Saviour. On this point there can be no question; while it is evident, from the testimony of Plutarch, a heathen, and an admirer of oracles, that they had begun to fall into decay and lose their credit before the Christian era.

The principal subject of inquiry here is, what regard is due to the statements of the fathers, as they are generally called, when they declare that the oracles were frequently silenced in the way which has just been mentioned? They make positive and yet strange assertions on this point. It is evident, that most of them believed that the oracles were delivered, partly at least, by devils, and that these devils themselves confessed that they were silenced and deprived of their power by the religion and followers of the Saviour; that these obliged the evil spirits who presided over the oracles to own, even in the presence of the heathen, that they were seducing spirits; and that they constrained them, by the mere invocation of the name of Christ, to come out of the idolatrous priests and priestesses whom they had possessed.* It does not appear, however, that the Pythian priestess was ever, properly speaking, possessed by a spirit, even if we believe all that is recorded of her, but only influenced by one once a year or once a month. A few of their statements must be given.

Tertullian, in his Apology, (cap. 23,)† thus writes: "Hitherto, I have brought reasons; now I will add facts which demonstrate that your gods are no more than devils. Let them bring before your tribunals any one really possessed with a devil; if a Christian commands him to speak, the wretched spirit will then as truly own that he is no more than a devil, as at other times he falsely says that he is a god. Likewise, let them produce any one of those who pretend to be inspired by a deity, which they receive into them by the smoke and odour of sacrifices, and draw their words from their stomachs with great pain. If that celestial virgin who promises rain; if that Æsculapius who prescribes medicine, and has prolonged the lives of three men who were dying;" (Tertullian seems to believe that Æsculapius could work miracles;) "if they do not own themselves to be devils to the Christian who shall ask them, because they will not dare to lie in his presence, put this rash Christian to death immediately." Similar to this is the testimony of Lactantius. "Let them bring," says he, "one really possessed, and let the priest himself of Apollo of Delphos, come with him; they will both of them equally

* See Appendix M.   † Answer to Fontenelle, p. 71.

tremble at the name of God; and Apollo will come out of his false prophet with as much haste as the devil out of the demoniac; and this god being thus exorcised and driven out, his false prophets will become dumb, and never speak more. The devils, then, which the heathen had in execration, are the same with the gods they adore." Cyprian expresses himself with equal confidence. After having said that they are evil spirits that inspire the false prophets of the Gentiles, that stir up the fibres of the entrails of victims, govern the flight of birds, dispose lots, and deliver oracles, by always mixing truth with falsehood to prove what they say, he adds, "Nevertheless, these evil spirits, adjured by the living God, immediately obey us, submit to us, own our power, and are forced to come out of the bodies they possess." And he invites Demetrius to come and see with his own eyes the truth of what he asserts. Athanasius asserts that the bare sign of the cross made the cheats and illusions of the devil to vanish; and then adds, "Let him that would make trial of this come, and amidst all the delusions of devils, the impostures of oracles, and the prodigies of magic, let him use the sign of the cross, which the heathens laugh at, and they shall see how the devils fly away affrighted, how the oracles immediately cease, and all the enchantments of magic remain destitute of their usual force." Father Baltus* maintains, though he does not cite any passage in support of his opinion, that the presence of only one Christian, though unknown, nay, even of an infant, armed with the sign of the cross, put all the oracles and false prophets to silence, and confounded all the augurs and soothsayers, to the great astonishment of the heathen and of the emperors themselves. Lactantius asserts, that "when the heathen sacrifice to their gods, if there be any one present whose forehead is marked with the sign of the cross, the sacrifices do not succeed, nor the false prophets give answer. This has given frequent occa-

* Baltus, p. 78.

sion to bad princes to persecute the Christians. For some Christian servants attending on their masters in their sacrifices, having made the sign of the cross on their foreheads, had put their gods to flight, and hindered them from describing things to come by the entrails of the sacrifices, which the soothsayers having learned from the devils themselves to whom they were sacrificing, they complained that profane persons were present, and thereby put the emperor in a rage, and in order to purify their temples, urged them to defile themselves with a real sacrifice, that ought to have been expiated with the punishment of these persecutors."
"Prudentius," says Baltus, "elegantly describes an event of this kind which happened when he was young, in the presence of Julian the Apostate; that at the very time that he was sacrificing to his demons, one of the pages that waited on him, being a Christian, did, by his presence and the sign of the cross, hinder the success of his sacrifices and magic enchantments, confound the soothsayers and enchanters, and make the devils whom he had raised vanish. And this is attested by both Theodoret and Gregory Nazianzen." "It has often happened to me," says the latter, "that I have hardly pronounced the venerable name of Christ, but the devil took flight, murmuring and raging for grief. The same thing has happened when I have only made the sign of the cross in the air."

Gregory Thaumaturgus, who lived in the third century, is said to have had such power over devils, that when he once entered a temple where Apollo delivered oracles, he drove out this false god by the sign of the cross, so that he could answer his priest no longer, even though he redoubled his sacrifices and enchantments, and used all the secrets of his art. At last Apollo appeared to him, and told him that he could not dwell in his temple any longer, because of the person who had slept there last night. The priest immediately ran after the holy bishop, and begged of him, by all the hospitality he had experienced in the temple, to restore his oracle. The saint consented, and immediately wrote to Apollo, or the devil, in these terms: "Gregory to Apollo; re-enter." The demon instantly obeyed, and the priest being thereby convinced of the power of Gregory over his gods, forsook them and became a Christian." " I know," says Baltus, " that your Anabaptist physician will laugh at this;" and really, if sorrow and indignation would permit, the laughing would not be confined to either Anabaptists or physicians.

Now what are we to think of these statements, and what conclusions are we to draw from them? Father B., who was a Roman Catholic and a Jesuit, believes them all most implicitly, and glories in them; and maintains, that similar miracles (this is a fact worthy of notice, and one which should be kept in mind in forming an estimate of the testimony of the fathers) are wrought in the Catholic Church,—that is, according to him, in the true church, to this day, and that they will be wrought to the end of time. And it is natural to ask, have we not here the testimony of pious, able, learned, acute men, who could reason most correctly and powerfully in defence of the Christian religion against the heathen, to what they themselves heard? nay, in some instances, to what they saw, and felt, and did? How can we reject their statements without undermining all testimony as a ground of faith? The question is important: the subject is difficult. The fathers, with all their defects, were a pious, noble, devoted class of men. With how much heartiness did they embrace the religion of the cross! How firmly did they believe it! How fearlessly did they advocate its cause! How did they, in some respects, adorn it by their lives! How ready were they to die [on its behalf! How certain is it that they are now receiving the reward promised to those who confessed Christ before men! Well would it be for their successors in the present day, if, in addition to their more extensive and accurate knowledge, they had the heartiness, and zeal, and faith of these ancient supporters of the Christian religion. I am far from joining with those who despise and revile them, and are disposed to think that it would be well for the cause of religion and of the church, if all their writings were blotted out from existence. Were this done, to say nothing of the chasm that would be made in the history of religion, were no other loss sustained, a most interesting specimen of human nature, in very peculiar circumstances, would be entirely lost. Still, I must say, I cannot place much dependence on their testimony, or rather their powers of observation and reasoning, or even on their fidelity, in the particular under consideration; and that for the following reasons.

It is only too evident, that with all their excellences, some of them were weak men, and all of them superstitious, and many of them under the influence of false views and maxims. I am afraid that the observations of Principal Campbell, in his Ecclesiastical Lectures,* on the writers and clergy of a later age, will apply, in some degree, to those whose sentiments and testimony have been quoted, in relation to oracles, and the way in which they were silenced. "The term 'pious fraud' was, in some places, and for several ages, not introduced sarcastically, as it is used with us at present, but employed to denote an expedient not only innocent but commendable. The patrons of ecclesiastical power had every advantage; their tricks, when undiscovered, wrought powerfully in their favour; and when discovered, (such was the superstition of the times,) were, on account of the supposed holy purpose to be effected by them, easily excused by all, and highly approved by many." I know that the system of pious frauds was not avowedly adopted in the age of Justin, and Origen, and Cyprian. But the spirit that produced them was even then working. It could not be matured and bear its fruits all at once. And when we consider that even

* Vol. ii. p. 50.

Augustine is said to have approved, in the latter part of his life, of these impious expedients, we can scarcely expect that Justin or Tertullian, with all their enthusiasm, would very strictly guard against them. It is evident that they were superstitious to a degree which would render them the easy dupes of impostors, as well as incline them too readily to believe what they heard on this subject, and even to misinterpret what they saw. Abundant proofs might be adduced of this, did our limits allow. Again we exclaim, What a falling off was immediately discerned when the Spirit of inspiration was taken from the church! What a contrast betwixt the apostles, and even the apostolic, and especially the primitive fathers!

And what a contrast, too, betwixt the ideas of Justin and Tertullian, &c., respecting oracles and the silencing of oracles, and the power of the very sign of the cross, and of the mere presence of a Christian,—and those of Jesus Christ and his apostles! From them we never hear a word respecting oracles managed by demons, or silenced by the sign of the cross: and though Peter and Paul preached the gospel in Greece and Asia Minor, in the very vicinity of oracles and amongst their votaries, and no doubt, in the very cities where they were established, yet we do not find a syllable respecting them in the preaching or epistles of these champions of the cross. We never find them glorying in silencing these oracles by their very presence, or by the sign of the cross, much less by the relics of a saint or martyr. But why is this? Oracles were as much in repute in the time of the apostles, as of Justin, or Tertullian, or Eusebius. Paul was as able to silence them as Gregory Thaumaturgus, or any one else. And his doing so would have been as good a proof of the truth of the Gospel, as any of their supposed miracles could have been. We cannot help suspecting, nay, feeling certain, that his views and practices were essentially different from theirs, and, consequently, that the latter were not correct. It deserves to be noticed likewise, that it was not till a considerable time after the death of the apostles, that so much importance began to be attached to the silencing of oracles. Justin Martyr, who died about the year 167, is, as far as I can find, the first who has mentioned their being silenced in the ways which have been specified above. And it is correctly observed respecting him, that "his judgment is not to be trusted, for he has made strange mistakes. The corruption of Christianity, by what was called philosophy, may be traced to Justin, who is at once fanciful and dogmatical, founding arguments on allegories, to the neglect of substantial verities nearer at hand, and then making assertions where he had no proofs."* And it is only too evident, that as the age of the apostles and of inspiration receded, superstition and corruption increased, and the fathers, as they are called, became more childish in their views and habits, and were more and more disqualified either to form correct sentiments, or to give faithful reports. But it may be said, whatever we may think of their judgments, or of their theoretical views, they were certainly entitled to credit as competent witnesses of what they saw and heard. In answer to this it is sufficient to reply, that the silencing of oracles, and the expulsion of demons, were precisely those facts, or supposed facts, respecting which there was the greatest danger of error, even if they had been always sincere and honest; for in regard to these, there was the most ample room for imagination on the one hand, and for imposture on the other. For instance, in the example which has already been quoted from Lactantius, in which he asserts, that the silencing of demons by the sign of the cross on their foreheads "often gave occasion to bad princes to persecute them, because this put their gods to flight, and hindered them from foretelling things to come by their sacrifices, and the soothsayer having learned this from the devil, that profane persons were present, &c.,—how easy

* Bennett's Theology of the Early Christian Church.

was it for those soothsayers, if they could not succeed in their auguries, or if they wished to excite the emperors against the Christians, to pretend that it was the presence of the latter, and the sign of the cross, that prevented them from being successful, and to affirm that their demons told them so! and the Christians were only too prone to believe such statements. How many cases are there in which the views, and feelings, and wishes of men will prevent them from being correct observers of the most palpable facts! That which blinds the eyes of the understanding, will pervert in many cases the eyes of the body. I knew a very sensible, pious, and clever man, whose mind too was far from being uncultivated, who had brought himself, by some means, to believe that if a half-crown piece were suspended by a string, held between the finger and the thumb, in a common drinking glass, it would strike, against the sides of the glass, the nearest hour of the day; and, when held by himself, it did so pretty exactly. I could not convince him by argument, or by my own example, that he gave it the impulse, and so managed it as to make it strike the requisite number of times. But when I grasped his hand in mine, and rested my arms on my knees, and kept it quite steady, the striking was at an end; though I do not know that he was convinced, or is so to this day, but that he was correct, and that the half-crown piece will indicate the hour, in the specified circumstances. And when I mentioned the fact to another intelligent person, I was surprised to find that he believed it likewise, and maintained that he had tried the experiment. How many, under the influence of imagination, and credulity, and earnest wishes, are, amidst all their honesty and abhorrence of deceit, deceived by their eyes and ears! And then, does not the sign of the cross and the mere presence of Christians, without their exercising any faith, or presenting any prayers, nay, the very presence of a child, being sufficient to work those miracles, render the whole suspicious? We find nothing like this in the New Testament, or amongst the miracles of the Saviour or his apostles. And farther if we credit the fathers, why not also, with Father Baltus, Gregory Thaumaturgus, and his letter to Apollo? And can we stop here? Must we not go a step farther, and believe with him in the efficacy of the relics of martyrs to silence oracles, and put Satan to flight? We find in Mark xvi. 17, that the power of casting out devils, and consequently of expelling them from heathen temples, was, in the gift and promise of the Saviour, connected with the ability to speak with new tongues. What reason can be assigned for the continuance of the former, and the withdrawing of the latter? If the believers, in the time of Tertullian and Lactantius, could expel demons, why could they not speak with tongues? but to this I believe they seldom pretended.* I have no doubt that the power of working miracles of any kind was confined to the apostolic age; that when the followers of Christ ceased to be able to speak with tongues, they were unable to cast out devils; but it was much easier for men to deceive both themselves and others in the one case, than in the other.

In one sense it is quite true that the oracles were silenced by the birth of Christ,—by the power of him re-

* "Irenæus declares that the gift of tongues was indulged to many in his days. But it is very remarkable, that this primitive bishop, who ascribes it so liberally to others, appears to have been in great want of it himself. It was not the least part of his trouble that he was forced to learn the language of the Gauls, before he could do any good amongst them. And from the time of Irenæus, there is not a single father, in all the succeeding ages, who has ventured to make the least claim to it, or to speak of it in any other manner than as a gift peculiar to the first Christians in the time of the apostles. And I might risk the merit of my argument on this single point: that, after the apostolic times, there is not, in all history, a single instance, either well-attested, or even so much as mentioned, of any particular person who had exercised this gift, or pretended to exercise it, in any age or country whatever."—Middleton, p. 119. Dr. Chapman's *à priori* reasoning, and his apology for the mistakes and weaknesses of Justin, and the fathers in general, are very far from being a satisfactory answer to Middleton's facts and arguments.

specting whom the whole church may gratefully and triumphantly say, " Unto us a Child is born ; unto us a Son is given." I am far from thinking with Fontenelle, that if Christianity had never been introduced into the world, the oracles would all have been silenced. They would probably have been carried on by the craft of men till the end of time ; though I must think with him, that the presence of Christians, and their known sentiments respecting oracles, that they were, in many cases at least, the work of imposture, and consequently the keen and suspicious eye with which they would scrutinise their pretensions, and the sentiments which they diffused all around respecting them, would necessarily disconcert the priests and their assistants, and cause them to fail in some of their exhibitions. What juggler could perform his tricks successfully, if he were afraid that his art was known, and if disgrace and punishment were to be the result of his failure? The oracles, then, were silenced by Jesus Christ, by the light which he, as the Sun of righteousness, spread abroad, and by the spirit which his Gospel elicited, or rather formed. He turned men from darkness to light, and from the power of Satan unto God.

I know and feel the difficulties of the subject which I have been discussing; the plausible arguments which may be advanced on the other side of the question; and how undesirable it may seem to some, to bring such charges as are implied in what I have advanced, against the successors of the apostles in the great work of evangelising the world, and establishing the cause of God.* But religion has nothing to fear from exposing the weaknesses and mis-

---

* See Middleton's "Free Inquiry," *passim*, and Isaac Taylor's masterly and interesting "Ancient Christianity," for proofs, alas! only too numerous and convincing, that the fathers were not only superstitious and easily deceived, but that they were quite capable of practising imposition; and that where miracles, and Jews, and especially oracles, and casting out of devils, are concerned, very little credit is due to their testimony, even respecting what they profess to have seen and heard.

takes of its professors and advocates. It is injured by being encumbered with their errors and faults. Let it have free course, let it be seen as it is, and it will be glorified. The truth of God will never abound by any man's lie, however they may think that it is " to his glory."

LECTURE V.

THE AGENCY OF EVIL SPIRITS.

DEMONIACS; AND ESPECIALLY THOSE TO WHICH OUR ATTENTION IS DIRECTED IN THE NEW TESTAMENT.

We come now to consider the difficult, yet interesting subject of demoniacs, or possessions, as this directs our attention to one of the ways by which evil spirits have, in the estimation of most professing Christians, carried on their intercourse with this world, in order to oppose the plans of God, as well as to injure mankind, and to gratify their own love of mischief and sin. Here it is natural to ask, What is meant by possessions, or by demoniacs? To this question Farmer would answer, "A man is said to be a demoniac, or to be possessed, when the demon within him is supposed to occupy the seat of the soul, and perform all its functions in the body. During his possession, the demoniac was silent: it was the demon alone that spoke in him. He was considered as being the very spirit by which he was possessed. Hence, the demon and the demoniac were often, in common speech, confounded together." He affirms, that "the doctrine of possessions implies that demons can unite themselves to the human body, in the same way that the soul is united to it by God, so as to govern all its organs." And he maintains, that "if they can thus deprive men of their speech, and sight, and reason, and then restore them to the use of these faculties, they can rival the glory of the prophets of God."* But there is much in these statements that is objectionable, and there

* Farmer on Demoniacs, p. 250.

is reason to fear, that, though he might not be sensible of it, he gave this description of possessions in order to place the theory of those who maintained their reality in as disadvantageous a light as possible, that it might be more easily refuted. However that may be, his definition will not be accepted by his opponents; all that we mean by possessions is, that the evil spirits brought those to whom the term could be applied so far under their influence, as to be able to vex and torment them, both in their bodies and in their souls, in various ways and degrees, and to cause them to think, and speak, and act, as they otherwise would not have done. By a possessed person, we mean one who, according to the language of the New Testament, is held, or afflicted, or grieved by a demon; according to the language of the woman of Canaan, " My daughter is grievously vexed with a devil," Matt. xv. 22. And it is evident from some of the cases of demoniacs which are recorded in the Scriptures, that they were not at all times equally under the influence of the demons; that they had their paroxysms, and their intervals of comparative freedom and ease. Luke ix. 38, "And behold a man of the company cried out, saying, Master, I beseech thee look on my son, for he is my only child; and lo, a spirit taketh him, and he suddenly crieth, and it teareth him, that he foameth again, and bruising him, hardly departeth from him." This is quite different from the spirit's uniting itself with the person as the soul does to the body. Indeed, it may be questioned whether ever the possession was perpetual, so as to imply that the demon was always present with the person whom it harassed and vexed. And this reminds us of the unfairness of one part of Farmer's description of a demoniac. We by no means allow that the evil spirit could restore sight, or speech, or hearing to those whom it had deprived of them; at least, if the deprivation had been caused by a derangement of the organs, and not merely by an influence exerted by the power of the demon during the interval of possession. Whenever the Saviour expelled the devil, he always restored the use of the faculty that had been lost.

Now, perhaps, it might almost be expected, on account of the sentiments which I have advanced respecting witchcraft, and Sibyls, and oracles, that I should adopt the theory of those who maintain that no one was ever really possessed by a demon, but that demoniacs were all either epileptics or madmen; and that our Saviour and his disciples, in miraculously curing them, merely humoured the prejudices of those with whom they were conversant, and adopted the current language of the day. And it must be owned, I should suppose, by all who have seriously considered the subject, and grappled with its difficulties, that this hypothesis possesses several advantages, and has been supported by very plausible arguments, especially by Whiston, Lardner, and Farmer. The latter, in particular, has compassed sea and land, and put in requisition all his learning and abilities, which were by no means small, to prove, that there never were any real possessions in the world; and that all the cases which were thought to be such, were different forms of insanity. And I readily allow, that there is much in his theory to recommend it. The principal objection to it, but it is a fundamental and insuperable one, is a deficiency of evidence; and especially the necessity under which it lays him, of explaining away the plain statements of the Bible, and of giving representations of Jesus Christ and his apostles, altogether unworthy of their character and station. His hypothesis affords at once an easy solution of the difficult questions:—Why were possessions so numerous in the days of Jesus Christ and his apostles? Why do we so seldom hear of them before that period? and why are there no decided cases of them now? How are we to account for the great resemblance betwixt them and epilepsy and insanity? And what are we to think of the stories which are recorded respecting exorcists in the primitive church? And why did the power of casting out devils appear to continue so long after the ability to work other miracles was withdrawn? I must candidly own, that were there not much more abundant evidence in the Scriptures—and that, too, of a different kind—for possessions, than for witchcraft and oracles; had the inspired records said as little respecting the former as the latter; had not the Saviour, and those whom he commissioned to establish his Gospel, met with *demoniacs everywhere*, and with *oracles* and *witches nowhere*, I should have adopted Farmer's hypothesis. But when I appeal to the law and to the testimony, and take into the account the absurd conclusions to which Farmer, notwithstanding all his ingenuity, is driven, and the charges which he is obliged to insinuate, or which, at least, are involved in his statements, against Jesus Christ and his disciples, I must reject his theory, and embrace that of real possessions. Whatever be the difficulties with which the latter is attended, they are, in my apprehension, fewer in number, and less in degree, than those of the opposite hypothesis.

Now surely it will be allowed by all, that the *onus probandi* lies on those who deny the reality of possessions. All who read the Gospels and the Acts of the Apostles, either in the original or in a good translation, without any previous ideas on the subject, or without any system to maintain, wishing merely to understand the language of the sacred writers, and regardless of consequences, or of any opinions or hypotheses, would conclude that the Bible teaches the doctrine of demoniacal possessions; especially as all allow that this doctrine was firmly believed when the Scriptures were written, and that those to whom they were addressed could understand their language in no other way. They never for a moment imagined that demoniacs were either lunatics, or epileptics, or insane. The persons themselves, and all who were connected with them, thought that they were under the influence of invisible, malignant spirits. There were many of their actions which, to say the least, could most easily be accounted for on this supposition. These spirits are spoken of as speaking and acting, and causing those who were under their influence to speak and act, as they otherwise would not have done. They are represented as entering into men, as tormenting and injuring them in various ways, as coming out of them, in consequence of which the possessed were immediately delivered from their power. We read of their speaking, presenting requests, and even entering into conversation with him who came to expel them; as making confessions; and as possessing a knowledge of the Saviour's character and mission superior to that of his own apostles. Jesus Christ gave his disciples a power to cast them out, as well as to heal all manner of diseases, which must of course have included epilepsy and insanity. He appealed to the ejection of demons as one great proof of his Messiahship; nay, as *the* grand proof that the kingdom of heaven was come nigh to the Jews. He viewed the casting out of devils as one of the greatest of his works, and allowed to his disciples, that next to their names being written in heaven, it was a cause for joy that the "spirits were subject to them." In short, whether we consider the actions and language of those demons themselves, or of those who were under their influence, or of Jesus Christ and his apostles, we are led to the conclusion that they were real possessions; or, as has already been said, that invisible malignant spirits had brought the demoniacs under their influence, and exerted over them a mysterious, but real and fatal control. On all these particulars, I may have occasion to enlarge a little hereafter, in answering objections against them. Now certainly it is the duty of those who maintain that possessions are only the chimeras of imagination, nay, that to believe in them is absurd and dangerous, dishonourable to God, destructive of piety, and injurious to men, to assign some very substantial reasons in support of their views; and it is only doing justice to those who adopt the contrary hypothesis to say, that they have laboured hard to maintain their opinions, and that they have at least *endeavoured* to answer all the arguments and objections of their opponents. I shall examine the system of Farmer in his works on Demoniacs, and Miracles, and Human Spirits, and in his answers to those who have refuted him; for he has exhausted the subject, and has advanced everything material that can be said, either in defence of his own sentiments, or in refutation of the contrary.

The foundation of his whole system is, that the term " demons," (which our translators render " devils,") does not mean Satan and his angels, or those fallen spirits which were expelled from heaven, but the souls or spirits of dead men;* that these were the principal and more immediate objects of worship by all the heathen; that the term " demons " was employed in this sense by the Seventy, and by the Jews in the time of our Saviour. He maintains, that to suppose that Christ and his apostles would use the term in any other sense, would be to cast on them a foul reproach, and charge them with guilt of the deepest dye;—strong language, implying a heavy charge against his opponents. And his inference from all this is, that as these souls of dead men could not be present in this world, could not possibly possess any person, the whole doctrine of actual possessions falls to the ground at once; and there is an absolute necessity, arising from the very nature of the case, to understand all the language which Christ and his apostles have used on this subject, in a figurative sense, and to consider it, and all their actions in relation to demoniacs, as being accommodations to the prejudices of the age in which they lived. On the contrary, Fell and others maintain, that Farmer's theory here is fundamentally false; that the heathen worshipped

* Demoniacs, p. 43.

other gods before ever they thought of deifying their departed friends and great men; and that they applied the term "demon" to the former as well as to the latter, and even before it was ever used in relation to the latter; and that some of them at least believed that there were evil demons who had never been men; and that the authors of the Greek translation of the Bible, the Jews in general, and our Lord and his disciples in particular, meant by the term "demons," spirits which had fallen from heaven, and had become the malignant and active enemies of God and man. It is obviously impossible, in the compass of a part of a lecture, to enter into a critical examination of their reasoning and learned proofs taken from writers of every description. All that can be done, and all that will be required, is to give the result of a serious perusal and a critical examination of them both.

In the first place, then, I must think that Farmer has completely failed in substantiating his assertion, that "the more immediate objects of worship among the ancient nations, particularly amongst the Egyptians, Greeks, and Romans, were beings of an earthly origin, or such departed souls as were believed to become demons,"* or, as he elsewhere expresses it, "dead men." Fell proves by quotations from Hesiod, Herodotus, Xenophon, and others, that the most ancient gods of the Egyptians, Ethiopians, Persians, and other eastern nations, were supposed celestial beings of some description, and not dead men. It would appear that the first objects of their worship, after they forsook the living and true God, were the sun, and moon, and stars, or beings by whom they supposed these were animated. Indeed, that this was the case is very evident from the Scriptures. Job xxxi. 26, "If I beheld the sun when it shined, or the moon walking in brightness, and my heart hath been secretly enticed, and my mouth kissed my hand, this also were an iniquity to be punished by the

* Farmer on Miracles, p. 187.

judges, for I should have denied the God who is above," as I should have been guilty of idolatry. Deut. iv. 16, " Lest ye corrupt yourselves, and make you a graven image, the similitude of any figure, the likeness of male or female, the likeness of any beast that creepeth on the earth, the likeness of any fish that is in the waters beneath the earth; and lest thou lift up thine eyes unto heaven, and when thou seest the sun, the moon, and the stars, even all the host of heaven, shouldest be driven to worship them, and serve them." There is no mention made in this enumeration of the idols or gods, whom the Jews were in danger of worshipping, and those whom the nations with whom they were surrounded served, (for we know that they adopted these,) of the souls of dead men, or of demons, unless it should be supposed that they are included in the expression "male or female," and this is by no means certain. Again, Acts vii. 41, "And they made a calf in those days, and offered sacrifice unto the idol, and rejoiced in the work of their own hand. Then God turned and gave them up to worship the host of heaven." Deut. xvii. 2, 3, "If there be found among you, within any of thy gates which the Lord thy God giveth thee, man or woman that hath wrought wickedness in the sight of the Lord thy God, in trangressing his covenant, and hath gone and served other gods, and worshipped them, either the sun, or the moon, or any of the host of heaven, which I have not commanded." In short, Moses never supposed that they were in any peculiar danger of falling into the worship of dead men. The only passage which even Farmer, after all his industry in research, and anxiety to establish his own hypothesis, could find, which even appeared to favour it, is, to say the least, capable of another application. Deut. xxvi. 14, "I have not given ought thereof" (that is of the tithes) "for the dead." But by comparing this passage with another, Psalm cvi. 28, "They joined themselves to Baal-peor, and ate the sacrifices of the dead," it would appear that by "the dead" here it is probable dead idols are meant, which, as the Scriptures represent them, can neither see, nor hear, and have no breath in them. Now the representations which the other prophets give of the heathen deities are similar to those of Moses. 2 Chron. xxxiii., 2 Kings xxi., xxiii., Jer. viii. 1. In these minute descriptions of idolatry, no mention whatever is made of the souls of the dead, which there would have been, had they been the objects of worship amongst the Jews. Nor has Farmer been able to prove his assertion, that "deified human spirits were, according to the pagan system of theology, associated with, and represented the natural gods, and both were called by the same name."* But were we to allow that this was done in some instances, the practice was far from being universal, and it was not introduced till many ages after the worship of supposed celestial gods had been practised. The truth of the matter seems to be this—that at first the Greeks, and afterwards the Romans, deified and worshipped their great men, and that they introduced their own gods and superstitious practices amongst the nations whom they conquered, and attached the names of their deities, such as Jupiter, and Apollo, and Mercury, and Venus, to those reputed divinities which were formerly worshipped in these countries. And as the greater part of the Greek and Roman gods were deified men, a pretext has been afforded to Farmer and others to maintain that all these nations paid their religious homage to demons, and that these were the souls of the dead. The fact is, however, that the term was not confined to the latter. Amongst many other proofs of this, Fell adduces the following from Plutarch, De Defectu Oraculorum:—"Hesiod was the first who did properly and distinctly lay down four rational natures, (that is, created natures,) the gods, the demons, many in number, and good in their kind, the demi-gods, and men; for

* Miracles, p. 179.

heroes are reckoned among the demi-gods." But it is not necessary to dwell on this point, for Farmer himself confesses that the most ancient gods were not deified heroes, and that there were always other gods worshipped besides them. The following are his own words:—"These," that is, the sentient nature of the sun, moon, and stars, "were the first deities of all idolatrous nations, and they were esteemed eternal, sovereign, and supreme. These were distinguished by the name of natural gods."* The heathens also believed that there were certain spirits who held a middle rank betwixt the gods and men on earth, and carried on all intercourse between them. These spirits were called demons, distributors, or dispensers of good and evil to mankind. They became the grand objects of the religious hopes and fears of the pagans, of immediate dependence, and Divine worship." He also confesses that the heathen philosophers believed in the existence of evil demons, beings which bore a great resemblance to fallen angels.† Both the fathers and the heathen philosophers asserted that "those beings whom the heathen world worshipped as gods, were evil demons. Both of them, in support of this assertion, urged the same arguments; such as the actions ascribed to the heathen gods, &c. Both taught that evil demons were spirits of a celestial origin, and that they were inspirers and authors of prophecies and miracles."‡ These concessions do in fact subvert the very foundation of Farmer's system. He is also obliged to own that the *shedim*, (שֵׁדִים) Deut. xxxii. 17, and the *sengnirim*, (שְׂעִירִים) Lev. xvii. 7, to whom the Jews were forbidden to offer their sacrifices, were the idols or gods of Egypt and Canaan, and these were not the spirits of dead men. Fell thinks that they were the natural gods of the heathen. Whatever they were, they do not favour the hypothesis that the term "demons" and "vanities,"

* Farmer on Miracles, p. 172.   † Ibid. pp. 174, 175.
‡ Ibid. pp. 219, 220.

by which they are rendered in the Septuagint, refer to the spirits of the deceased; and very important considerations may be assigned in support of the version in which the words are translated "devils." And if they should be rendered "demons," still the question would be, what kind of beings are those demons? and I apprehend they would be found to be very different from the ghosts of dead men.

But if it should be granted, for the sake of argument, that by the term demons are meant the spirits of those who once had been inhabitants of this world, would it follow from this, as Farmer maintains, that there could be no real possessions? He allows, at least he does not deny, that the soul exists after its separation from the body, in a state in which it is capable of action, and happiness or misery; and, consequently, he must admit, I should think, that in the latter case it is in a state not dissimilar from that of fallen angels; and as we are assured that, after the judgment, the wicked are to be condemned to the same punishment with the devil and his angels, where would be the absurdity of supposing that they may, immediately after death, be associated with them in their impious opposition to the plans of God, and to the Gospel of Jesus Christ, and that therefore they might be able to act the part of the demons mentioned in the New Testament, and that they might be permitted to do so? I know it will immediately be replied, they are confined to their place of punishment. They are represented, 1 Peter iii. 19, as "spirits in prison." But are not Satan and his angels, likewise, "cast down to hell and delivered into chains of darkness, to be reserved unto judgment?" and yet I suppose Farmer would not deny that they are able to tempt men, though they are not exempt from punishment. It certainly follows from some principles which Farmer labours hard to establish, and which we may afterwards have occasion to notice, that neither angels nor devils can have any intercourse with this world, since this would be an infraction of the immutable laws which God has established.

But, thirdly, it is not possible that the Jews, and especially the apostles, could have the same notions respecting demons that the heathen had. Were we to grant, that by the term "demons," the Gentile nations meant the spirits of the dead, and much more when it is certain that they used the term to signify beings of a different order, still we must consider what were the religious knowledge and belief of the chosen people of God, respecting the invisible world. They knew that the gods of the heathen were vanity, and had, in reality, no existence. They believed, as is very evident from many passages of Scripture, and from the testimony of Josephus, in the existence of angels both good and bad; in other words, of fallen angels. Hence we are told that the Pharisees maintained the existence of both *angels and spirits;* and the Saviour, and the apostles Paul, and Peter, and Jude, speak of "the holy angels," and "the elect angels," and "the angels that kept not their first estate," as beings the existence of which was commonly believed amongst Jews and Christians, so that it was no more necessary to prove it, than to demonstrate that of God himself, and therefore any argument fairly deduced from this acknowledged fact would be valid; and at the same time, the *general character* of these spirits was well known. The same remark will apply to the Christian fathers. Now taking into the account these two things, that the Jews did not believe in the existence of the heathen gods which were called demons, and that they believed in that of fallen angels, who were engaged, to the utmost of their ability, in tempting and injuring men, would they not inevitably, when they used the term demon apply it according to their own views and belief, and, therefore, to fallen angels? And they were justified in doing so. The heathen applied the epithet in question, when taken in a bad sense, to certain invisible spiritual agents, that were inimical to men, and bent on doing them mischief. The Saviour and his apostles knew that though the ideas of the heathen were grossly erroneous, yet there were agents to whom the attributes of the supposed evil demons did belong, and in designating whom the word in question might well be used. How much more natural was it for them to employ it in this sense than to apply it to beings (as Farmer contends they must have done,) who either did not exist at all, or else could not possibly act the part which was assigned to them! Fallen angels could, and did. They were really evil demons. In this way we may account for the fact, that many of the Christian fathers assigned possessions to them, and I apprehend we are necessarily led to the conclusion, that Jesus Christ and his apostles applied the term demons to these evil spirits in the case of demoniacs. How often is it the case, that words are employed in a sense different from their original meaning, because of the views of those who have borrowed them and used them to express their own sentiments, and on account of some similarity in the objects with which, in the two cases, they are connected!

But Farmer, in his work on Miracles, advances and endeavours to support another proposition, which, if established, would render real possessions impossible, and therefore would reduce us to the necessity of considering all demoniacs as epileptics, or insane. It is this: "That the same arguments which prove the existence of superior created intelligences, do *much more* strongly conclude against their *acting out of their proper sphere.*" It is evidently implied in this, that the evidence which we have for the existence of angels and devils is not so clear and conclusive as are the proofs which assure us, that if they do exist, they can have no intercourse with our world; and, therefore, that they can neither benefit nor injure us. And though this is advanced to prove that miracles can be performed by none but God, yet it is not uncharitable to suspect that it is intended to support his favourite doctrines, that all cases of supposed possessions are only diseases, and that the temptations of Jesus Christ took place in a vision, and that this was presented to him by the Holy Spirit, and not by Satan.

Now it must immediately occur to all here, that this proposition is directly contrary to the general doctrine of Scripture respecting both good and bad angels. The former are represented as "ministering spirits, sent forth to minister to the heirs of salvation;" and numerous instances are recorded of their being employed in works both of mercy and vengeance, and no extraordinary ability seems to have been imparted to them on these occasions; they executed the commission given to them by their own native powers, which they could exert at any time, in obedience to the Divine command; and yet our world is not represented to us as that which Farmer would consider as their *proper sphere;* this is heaven, where they are always employed in serving and praising God. And we learn from the same infallible records, that fallen angels are incessantly engaged in tempting men to sin, and that they have been permitted to interrupt, to disarrange, in the most dreadful manner, the beautiful moral order which God established, and indeed to throw it all into confusion. Before Farmer's principle, then, can be established, so as to furnish an argument against real possessions, all the evidences which the Bible affords us, that either angels or devils have any intercourse with this world, must be nullified.

But further, who can tell how extensive is the sphere of action allotted to superior beings? Are we warranted to conclude, that because men, who are probably the very lowest order of rational creatures, are, at present, confined to one small province of Jehovah's dominions, none of his subjects, whatever be their natures, or powers, or privileges, can pass beyond the limits of that in which they were brought into existence, or in which they may generally reside? or that because man, on account of the grossness of his body, and the influence of the laws of gravitation, is confined to this earth, that angels, whether good or bad, must be unable to visit various parts of the universe? This notion is not supported by either reason, or analogy, or Scripture. It is just as if a horse or a sheep, supposing it capable of thought and reflection, were to conclude, that because it cannot navigate the ocean, and leave the little island in which it is located, therefore no creatures in existence can visit those parts of the earth which are separated by the mighty deep; or as if a shell-fish, were it able to reason, were to conclude, that because it cannot leave the rock to which it adheres, therefore every living thing must be so confined, and that the law under the influence of which it exists, must be universal. Who can forbear hoping at least, and pleasing himself with the idea, that after death, and when the soul is united to a glorified body, such as that which is described in 1 Cor. xv., he may be able and permitted to range through a large part of the universe, to pass from world to world, and from system to system, converse with various orders and ranks of creatures, and contemplate and admire the perfections of Jehovah, as manifested by the essential unity, the rich and endless variety, and complete harmony, of his mighty works? Must we always behold these glorious suns, those centres of mighty systems, and all their attendant worlds, at such a distance, as that, with the exception of one, they will appear like shining points, while multitudes of them can never be recognised at all; and shall we never be permitted to gratify a hallowed, a pious curiosity, which must surely at times arise and work in every breast? I ask again, what passage of Scripture or principle of reason authorises the conclusion? Allowing, therefore, that the mightiest spirits, both good and bad, have their allotted spheres of action, we are not warranted to conclude that this world may not be a part of that sphere, as the Scriptures teach us that it is. It does not follow, however, from this, that either angels or devils are able to work miracles, or, in other words, to change or supersede the great established laws of nature. But to take possession of the person of a man, and to torment his body and agitate his mind, surely do not involve anything miraculous. We find that men can influence one another, and derange each other's bodies and minds, and also control, to a certain extent, some of the laws of the universe, and render them subservient to their purposes; why, then, should it be thought impossible that angels, who "excel in strength," should do the same? It does indeed follow, that if spirits are able to operate on matter, they may be supposed to be able to effect, on account of their invisibility, some things which would appear to us miraculous. For instance, they might raise a ponderous rock into the air, or shiver it to pieces, without any apparent cause. But this would not be a miracle in itself, nor would it necessarily appear to be so to those who saw it; it would only be unaccountable. They might conclude that both the one and the other were effected by some unknown agent or force in nature. To render it a miracle, even in appearance, it would be necessary that it should be announced as such; that information should be given to those who beheld it that the rock would be raised into the air, or the tree would be shivered in pieces, without any natural cause, and at a certain time. The earth might have opened and swallowed up Korah, Dathan, and Abiram, without any miraculous interposition. It was a miracle when it was announced, the time specified, and supernatural power exerted to produce the predicted phenomena. So that though spirits, by their natural power, might do many things astonishing to men, as some of these can to others, yet it does not follow that they can work real miracles; and we may be certain that holy angels will not sport with the ignorance of men, and wicked spirits will never be permitted to do so, or to perform anything which, if it be carefully examined, will exhibit the properties of real miracles. Because, as these are one of the great proofs of a Divine interposition in giving a revelation to the world, God will not suffer any of his creatures, any rebels against his government, and no other would attempt it, to forge the great seal of heaven, in such a way as that the imposition could not be detected, even by his loyal subjects who were desirous to know his will, and to obey his commands. But though they cannot work miracles, yet, as Wollaston well observes, "As men may be so placed, as to become, even by the free exercise of their own powers, instruments of God's particular providence to other men or animals; so may we well suppose that these higher beings may be so distributed through the universe, and subject to such an economy, (though I pretend not to tell what it is,) as may render *them also* instruments of the same providence; and that they may, in proportion to their greater abilities, be capable, consistently with the laws of nature, some way or other, though not in our way, of influencing human affairs in proper places."*

The other arguments which Farmer employs in support of his system, we shall have occasion to consider, in examining more particularly the scriptural evidence for real possessions, and some of the principal cases of demoniacs. To these, therefore, we shall now proceed, after just remarking that from what has already been observed, there is nothing irrational in the doctrine, that wicked spirits may bring men under their power, and harass and injure them, according to the accounts which are given us in the New Testament. On the contrary, we should be led from reason, supposing that there are such beings as fallen angels, to expect that something of this kind would take place; and the wonder is, that instances of it are not more numerous. On Farmer's principles, indeed, we should

* Religion of Nature, sec. v. No. 18.

need no protection from evil spirits ; we might rest satisfied that they cannot hurt us. But on the principles of the Bible, our safety from them, as well as from evils and enemies of every kind, must arise from the power and vigilant care of God. He bruises Satan under the feet of his people. It has indeed been urged, that if Satan possessed such power as has been attributed to him in the observations which have just been made, he could not be restrained, without a perpetual miracle, from doing mischief of every kind. But does this follow ? Can men, by the influence of their authority, by the laws and arrangements which they make, and by the threatenings which they utter, restrain their fellow-creatures, however vicious, from perpetrating many crimes to which they are strongly inclined ? And cannot the Sovereign of the universe, who is everywhere present, and infinite in power, restrain all the wicked spirits in existence within the bounds which he is pleased to appoint them ? and that without the performance of a perpetual miracle, or of any miracle at all ; and without depriving them of their power ? Most certainly he can. He causes their wrath, as well as that of men, to praise him, and the remainder of it he restrains.

I shall now make a few remarks, first, on those passages which evidently imply, that the demons which were ejected by our Lord and his disciples were evil spirits or fallen angels ; and then consider some of the most remarkable accounts of possessions or demoniacs.

In Luke x. 17, we are informed that the seventy, after having fulfilled the commission which had been given them by the Saviour, "returned again with joy, saying, Lord, even the demons are subject to us through thy name. And he said unto them, I beheld Satan as lightning falling from heaven. Behold, I give you power to tread on serpents and scorpions, and over all the power of the enemy, and nothing shall by any means hurt you. Notwithstanding, in this rejoice not, that the spirits are subject to you ; but rather rejoice that your names are written in heaven." Now, whatever is meant by Satan falling as lightning from heaven; whether it refers to his first expulsion from the realms of perfect holiness and happiness, or to the approaching overthrow of idolatry by the preaching of the apostles, is indifferent to our present purpose. The term "Satan," with the article, (τὸν Σατανᾶν,) is used as a proper name, and refers, as has already been shown, to the leader of the apostate angels, the great adversary of God and men. The demons that had been ejected by the seventy are evidently considered as belonging to him, and as engaged in maintaining his cause. Their expulsion was a victory obtained over him, the overthrow of his power, and either one consequence of his being expelled from heaven, or an indication that by the approaching subversion of idolatry in the Roman empire, he was to be, as it were, cast down from the skies; and the Saviour calls those demons which were subject to the seventy, "*spirits*," τὰ πνεύματα, *not diseases*. Now surely, whatever might be the original meaning and application of the term "*demon*," and whatever the ideas of the Jews, and even of the seventy themselves, respecting them, *our Lord* knew that they were not the souls of dead men; and if they were diseases, he knew this also. How could he then, consistently with his character and the design of his mission, call them spirits, and represent them as in league with Satan, so that their ejection was connected with the overthrow of his power, with his expulsion from heaven? Allow that they were some of the angels who kept not their first estate, and who are represented as the angels of Satan, and then everything in the passage is plain and natural. On the other supposition, everything is strained and unnatural, and our Lord employed language which his disciples could not possibly, in their circumstances, understand; nay, which necessarily confirmed, I had almost said sanctioned, some grossly erroneous views which they entertained; and he has thus contributed much to lead his followers, in all subsequent ages, into mistakes on a very important subject. Who can believe that the great Prophet and Teacher would act in this way? and that, too, when the great end of his mission, the destruction of the works of the devil, was concerned? The interpretation which has been given is confirmed by the language of the 19th verse, compared with Mark xvi. 15, 16, and Acts xxviii. 3—6. To whom can the term " enemy" refer but to Satan? And the idea conveyed is, that those demons which the seventy had expelled, were a part of his power; and in the words *serpents* and *scorpions*, there is evidently a reference to the deception of Eve by the serpent, and to the curse which in consequence was pronounced on it, and the enmity which was put between it and man.

Another Scripture which plainly teaches that the demons of the New Testament were fallen angels, is Luke xi. 14— 26, and the parallel passages. The Pharisees brought against the Saviour the heavy and impious charge, that he cast out demons by Beelzebub the prince of the demons. It is not requisite, for the limits of this discourse will not allow, to enter into any long discussion respecting Beelzebub or Beelzebul. The views of Fell respecting him appear to be correct. " The Phœnicians worshipped the sun, which was undoubtedly meant under the term Beelzebub, the most famous of all the heathen deities for his oracles. But that the Pharisees, in their accusation of Christ, alluded to this god of Ekron, is by no means evident, since they do not even mention his name."* But whoever Beelzebub was, and whatever was the import of his name, the question here is, What was the charge which the Pharisees brought against Christ? what did they mean by " demons," and by " the prince of the demons?" Now it appears to me impossible, ignorant and superstitious as they might be, with the Old Testament in their hands, and firmly be-

* Fell, Demoniacs, p. 133.

lieving it as they did, that they could for a moment believe any heathen deity had the power which they here attribute to the prince of the demons. But they knew that there was a being who was in reality the prince of all wicked demons; would they not then be led by their views to refer to him in the charge, "By the prince of the demons he casteth out demons?" Accordingly we are informed, that Jesus Christ "knew their *thoughts;*" and in reference to *these*, to the sense in which they used the term Beelzebub, he framed his answer, "and said unto them, If Satan cast out Satan, he is divided against himself; how shall then his kingdom stand?" Does not this imply that he knew that they intended to charge him with ejecting demons by the power of Satan, and that by Beelzebub and his demons they meant the devil and his angels? The Saviour did not use the word *Beelzebub* in his answer to them, but *Satan*, (ὁ Σατανᾶς,) replying according to their intention, rather than the original import of the words which they employed. But does not this likewise indicate that the use of the name Beelzebub, as applied to the prince of darkness, was not unknown amongst the Jews? And the fact that our Lord charged the Pharisees with either having committed the sin against the Holy Ghost, or having approximated to it, confirms the interpretation that has been given; as his warning implies the greatest degree of malignity and guilt in those to whom it was addressed. He likewise assured them that he cast out devils by the Spirit of God, and that was an evidence that "the kingdom of God was come unto them," or that he was the Messiah, the Saviour of the world, and that his ejection of demons was an evidence of his being more powerful than Satan, that he was "binding the strong man, and spoiling him of his goods." There cannot be a rational doubt, that by "the strong man" here, he meant the devil, whose works he came to destroy. He farther informed them, that they might, if they would not believe him, apply to some of their own countrymen, of their own children, for evidence of the fact that he was not in league with Satan, but that he ejected demons by a Divine power. Luke xi. 19, "And if I by Beelzebub cast out devils, by whom do your sons cast them out? Therefore they shall be your judges." I cannot think, notwithstanding the learned and respectable names which sanction the interpretation, that by the "sons" of the Pharisees are meant the Jewish exorcists, who ejected demons, by adjuring them in the name of the God of Abraham. There is no allusion to any such practice in the Old Testament. None of the prophets were ever commissioned to work a miracle of this kind as a proof of their mission, and we have no instance of any besides prophets ever being employed to work miracles. The testimony of Josephus in this case is entitled to no credit,* connected as it is with his ridiculous stories respecting the root Baaras, and the charms which Solomon left behind him to eject demons, and cure diseases; and of applying a ring, with a portion of this root, to the nose of a possessed person, and thus drawing out the demon through the nostrils. Nor can I think that our Saviour here uses the *argumentum ad hominem*, however conclusive it might be. Many, perhaps I should say most commentators, think that by "the children" of the Pharisees are meant their *disciples*, and that some of them might be exorcists, who pretended to cast out devils, and that the meaning of the Saviour is, "You allow that your disciples eject evil spirits, by using the name of the God of Abraham, Isaac, and Jacob. I have come, I preach and cast out devils in his name, and therefore in charging me with a compact with Beelzebub, you condemn both them and yourselves." This reasoning the Saviour might employ, without allowing that these exorcists performed any real miracles. But Jesus Christ never used, as far as we know, their form of exorcism, and most certainly none of

* Josephus, Antiq. lib. viii. c. 2; Bell. Judaic. lib. vii. c. 23.

their arts. He "commanded with authority the unclean spirits to come out." And the probability is, that he did this in the same manner as he delivered his sermon on the mount—" I say unto you"—so that the people " wondered, because he taught them as one having authority, and not as the scribes." We have a specimen of the manner in which he acted on these occasions in Mark ix. 25 ; " Thou dumb and deaf spirit, *I charge* thee, come out of him, and enter no more into him." The Pharisees might therefore urge that though their disciples cured demoniacs in the name of the God of Abraham, he did it in his own name, and thus might derive his power from Beelzebub. For these reasons, I must coincide in opinion with those who think that by "children" in this passage are meant the disciples of Jesus Christ, who, as they were probably all comparatively young, might be called, in a general way, "the children" of the Jews, or even of the Pharisees ; and probably some of their parents belonged to that sect, as we know Nicodemus did ; and it is not at all unlikely that they who brought the charge in question against Jesus Christ were members of the sanhedrim. He communicated the power of casting out demons to his disciples; he might then appeal to them whether there was any compact with Beelzebub in the case, and assure the Pharisees that they should at last be judged by those who were, in a sense, their own children. On the whole, then, this passage clearly proves, both that by the term demons our Saviour did not mean the souls of dead men but evil spirits, and that the Jews were not unacquainted with this application of the word.

Again, in Acts x. 38, we read that "God anointed Jesus of Nazareth with the Holy Spirit and with power; who went about doing good, and healing all who were oppressed of the devil : for God was with him." By "the devil" here is evidently meant Satan. What other slanderer or false accuser in the universe oppressed, or brought under his power, those whom Jesus Christ healed during his personal ministry? And the term "*healed*" might with the greatest propriety be employed with regard to demoniacs; for possession in itself was a dreadful disease, and it was also frequently the cause of other maladies. The apostle undoubtedly refers here to the casting out of demons, and he represents them as the agents of Satan, in oppressing and injuring men. Could he with any propriety have used this language, if there had been no such thing as real possessions, and no diseases caused by the immediate agency of Satan; or if those to whom he addressed these words, had, on account of their own views, and the notions that commonly prevailed, thought that the spirits which agitated and oppressed demoniacs, were the souls of those who had once been inhabitants of this world; unless they had believed that these souls after death were wicked spirits, and were associated with fallen angels? Those who heard him would infallibly think that by " those who were oppressed by the devil," the apostle meant demoniacs; and after the Holy Spirit had been poured out on the day of Pentecost, according to the promise of the Saviour, Peter could not be ignorant of the truth on this important point; he could not be left to think, and to lead others to suppose, that those who were merely epileptics and insane, were possessed by fallen spirits.* Nor was there any necessity to accommodate himself to the prejudices of those whom he addressed; for if he had said, (suppose he had not believed in possessions,) that Jesus Christ cured all that were diseased, and healed all that were sick, it would have fully conveyed his meaning with-

---

* I am sensible that this reasoning will have very little weight with those who can say with Dr. Priestley, " Though we admit that Jesus taught the truth in a popular way, yet we very much doubt whether, in some instances, he properly and accurately understood it."—*Priestley on Necessity.*

What intolerable presumption! What must be the state of that person's mind and heart into which the thought could by any possibility enter, that he understood the truth better than Jesus Christ did!

out giving any offence. We must conclude, then, that this passage affords an irrefragable proof of the reality of possessions, and that demoniacs were not merely the subjects of disease.

We shall now proceed to examine, as far as our limits will allow, one or two of the accounts which are given us of demoniacs in the New Testament; from which it will appear that the facts which are recorded respecting them, and the way in which the Saviour acted in performing his miraculous cures, as well as the general principles and declarations of the Scriptures, prove that possessions were real, and not imaginary. One of the most remarkable of these cases is that which is recorded in Matt. viii. 28—34, Mark v. 1—20, Luke viii. 26. It is not necessary for the object of this lecture, to reconcile the apparent discrepancy in the accounts of the evangelists. Mark and Luke mention only one demoniac, while Matthew informs us that there were two. Perhaps, as Doddridge supposes, one was much fiercer than the other, and was therefore alone thought worthy of particular notice by two of the writers; or, perhaps, there was at first only one, and the question respecting his name was proposed to him only, and another joined him afterwards. There is certainly nothing improbable in this supposition. We cannot imagine that these unhappy creatures were very sociable, or that they were much together. The most prominent circumstances of this remarkable and difficult case are the following:—

First. The demoniac was so fierce and powerful that no man could tame or subdue him, and no chains could be found sufficiently strong to bind and confine him. To account for this, one writer has suggested that "perhaps they were not so expert at making chains as men are now; that madmen are very powerful, their disorder furnishes them with almost supernatural strength, or at least causes them to exert what they have in almost a supernatural way; and that therefore it is not wonderful that no chains sufficiently strong to bind this demoniac could be found." Surely this does not deserve refutation. When we consider the houses, temples, and cities they could build, the huge stones they could raise to a great height in their walls, we feel certain that they could have formed chains sufficient to bind effectually any insane person, even if he had possessed the strength of twenty men. How comparatively weak a chain will confine the strongest giant!

Secondly. The next remarkable circumstance is that when he saw Jesus, and the unclean spirit had been commanded by the Saviour to come out, the demoniac fell down before him, and exclaimed, "What have I to do with thee, Jesus, thou Son of God, most high? I beseech thee torment me not." Also the man with the unclean spirit, in the synagogue at Capernaum, said, "What have I to do with thee, thou Jesus of Nazareth? I know thee who thou art, the Holy One of God," Luke iv. 34. And we read that "*demons*" (not the *demoniacs*, as Farmer asserts, but the *demons* when they came out—δαιμόνια ... κράζοντα καὶ λέγοντα) "cried out, and said, Thou art the Christ, the Son of God." Whiston and Farmer endeavour to account for this, by saying that the testimony of John the Baptist, and the miracles which Jesus had performed at the very commencement of his public ministry, had rendered him the object of universal attention, and had produced a strong persuasion that he was the Messiah; that the reputed demoniacs were epileptics or madmen; that in the intervals of their fits and insanity they had heard the common report respecting Jesus of Nazareth; or that, long before they were seized with their disorder, they might have learned the high character of the Messiah; that their disorder might not only be temporary, but partial, not affecting their understandings, naturally quick, except on a single subject, and that on all others they might be left in full possession of themselves: that perhaps by the words, "the Son of God," they meant nothing more than a godly man, and that their very disorder would enable them to judge better than others of the character of Jesus Christ.* In the same way he explains the history of the Pythoness at Philippi. He thinks that she laboured under melancholy, or some species of insanity; that this fixed her mind strongly on this one object; that she had heard before of the character and doctrine of Paul, and thus was led to follow him and his companions, and exclaim, "These men are the servants of the Most High God, who show to us the way of salvation!"

But this interpretation is worse than unsatisfactory. Though "all men mused in their hearts of John, whether he were the Christ," and though great curiosity and much discussion were excited by the preaching and miracles of Jesus Christ, yet the people, in general, were very far from believing that he was the Messiah, much less that he was the Son, and the Holy One of God. There was not an individual amongst them, who was prepared to confess this, with the exception of the disciples of the Saviour; and their views on this subject, especially on the latter part of it, were far from being clear. Hence, when Peter made the declaration, "Thou art the Christ, the Son of the living God," Jesus replied, "Blessed art thou, Simon Barjona; for flesh and blood hath not revealed it to thee, but my Father which is in heaven." Can we suppose, then, that these madmen or epileptics, even when under the influence of their fits, possessed that knowledge which was exclusively the result of Divine teaching and influence? And not only did the demons confess this, but they also knew the design of the Saviour's coming, to subdue and punish them, in other words, to destroy the works of the devil; and that in the very commencement of his ministry, before he had wrought many miracles of this kind; nay, it would appear when he wrought the very first, soon after

---

* Farmer on Demoniacs.

his return from the wilderness where he had been tempted of Satan, Mark i. 24, Luke iv. 34. This can never be rationally accounted for, on the supposition that the demoniacs were madmen. And why were they afraid of Jesus Christ, and why did they beseech him not to torment them? Farmer is obliged to grant that this might be the effect of some supernatural impression. He finds that his hypothesis fails him, and he is willing to believe that the request was produced by the mere rebuke of the Saviour, and by the awe in which the demoniac stood of him; and that on this account he forbore from assaulting the company, as he had intended to do when he first ran to meet them. And Farmer quotes with approbation the sentiments of Wetstein, who supposes that " the demoniac was afraid of being *beaten* or *bound*, or having some *ungrateful purgative* administered to him." Here again the causes assigned are utterly inadequate to the production of the effects. If the demoniacs had been so much afraid of Jesus Christ, they would have fled from him rather than have run to meet him. It may be said, would not the demons have acted in the same way? But *they* knew that they could not escape by fleeing from him, and they might hope to be able, by their requests, to induce him to defer their punishment. And what imaginable reason could the demoniacs have to think, that Christ came to torment them? Especially if they knew, as Farmer supposes they did, that he was the Son, and the Holy One of God, they might have rather supposed that he came to do them good, to deliver them from demons, by which they thought they were possessed. And why should they request him not to torment them *before the time?* To what time could a demoniac refer? Farmer is obliged to confess his inability to determine the precise ideas of the madman here. And why implore him not to send them into the deep? What deep could an insane person have in view? And what could he possibly mean by a request to enter into the swine? But let us grant, according to the account of the evangelist taken in its obvious sense, that those persons were really possessed by fallen spirits, and then every thing appears natural; the causes are sufficient to produce the effect. It may be asked, But why did the demons come to the Saviour, or induce those who were under their power to come to him; and why did they confess him, and bear a most honourable testimony to him, in a way that was calculated to promote his cause, and to overthrow their own? To this I answer, The Saviour intended to cast them out, and to relieve those whom they oppressed: and the same power or influence by which they were ejected might constrain them to approach him; and then their fear would naturally lead them to make the confession, hoping, perhaps, that it would flatter the Saviour, and induce him to comply with their request, not to torment them. Here, again, the hypothesis that they were actually possessed accounts for everything; the contrary accounts satisfactorily for nothing.

The next circumstance which requires notice is the question which Jesus Christ proposed to him, and the answer that he returned. Verse 30, "And Jesus asked him, What is thy name? And he said, Legion; because many devils were entered into him." The proposal of this question is utterly unaccountable, and I cannot help saying, with reverence, altogether inconsistent with the character of the Saviour, on the supposition that the man was merely insane. He could not be under any necessity here, as it is alleged he was in some other instances, to accommodate his language to the prejudices of the people respecting demoniacs. He might have wrought the cure without saying anything that would have implied possession, or that would have led to the statement respecting the legion. It appears evident that he knew, though none else did, that a number of evil spirits were concerned in tormenting this unhappy person; and that he thought it proper that this remarkable fact should be known to his own attendants, and to the world in general. There is no necessity, however, to determine the number of the demons, or to suppose that there were six thousand of them. The explanation of Doddridge and others is quite satisfactory. "There is no need of concluding from hence that the number of these evil spirits was exactly the same with that of a Roman legion, which was upwards of six thousand. It was a phrase that was often made use of to denote a great number. It is observable that Luke here adds, that 'many demons were entered into him;' so that it is evident that they thought it not a lunacy, but a real possession. Probably a band of evil spirits united in the vexation of this unhappy creature; but in what manner and order it is impossible for us to say, who know so little of invisible beings."* To this it may be added, that as a legion was united under one commander, so might it convey the idea of union, or of a band. And a number, though small in itself, might be considered great when applied to beings of a hateful or repulsive character. So the term legion might figuratively, and in ordinary language, be applied to these hateful spirits when engaged in the work of mischief, though their number, instead of being six thousand, fell far short of a hundred. On the supposition, then, of lunacy or insanity, this part of the narration is altogether unaccountable.

Still more so, however, if possible, are the next circumstances, namely, the leave that was asked and given to enter into the swine, and the consequence of this, the rushing of the whole herd down a steep place into the lake, so that they were all choked. If the man had supposed that he was possessed, he might have asked that the *demons* might enter into the swine; *he* could not wish to enter *into them*. But if we were to grant that this wild idea might enter into a madman's head, and this incoherent language might be

* Doddridge in loc.

uttered by him, (though the language was uttered by the demons, and not by him,) how are we to account for what follows? Jesus Christ knew the facts of the case. Would he have humoured the madman, and deceived those who heard the conversation, by saying, "Go," and thus treating a case of insanity as if it had been a real possession? And how are we to account for the effects which immediately followed? Would the demoniac's whim, and the Saviour's humouring of it, cause two thousand swine to rush into the lake? This, I need not say, is an absurdity—an impossibility. And hence those who deny the reality of possessions are altogether at a loss here. Some of them, as Dr. Lardner, say the swine were frightened by the two madmen, and so were driven down the precipice into the sea. This is altogether unsatisfactory, as it well may be, to Farmer. He allows that it was impossible for two men, however fierce, to put so vast a herd of swine into motion in an instant, and to cause them all to rush with violence into the sea; particularly since they, perhaps more than most other animals, commonly run in a direction contrary to that in which they are driven; and that it was next to impossible that these two men could have overcome all those who tended the swine, especially as, in order to compass the herd, they must have separated from each other; and had they, under the influence of their disorder, driven the swine into the sea, it is strange they did not follow them thither. And it appears from the history, that at the time when the demoniacs were cured, they were present with Christ, and the herd of swine at a distance from them; yet no sooner was leave given them to enter the swine, than immediately the whole herd ran down the steep place. The demoniacs therefore were cured before the herd commenced running into the sea. How then could the madmen drive it? Not a single word more need to be said in refutation of this absurd hypothesis, which is certainly more worthy of an insane person, than of a learned divine.

Not less absurd, however, nay, in my opinion, more so, in some respects, is the supposition of Farmer himself. He supposes that "the madness or insanity of the demoniacs was miraculously transferred to the swine by the power of God, to humour the madmen, and to punish the owners of the swine." But there is not a word said about any power or influence being exerted by Jesus Christ or by God. The Saviour *gave them leave*, which plainly implies that they *had the power;* all that they needed was the permission. And could he possibly have done anything better calculated to sanction and confirm the erroneous ideas which, according to Farmer, were entertained respecting demoniacs and possessions, than to ask questions of the supposed demons, to receive their answers, to grant them their request, and then to work a miracle to confirm, I had almost said, the delusion, and to cause all who were present to think that demons went out of the man, and entered into the herd? An hypothesis must be false which needs such support as this. Farmer, indeed, pleads that this miracle, transferring the madness of the demoniacs to the swine, would ascertain the reality and spread the fame of the miracle. There was no need for either of these. The demoniacs had been in their miserable situation for a considerable length of time; perhaps for years. They were known to multitudes. There could not be any collusion, any agreement betwixt Jesus Christ and them; and all who saw them believed in the reality of possessions, and thought the expulsion of demons amongst the most wonderful miracles that could be performed. They would, therefore, not be backward to spread the report of what had been done, even if nothing had happened to the swine.

But what is strangest of all, Farmer maintains that the miracle performed, according to his ideas, on the swine, was calculated to correct the false notions that were entertained in that age respecting the power of demons. It is surely not necessary to confute this hypothesis. Certainly nothing could be better calculated to sanction those notions, however false they might be. And as one evidence of this, we find that those who believe in the reality of possessions, bring some of their strongest arguments, to this day, from what took place with regard to the swine; and it presents the greatest difficulties to their opponents. What then must have been its effects on those who beheld it, with all their ideas respecting the existence and power of demons, and the reality of possessions? I leave it to common sense to return the answer. Farmer urges, that the spectators could not see the demons, and, therefore, their expulsion and entering into the swine, could not be to them a proof of the Saviour's power; all that could be witnessed were the sensible effects. But they could see the *demons* just as well as they could see *insanity* or *epilepsy*, in other words, the cause of those disorders; all that they could see in either case were the sensible effects, from which they judged when the cause was removed. It is an egregious mistake, however, to say, as Farmer does, that the demons acknowledged their own impotence, when they asked for leave to enter into the swine, and that it took place at the command of Christ, and is to be referred to his power. The language employed by the evangelist most plainly conveys the idea, that he gave only permission, and that the demons possessed the requisite ability. It is trifling to say, that they *would* not have destroyed the herd, because that would have exposed them to some terrible punishment; just as if they must either keep possession of those animals, or else go into the deep, which they so much dreaded! The Saviour had not commanded them to go into the deep, whatever it was; rather, by acceding to their request, he had intimated that he would not punish them at present, and then they had no more cause to fear his vengeance, after the destruction of these animals, than before.

Farmer endeavours to support his theory, by saying,

that "it was necessary for Christ and his apostles to use common language on the subject of possessions, just as the sacred writers do in other instances, when they say that the sun rose and set, and that he runs a race, and that God lays the foundation of the earth, and that the dew descends," &c. But there is no analogy between the two cases. The employment of popular language on natural or philosophical subjects, could not lead to any errors in religion. No other expressions could have been used, unless the sacred writers had first taught the world a new system of philosophy, which they were not commissioned to do, and which they could not have done. But the doctrine of possessions related immediately and directly to religion, and was intimately connected with several of its most important doctrines, and with the very design of the Saviour's appearance in our world, namely, "to destroy the works of the devil." If there were no real possessions, the common belief respecting demoniacs was injurious, in ways innumerable, both to the temporal and spiritual interests of men. It filled with imaginary superstitious fears; it caused the improper treatment of those who were thought to be possessed; and prevented the adoption of proper means to effect their cure. It led to all the absurdities of exorcism. Amongst the heathen it was connected with idolatry, and amongst the Jews it was the source of many superstitious notions and practices. It caused men to form wrong ideas of the miracles of the Saviour, and led them to admire him, and to praise God, for that which he never effected. Farmer himself has laboured to prove that the doctrine of real possessions has done, and does, Christianity the greatest injury in many respects.* "It gives occasion to numberless superstitions; particularly to those shameless impostures, the possessions and exorcisms of the Romish church, with all the mummery of fanatic agitations. It affects the very

* Farmer on Miracles, p. 400.

foundation of Christianity, and discredits the evidence. It sets revelation at variance with reason and experience, and fixes an indelible reproach on those who professed to be commissioned by God to publish it to the world!" Heavy charges, indeed! It is not too much to assert that, if this is true, it is a doctrine of devils!—one of the most injurious errors that the prince of darkness ever introduced into the world; and surely it was just as false and pernicious in the time of the Saviour and his apostles, as it is now. Nay, the foundation of all the mischief which it has done was laid then, by the way in which they treated supposed demoniacs, and by their just omitting to utter a few plain words respecting them. It evidently fell within the compass of their mission; for it belonged to religious truth and practice. This is evident from what Farmer himself advances. Nay, it may be asserted with truth, that it entered into the very essence of religion. Jesus Christ could easily have condemned the tenet in question, if it had been an error. When he cured the reputed demoniac, if he had expressly asserted that there was no possession in the case; that there never had been such a thing as a person possessed by evil spirits; that supposed demoniacs were insane or epileptic; and that as a proof of this he would miraculously cure them; and then commanded the epilepsy, or the insanity, to depart, as he did the fever in the case of Peter's mother, who could have disbelieved him? Many converts, at least, would have been made, and a foundation would have been laid for the subversion of the whole error. But to take lower ground than this, (though it is not at all too high—it is furnished by truth and reason,) in curing demoniacs, the Saviour might have abstained from using language which implied possession; he might have spoken a word, or laid his hands on them, and healed them; and he might have explained the matter to his disciples, and informed them that there were no real possessions; that all supposed cases of them were merely diseases; and thus have prevented them from sanctioning and propagating the error. It is in vain (as Farmer owns,) to plead the prejudices which prevailed, and the offence which would have been given, as a reason why the Saviour employed the common language on this subject, and forbore to state the truth. He spoke with the greatest plainness, and published the most offensive doctrines, in instances when the prejudices of those whom he addressed were much stronger than they were even in this case. He did not forbear from foretelling his death, because his disciples could not understand his statements, and Peter even dared to rebuke him; or to insist on the necessity of eating his flesh and drinking his blood, because some exclaimed, " This is a hard saying; who can hear it?" or from asserting his divinity, because the Jews were so exasperated, that they endeavoured to stone him. It is true that, as Farmer states, " the sacred historian calls a certain disorder lunacy, using its ordinary name, without sanctioning the idea that it was caused by the moon." But it is the opinion of many philosophers and physicians, and facts seem to corroborate the idea, that it is at least *influenced* by that luminary; and there is nothing more wonderful or improbable in this, than that the tides should be subject to lunar influence; and in curing lunatics the Saviour never used language which implied that the moon was the cause of the disorder which was called lunacy; so that the cases are not at all similar.

It does not follow from the reality of possessions, that fallen spirits can work miracles. For how easily can men produce diseases in others, and deprive them of sight or hearing! To constitute the infliction of blindness, or dumbness, or epilepsy, as caused by a demon, a miracle, it would be necessary, as has already been shown, that the evil spirit should announce his design, so as to arrest the attention of some spectators, and then immediately inflict the disease, without the employment of any natural means.

This I apprehend is essential to the nature of a miracle, at least to constitute it a proof of any doctrine or fact: and hence, when Moses was sent to work miracles in Egypt, he always foretold what he was about to effect, and directed the attention of Pharaoh and his servants to the outstretched hand of God; and the same observation may be applied to the prophets in general, as well as to Jesus Christ and his apostles. Had the Saviour caused the fig-tree to wither away in a night, without pronouncing a malediction on it, or giving any intimation of his intention, though the power exerted and the phenomenon would have been the same, the act would not have been a miracle demanding attention and belief. It might have arrested notice, and excited wonder; but it would have been attributed to some natural causes; no interposition of the Divine power would have been pointed out or recognised. On the whole, I must think that the pernicious consequences, which Farmer and others attribute to the doctrine of real possessions, imply very heavy charges against the Saviour and his apostles. And I cannot see how their character can be vindicated, but by maintaining that the persons generally called demoniacs were actually under the influence of evil spirits. There is no difficulty presented by the fact that many of them were affected by epilepsy or insanity; for Satan or any of his angels might cause these, as well as any other disorders.

The limits prescribed will not allow me to examine any other cases of possession; nor is it at all necessary. The principles already laid down, and the observations which have been made, will apply generally. And if they are correct, it will follow that the Pythoness, as she is generally called, of Philippi, was neither a pretender nor insane, but actually possessed by an evil spirit. I had almost forgot to notice the objection which has been urged by some, that it is inconsistent with the goodness of God to leave men under the power of malignant demons in such a way as is implied in the doctrine of real possessions. But it scarcely deserves an answer. A single glance at the facts which are presented to us all around, is sufficient to enable us to refute it, and a thousand others of the same kind. To say nothing of Satan being permitted to tempt men to sin, one fell oppressor, or avaricious, merciless slaveholder, has caused more misery to the human race, than has been the result of all the possessions which have ever been permitted in the world. If it be thought strange that, if evil spirits have been suffered to act in the way supposed, they should not have tormented men more than they have done, or even destroyed them, we can account for this only on the principle which is implied in the language of God respecting Job, "Behold, he is in thy hand, *but spare his life;*" and this is quite sufficient.

On the questions, why were possessions so much more numerous in the time of our Saviour than they were before, or have been since his advent? and are there any instances of possession, or does Satan cause diseases, now? very few observations must suffice. To the first it may be replied, that as the evil spirits inflicted maladies of various kinds, and thus, as it were, concealed their presence and agency, it might require the knowledge of the Saviour, and of inspired men, to determine whether any epileptic, or lunatic, or insane person was possessed or not; or whether blindness, or deafness, &c., was caused by a demon. And it is *possible* that the same may be the case now. But I must own that I am very much inclined to think that they were really much more numerous in the time of our Lord and his apostles than ever they were before, or have been since; or that, possibly, they were confined to that period. We read, as has been already stated, nothing of them in the Old Testament. All that is recorded respecting the Jewish exorcists is, to say the least, very suspicious. Satan, we know from the character which is given of him in the Scriptures, is going about seeking whom he may devour. Evil is his good; mischief, and misery, and sin are his element. He needs no impartation of power to enable him to take possession, either immediately or by his agents, of the bodies of men. The idea of impartation of ability, connected with what is recorded of him, is in my apprehension very dishonourable to the Divine Being; permission is all that was requisite. Satan has been ready at any time to exert his influence on the bodies of men, as well as to tempt them to the commission of sin, had he not been laid under restraint. When, therefore, we take into the account that the great purpose of the Saviour's appearance in the world, was that he might vanquish Satan, bruise the head of the serpent, and destroy his works, what is there irrational or unscriptural in the supposition, that evil spirits, who are amongst the principal agents of Satan, should be permitted, when the Saviour was here below, to take possession of far greater numbers of men than they had ever done before, or have done since? Thus there would be afforded to the world a striking manifestation, on the one hand, of their power and malice, and of our obligations to God for protection from them, and of the misery of those who shall be their victims for ever; and on the other, of the authority and glory of the Lord Jesus Christ, of the importance of the end for which he appeared in our world, and of his ability to accomplish it in all its extent. The wrath of devils as well as of men is caused to praise God, and the remainder of it is restrained. For the same reason, after the Saviour had finished his work and ascended to heaven, and the age of inspiration and of miracles had passed away, a restraint might be laid on Satan, and on evil spirits in general, and, consequently, possessions may have been much fewer since. Nay, what is there irrational in supposing that an entire prohibition is laid on Satan in this respect, so that he is not permitted to bring any under his power as he did then? We can scarcely see how evil spirits could wreak their malice on men, when they were permitted to bring their persons under their power, but by disordering either their bodies or their minds, or both, and consequently, producing either epilepsy, or palsy, or insanity, or blindness, or disease of one form or another. I cannot conceive of the results of possession, but in some of these, or similar forms. It must then be always difficult,—perhaps, to those who are not inspired, impossible, to tell when disease is the result of Satanic influence, and when it is not. There is always, as facts abundantly and lamentably prove, a wide scope for craft, and imposture, and collusion here. Men have ever been able to cast out devils when they could work no other miracle; and yet the ejection of evil spirits is numbered amongst the most splendid of the miracles of Jesus Christ. According to the passage which has been already quoted, it was when Jesus Christ cast out an unclean spirit, that the people were amazed, and exclaimed, "What *thing* is this? what *new* doctrine is this? for with authority commandeth he even the unclean spirits, and they do obey him." How could they with propriety, or why would they have used this language, if they had been familiar with the ejection of spirits by their exorcists? Taking all these things into the account, is it not probable, I had almost said certain, that the power of Satan, in this particular, would be very much restrained, if not entirely destroyed, after the death of the apostles, and of those on whom they conferred miraculous powers, and amongst others the gift of discerning spirits? When the Spirit of prophecy departed from the Jewish church, the power of working miracles ceased likewise. Is it not reasonable to suppose, that a similar rule would be observed in the case of the Christian church? so that when the Spirit of inspiration had uttered its last accents, and declared, "If any shall add to the words of the book of this prophecy, or take away from them, God shall add to him the plagues that are written in this book, or take away his part out of the book of life;" and when all those died on whom the apostles had laid their hands, that they might receive the extraordinary gifts of the Holy Ghost, (and we have no evidence that any besides the apostles ever could impart this precious boon, but much evidence to the contrary;) is it not reasonable to suppose that the power of working miracles would be recalled, as the end to be answered by it was answered? I repeat it, and I think it an important fact, we have no evidence that any but apostles, and prophets, and those to whom they imparted the power, could ever work miracles. And I do not see why any have a right to think they shall be able to eject demons now, any more than to raise the dead, or open the eyes of the blind, or why God would grant the former in answer to prayer, any more than the latter. Far be it from me to limit the power of God, or the efficacy of prayer: but we must look for the exertion of the former, and the answer to the latter, in the way which God has prescribed and warranted. If, then, the question is asked, Whether there are any instances of possessions and dispossessions in our day, I would answer, I do not deny the possibility of them; I do not positively say there are none; but I must say I have never met with a well-authenticated instance of either; never one respecting which I could say, This person was undoubtedly possessed by a demon, and cured by the prayers and efforts of men. One of the most remarkable cases of this sort, as far as my knowledge extends, is that recorded by Mr. James Heaton, and entitled, "The Extraordinary Affliction and Gracious Relief of a Little Boy, whose name was John Evans, supposed to be the effects of spiritual agency, carefully examined and faithfully narrated." The account is certainly a very astonishing one. I have no suspicion of the integrity and good intentions of the narrator, and of his sincere wish to discover and narrate the truth. Still, I can have little doubt that it was a case of epilepsy, united, perhaps, with some other disorders. And it is well if there was not something of craft and management in the boy, and in some of his friends; and from the account which Mr. Heaton himself gives, this was the opinion of some of the medical men who attended him. I have myself seen a decided case of epilepsy, in which there was no suspicion of any agency of evil spirits; and yet all the symptoms of this boy's case, as it regarded staring, grinning, gnashing with the teeth, attempting to bite, almost supernatural strength, so that it required four persons to hold him, and frightful cries, were exhibited. What might have taken place with regard to leaping, and dancing, and answering questions proposed to him, on the supposition that he was possessed, I cannot say, for he was always held during the fits when I saw him. But certainly his looks, and cries, and motions were sufficiently fiendish. No attempts were made to exorcise him, for no one thought he was possessed. Prayer was certainly made to God for him, both by himself, (for he was a pious young man,) and others; proper medical means were used; and at last, I think after the lapse of a year or two, he got permanently well, after some returns of the fits, as in the case of John Evans, and continues so to this day. I cannot avoid the suspicion, that if he had thought he was under the influence of an evil spirit, and had fallen into the hands of those who believed in possessions, almost every symptom, which was exhibited in the case of John Evans, might have been found or produced in him; and had the same means been used to dispossess the supposed demon, joined with similar perseverance and devotional exercises, it might have been supposed that his recovery was owing to a special interposition of Divine power in answer to prayer. Some circumstances in the account of Mr. H. are of such a nature, as to excite a suspicion that the good friends, who were so laudably concerned for his recovery, were rather credulous, and that the boy was not free from craft and design. I shall give one paragraph of the account, as an illustration of what I mean. "His attention and ghastly look were generally directed to those who gave out a hymn, or prayed. But as he dreaded adjurations more than anything else, the person who adjured shared most of his resentment. I had frequently proved that he was sensible of what I said to him in *thought* only, without the motion of my lips or eyes, or any visible indication of my meaning whatever. I this morning tried it again and again. Some of the brethren observed, that his attention was directed to me more than to those who were praying, and wondered what could be the cause. I was then mentally adjuring the evil spirit, and he knew it, felt it, and resented it. This was an astonishing fact; and wishing others might try and witness the experiment as well as myself, I whispered into Mr. Coath's ear, 'Adjure in your own mind, and watch the effect.' He did so; and when he saw how the evil spirit, in a moment, resented it, through the boy, in his astonishment he lifted up his hand and eyes. This attracted the notice of Mrs. J. Kennard, T. Sibley, and the Rev. Mr. ——. In whispers they inquired, 'What is that?' In whispers they were informed. They all tried it, and they all proved it, to their utter astonishment, that the *evil spirit knew as well, and felt as much, what was only mentally addressed to him, as what was spoken aloud*. The moment one of them addressed the demon mentally, the demoniac fastened his eyes on him, and grinned, and growled, and would sometimes spit on him if he could. In whatever situation the man stood who did this, whether at his head or feet, right hand or left, he would instantly stare him horribly in the face, and by various gestures and struggles to bite or get at him, show how he felt, dreaded, and hated the mental stroke."* Now I would ask, are we warranted by either Scripture or reason to believe that any evil spirit, if it had been Satan himself, can know the thoughts, the most secret workings and

---

* Heaton's Account, p. 90.

prayers of the heart, in the way in which this is supposed to have been done? I must think we are not. It is recorded of the Saviour, as an evidence of his superhuman wisdom, that "he needed not that any should testify of man, for he knew what was in man." But if the account which is given of this demoniac be correct, the same might be asserted of the evil spirit by which he was possessed. He knew, it seems, the thoughts of all, at least of any who were present. But all who have seen any person in a fit of epilepsy, know well that, when he is held, as it seems this boy was, he turns his eyes and his head rapidly in every possible direction, so that any spectator may be sure he will soon look him in the face. By a little help from the imagination, his eyes will appear to be in any direction at any time. Nor can I form any very definite ideas of those mental strokes given by the words of adjuration. I cannot conceive of any influence they could have of themselves. If there was a spirit present, which was to be ejected, this could be done only by the power of God in answer to prayer; and have we any scriptural warrant to think that the omnipotence of God would be exerted in such a way, by repeated strokes, and yet not producing the desired effect; only irritating the malignant fiend, and not expelling him? It was not in this manner that the Saviour and his apostles expelled demons.

I have already stated my suspicions that the boy was the subject of epilepsy; there is reason to fear that he also acted deceitfully, and imposed on those who attended him. I shall mention only one instance in proof of this. "I have before stated," says Mr. Heaton, "that at the door was his oracle. He now went to consult it, or rather the evil spirit."* Does it not appear strange and inconsistent that this evil spirit, which had possessed and was tormenting the boy, should keep an oracle at the door? Or had

* Heaton, p. 88.

it an assistant spirit there? Or if the boy was free from its influence at that time, and wished to be delivered from it, as appeared to be the case, from his desiring the prayers of others for him, why did he go to consult it? Could not the spirit, which was so wise as to know the very thoughts of men, have suggested to him at once what were the intentions of those who were consulting where to meet? At least, what additional information could be obtained by going to the door, I cannot conceive. There are other parts of the narrative on which similar remarks might be made. On the whole, I cannot see anything in the narration, which may not be accounted for by supposing it a case of epilepsy treated as if it had been a possession. And many other evidences of collusion and management, besides those which have been specified, will suggest themselves to those who critically examine the volume.

To the question, Do evil spirits inflict any diseases now, as they did in the case of Job, and of some of whom we read in the Scriptures? all the answer I have to give is, I would not assert that they do not; but if they do, I should not think it possible to distinguish them from other diseases; nor do I see any absurdity in maintaining that they may yield, in some cases, to medical treatment. Satan can cause them only by disordering the body; and he may be so restrained, that these disorders may be counteracted by the blessing of God on the virtues of medicine and the skill of physicians. We pray for that blessing, and we return thanks when we think it has been bestowed, so as to secure the restoration of health; and that blessing can counteract the craft and power of the devil, as well as the malignity of disease. On the whole, however, I must think that it is far more irrational and unscriptural to deny that there were real possessions and ejections in the days of our Saviour and his apostles, than to believe that evil spirits may still take possession of the bodies of men, and cause various diseases; but the belief of the former by no means necessitates that of the latter; and I must think, that as the power of Satan to inflict diseases must have been always very much restrained, so the probability is that it is now entirely taken away.

LECTURE VI.

THE AGENCY OF EVIL SPIRITS.

ON TEMPTATION :—THE SAVIOUR'S TEMPTATION IN THE WILDERNESS.

THE principal way in which evil spirits have intercourse with this world, and that in which their influence is most destructive, is by tempting men to the commission of sin. This I apprehend all who believe in the fact will allow, whatever may be their opinion respecting the subjects to which our attention has already been directed. It was in this way that Satan first obtained the advantage over men, and brought them under his power, and in which he still endeavours to maintain his empire on earth. Those who can detect and resist him here, have little to fear from him on any other account. And as it was in the character of the tempter that our Lord met and vanquished him, and that, it would appear, before he triumphed over any of his agents by casting out devils; and as he did this in the name and on the behalf of his people, in entering on this part of the subject, our attention is naturally directed to the account which is given by the pen of inspiration, of our Saviour's temptation in the wilderness.

And as we have a very plain and circumstantial narration of this remarkable event, given by two of the evangelists, while it is alluded to by a third, we might suppose that it can present but little difficulty, and that respecting it there could not be two opinions. Nor, I must think, would there have been, had not the statements been of a very extraordinary kind, such as men cannot reconcile with their preconceived opinions, and with what they think Satan can or cannot do, or would have done, on the one hand, and with what they suppose is consistent with the dignity of the Saviour, and with the wisdom of God, on the other. I must here repeat the remark which has been made in substance already, that if any number of persons were to read the statements of the inspired penmen, just to learn what is the most natural and obvious sense of their language, all of them would adopt what is called the literal scheme, namely, that Satan appeared to our Saviour, urged him to turn stones into bread, set him on a pinnacle of the temple and solicited him to cast himself down, conducted him, by some means, to a mountain, gave him a striking view of all the kingdoms of the world, and promised them all to him, on condition of receiving from him one act of homage. Now, such a mode of interpretation as this has always one powerful recommendation. If it is not received, very cogent reasons should be assigned for its being rejected.

As far as my knowledge of the subject extends, five different theories have been advanced respecting the way in which our Lord was tempted. Some think this was done in what may be called the common way, merely by suggestion; others that his temptation was a diabolical vision, exhibited to his imagination by the power of Satan; others, that it was a visionary, symbolical representation, presented to him by the Spirit of God, of the trials to which he was to be exposed during his personal ministry; while it might also answer the purpose of a present probation. A fourth class maintain, that all the temptation arose from the reflections and anticipations of the Saviour's own mind, seriously meditating, amidst the solitude of the desert, on his situation, the work in which he was engaged, and the difficulties and obstacles which presented themselves in various forms. And they imagine that these would appear peculiarly formidable to him, on account of the languor of his frame, reduced by his (according to them) partial fasting, or subsisting for forty days and forty nights on the spontaneous productions of the earth in that mountainous region, as John the Baptist is said to have come "neither eating, nor drinking." They deem the whole narrative highly figurative. All the refutation which this scheme deserves will be included in the remarks which are made on some others. A fifth class contend for the literal interpretation, and think that everything took place just as it is recorded by the evangelists.

On the first of these hypotheses, it is not necessary to dwell. As far as I know, it is not adopted by many, and by them it is suggested, rather than maintained. We can easily allow that in this way the devil might urge the Saviour to turn stones into bread; but how he could set him on a pinnacle of the temple, or take him up to a high mountain, it is not easy, or rather, it is impossible to conceive. When Satan tempted Judas and Ananias in this way, it is said that he "put it into their hearts," implying, I apprehend, that he suggested it to their minds, and that they were led by their own wicked hearts to adopt the suggestion. But in the narrative under consideration, it is said that the tempter came to Jesus Christ, addressed him in specified words, to which a verbal reply was given, and took him from one place to another. In short, this interpretation seems altogether inadmissible, however simple it may be, and free from some difficulties with which others are incumbered.

The second theory to which I have adverted, is that of those who, allowing that the whole of this history is to be understood as a recital of visionary representations, contend that those visions were framed by the devil, and that the temptations are to be ascribed to his immediate agency.* This, it appears, was the opinion of Le Clerc, and to it

* Farmer's Inquiry, p. 27.

Bishop Warburton was also inclined. But besides its being contrary to the obvious meaning of the language employed, there are two objections against it which immediately present themselves, and which I must own, did no others occur, prevent me from adopting it. The one is, granting that Satan could present such visionary scenes to the eyes and imagination of the Saviour as this theory supposes, yet is it possible that he could exert such power over his mind and rational faculties, as to cause him to think that he was carried first to the pinnacle of the temple, and then to a high mountain, and that he actually heard Satan addressing him? Were we to allow that this could have been done, would it not follow that, during the time that he was subject in this degree to the power of the tempter, he scarcely could have that command of himself, and that use of his rational powers, which were necessary to enable him to act voluntarily, and therefore to be the subject of temptation, and to resist and vanquish the adversary? And, farther, it is a greater difficulty to suppose that Satan could exercise this power over the *mind* of the Redeemer, than that he should transport his body from place to place, through the air. To deceive Jesus Christ, and to cause him to imagine that he was placed first on a pinnacle of the temple, and then on a lofty mountain, implies a far greater degree of influence over him, than what is supposed in the literal interpretation.

The hypothesis of Farmer is the third that was mentioned, and this, on account of the ability with which it has been stated and supported, and its plausibleness in many respects, will require a more extended examination than has been given to the others.

His theory is, that the temptation was neither an outward transaction nor a diabolical delusion, but a Divine vision; or that " Christ was carried or brought into a wilderness by a Divine afflatus, in a prophetic vision, that he might be tempted by the devil, and was so tempted, during his vision; and that, therefore, what is called his temptation by the devil was a Divine vision and revelation; the presence and agency of Satan was not real, but apparent, or a part of the prophetic scenery; and the history represents Satan as coming to Christ and tempting him, and removing him from one place to another; because the vision consisted of a representation of Satan as appearing and acting in this manner, and it was necessary the scenes should be described just as they were represented to Jesus Christ."* In support of this theory, Farmer commences by asking, "With what propriety could it be said that Jesus went into the wilderness in person at this time, when he was there already? It was in the wilderness that John exercised his ministry, and he baptized our Saviour there."† But is it not very probable, nay, is it not certain, that some parts of this region, which was denominated a wilderness because it was thinly inhabited, were a desert when compared with others? He was driven into that part of it which was the resort of savage animals, and not of men; for he was forty days with the wild beasts. This could not be in that locality where John was preaching, and to which all Judea and Jerusalem went to be baptized. Lightfoot‡ says, "The wilderness of Judea had indeed both cities and villages and dwellings of men in it, but it had also some places wild, without any such habitations, and it had wild beasts in those parts." 1 Sam. xvii. 34, and xxiii. 14; 2 Sam. xxiii. 20; Psalm lxi.; Jer. xlix. 19. So that it is easy to see how the Saviour was, in one sense, in the wilderness before the temptation commenced, and yet how he was driven into it in order to be tempted. The long discussion of Farmer, in which he labours to prove that "the Spirit often signifies the gifts or influence of the Spirit," is nothing to the purpose. Who ever thought that the Spirit could act, or, in any way, lead Jesus Christ into

---

* Farmer's Inquiry, p. 7, Contents. † Ibid. p. 46, Contents.
‡ Works, vol. i. p. 502.

the desert, but by some afflatus or influence? Nor can there be any objection to translating the word ἀνήχθη, " brought." The great support of his system, in his opinion, is that the phrases, 'Ἀνήχθη ὑπὸ τοῦ Πνεύματος, Matt. iv. 1, Τὸ Πνεῦμα αὐτὸν ἐκβάλλει, Mark i. 12, Πνεύματος ἁγίου πλήρης, Ἤγετο ἐν τῷ Πνεύματι, Luke iv. 1, are equivalent to the expressions which are used respecting the ancient prophets and the apostle John in the Apocalypse, when the meaning evidently is, that they had visions and imaginary scenes presented to their minds, so that they appeared to themselves to be carried from one place to another, whilst they never changed their locality, and to see and hear that which was merely impressed on their imagination. Now to substantiate his position here, Farmer ought to have proved, not only that the phrases which have been quoted, are used with regard to those who were favoured with visions, or prophetic inspiration, or miraculous gifts, but that they are exclusively so, and to no others, which, as I hope to be able to prove, is not the case.

The quotations which he has given from Ezekiel do not prove his assertion, nay, they militate against it; for the sacred historian did not think it sufficient to say, " The Spirit took me up;" " the hand of the Lord was upon me, and carried me by the Spirit of the Lord," &c., Ezek. iii., viii., xi., xxxvii., though these expressions are stronger than those used by the evangelists; but he also expressly informs us that all took place " in the *visions* of God," and that " the Spirit took him, and brought him in *vision;*" so that we have in those places a professed description of a vision. And the inspired penman does not seem to have thought that the expressions " in the Spirit," or " by the Spirit," necessarily implied that a visionary scene was presented to the mind, or else why should he have added " *in vision,*" or " *in the visions of God,*" but because the former words alone might signify that Ezekiel was actually carried from one place to another, as Philip was, Acts viii., and that the scenes which are afterwards described were real? And with regard to the evangelist John, Rev. i. 10 and iv. 2, though the phrase 'Εγενόμην ἐν Πνεύματι is used, it is not synonymous with those used by the evangelists Matthew and Mark, 'Ανήχθη ὑπὸ τοῦ Πνεύματος, Τὸ Πνεῦμα ἐκβάλλει αὐτόν· and as it respects the ἐν τῷ Πνεύματι of Luke, all must allow that ἐν often signifies *by* as well as *in;* and in this very place Schleusner renders it *à, ab,* so as to signify either the efficient or instrumental cause, and refers to the parallel passage in Matt. iv. 1, in support of his rendering. And besides, the whole of the scenery, and all the events recorded in the Revelation, are of such a nature, that it is necessary to understand them as having been presented to the apostle in a vision. Many of them could not possibly be facts and realities. This is obviously not the case, notwithstanding all the efforts of Farmer to prove the contrary, with the narration of the evangelists. It is given as a simple statement of facts; its connexion both with what precedes and follows, as a part of a historical account, requires us to understand it literally. As one proof of this it may be observed, that no commentator, I should suppose no reader, ever understood the Revelation so; all have seen at once that it was a vision; on the other hand none, till Farmer suggested the idea, (as he himself labours to prove,) ever thought that the temptation of the Saviour was a Divine vision, or that Satan was not the actual tempter. How can we account for this, but from the difference of the connexion and the language, in the two cases? Surely, if it is just as plain, as Farmer intimates, that Christ was tempted in a vision, produced by the influence of the Holy Spirit, as that Ezekiel and John saw visions of God, the fact could not have escaped the notice of all the learned and acute readers, and commentators, and critics, who have studied the word of God before Farmer was born. It may be

THE AGENCY OF EVIL SPIRITS. 285

observed, that the language used by the evangelists does not refer the temptation of Christ to the Holy Spirit at all, but merely his *being led into the wilderness*, doubtless by a Divine influence, or by the afflatus of the Spirit; but it was in order " to be tempted by the devil," not to have any communication made to him by the Holy Ghost. I have said that there are several places, in which the terms in question, ὑπὸ τοῦ Πνεύματος and ἐν τῷ Πνεύματι, cannot refer to a vision, but to plain facts and realities. For instance, Luke ii. 27, Simeon "came by the Spirit, ἐν τῷ Πνεύματι, into the temple." It is evident that he came *actually*, and not in a vision or in imagination. Again, Luke iv. 14, "Jesus returned in the power of the Spirit into Galilee," ἐν τῇ δυνάμει τοῦ Πνεύματος. This most certainly means that he *actually returned*, in the literal sense of the word, and not in a vision. And let it be noticed here, that this passage refers to his returning from the scene of his temptation to preach the Gospel; as his *returning* then is literal in the one case, is it not necessary to understand his *going* in the same sense in the other? His returning "in the power of the Spirit," or "by the power of the Spirit," into Galilee, signifies, not that he returned in a vision, but actually; and as the same preposition is used, is it not fair to say that it has the same meaning in the other place? Farmer maintains it means that he was furnished with the gifts of the Spirit, to enable him to preach and work miracles. Were we to grant this, it by no means excludes the leading and guidance of the Spirit, causing him to go into the place specified; but this is not its natural signification here; as the Holy Spirit had been poured out on him before, when he was baptized, for the purposes specified by Farmer, and that very recently. Again, we read, Acts viii. 39, "The Spirit of the Lord caught away Philip, so that the eunuch saw him no more," Πνεῦμα Κυρίου ἥρπασε. Here, also, it is plain that this was not done in a vision, but really; and if it should be said, "Perhaps this means no more than that the Spirit rendered Philip invisible to the eunuch," it may be replied, that this is not the natural meaning of the word employed, or rather, it is never used in this sense; and even were we to allow this, it makes no difference in the force of our argument, for there was no vision, or ecstasy, or trance, in the case. Again, Acts xiii. 4, we read, "So they being sent forth by the Holy Ghost, ὑπὸ τοῦ Πνεύματος τοῦ ἁγίου, departed unto Seleucia." Here, again, the formula ὑπὸ τοῦ Πνεύματος cannot relate to a vision; it can mean nothing else than that by the influence, and in obedience to the command of the Holy Ghost, they actually went unto Seleucia. Other instances might be adduced; but these are quite sufficient to prove that the expressions under consideration do not, by any means, naturally signify a vision or trance caused by the influence of the Spirit. Thus, I hope, it is manifest that one main pillar, or rather the main pillar, of Farmer's system is utterly insufficient for its support.

As a recommendation of his hypothesis, Farmer urges the advantages which are secured by his view of the subject. I must think it is easy to show that all the advantages which he specifies, are more obviously and effectually secured by the common hypothesis. For instance, he maintains that "the several scenes of which it is composed contain a real trial, such as occasioned a very bright display of the virtue and piety of our Redeemer, and yet he was not accessary to his own temptation; the mind being passive to all the scenes which are presented to it in a vision." And then he strangely asserts, "But upon the common hypothesis there was no temptation at all, and if there had been any, his being exposed to them was the matter of his own choice."* But his assertion, that on the common hypothesis it was no trial at all, is founded on something which many of the maintainers of the ordinary interpretation will by no means grant, nay, on what they

* Inquiry, p. 116.

positively *deny*, and think they can disprove; namely, that the devil appeared in what may be called his own form, or in such a way that he could be immediately recognised. They think that he would, doubtless, put in requisition all his power and craft, in order to conceal himself. This he did when he seduced our first parents, and it may confidently be asserted, that whenever he tempts, he always, in one respect or another, puts on the appearance of an angel of light. And there are some at least of the advocates of the common hypothesis, who never felt any difficulty in the question, " Why the devil should assault our Lord at all, and what advantage he could possibly hope to gain over him?" On the contrary, it would have been a much greater difficulty and wonder, in their estimation, if Satan had not, as far as he was permitted, tempted him. What right have we to suppose, however it may have been asserted by some, and taken for granted by others, that Satan knew in what sense Jesus Christ was the Son of God, or that he was acquainted with the doctrine of his divinity? These truths were but obscurely revealed in the Old Testament; they were but very imperfectly known by the Saviour's own apostles till after the descent of the Spirit on the day of Pentecost. Who was to teach them to Satan? He saw the Redeemer in his human nature, like others, frail and mortal, and the subject of all sinless infirmities. He had prevailed against our first parents notwithstanding their innocence and holiness, and the peculiar privileges which they enjoyed; why might he not hope to vanquish the Saviour also, who, in some respects, was apparently inferior to them, and placed in much more disadvantageous circumstances? And if he knew the design with which our Lord appeared in the world, could his malice and rage suffer him to forbear attacking the great Captain of salvation? Nay, were we to allow that Satan was acquainted with the divinity of Jesus Christ, there would be no inconsistency or difficulty in conceiving that the assault would be made, for he might hope to harass and impede the Redeemer, which, to use the language of the poet,

"If not victory, is yet revenge."

But we must likewise remember, that with all the craft, and policy, and natural sagacity, which Satan possesses, he is the most foolish, because the most wicked being in existence, and it is the very property of folly and wickedness to act irrationally. "Though the devil be exceedingly cunning and subtle, yet he is one of the greatest fools and blockheads in the world, as the subtlest of wicked men are. Sin is of such a nature, that it exceedingly infatuates and stultifies the mind; men deliberately choose eternal torments, rather than miss of the pleasure of a few days. Sin has the same effect on the devils, to make them act like fools; and so much the more, as it *is greater* in them than in others."* What success, what benefit, could Satan propose to himself, on any rational principles, in rebelling against the Most High at first, or in continuing his course of opposition to him? and if he could act thus foolishly and irrationally in heaven, of what folly is he not capable in hell? He must know that he is only increasing his own misery, plunging himself deeper and deeper in the bottomless gulf of guilt and wretchedness. He must know that to desist from provoking God, and to endeavour to propitiate him, would, at the least, render him less miserable than he must otherwise be; and yet he perseveres, and omits no opportunity of provoking the Almighty. This is just as irrational as to make an attack on Jesus Christ, even if he knew his divinity. It may be said that despair urges him on, in the first case; it would equally do so in the second.

The difficulty, then, which Farmer here has in view, as incumbering the hypothesis of his opponents, exists, I must say, only in his own imagination. And although he

* Edwards, vol. ii. p. 612.

asserts, in the quotation which has been made, that "each of the scenes of which the temptation was composed, contained a real trial, such as caused a bright display of the virtue and piety of our Redeemer," yet in another place he speaks doubtfully on this point. For he says that "it is *possible* this vision *might* contain a present trial."* Without denying the *possibility* of this, or the fact that it would, *in some* degree, have caused a development of the principles and character of the Saviour, surely it must be evident, that if the temptations were real, and carried on by Satan himself, the trial was far greater, and the manifestations of the virtue and piety of the Redeemer much more effectual and conspicuous; for we suppose that Satan concealed himself as much as possible from the Saviour, and assumed in one way or another the appearance of an angel of light, and that he proposed his temptations in the most artful way. On Farmer's hypothesis, Jesus Christ must have known the tempter, so that all the objections which, on this account, are urged against the common interpretation, apply to his with more than double force; and on his scheme there was no pressure of *real want* in the first temptation, and no influence of external circumstances and concealment of the tempter in the other. Farmer thinks that one advantage of his scheme is that, according to it, "the Saviour was not accessary to his own temptation; and on the common hypothesis his being exposed to it, was the matter of his own choice." And what then? Was not his being exposed to temptation at all, was not his undertaking the work of human redemption, and all the labours, and temptations, and sufferings attendant on it, the matter of his own choice? And was not this his glory, and one thing that contributed essentially to the perfection of his work? But it is not true that he exposed himself to temptation, without a call from the very highest authority; for he was "*led*

* Page 83.

by the Spirit into the wilderness to be tempted." And whenever the Spirit leads any one into temptation, it is his duty to go.

Farmer attaches great importance to the *symbolical design* of the vision on his theory. He thinks it gave Jesus Christ an interesting and instructive view of all the temptations which awaited him during his ensuing ministry, and, therefore, had a tendency to prepare him for them. But we ask, was it at all necessary on this account? Did he not know well, before this, from the experience which he had, ere he commenced his public labours, and especially from the influence of the Spirit which descended on him at his baptism, all that awaited him, and all that he had undertaken? Could such a comparatively obscure, symbolical representation, as that which Farmer thinks his temptation was, add to the clearness of his views, or the extent of his knowledge? Rather, had it been intended to answer this purpose, it would have required his previous knowledge to understand and apply it. This supposed vision did not give him the least intimation respecting his death, or the treachery of one of his disciples; and yet he knew from the beginning that he was to be delivered to be crucified, and who believed not, and who should betray him; so that, on Farmer's hypothesis, I cannot see any important end whatever that was answered by his temptation.

He thinks that his scheme will "teach the adversaries of the Gospel, that they ought to be cautious in taking offence at any particular passages in it, that may have been injudiciously explained." But I must think, that to explain away the obvious meaning of the Scriptures, and to wrest their language to suit a favourite hypothesis, will give the adversaries of the Bible a greater advantage over it, and do more to prejudice them against it, than a plain statement of its facts and doctrines, with all their attendant difficulties and mysteries, can possibly do. " The foolishness of God is wiser than men, and the weakness of God is stronger than men."

Another advantage which Farmer thinks his system secures is, that it exalts the character of Christ, and confirms our faith in his Divine mission, because of the trial to which it exposed him, and the view which it gave him of the future difficulties of his ministry. "He foresaw all the evils which he was to combat, the very worst to which human nature is liable. He knew that he was to spend his life in want and contumely, and then to finish it on the cross."* True; but, as we have just seen, he did not, he could not, obtain that knowledge from anything that occurred during his temptation in the wilderness, not even if it had been a symbolical representation; for there was no allusion to his *death*, much less to his death on *the cross*. He evidently learned what was to come upon him from another source, which afforded him a much clearer foreknowledge "from the beginning" of all the trials and sufferings he was to undergo in the execution of his office. This knowledge did, indeed, "add the highest lustre to his character." And, as we may afterwards show, so did the temptation in the wilderness, but in a way different from that which Farmer supposes, and in a degree far superior.

I would not be uncharitable, or bring anything like unfounded or rash charges against any one; especially against a man of Farmer's ability and learning. I am willing to allow that he was sincerely desirous to serve the cause of religion, and that he was convinced that his scheme was calculated to do so. But I cannot avoid saying, that surely nothing but a strong propensity to fancy everything good in his own hypothesis, could have led him to add, in the third place, that his account of Christ's temptation "furnishes ample instruction and consolation to his disciples under those manifold and great

* Inquiry, p. 119.

temptations that they may have to encounter."* What great consolation and instruction can they derive from his having an imaginary scene presented to him in a vision, where the temptations were very feeble, if they existed at all; where the scenes and the trials were such as they can never realise? Abundant consolation and instruction are indeed afforded by our Saviour's temptation in the wilderness, as well as by his previous knowledge of all that he had to perform and suffer, and the part which he acted through his whole life; but this will be the case *only* when the temptation is considered as real, and his knowledge as being much more accurate than what could possibly be obtained from any symbolical representations that could be given him in such a vision as Farmer imagines.

Such is a short, but, as far as I have been able to accomplish my design, a correct representation of the arguments by which Farmer supports his system, and the advantages with which he thinks it is attended. The former I must deem fallacious; and the latter are, in some cases, only imaginary, and in others, the alleged advantages result more abundantly from the ordinary interpretation. The only advantage, as far as I can see, which it secures, is that it avoids the necessity of supposing that Satan conveyed Jesus Christ through the air, or persuaded him to go, first to the pinnacle of the temple, and then to the mountain where he was shown all the kingdoms of the world, and all their glory. On these statements we may afterwards make a few remarks. But, in addition to the want of sufficient evidence, his system is liable to very serious objections. It departs, without necessity and without warrant, from the plain and obvious sense of the narration. It attributes, in the plainest language, to the devil that in which he had no influence, in which he acted no part, any more than if he had had no existence; nay, I

* Inquiry, p. 123.

had almost said, it represents the Spirit of God as ascribing that of which he himself was the author, to Satan. Had Farmer's scheme been correct, I must think, notwithstanding all he has advanced to meet the objection, that the sacred historian would have said, The *Spirit* set him on the pinnacle of the temple, and, The *Spirit* took him up to a high mountain. It might be necessary, on Farmer's hypothesis, to represent Satan as tempting, but not as conveying the Redeemer from one place to another. *This*, if Farmer's sentiments respecting Satan are correct, is what he not only *did not*, but what he *could* not do; for he supposes he has no power over matter. Farmer confesses, or rather maintains, that to the view and apprehension of Christ at the time, the vision contained certain *alluring proposals,* made to him by the devil, in order to solicit him to *evil;* * and he does not mean here that Christ learned from the vision, that these alluring representations would be made to him afterwards, in the course of his ministry, but they were made to him *at that time,* as he is showing that " the vision *bore the form of a present trial.*" If so, then inevitably the Spirit of God, according to Farmer's scheme, presented "alluring proposals to the mind of Christ, which had a tendency to solicit him to evil." And farther, I must maintain and repeat it, that on this scheme, there was no adequate important end answered; as Christ already possessed all the knowledge professed to be communicated, and was soon to be exposed to much severer trials than any by which he could possibly be exercised in a vision.

For all these reasons, and for others which may be afterwards stated, I must reject Farmer's scheme, and adopt the common interpretation of this important passage; and believe that Jesus Christ was actually led by the influence of the Holy Spirit into a sterile, uninhabited part of the wilderness; that Satan really appeared to him in dis-

* Inquiry, p. 149.

guise, and endeavoured first to induce him to change stones into food; and then to cast himself down from the pinnacle of the temple; and then, in order to obtain the possession of all the kingdoms of the world, to fall down and worship the being who had shown him this wonderful sight. Before making any particular remarks on these various temptations, I shall consider the objections which Farmer urges against what is called the literal scheme.

First. He objects that "it is unsuitable to the sagacity and policy of Satan, because his personal appearance could serve only to frustrate his intention." But this objection is founded on a false hypothesis. None of those who adopt the literal scheme think that Satan appeared in his proper character. We may, as has already been stated, be certain that he did not. It would not be difficult to show that Farmer's attempt to prove that he must, if he appeared at all, have done so in his proper form, is an entire failure. The question is not, what our Lord *knew;* but what Satan attempted, what was the imposition which he endeavoured to practise. And even our Lord's calling him Satan in the last temptation will not, of itself, prove that he knew him; since he called his own disciple Peter, Satan, when he merely meant that he was acting the part of Satan, or of an adversary.

Secondly. He objects that "this explication is very ill calculated to promote the honour of the Saviour, or the instruction and consolation of his disciples. We can scarcely preserve on our minds a sufficient reverence of the sanctity of the Redeemer, when we behold him in such familiar conference with, and under the power of an unclean spirit, who at pleasure transports his Sovereign and his Judge from place to place, raises him to the most conspicuous stations to expose him to public derision, and wantonly and arrogantly propounds to him one foolish enterprise after another."* Now it deserves consideration

* Inquiry, p. 12.

whether this objection, if it has any force, does not militate against his own hypothesis, partly at least, as well as against that of his opponents; for if it would not be consistent with the dignity of the Redeemer to *be* thus treated, would it be consistent with his dignity to be *caused to think* that he was thus treated, or with the veracity of the Spirit of truth to produce the deception? But, not to insist on this, there is nothing in the literal scheme which represents our Saviour as exposed to public scorn; for if he was seen when on the pinnacle of the temple, which is not certain, his position and appearance would excite *wonder* rather than *scorn*. And it is not at all intimated or granted, that he remained long there, to attract much public notice; and in the other temptation none saw him. And with regard to foolish enterprises being proposed to him, sinful enterprises are always foolish; but what other has Satan to propose? It was a foolish enterprise that he proposed to our first parents, to try to become as gods, and yet he succeeded; and how often have his most ridiculous proposals been accepted! And why should it be thought inconsistent with the dignity and power of the Saviour to be transported by Satan from place to place, when "he hid not his face from shame and spitting," and did not refuse patiently to endure the most ignominious treatment from the most wicked and worthless of mortals? Nay, he suffered himself to be nailed to the cross betwixt convicted thieves. How foolish is it to urge, that because the Saviour permitted Satan to place him on the pinnacle of the temple, he was accessary to his own dishonour, danger, and temptation! There was no dishonour in the case, any more than in being crucified. And it was as necessary that the Saviour should obtain a spiritual and moral victory over Satan by resisting his temptations, as it was that he should die on the cross. Farmer might with just as much propriety maintain, that Jesus Christ was accessary to his own disgrace and death, by becoming incarnate. Nor was there any real danger of falling from the pinnacle on which he was placed; at least, none but what the Saviour knew he could avoid. And as to *temptation, he came into the world for this very purpose, that he might meet and vanquish temptation;* and it was only by doing so that he could accomplish his work, and become the Saviour of his people, and be "able to succour these that are tempted."

On this part of the subject, Farmer maintains that the passage, Heb. iv. 15, "He was in all points tempted like as we are, yet without sin," cannot, on the common hypothesis, refer to our Saviour's temptation in the wilderness, because we are not tempted by Satan in person, appearing in a visible form, as he is supposed to have done to our Saviour. But did he never appear in a visible form to any of those who were saved by Christ, and rescued from the power of the devil? Did he not appear in a visible form (not his own) to our first parents, when he tempted them? and have we not reason to hope that they were saved by Jesus Christ? And as the first Adam was tempted in this way, and Satan might suppose that it gives him some peculiar advantage over those whom he assaults, does it not appear fit and becoming, in some respects, that he should be permitted to attack the second Adam, the Saviour, the seed of the woman, in this way also, that in all things Jesus Christ might be "made like unto his brethren," in all the forms in which ever any of them were assaulted by the tempter? And with regard to his example not being a complete pattern of virtue if he voluntarily exposed himself to temptation, it is enough to observe that it is not only our duty to pray against temptation, and to flee from it, but also to *face it in all its forms* whenever we can be sure, as Christ was, that we are in the path of duty, and following the guidance of the Spirit of God.

Another objection which is urged against the literal scheme is, that it "ascribes to the devil the performance of the greatest miracles,"* such as assuming a visible form, speaking with an audible voice, and conveying men from place to place; and the principal argument which he employs against his being able to do these is, "that we have no proof from experience, our sole instructor in the established laws of nature, that Satan can do any of these." But how limited is our experience! How egregiously shall we err, if we make it the measure of all that is possible, of all that spirits can do, of all that has been! We have no experience of the performance of miracles; but shall we therefore conclude that none were ever wrought? This is exactly Hume's argument against miracles in general, which has been so effectually refuted by Campbell and others. But this objection is founded entirely on Farmer's theory respecting evil spirits, which is by no means granted. It is evident from many examples recorded in the Scriptures, that good angels have the power of assuming a visible form, of speaking with an audible voice, and of removing bodies from one place to another; and that doing so does not imply a miracle in the proper sense of the word. But on this subject some remarks have already been made, which need not be repeated here. The rest of his objections will be noticed in the review of the different temptations, to which I shall therefore now proceed; noticing only such particulars as bear more directly on the subject of this Lecture. And it will be evident, from what has been said, that I adopt the literal scheme, as being that which is suggested by the language of the evangelist, agrees best with the scope and connexion of the passage, is most honourable to the Saviour and to the Spirit of God, and most instructive and consolatory to the Christian, as implying the greatest victory over Satan, and with him, over all the hosts of hell.

In the account which we have of the first temptation, Luke, chap. iv. 1, informs us that Jesus " being full of the

* Inquiry, p. 19.

Holy Ghost, returned from Jordan," where he had just been baptized by John, and it was at his baptism that the Spirit descended on him; so that if this phrase denotes, as Farmer would have us to believe, that he was wrapt up in a vision or trance, it would seem to follow that his return from the river was only imaginary or visionary, and not real; for his return from Jordan, as well as his being led into the wilderness, took place under the influence of the Holy Ghost. He was led by the influence of the Spirit, or, as Mark expresses it, "was *driven*," that is, urged by strong impulse to go, into the wilderness. It is of no importance where this wilderness was, whether, as some suppose, it was the desert of Horeb, which they think was called by way of eminence "the wilderness," or some desert part of the wilderness of Judea. Maundrel, who inspected those places, gives it as his opinion that it might be the wilderness near Jordan, which, as he assures us, "is a miserable and horrid place, consisting of high barren mountains, so that it looks as if nature there had suffered some horrid convulsions."* In such a place it is natural to suppose wild beasts would be found, and accordingly Mark informs us that "he was with the wild beasts." In this dreary region he remained all alone forty days, during which time he abstained from food, partly, perhaps, because the exercises of his mind and his conflicts with Satan were so interesting and absorbing, that he disregarded the demands of nature, or scarcely ever felt them. Still there was something miraculous in his being preserved so long without food, and, perhaps, he was preserved from the cravings of appetite, for it was not till he had fasted forty days, that " he afterwards hungered:" doubtless he was engaged all the while in prayer and meditation, subject to the attacks of Satan, made on him with all the skill and power that this great enemy could put in requisition. The attention of Satan must have been arrested by the extra-

* Maundrel's Travels, p. 78.

ordinary birth of Jesus Christ, and the remarkable scenes of his childhood and youth; but especially by the testimony and preaching of John, and by what took place at his baptism. Whether, then, the tempter knew in what sense Jesus Christ was the Son of God or not, he had heard and seen enough to assure him that the son of Mary was some extraordinary being, and that he was probably the Messiah promised to the fathers. This was sufficient to excite his malice and rage, and God was pleased to permit him to assume a visible form, and make a personal attack on the blessed Redeemer, and that in circumstances the most favourable for his purpose; in consequence of which the defeat of the great destroyer, and the victory of the Saviour, were the more conspicuous. It was a remarkable coincidence, nay, much more than a coincidence, for it was doubtless the arrangement of infinite wisdom, and designed for the instruction of the church, as well as the trial of the Redeemer, that as Moses fasted forty days when the law was given, (or rather twice, forty days and forty nights) and Elias, when the honour of the law was, in a special manner, vindicated by him, so that he has been called its restorer, abstained from food during an equal period; so Jesus Christ, when he publicly commenced that course of obedience by which the law was fulfilled and honoured, fasted the same length of time. It is by activity and labour, and self-denial, and not by indulgence, that great things are accomplished, that God is glorified, temptations are overcome, and high honours are secured. "Forasmuch, then, as Christ hath suffered for us in the flesh, arm yourselves also with the same mind; for he that hath suffered in the flesh hath ceased from sin." Such coincidences as these show the unity of the Scriptures, that all things were known to their Author from the beginning, and that one great, simple, yet complex plan is developed and carried into execution by all the different dispensations of providence and of religion which the Scriptures have introduced or presented to the world. "There are diversities of administrations, but the same Spirit, and the same Lord."

During the whole of these forty days, he was tempted of Satan. Farmer thinks that his visionary temptation continued through all this period; and that the *time* is to be taken literally, however figurative everything else may be; though, after all his special pleading and criticism, I cannot see his consistency here. In Daniel and the Revelation the time is not given literally; in these visions, we have "times, and a time, and a half," in days, for years. This is one argument for the literal scheme. How Satan tempted him during these forty days, how the conflict was carried on, we are not told; and conjecture would be fruitless, and entirely unsatisfactory. We may conclude, however, that the great adversary would vary his mode of attack; and it is by no means certain that he did not assume some visible form before the close of the forty days, when he made his last, and it seems his grand assault, for that time. Hence, as Doddridge correctly observes, the words of Matthew should be translated, "And the tempter *coming* to him," which rather implies that he had attacked him before. At the end of these forty days he felt the demands of appetite; nature craved its appropriate supply. Of this Satan took advantage, as we may be sure he always does of the circumstances, and feelings, and appetites of those whom he wishes to seduce, and said to him, "If thou be the Son of God, command that these stones be made bread," or become loaves. Now it is most absurd to suppose, as Farmer would have the maintainers of the literal scheme to do, that he "appeared in his own proper shape," (what that is, I am at a loss to determine,) or in any form which would betray him, or in which he would be easily recognised. Perhaps he assumed the form of a man wandering in the desert, and professed to have heard of the character and claims of Jesus Christ, and that he wished to ascertain the truth respecting him; and suggested that if the Saviour would work this miracle, he would both satisfy his own appetite, which he might surely do with the greatest propriety, when his fast of forty days was ended, and would also enlighten and guide an inquirer after truth ; which was one purpose of his coming into the world : or Satan might assume some other form, and try to provoke and irritate the Saviour to show his power. He could not, on this occasion, assume the appearance of a good angel ; for no inhabitant of heaven would have expressed a doubt whether or not Jesus Christ was the Son of God, or would have undertaken to suggest to him what he should do. Now this was a temptation not only to distrust the goodness and providential care of his heavenly Father, and to question whether he would provide for him, in due time, or not, but also to impatience under his present trial, as well as to prefer the gratification of his senses, to following the dictates of reason and conscience, and to entire obedience to the command of God. Satan had prevailed against Eve, partly, by appealing to her appetite, and by exciting its cravings ; by directing her attention to a tree good for food, and pleasant to the eyes ; (how many victories has he gained by the same means !) and he hoped in this way to overcome Jesus Christ likewise. But how much more powerful was the temptation in the case of our Saviour, than in that of our first parents ! *They* had access to all the trees of the garden, numbers of which were doubtless " good for food, and pleasant to the eyes :" they could not have felt the painful cravings of appetite. *Jesus Christ* was in a desert, where no supplies could be obtained, and had fasted forty days, and nature was urgently demanding a supply for her wants. They transgressed an express positive command. There was no such command, as far as we know, given to the Saviour ; he was left to infer from circumstances how it was proper for him to act. And yet they were overcome, and he triumphed. It is impossible to prove, as some attempt to do, that this temptation was weak, or that it scarcely deserves the name of a temptation, but on principles, or for reasons, which would equally apply to all his trials; and thus it would follow, that instead of being "in all points tempted like as we are," he was never so tempted at all. And likewise, let it be observed, that he would be much more clearly and forcibly taught what temptations of a similar kind awaited him, and therefore that he must never, amidst all the poverty to which he submitted for the sake of man, and all the sufferings to which it exposed him, work a miracle for the supply of the most urgent necessities of nature, than he could have been by any visionary representation, exhibited to his mind by a trance or ecstasy; so that the literal scheme answers even the end to which its opponents think the whole temptation was intended to be subservient, much better than the visionary one could possibly do.

Jesus Christ was clad in the armour of righteousness on the right hand and on the left. He was effectually fortified against temptation by correct views and holy principles. He was furnished with the sword of the Spirit, and he knew well how to wield it, and by it he overcame. He immediately answered, "It is written," in the history of the Israelites, when they were, as I now am, in a desert, and were entirely dependent on the special providence of God, and therefore the declaration is in every point of view applicable to my circumstances, "Man shall not live by bread only, but by every word that proceedeth out of the mouth of God shall he live." Deut. viii. 3. It is of greater importance that he should obey the command of God, than that he should procure his necessary food in the most pressing exigencies. The meaning of this expression, as applied by the Redeemer to himself, may perhaps be learned from his declaration on another occasion, John iv. When the disciples besought him, saying, "Master, eat," he replied, "My meat and my drink is to do the will of my heavenly Father, and to finish his work." This was more important in the estimation of the Redeemer, and more refreshing and animating to his frame, than the choicest viands could be; and he perhaps knew it was the will of God that he should fast till angels came from heaven to minister to him: though, when we consider the connexion in which the words stand in Deuteronomy, and their original application to the Israelites, their meaning would seem to be, God can support me without bread by his powerful word; or he can furnish me, as he did them, with a miraculous supply; and therefore I will depend on him, and wait for him, and not abuse my power of working miracles, by an application of it to a purpose which it was never intended to serve. Whatever may be in this, we learn, from the answer of the Saviour, the important truth, that all things which God has spoken and recorded in the volume of inspiration will, if believed and obeyed, contribute to *spiritual*, and therefore to *eternal* life, and that disobedience to any of them produces *spiritual*, and exposes to *eternal* death.

The next temptation includes the greatest difficulty to those who adopt the literal scheme. We are informed, Matt. iv. 5, "Then the devil taketh him up into Jerusalem, the holy city, and setteth him on a pinnacle," or on a wing, or on one of the battlements, "of the temple." Now there is plainly no necessity for maintaining or allowing that this temptation immediately followed the other. We are at liberty to suppose that Satan retired, and assumed another form, probably that of a celestial spirit, sent to render some service to Jesus, or to give him the opportunity of performing a miracle; and for this purpose to convey him to the pinnacle of the temple. The great difficulty which presents itself here,—and it is one which all who adopt this interpretation must have felt, — is, how did Satan accomplish this? and how was it consistent with the dignity of the Son of God, to permit himself thus to be transported from place to place, by the prince of hell? We have already answered the latter part of the objection. It was as necessary for Christ to be tempted, and to vanquish temptation, as it was to die and to overcome death. He could do either the one or the other, only in consequence of his voluntarily exposing himself to it, only by determinately, as it were, entering into a contest with the enemies of his people; and it was no more inconsistent with his dignity to permit Satan to take him from place to place, than to suffer his enemies to bind and buffet him, and to spit on his face, and to nail him to the tree. "He humbled himself, and became obedient unto death," exposing himself to the attacks of Satan and to every kind of indignity. Those who adopt the hypothesis that the temptation of the Saviour took place in a vision, are fond of representing the matter as if, in the literal scheme, it is supposed or allowed, that Satan appeared in his *own form*, or in such a way that he could be recognised by even the spectators, who might behold him as the prince of hell; carried the Saviour through the air in some such way as a ravenous bird does its prey; or persuaded or forced the Redeemer to accompany him, and to engage in conversation all the way. This is to caricature the matter, not to describe it. The evangelist has not informed us how he took or brought him, first to the temple, and then to the mountain. We know little or nothing of the powers of unembodied spirits, especially of one so mighty as Satan doubtless is; and therefore we are not concerned to specify the mode, nor do we think it incumbent on us to answer objections founded on any imaginary schemes. But if Satan appeared as a man, and induced the Saviour to accompany him, he doubtless assumed the form of a good man; and as the knowledge of Jesus Christ, in his human nature, *was not infinite*, as it was capable of increase, Luke ii. 52, he might be left in ignorance of what Satan was till he discovered himself by the proposal he made; and then, if the Jews saw him, they could have no conception of the character of the being who accompanied Jesus Christ; or if he was carried through the air, it was done by Satan in the guise of a good angel, and perhaps, in such a way as to be visible to none. Lightfoot* indeed asserts that "our Saviour, as he flew in the air, and as he stood on the temple, was visible and conspicuous to the people;" but we have no evidence that this was the case; and it is very unlikely, were we to grant that he was conveyed through the air, that this would be done in such a way as Lightfoot supposes. As to the part of the temple on which he was placed, those who have paid far more attention to the form of that edifice than I can pretend to have done, are not agreed, nor can it be *determined* from the word πτερύγιον, which is employed by the evangelist. Farmer, indeed, raises vast difficulties here, as if there was no part of the temple on which he could be placed, or to which he could ascend. The remark of Doddridge is as pertinent, and his conjecture as likely, as any I have met with,—that though "pinnacle" agrees very well with the etymology of the Greek word, yet according to its use amongst us, it leads the English reader to suppose that he stood on the top of a spire. The truth is, the top of the temple was flat, and had a kind of battlement round it; and on the edge of this battlement we may suppose that Satan placed Christ in attacking him with this temptation."†

Perhaps, as Satan saw that Jesus Christ was subject to the common infirmities of human nature, he thought that if he could induce him to cast himself down, and if no angel should come to his rescue, he might be dashed to pieces at the bottom, and being found by the Jews in this condition, he might be charged with self-destruction, and thus he would be ruined both as regarded his life and his character. But, doubtless, his great design was to induce the Redeemer to work an unnecessary miracle, to presume

* Works, vol. i. p. 507. † Doddridge in loc.

on the providence of God, and on a miraculous preservation, without a warrant, and in such a way as would amount to a tempting of God, and thus to lead him into sin; and perhaps also Satan wished to excite ostentatious feelings in his breast, as the miracle would arrest the attention of all who were about that part of the temple, and thus a striking proof would be given that he was the Son of God and the Saviour of the world, as well as an evidence that he could depend on the promise of his heavenly Father for preservation as well as for food; though I must own I am disposed to question whether the proof of his Messiahship, or of his being the Son of God, was any part of this temptation, or of the end proposed to be answered by throwing himself down from the temple. To have answered this end the claim should have been announced to the spectators, and their attention should have been arrested, and then the miracle performed in confirmation of the doctrine which had been stated. And Jesus Christ had not yet commenced his ministry, and therefore had not claimed to be regarded as the Son of God and the Saviour of the world, unless indeed by the preaching of the Baptist. However, presumption, by a wanton exposure of himself to destruction, and an unwarrantable dependence on the promise of God, were the only ends, as far as we know, that Satan proposed to him, and to which the Saviour alluded in his answer, "Thou shalt not tempt the Lord thy God." Satan had endeavoured to wrest from the Redeemer the sword of the Spirit, and thus to vanquish him with his own weapons; but he was immediately baffled in his attempts, and laid prostrate at the feet of him who, amidst all the weakness of humanity, was still the Lord of hosts, mighty in battle, and able to spoil principalities and powers. We are taught by the reply and example of the Saviour, that we tempt God whenever we expose ourselves unnecessarily to danger, and hope to be preserved by a special interposition of providence; or whenever we expect the end, without using the means; or place unwarrantable trust on the Divine promises.

The objections which the opponents of the literal scheme urge against it, because it implies that Satan performed miracles, (Farmer is pleased to say, the greatest miracles, such as appearing in a visible form, conveying the Saviour through the air, &c.,) have already partly been answered. No miracle, properly speaking, was performed. The laws of nature were neither suspended nor contravened, unless it can be proved, which has not yet been done, that Satan cannot assume a visible form, or exert any influence on matter. The contrary appears to be the case, from the facts which are recorded in the Bible respecting the ministry of angels. Something wonderful indeed may have been effected, which might have appeared a miracle to those that did not understand it. But how often do men perform that which appears wonderful or even miraculous to some of their fellow-creatures, by taking advantage of the laws of nature, and rendering them subservient to their purpose! If Satan has the power of rendering himself visible, and of removing a quantity of matter from one place to another, no law of nature was controlled or suspended, even were we to allow that he conveyed the Saviour through the air.

Perhaps to add force to this temptation, Satan assumed the appearance of a good angel, and pretended that he was sent to guard him, and thus to afford him a striking proof of the care of his heavenly Father, and of the truth of his word, and to show him that he might securely depend on it in time to come. And if the promise related to the saints in general, most assuredly the Son of God had a special interest in it; *He* might *depend* on its accomplishment.

Many of the remarks which have been made, will apply to the third temptation, especially as it regards the conveyance of the Saviour to the top of a high mountain. It is of no importance, as it is impossible to determine where this mountain was. The principal difficulty that presents itself here is, how could all the kingdoms of the world, in their glory, be shown in a moment of time, or shown at all? By what means was this done? Great importance is by some attached to the words, "a moment," or "an instant of time," ἐν στιγμῇ χρόνου. Farmer strangely maintains, that the literal scheme supposes the performance of what was not only miraculous, but absolutely impossible, because, at the least, Jesus Christ must have had time to turn himself round, and survey all these scenes, and this could not be done in an instant. But surely this is mere trifling. It is not said that all these were presented to him, or exhibited to his view, so that he might *survey* them in a moment of time. Besides, what occasion is there to take these words literally? How often do we say that we will do things in a moment, when we mean, and are well understood to mean, that we will do them immediately, or in a very short time! And similar forms of speech are, doubtless, found in all languages.

Not to dwell on the different theories which have been advanced respecting the manner of the exhibition in question, that which supposes it was done in a kind of panoramic scene, or visionary representation, seems by far the most eligible. There is a great difference between allowing that Satan could operate on the senses and mind of the Saviour, and throw him into a trance, and cause him to believe that a thousand things which had no existence were realities, so that he should be affected by them as if he had actually seen and heard them, and supposing that he could present a striking scene, by exhibiting a beautiful picture of actual realities, which would excite lively ideas of the original, while the Saviour was not deceived, but still knew that it was but a picture. Men can do the latter; what difficulty, then, is there in supposing that Satan, with all his powers, and knowledge, and experience, can do it more effectually? He probably intended to deceive Jesus Christ here, to cause him to think that what he saw was a reality; and to aid the deception, he took him up to a very high mountain. There is no necessity, however, for allowing that Jesus Christ was deceived; though if he had been the subject of what is called a *deceptio visûs*, this would not have been at all dishonourable to him; it would have been an illustration of an important fact, that in all things, as far as the innocent weaknesses of human nature were concerned, "he was made like unto his brethren." Lightfoot* says, "Now the acting of Satan in this delusion was the framing of an airy horizon before the eyes of Christ, carrying such pompous and glorious appearances of kingdoms, and states, and royalties, and riches in the face of it, as if he had seen those very kingdoms, and their very state indeed;" and he applies to the illustration of this theory the difficult passage, Eph. ii. 2, "The prince of the power of the air," τὸν ἄρχοντα τῆς ἐξουσίας τοῦ ἀέρος, as if Satan was called "the prince of the power of the air," because he can operate on it, and by it form shadowy representations of things, causing them to appear as if they were realities.† This seems much more probable than that he showed him all the land of Judea, or any other part of the world. How could any view that could be given from a mountain, however lofty, even if the vision of the Saviour had been strengthened or assisted in the most remarkable manner, be with any propriety called, "showing him *all* the kingdoms of the world, and all their glory?" How small a portion of the earth, and in how indistinct a manner, can the strongest eye behold at once, from the most advantageous position!

The temptation was a promise, that if the Saviour would perform to the tempter, whoever he might be, one act of homage, all these kingdoms, and glory, and riches, should

---

* Works, vol. i. p. 599.   † See Appendix N.

be his; "for," says the father of lies, "all these are delivered to me, and to whomsoever I will, I give them." And Satan might think that the fact of his presenting them to him in so extraordinary a manner might aid the delusion which he was endeavouring to practise, and be considered as a proof that he indeed had them at his disposal, and might, therefore, induce Jesus Christ to comply with his terms. Lightfoot applies the promise to the Roman empire, and endeavours to show with how much truth Satan might say that all these were delivered to him; and he thinks that he might have actually fulfilled his promise to Jesus Christ, by raising him to the throne of the Cæsars. His remarks and reasonings, however, appear to me to be much more ingenious, if not fanciful, than solid.

Now, whatever may be thought respecting the strength of this temptation, it was much more powerful as a reality than in a vision; and it included in it all that Satan could offer,—all the pleasures and honours of the world, as well as all its riches and power. Satan was sure that Jesus Christ was a man, whatever he might be besides,—that he was subject to the sensibilities and affections of human nature. He well knew what sacrifices men will make, what crimes they will commit, how they will dare the wrath of the Almighty, in order to obtain possession of one kingdom. He might, therefore, rationally, in a sense, hope to excite the passion of ambition in the breast of Jesus Christ, to receive from him the required act of homage, and thus to accomplish his ruin, and that of the cause of God and of human happiness.

Promptly, and with becoming holy indignation, was the offer rejected, and the tempter rebuked, and commanded to depart. And here again, he was put to flight by the sword of the Spirit. "Get thee behind me, Satan." "Get thee hence; for it is written, Thou shalt worship the Lord thy God, and him only shalt thou serve." Satan was now caused to know that he was recognised, and his plans detected, and that it was in vain for him to make any further attempts; and, perhaps, Jesus assumed his authority as the Son of God, exerted his power, and positively commanded Satan to depart. Whatever may be in this, we are informed that "the devil departed from him for a season," which plainly implies that he intended to attack him again, and that he actually did so, though, as far as we know, not in the same manner, appearing in a visible form, and transporting him from place to place. This is by no means implied in the language of the evangelist. But that he did assault him afterwards is certain, from John xiv. 30, "The prince of this world cometh, and hath nothing in me." On the symbolical scheme, indeed, the words could not with propriety be used, for according to it, Satan had not attacked him at all, and he never, as far as we know, was the subject of another vision. Hence, Farmer labours hard, but very unsuccessfully, to explain this expression in a consistency with his hypothesis; and though he refers his implied returning to the realisation of the vision in the trials and temptations to which the Saviour was exposed, it could not be said, on this principle, that the devil departed from him even for a season; for as Jesus Christ entered forthwith on his personal ministry, these immediately commenced. The angels, we are informed, came and ministered to the victorious Saviour. They supplied him with the food which was necessary to recruit his exhausted frame. Doubtless this, as well as his fasting, is to be taken literally. This Farmer is obliged to allow; and this is another evidence that the whole account of the temptation is a literal record of what actually took place.

How insignificant are the victories of the most celebrated earthly conquerors over all the power of their fellow-men combined in the mightiest armies, when compared with the moral and spiritual victory which the Redeemer, on this occasion, gained over the prince of darkness, flushed and animated with the recollection of all the triumphs which he had achieved during four thousand years over multitudes of the human race, including many of the wisest and best that had ever appeared in the world; an Abraham, a Jacob, a David; commencing with their great progenitors in a state of innocency! The victory was gained in human nature, in circumstances the most advantageous to the tempter, and most unfavourable to the Saviour. What a contrast between his situation and that of our first parents in paradise! and yet he conquered, and they were overcome. Whatever the influence of the union of the Divine and human natures in the person of the Redeemer, the victory was achieved in the latter, amidst all its innocent infirmities, by the force of wisdom and noble principles, and holy dispositions; of love to God, and benevolence to the human race. What would have been the consequences if the Saviour had been overcome, if we may be allowed to make such a supposition! How direful were the results of the victory which was gained over Adam in paradise! What confusion, and crimes, and misery, have deluged the earth in consequence! But what must have been the result, if the second Adam, the champion of heaven and earth, of God and men, against the prince of darkness, the hosts of hell, had been vanquished! He fought and triumphed for us. And he says to all his people, "Be of good cheer; I have overcome the world." I have overcome Satan, and death, and hell. I have overcome temptation in all its forms; and, therefore, you shall overcome also. And hence the promise, "The God of peace shall bruise Satan under your feet shortly." What benefits and blessings may we all derive from the victory gained by the Redeemer on the occasion to which our attention has been directed! If we are still overcome by the great enemy of souls, because we will not enlist and fight under the Saviour's banner, our state is desperate, we must be as miserable for ever and ever as Satan can make us. On the contrary, if we gain the victory, the kingdom of heaven and all its glories are ours; and we can overcome only through the "blood of the Lamb," and by taking to us "the whole armour of God."

LECTURE VII.

THE AGENCY OF EVIL SPIRITS.

THE TEMPTATIONS OF SATAN IN THEIR COMMON OR ORDINARY FORM.

"We are not ignorant of his devices."—2 Cor. ii. 11.

We come now to the last, but in some respects the most important part of our subject, viz. the manner in which Satan exerts his power or agency through the medium of ordinary temptation. To his attacks in this way we are all exposed, at any time, and in ways, perhaps, of which it is difficult for us to form any idea. And were he permitted now to take possession of the persons of men as frequently and as far, as he did in the time of our Saviour; did we behold them every day, wherever we went, reduced on this account to the most deplorable situation by his power and malice, we should have much more to fear—as surely as the representations of the Scriptures are correct—from his invisible attacks, from his efforts to cause us to break the law of God, and to prevent us from availing ourselves of the provisions of the Gospel, than from anything he could do by inflicting either bodily or mental diseases. Nay, were we to admit all that the most credulous have reported and believed respecting oracles and witchcraft, and all the delusions that Satan has practised, and all the misery he has caused by these means, still his influence as a tempter has been more destructive than it would have been by all these practices and arts. In possessions, as far as he brought men under his power, so as to produce insanity, he deprived them, at the same time, of their responsibility, so that he could not involve them in guilt; and witchcraft and oracles have always been limited to a few persons and localities; but as tempters to sin by their invisible influence, evil spirits have ranged through the whole world; and we have no reason to think that any son or daughter of Adam has been exempted from their attack, or has not been led by them into the commission of sin. Every truly good man has constantly to wrestle with these fallen principalities and powers; and facts prove that delusions as gross have been imposed on men, and crimes as horrid have been practised, where oracles were unknown, as where they exerted all their power, and uttered the most egregious falsehoods as revelations from heaven, and enjoined, as the only way of escaping the vengeance of their supposed deities, the commission of the most shocking crimes. Though the Mexicans had their temples, and altars, and priests, they had not, as far as I have been able to learn, any oracles like those of Greece and Rome; and yet where was ever the human mind more fearfully darkened and perverted by ignorance and error, or the heart of man more depraved and debased by superstition? Where was ever *that* which is at once one of the most cruel, impious, and revolting crimes, to which Satan ever tempted, or which infatuated mortals ever perpetrated, practised to so great an extent as in Mexico? Or where did the genius of cruelty ever glut itself more with the most barbarous infliction of torment? What are all the human sacrifices that ever were demanded by the oracles of ancient heathenism, compared with the twenty, or sometimes fifty thousand, which, we are informed, were presented to his sanguinary deities by Montezuma in one year? Nay, where have greater abominations been practised, than among Jews and professed Christians, to whom were committed the oracles of God? And in the production of all these, Satan, as a tempter, has had a large influence. Who, then, has not cause to dread his craft, and malice, and power?

Who may not be injured, if not ruined, by his devices? How important, then, is it to know them! How arduous, and yet how necessary, is the attempt to point them out!

On the nature of temptation, and on the import of the word, it is not necessary to dwell. It signifies in general to try or prove, to put to the test of experiments: the word נָסָה, which is generally used in Hebrew to signify trial or probation, and hence temptation, comes from one that signifies to try by the smell; and this sense will sometimes enable men to ascertain the most subtle, hidden qualities of objects; and in a general way it means to try, to prove, in order to ascertain. In Greek, the word that signifies to tempt, πειράζω, comes from one, πείρω, which means to pierce, to bore through, "to pierce a vessel, that the liquor which is in it may be known;"* and, therefore, it signifies a thorough, effectual trial, by experience and facts. It is employed in either a good or a bad sense, for a trial or experiment made either by God, for the most holy and benevolent, or by Satan, for the most wicked and malignant purposes. Hence the old distinction, "*Diabolus tentat; Deus probat,*" "The devil tempts; God proves." God tempted, or tried, and proved Abraham, that his faith might be found unto glory, and honour, and praise, might be exhibited to the admiration and imitation of the whole church, and might obtain a great reward in heaven. Satan tempted Judas and Ananias, that he might draw them into sin, and thus ruin them for ever. God, indeed, may tempt, or try men, when he knows that they will not abide the trial, but that they will fall, as he did the Israelites in the wilderness. He there proved them, and discovered all that was in their heart, though he knew how perversely they would act; but he never tempts men in order to lead them to commit sin. We are warranted by the nature, the commands, the

---

* Dr. Owen on Temptation, p. 439.

threatenings, and promises of God, to say, that there never has been in the universe a rational creature that has fallen before temptation, whose victory over it would not have been pleasing to the Divine Being, and followed with his approbation. Satan is always gratified, he ever feels an infernal pleasure, when men fall before temptation; when it is successfully resisted, he is mortified. He tempts under the influence of the most malignant dispositions, and for the attainment of the basest and the most cruel purposes.

Much as there is that is mysterious on this subject, there are several things which, if the principles that have been advocated in these lectures are correct, are as obvious as they are important. First, that Satan *does* tempt men, nay that, if the expression might be applied to spirits, it is his meat and his drink. When we consider the character and circumstances of Satan and his associates, the part which they acted in heaven, their eternal exclusion from thence, the way in which wilful sin, and obstinate impenitence, amidst constant punishment, and irritating collision with the object of dislike and hatred, while its glories are more and more displayed by every attempt to obscure them, must operate, we may be certain, as has already been shown, from what we observe amongst rational creatures in this world, nay from experience itself in some degree, that Satan will be disposed, will be determined to tempt as far as he has it in his power. And there is nothing more mysterious in the fact that God permits him to carry on the work of temptation, throughout the whole extent of this earth, and that for ages, than that he suffers large portions of it to be brought under the dominion of some wicked human spirits, and filled, through their influence, with miseries and crimes; so that they have been correctly designated "incarnate devils." It has been properly observed. by an old writer,* " Nothing is more

* Gilpin, Demonologia Sacra.

likely to beget malice, than hurts, and punishments, and degradations from happiness. Satan's curse, though just, fills him with rage and fretting against God, when he considers that from the state and dignity of an angel of light, he is cast down to darkness, and to the basest condition imaginable. Where the heart is so wicked that it cannot accept the punishment of the iniquity, all punishment is as poison, and envenoms the breast with rage against the hand that inflicted it. Thus doth Satan's fall enrage him, and the more when he sees man instated into a possibility of enjoying that which he has lost. Hence it may be concluded that Satan, being a wicked spirit, and his wickedness being capable of working higher or lower, according to occasions, and with a suitableness thereto, cannot but show an inconceivable malice against us; our happiness and his misery," (and it may be added the glory of God, and his own conscious deformity and vileness,) " being such proper occasions for the wickedness of his heart to work upon."

But to dismiss all general analogical reasoning on this subject, the word of God clearly reveals and states the fact, that Satan and his angels are constantly, assiduously engaged in attempting to render men like themselves in moral impurity and wretchedness. From it we learn the alarming, important fact, that he introduced, by his craft and influence, as a tempter, sin into our world; that he prevailed against our first parents amidst all the innocence, and privileges, and happiness of paradise; and it gives us a most instructive view of the manner in which he conducted the first temptation, and triumphed over all the wisdom and virtue of the progenitor and representative of the human race. Not only have we several instances given us in the Scriptures of his tempting individuals, but he is represented to us as " the god of this world," 2 Cor. iv. 4. He has subjected men to his power, he renders them subservient to his purposes, imposes on them his yoke and his laws, and in a sense receives their homage, indirectly, if not directly. He is also called "the prince of the power of the air, the spirit," or the ruler of the spirit, "that worketh in the children of disobedience," Eph. ii. 2. When men are converted and brought to embrace the Gospel, especially when they are delivered from idolatry, they are, according to the representations of the Bible, "turned from darkness to light, and from the power of Satan unto God," Acts xxvi. 18. As it is expressed in another passage, they are "delivered from the power of darkness, and translated into the kingdom of God's dear Son," Col. i. 13. The "enemy," that sowed the tares in the field of the world, in which the Son of man sowed the good seed of the word of God, "is the devil," Matt. xiii. 39. "For this purpose the Son of God was manifested, that he might destroy the works of the devil," 1 John iii. 8. "The old serpent, called the Devil, and Satan, deceives the whole earth," Rev. xii. 9.

Now from these and similar representations, it clearly follows, that every system of error, and superstition, and idolatry, everything that has caused the moral darkness in which the nations have been involved, the pollution in which they have wallowed, and the absurdities and cruelties which they have practised, has been, in an important sense, the work of Satan. He has indeed found the materials in abundance, in the human heart, of which he has constructed his systems; men have been his ready coadjutors in erecting them. In their dispositions and passions there has ever been something congenial to every error which he has wished to disseminate, to every corrupt and wicked practice to which he has tempted. May I not say that in some cases they have even tempted the tempter, and furnished him with the hints which he has improved? Still, these systems and crimes, to which I have alluded, are his works. The darkness, in all its ignorance, and errors, and pollution, and cruelties, is the kingdom in which he reigns. He is "the ruler of the darkness of this world." He can, in some way or other, exert an influence to involve men in ignorance, or keep them in it; to induce them to embrace error, and to commit crimes of every description. And that he is constantly engaged in this infernal work, is plainly implied in those passages which have been already quoted, as well as in many others. Whether there be any other revolted region of Jehovah's dominions, into which he is permitted to roam, any other rational beings whom he has brought under his control, it is not for us to say. It is easy to make assertions, and to take things for granted; but certain it is, that this world occupies a large share of his malignant regards, and that here he is dreadfully successful in the work of destruction. There is not an error or false doctrine to be found in all the records or systems of error, there is not a crime in the long black catalogue of crimes, which the depraved ingenuity, and appetites, and passions of men have led them to commit, that is not, directly or indirectly, the result of his influence; nay, not one of which we can positively say that he is not the instigator. But as he has revolted from his rightful sovereign, "the King eternal, immortal, and invisible," and erected the standard of rebellion against the Most High, and has had the audacity, the dreadful temerity, to enter the lists with Almighty Power, to "defy the Omnipotent to arms," (oh, what abundant evidence have we in the history and present deeds of our own species, that rational beings are capable of this! otherwise, it might be deemed almost incredible,) and as he, probably, fell by aspiring after that to which he urged our first parents, seeking equality with God,—idolatry, in some one of its forms, nay, in all its forms, must be in a special manner his invention, his work, because it is a worshipping and serving the creature more than the Creator. Whether the comparatively refined and elevated system of Persia, and Chaldea, and Peru, in framing and practising of which, though men forgot Jehovah, the self-existing, eternal, infinite Source of life, they still directed their eyes and their attention in a sense to heaven, and adored the fire, the sun, and moon, and stars, and all the host of the spacious firmament; or the absurd mundane mythology of Greece and Rome, with its gods and goddesses of terrestrial origin, and human passions of the lowest, grossest order, the deformity, and folly, and abomination of which could not be hidden by all the genius and splendid achievements of their great men, and by all their magnificent and beautiful temples, and altars, and statues, and paintings;—nay, these rendered the darkness, and deformity, and folly only more palpable;—or the extravagant, monstrous, libidinous, murderous idolatry of India, with its myriads of gods, and nameless obscenities, and revolting self-murders, and worse than self-murders, in the cruel, unnatural destruction of those whom nature, and justice, and religion recommend to the most affectionate love;—or the fierce, diabolical superstition of Mexico, slaughtering its hecatombs of human sacrifices;—or the stupid, grovelling idol-worship of Africa and the Southern Ocean, whose images seem to have been devised and formed by the very genius of ugliness, the spirit of deformity;—all of these systems breathe his temper, bear his image and superscription, in their absurdity, impiety, unnaturalness, lust, and cruelty; all are the worst, the grossest that he could induce men to adopt in their various circumstances; and all answer, in a greater or less degree, his purpose,—to affront the God of heaven, and degrade and destroy the sons of men.

We may also conclude from the general principles and statements of the Bible, and from what we know of the nature of Satan, that he has had a large share in producing all the various corruptions of Christianity that have destroyed its spirit, deformed its heavenly beauty, and counteracted the design of its Author; nay, rendered it the savour of death unto death. Alas, how soon were effectual substitutes for all the gods and goddesses, and superstitions, and festivals, and mysteries of Greece and Rome, introduced into the Christian church under the form of canonised mortals; while Satan found a more efficient vicegerent in the Man of sin, than ever he had done in the pagan emperor! The mystery of iniquity was operating in the time of the apostles; and soon, and most conspicuously, when beheld either in the light of prophecy, or of Christianity in general, was "that wicked one revealed, whose coming was after the working of Satan, with power, and signs, and lying wonders, and with all deceivableness of unrighteousness in them that perish."* Error was most artfully arrayed in the garb of truth, and vice adorned with the name and habiliments of virtue; and both were caused to exhibit all the attractions of which they are capable, to hearts that secretly hated holiness and relished sin, and therefore would not receive the love of the truth that they might be saved.

What allurements could unrighteousness possibly present, which were not found in this Antichristian system? It had (and it has) its austerities and mortifications to gratify the morose and the proud; its indulgences and carnivals to gratify the voluptuous. It had its honours and high stations to allure the aspiring, and its monasteries and nunneries for the recluse and the ascetic. It had its merits and works of supererogation for the lovers of pleasure. It presented its riches to the votaries of money, and its voluntary poverty to those who, in this way, sought the reputation of superior sanctity. It had its vows of celibacy for those who, notwithstanding the express denunciations of the Bible, thought there was something holy in refusing to marry, and forbidding it to others, and its concubinage to enable them at the same time to gratify the flesh. It had its miracles for those who de-

* See Sortain's Lectures.

sired signs and wonders, and its infallibility for those who wished to dispense with the labour of thinking and answering for themselves. It had its confessions for those who desired to live in sin, and yet preserve an easy conscience; and, what would be incredible, were it not proved by fact, its confessions before the perpetration of the act, to diminish the guilt of the most horrid crimes, nay, in some degree to sanction them, and its ritual observance for those who disliked the spirituality of religion : its baptismal regeneration, (we heartily wish that this was confined to the church of Rome,) for those who did not care to examine whether they were born again, and to labour to enter in at the strait gate, and its extreme unction and priestly absolution for those who had neglected all attention to religion to the very last, and after all, its purgatory, as the forlorn hope for those who have no other hope, from even all *its* provisions. It had its palaces, and its titles, and its thrones for the rich and aspiring, and its alms and holidays for the poor. It had its visible head for those who could not, or would not, look by faith to the invisible Head of the church in heaven, and its images and sacrifices for those who had no spiritual perception of the " one sacrifice, which has for ever perfected those who are sanctified," and who could not realise the cloud of witnesses, nor read their Bibles to learn the character of those whom they ought to follow, and " who, through faith and patience have obtained the promises." In short, what had it not, that could possibly be included in the comprehensive term, " *the deceivableness of unrighteousness,*" suited to the taste of those who wished to serve God and mammon ? *And it has all these still, in the present day;* and all connected apparently, in the most artful manner, with the authority and institutions of the great Head of the church, and therefore calculated to bind the conscience in the chains of priestcraft and superstition. This system has been called by one, who was no mean judge,* "Satan's master-piece which exceeded all that he had ever contrived before, and which he can never equal again." It threw into the shade all the superstitions and idolatry of Greece and Rome, as it regards art, subtlety, and accommodation to the various tastes of men; and fascinations, and provisions for gratifying the passions, and enslaving the conscience. What a proof have we of this in the fact, that notwithstanding all the knowledge, and fidelity, and love to the truth, and noble boldness of the reformers, of a Luther, and a Zuingle, and a Knox, and many others, they could not unravel all these arts of Satan, they could not break through all the trammels in which they were held, and cast off the whole of the yoke which had been imposed on the church of God, nor escape from all the fascinations of "the deceivableness of unrighteousness!" But they carried much of the spirit of the Antichristian system which they exploded, into the churches which they formed, and there it remains, to a lamentable extent, to this day, and is operating to produce a retrograde movement. When will the command be universally heard and obeyed by the professed disciples of Jesus Christ: "Come out of her, my people, that you be not partakers of her sins, and that you receive not of her plagues?"

On the same principles, we may be certain, that Satan has exerted a powerful influence in the introduction of every error, and every system of error, by which the peculiar doctrines of the Gospel have been obscured or denied, in every age of the church or part of the world. Even if those errors have had their source in the perverse mind or corrupt heart of man, he who abode not in the truth, and who maintains his cause by means of falsehood, would, doubtless, endeavour to render them subservient to his design. As it is by means of the truth that Jesus Christ converts sinners, and sanctifies and saves his own

* Cecil.

people, the great patron of sin and enemy of souls must labour, with all his craft and energy, to counteract that by which his works,—ignorance, and delusion, and sin in all their forms,—are destroyed. The locusts which so terribly devastated the earth, came, we are informed, out of the smoke which arose from the bottomless pit. How extensively injurious and even fatal may be the influence of but one error respecting the nature and character of God, or the relations in which he stands to men; the obligations of the Divine law, the criminality and destructive tendency of sin, the way in which it may be forgiven, and its punishment in a future world; or the glories, and dignity, and work of the Redeemer, or the way in which sinners may be interested in his work; or the danger to which men are exposed in consequence of the existence and character of their spiritual foes! As surely as there is a tempter, an adversary to the cause of God and truth, he will endeavour to render all these errors subservient to his cause. Hence we may be certain that he puts in requisition all his energies and resources to oppose the ministers of the Gospel and missionaries of the cross. He will doubtless hate the leaders and standard-bearers in the army of Immanuel. We cannot wonder in this respect, however we may in another, at the corruptions which have been introduced into the Gospel ministry, or at the way in which it has been perverted to subserve the cause of error and vice, and rendered subservient to the lowest, vilest purposes of avarice, ambition, voluptuousness, tyranny, and spiritual domination; or that some of the most revolting scenes that hell has ever enacted, or earth witnessed, should have been presented in connexion with its sacred offices, and by men who have professed to minister at its altars. John might well marvel when he "saw the women drunken with the blood of the saints, and of the martyrs of Jesus." In a special manner those who are engaged in making inroads on the territories of the prince of darkness, attacking him in his own kingdom, disturbing him in his very seat, where he keeps his house and his goods in peace, must expect his fiercest opposition; and when they are successful he must hate them and their converts with a peculiar hatred, and commission against them his most effective squadrons. They, in particular, "wrestle not with flesh and blood, but with principalities and powers." How Satan arranges his forces, or whether he leaves any region of the earth, where his dominion is already firmly established, nearly vacant, that he may bend all his efforts against another, where his empire of error and vice is attacked, according to the supposition of an ingenious and excellent writer,* I do not undertake to say: though I am afraid his motions are so swift, and his forces so numerous, that we cannot safely reckon on his absence from any part of the world; and his agents are impure as well as malignant, and will tempt to lust as well as to error, or impiety, or cruelty. The former is offensive to God and ruinous to men, as well as the latter; and "the adulteress hunts for the precious life." Moloch and Venus were worshipped by the same individuals amongst the heathen. I cannot conceive that there can be any depraved propensity in the frame of man of which Satan will not avail himself, or any sin to which they are prone, or which easily besets them, to which he will not tempt. The heathen, before they are turned from the power of Satan unto God, are as notorious for *uncleanness* as for *cruelty*. I cannot, therefore, fully accord with the sentiments of the respected and excellent author of the instructive Life of Bunyan, when he says, "accordingly, the bloody and libidinous vices prevail most in those places where Satan does least, and visits but seldom."† I should rather say, they, as well as vice in all its forms, prevail most, where Satan *has done most*, and where he has accomplished his work, and entirely subverted the true religion, or prevented its establishment. Whenever this is known,

---

* Philip's Life of Bunyan, p. 154. † Ibid.

it must, just in the degree in which it prevails, prevent vice of every description. I am afraid too, that we cannot, by any inroad we can make on Satan's territories, however desirable it is that this should be done to the greatest possible extent, cause any sensible withdrawment of his forces from our churches at home. Whatever may be in this, the fact is certain that missionaries must expect and encounter his most determined opposition, and that he will, as far as he can, incite princes and rulers to impose restrictions on the heralds of the cross, to persecute them and their converts; and the emissaries of the Man of sin to insinuate error where missionaries preach the truth; and his vilest slaves, those who perform his lowest drudgery, to tempt their converts to drunkenness and sensual indulgence. And how will he rejoice if he can induce the various divisions of the army of Immanuel to turn their arms against one another—if he can involve the agents of missionary societies in mutual strife and contention, and cause them to oppose each other's progress; and thus furnish the world with objections against them! May all concerned in the management of missionary societies and churches, be able to say with Paul, "We are not ignorant of his devices!"

A second important and certain principle here is, that Satan cannot compel to the adoption of error, or to the commission of sin; he can only entice and deceive. The act must be voluntary. If such an application of a passage of Scripture might be allowed, it might be said that Satan makes his dupes, as Jesus Christ does his people, "willing in the day of his power." And when we consider that, as far as I can see, he can persuade, directly, only by suggesting thoughts or ideas to the mind, or by exciting the passions, and directing the attention to external objects, (if he can do this,) much as we have to dread from him, and well founded as are the warnings that are given us in the Scriptures, yet his power is not so great as some imagine, and therefore their efforts to lessen their guilt by criminating Satan, by pleading as Eve did, "The serpent beguiled me," will be fruitless. If he has some advantages in the work of temptation over men, they have, when they act the part of tempters, some over him. He cannot, when he tempts in his own person, like them, address those whom he wishes to delude, in verbal, eloquent discourses, and employ a train of specious reasoning and interesting illustration. He cannot avail himself of the fascination of the voice, or the eye, or the action, nor of excited feeling and sympathy, nor is he permitted to present to us written discourses, to which the attention may again and again be directed, and which are valued as literary treasures. He must, therefore, avail himself of the assistance of men who have embraced error, or who will plead for vice. It is principally through their instrumentality that he diffuses either the one or the other. How effective a minister of Satan is the learned infidel philosopher, metaphysician, or historian, or the atheistic, licentious poet, or the irreligious, scoffing novelist, who renders all the stores of his learning, and the creations of his imagination, and the colourings of his fancy, subservient to arraying piety in the garb of enthusiasm, or hypocrisy, or of a contemptible weakness; and heartless licentiousness and cruelty, in the attractions of sincerity and ingenuousness and nobleness of spirit! How dreadful the responsibility of those who thus pervert the most valuable gifts of the Father of spirits—of Him who puts knowledge into the heart, and wisdom into the inward parts! How much would the influence of Satan be diminished, were he thrown, as it regards every individual, entirely on his own resources and direct attacks! This deserves the attention and grave consideration of all, who, by purchasing and reading such works, and even recommending them, because of the genius and learning of their authors, contribute to preserve them from oblivion, and even to increase their celebrity. Can there be a doubt whether the mischief which they effect is not greater than any good of which they are the instruments?

I must own I scarcely understand what Gilpin and others mean by Satan's power of spiritual fascination, as something apart from, or more than, his ability to inject or suggest thoughts, and thus to inflame the appetites or passions. Gilpin describes it as follows: "Satan's own power of spiritual fascination is that by which he infatuates the mind of men, and deludes them, as the external senses are deceived by enchantment or witchcraft. That Satan is a cunning sophister, and can put fallacies on the understanding—that by subtle objections or arguments he can obtrude a falsehood upon the belief of the unskilful and unwary—that he can betray the judgment by the affections, are things of common practice with him. But that which I am now to speak of is of a higher nature, and though it may probably take in much of his common method of ordinary delusion, yet in this it differs at least, that it is more efficacious and prevalent. . . . He hath, by special commission, a power to lead those to error effectually, without missing his end, that have prepared themselves for that spiritual judgment by a special provocation ; and for aught we know, as he hath an extraordinary power which he exerts at such times, so he may have an extraordinary method which he is not permitted to practise daily, nor upon all. And thus some do describe it: ''Tis a delusion with a kind of magical enchantment;' so Calvin, 'A Satanical operation whereby the senses are deluded.' Thus Perkins, who after he had asserted that Satan can corrupt the fantasy or imagination, compares this spiritual witchcraft to such diseases of melancholy as make men believe that they are or do what they are and do not, (as the disease called *lycanthropia*,) and to the enchantments of Jannes and Jambres who deluded the senses of Pharaoh."*

* Gilpin, Demonologia Sacra, p. 181.

He might well add, "A particular account of the way in which the devil does this, is a task beyond sober inquiry." And then he proceeds to prove from Scripture that Satan does possess this power.

The first text which he quotes, and therefore I should suppose, one which he thinks most clearly proves his point, is Gal. iii. 1, " O foolish Galatians, who hath bewitched (or fascinated, or charmed) you, that you should not obey the truth?" This passage, however, is far from proving his assertion; for, in the first place, no mention is made of Satan—there is no allusion to him. On the contrary, it is evident from several hints which are given in the epistle, that Paul had false brethren or teachers in view. Chap. iv. 17, "They zealously affect you, but not well; yea, they would exclude you, that ye may affect them." Chap. v. 7, 10, 12, "Ye did run well; who did hinder you that you should not obey the truth?" "He that troubleth you shall bear his judgment, whosoever he be," &c. These passages render it evident that it was false teachers who had bewitched the Galatians. They might, indeed, well be considered the agents or ministers of Satan, as the apostle calls them in another place; but this is quite different from the spiritual fascination which we are considering. These advocates of error could not exert any direct spiritual influence on the mind; they could employ only the common arts of seduction. Farther, the apostle was far from considering the Galatians, with all their errors and faults, as given up by God, and entirely under the power of Satan; so that if he did possess this direct power of fascination, he had not employed it on them. On the contrary, Paul still had hope that those very persons whom he denominated "foolish," and "bewitched," were truly pious. Hence we have the following language, chap. v. 10, "I have confidence in you through the Lord, that you will be no otherwise minded." And hence he addressed them as "brethren," not as reprobates given over by God to the power of Satan; "And I, brethren," &c. And he thus concludes his epistle: "Brethren, the grace of our Lord Jesus Christ be with your spirit, Amen." It is evident that the word "bewitch" is used by him in a figurative sense, to intimate that the error which they had embraced was most palpably gross; that their conduct was egregiously foolish and irrational; or as Calvin expresses it, (for his language by no means implies the direct magical fascination, in defence of which Gilpin quotes it,) "Neque tantùm quòd se decipi passi fuerint, eas arguit, sed quâdam *veluti* magicâ incantatione deludi." "Neither does he censure them, that they had suffered themselves to be deceived only, but even to be deluded by a kind of magical incantation." Besides, as the allusion here is to the "practice of witches and sorcerers," it is more than doubtful whether they ever were able "by secret powers to bind the senses and effect mischiefs."*

The next passage he quotes is 2 Thess. ii. 9, 10, "Whose coming is after the working of Satan, with all powers, and signs, and lying wonders, and with all deceivableness of unrighteousness in them that perish, because they received not the love of the truth that they might be saved; and for this cause God shall send them strong delusion that they should believe a lie." Surely it is evident that there is no allusion here to any mysterious spiritual fascination, or bewitching, but to the lying signs and wonders that were wrought, and to the allurements that were presented to their appetites and passions. It is indeed said that God would "send them strong delusion." But this might be done, and was done, by giving them up to the influence of the lying wonders, and to the dispositions of their own hearts, as he did the Israelites in another case, when they embraced errors as gross as those which the apostle had in view. Psalm lxxxi. 11, 12, "But my people would not hearken to my voice, and Israel would none of me; so *I*

* Gilpin, p. 183.

gave them up to their own hearts' lusts, and they walked in their own counsels." Here we have the cause, and even in a sense, the *process,* of the spiritual fascination of which the apostle speaks.

The only other passage which Gilpin quotes, is Rom. i. 28, "God gave them over to a reprobate mind." These words, taken in their connexion, plainly show, that men, when given up by God to their own inclinations, to the lusts of their own hearts, and to the ordinary temptations of Satan, may embrace the grossest errors, and practise the greatest abominations, without any other influence. And in the same way, we may easily account for all the errors, and crimes, and abominations, however vile, and odious, and extraordinary, and unnatural, and suddenly embraced, or committed; or however earnestly pursued, which Gilpin adduces as facts which support his theory. In fine, I must consider this spiritual fascination, and his view of it, as altogether unintelligible; as ascribing a power to Satan, which we have no proof that he possesses; as utterly unsupported by Scripture; and as unnecessary to account for any facts which the history of error and vice presents to us. Were it possessed and exercised, those who are under its influence would, so far, be almost blameless; because it is represented as irresistible, and as, in a degree, depriving them of the power of thought and action, however culpable they might be, in committing those crimes which induced God to give them up, in the way and measure supposed, to the power of the great enemy of souls.*

This suggests a third general principle on this subject, namely, that as Satan is not possessed of omniscience or ubiquity, he carries on the work of temptation, to a great extent, through the instrumentality of those fallen spirits who are called his angels. This term denotes their inferiority, and subjection to him, and their being united

See Appendix O.

with him in his infernal occupation. We have already stated the opinion of Jonathan Edwards, with regard to the vast superiority of Satan to the angels who fell with him, and there is no absurdity, no improbability, in the supposition, that his pre-eminence is so great, that he can induce them all to submit to his dominion, and to obey his laws, and that he is, in reality and effectually, the prince of hell; and he has this advantage, that all his subjects, like himself, are influenced by the principles of hatred to God and man, and delight in perpetrating mischief, so that they enter into the spirit of the work which he appoints them, as far as temptation and seduction are concerned. And there is no danger of their so far revolting from him, as to desert his standard, join the army of Immanuel, and fight for the cause of holiness and heaven. May we not suppose, then, if what has been advanced is at all correct, that some of these evil spirits far exceed others in capacity, that they can manage the work of temptation with much greater craft and efficiency, and that some of the lower orders are not much superior to men in mental power; and that several of these were employed in harassing the man that had the legion; and that Satan, with the assistance of those who are next to him in rank, presides over them all, appoints them their various spheres, and even calls them to account, how they have acted and succeeded; and that *for this reason*, not only for his *personal efforts*, and *direct* influence, but also, and principally, for his *indirect*, because of the way in which he marshals, and prompts, and leads on all the armies of hell, we read so much in the Bible of Satan, and, comparatively, so little of his angels? Just as in the history of a warfare, we read so much more of the general, especially if he is one of consummate abilities, than of the inferior officers and soldiers. It is enough for us to know, that he has these under his command. The subject is thus stated and illustrated, by the eloquent pen of a master intellect:—

"It has been said, that to ascribe to Satan such an interference in the moral concerns of the world, as is implied in his incessantly tempting men to sin, is to suppose him omnipresent, a supposition repugnant to the nature of a finite being. It must be confessed, the Scriptures of the New Testament teach us to conceive of Satanic agency as occurring in almost every act of deliberate sin: he is said to have filled the heart of Ananias; to have entered into Judas, 'after he had taken the sop.' To infer from thence, however, that any proper omnipresence is attributed to this apostate spirit, betrays inattention to the obvious meaning of the inspired writers. We are taught to conceive of Satan as the head of a spiritual empire, of great extent, and comprehending within itself innumerable subordinate agents. The term Satan, in application to this subject, is invariably found in the singular number, implying that there is *one*, designated by that appellation. His associates in the principal rebellion are spoken of in the plural number, and are denominated his angels. Thus the punishment reserved for them at the close of time, is said to be 'prepared for the devil and his angels.' What their number may be, it is vain to conjecture; but when we reflect on the magnitude of the universe, and the extensive and complicated agency in which they are affirmed to be engaged, we shall probably be inclined to conjecture, that it far exceeds that of the human race. In describing the affairs of an empire, it is the uniform custom of the historian, to ascribe its achievements to one person, to the ruling mind under whose auspices they are performed, and by whose authority they are effected; as it is the will of the chief which, in an absolute monarchy, gives unity to its operations and validity to its laws, and to whose glory or dishonour its good or ill fortune redounds; as victories and defeats are ascribed to him who sustains the supreme power, without meaning for a moment to insinuate that they were the result of his individual agency. Thus, in relating the events of the last war, the ruler of France would be represented as conducting at once the most multifarious movements, in the most remote parts of Europe, where nothing more was intended than that they were executed, directly or indirectly, by his orders. He thus becomes identified with his empire, and spoken of as though he pervaded all its parts. Thus the sovereign of Great Britain, by a fiction of speech, perfectly understood, is represented as the direct object of every offence, and as present in every court of law. . . . .

" Conceiving Satan, agreeably to the intimations of the word of God, to be the chief or head of a spiritual dominion, we easily account for the extent of the agency he is affirmed to exert in tempting and seducing the human race ; not by supposing him to be personally present whenever such an operation is carrying on, but by referring it to his auspices, and considering it as belonging to the history of his empire. As innumerable angels of light fight under the banner of the Redeemer, so there is every reason to conclude, the devil also is assisted by an equally numerous host of his angels, composing those principalities and powers over which Jesus Christ triumphed in the making 'a show of them openly.' On this principle, the objection we are considering falls entirely to the ground ; and no more ubiquity or omnipotence is attributed to Satan by our system, than to Alexander, Cæsar, or Tamerlane, whose power was felt, and their authority acknowledged, far beyond the limits of their personal presence."

Now though it may be true, as Hall conjectures, that the number of these unhappy, malignant beings far exceeds that of the human race, we have no evidence that this is so. But even if this supposition should be correct, are we to imagine that this comparatively small, inconsiderable world is the only part of the universe assigned to them for their abode, or that they are all continually present on this earth, or that they are engaged in nothing else than in tempting men to sin? Will not the malice which burns in the heart of Satan against God and his holy, happy creatures, induce him to make attempts on other parts of the dominion of Jehovah? Whether he has been suffered to do so or not; or whether, if allowed to make the attempt, he has realised success in any other of them, it is not for us to say; our wishes and feelings would lead us to hope that he had not. That he should be permitted, however, to try, is not more mysterious than that he should be allowed to invade paradise, or to attack and harass the church of God, or the Saviour himself. It is true we have no hint given us in the Bible that such is the case; but we must recollect that the Bible does not contain the history of fallen angels, but of the fall and recovery of human beings. Now, if these suppositions are admitted to be probable, and I must own they appear to me to be exceedingly so, we are not left to conclude that, even taking into the account the great activity of Satan and his emissaries, they can always fill, as it were, the whole earth, and that there must constantly be a fallen angel at hand to tempt every man, or to take advantage of any opportunity that may occur of soliciting him to sin; though none can be sure that this is not the case. But with all the hosts of hell under his command, Satan cannot be, even in their persons, and through their instrumentality, everywhere present, or possessed of anything like ubiquity, according to the sneering representations of some of our opponents. And this view of the matter corresponds, as we have already seen, with the representations of the Bible. Satan, even considering the term as denoting the whole of the influence that he can exert, "*goes about* seeking whom he may devour;" he "goes *to and fro* on the earth, and walks up and down on it." His great aim, we may be sure, is to bring all men, whether nations, families, or individuals, into such a state as that they may be tempted, as the Scriptures express it, "of their own lusts," and prove tempters to one another, so that they may perform his work, and fall an easy prey to his agents. And he doubtless endeavours to render, as much as possible, the master-minds in every locality his instruments in diffusing error, in patronising vice, and opposing the cause of heaven; so that "the kings of the earth may set themselves, and the rulers take counsel together, against the Lord, and against his Anointed."

In the fourth place we may, I think, be certain that Satan endeavours, as much as possible, to conceal his operations, and to carry on the work of temptation in such a way that he may not be perceived or suspected. He did so when he attacked and ruined our first parents; and, probably, as we have already seen, when he assaulted our Saviour in the wilderness. And except in those two instances, we have no satisfactory evidence that ever he appeared in a visible form, or uttered any verbal language. He is too much in earnest to throw impediments in the way of his own success. For this reason, I must own it appears to me very improbable that, even if he were permitted, he would have acted as the believers in witchcraft think he has done, namely, that he would appear to any of his devotees, or conduct himself in such a way as that his operations might be detected, and his malignant character discovered. The craft that induces him to assume the form of an angel of light, would scarcely suffer him to show himself as a fiend of hell. He endeavours to ruin men by atheism and infidelity, by causing them to doubt of his own existence. Would he then appear in a visible form, furnish proofs of the existence of a God, and of spirits, and of the truth of the Scriptures? One of his devices is to lull men asleep in carelessness and disregard of religion. Would he then do anything to alarm them, and render them sensible of their danger? Will the fowler discover himself to the bird that he is endeavouring to ensnare, or the ambuscade to the army that it wishes to surprise and defeat? If *they* will, then may we grant that Satan will appear in a visible form, and expose his operations to those whom he is attempting to seize as his prey. It is true he "goes about as a roaring lion;" but even the lion will crouch and conceal himself till his intended victim is within his reach, and not unnecessarily alarm that which he wishes to destroy.

Fifthly. We may be certain that Satan will ever avail himself of all the advantages that are afforded him by the dispositions, the character, and the circumstances of those whom he tempts. As it has been sometimes expressed, he will never row against the stream or tide, when he can avail himself of its impetus. His earnestness in the work of destruction will effectually prevent this. He will tempt the proud, and those whose attainments, or situations, or performances, are calculated to produce elation of mind, to pride and ambition; the voluptuous and unchaste, to unhallowed indulgence and impurity; the discontented to fretfulness and repining; the irritable and passionate to anger; the malicious and envious to revenge; the peevish and dissatisfied to murmuring and impatience; the rich to "trust in uncertain riches;" to "deny God, and to say, Who is the Lord?" and the poor to discontent and envy, or to "steal and take the name of God in vain;" the self-righteous to "trust in themselves, and to despise others;" the profane to swear and desecrate the ordinances of religion; those who are naturally of a bold and sanguine disposition, to presumption; and the melancholy, timid, and dejected, to heartless, groundless suspicion or despair. He did not tempt Peter or John to betray the Saviour; probably he could not have succeeded with either; but Judas, who was dishonest and covetous, to whom, therefore, the paltry sum of thirty pieces of silver would be an object, while he was devoid of any real love to his Master.

It is true he tempted Peter, notwithstanding his zeal and boldness, to deny his Lord. But it was when that disciple was placed in peculiar circumstances, in which there was a probability that he might be induced to act contrary to his natural disposition; and, perhaps, while Peter's ardent temperament would often induce him to act rashly, he was rather warm, zealous, and forward, than truly courageous. Satan tempted Ananias and Sapphira, who were evidently under the influence of that love of money which is the root of all evil, to lie and keep back part of the price of the land, which they had sold. But before he could hope to induce Job to complain, and charge God foolishly, or Abraham to give way to unbelief, he must have the advantage, the assistance, of peculiarly favourable circumstances; the former must be overwhelmed with calamities, and the latter brought into such a situation, that he thought his life in danger. It is plainly implied in 2 Cor. ii. 11, that Satan is, as it were, constantly watching to take advantage of the circumstances of men, especially of professors of religion, in order to tempt them with success. "Lest Satan should get an advantage of us; for we are not ignorant of his devices." I know some would render the word Satan here, the *slanderer*, or accuser, and refer it to some of the enemies of religion. But, to mention nothing else on this occasion, their heathen neighbours would not concern themselves whether these Christians were or were not too strict in their discipline, whether or not they received and comforted the excommunicated person, of whom the apostle had been speaking. He evidently means, 'Lest Satan, the great adversary, shall be able to injure the church at Corinth, and the cause of religion in general, by taking advantage of their severity to the unhappy person who had fallen into sin.' For the same reason, the apostle exhorts the Ephesians, chap. iv. 26, 28, "Be ye angry and sin not: let not the sun go down upon your wrath; neither give place unto the devil." This plainly implies that Satan is ready to take advantage of our frame of mind to tempt us to the indulgence of that depraved disposition, or to the commission of that sin, whatever it may be, to which we are inclined; into which something that is lawful in itself may betray us, if we are not on our guard. He will always endeavour to push us over that precipice near to which we have been brought, or to hurry us down the declivity on which we may be standing. And this is one way in which we may account for the dreadful excesses of furious passion, into which some men are frequently wrought, and the shocking crimes into which, in consequence, they are plunged. No wonder that the vessel is dashed to pieces, when, under a full press of sail, it is driven by a tempestuous wind and a flowing tide against a rock.

The way in which some Christians have been harassed by blasphemous, abominable thoughts, suddenly, forcibly, and irresistibly suggested to their minds, and that sometimes for a length of time, wherever they were, or however they were occupied, may further illustrate our subject. Though it is difficult, or rather impossible, to tell how far these may be the native production of that depraved heart, out of which, the Saviour himself assures us, "proceed evil thoughts, and blasphemies," in all their various forms, yet surely none who believe in the agency of Satan, and that he has a power of suggesting anything to the mind, can doubt for a moment, that they are often to be attributed to him, and that in such a degree, that those who are harassed with them are unfortunate rather than guilty, are objects of pity rather than of blame. Bunyan is far from being the only person who has known from experience what it is to have "a storm of blasphemous thoughts burst upon him, stirring up questions against the very being of a God, and his only beloved Son, and whether there were, in truth, a God or a Christ, and whether the

Scriptures were not a cunning story, rather than the pure word of God." And some can add with him likewise, "I may not and dare not utter, by either word or pen, even at this time, other suggestions."* Some know by bitter experience, what it is to be haunted by such suggestions against the being of a God, the truth of the Scriptures, and of all the peculiar doctrines of the Gospel, one after another, as well as other "suggestions," which cannot be named, for months, and at times for years together, so as to have their lives embittered to such a degree, that they would not for worlds consent to be exposed to such buffetings again, or to be the subject of their former experience. They have found, as Bunyan did, that the blowing of the wind, the least noise, the most insignificant occurrence, excited the suggestion; nay, that it was habitually present to the mind, working in their breast, struggling for utterance, as if an evil spirit had taken up its abode there, and was endeavouring to usurp the office of the soul. Again I must assert, to deny that such thoughts are owing to the suggestions of Satan, would be equivalent to denying that he has any influence whatever over the human mind, or that he can suggest any ideas at all; still I apprehend, that careful observation would discover something in the frame, or the experience, or the circumstances of the individual, favourable to such suggestions: perhaps in his want of clear views of the evidence for the existence of God, or of the truth of the Scriptures, or of the perfect rectitude of the Divine dispensations; or in a secret dissatisfaction with something that God has permitted, or which he requires; or perhaps in the state of the bodily health. This may be in such a condition as to dispose to dissatisfaction with everything, and therefore to gloomy, melancholy musings and feelings; and of this Satan takes advantage. And, probably, without it, as such thoughts are directly contrary to all the principles of piety, and, there-

* Philip's Life of Bunyan, p. 114.

fore, to all the views and feelings of the Christian, Satan could not succeed with his blasphemous injections; and the morbid state of health, or the melancholy frame of mind, might not produce them, without his concurrence. I apprehend it has been found, when those who have been the subject of these distressing experiences have made accurate observations on themselves, and have recorded the result, that when the health has been improved, and the bodily frame has been invigorated, or anything has occurred to cheer and animate the mind, the blasphemous suggestions have immediately become less powerful and frequent, or perhaps have entirely ceased. When the Christian is in a state of *bodily, mental, and moral health*, he will not be troubled with these thoughts. I repeat it, the probability is, that Satan could not then produce them. He must in such cases have something in the subject on which to work, and therefore I do not hesitate to express my conviction, that though they proceed from him, and though prayer, and faith, and waiting on God, are the weapons with which the adversary must be encountered, temperance, exercise, and medicine may have some influence in counteracting them, and that, in some cases, without these, even religious considerations and exercises may fail of producing the desired effect, unless God should be pleased to appear for the individual in an extraordinary way, and even almost to work a miracle.

All will see that the subject now under consideration is very copious, and that to do it justice would require a whole course of Lectures, instead of a single discourse. There are many other topics on which it is desirable to touch, did our limits allow. If the principles which have been advanced are correct, it is evident that Satan can suggest thoughts to the mind. Indeed, could he not, it is difficult to see how he could tempt at all in ordinary circumstances. Spirits must have some way of communicating their ideas to one another; and, therefore, it is rational as well as scriptural to think, that Satan can, to a certain extent, impart or suggest his thoughts to men. Whether he can do so immediately, or whether he must employ the brain or some part of the bodily organisation, whilst the soul is intimately and wonderfully united to the corporeal part of our frame, is a subject on which we cannot now enter. Much may be said in support of the affirmative. It would seem, however, that he must carry on his temptations, in our circumstances, entirely by suggestion or injection. He cannot alter the appearances or the nature of external objects, nor, as he was permitted to do in the case of Jesus Christ, place us in circumstances favourable to his design. He can only take advantage of them, and tempt when the seducing object is before us; and this, perhaps, he can always do.

It may be asked here, Does he know our thoughts? Perhaps he does to a greater extent than is generally imagined. It is true that, in the full sense of the term, God only "knows the thoughts and tries the reins of the children of men." He only knows them immediately or directly, (being present, so to speak, with the very essence of the soul,) infallibly and universally as it regards all men, and all creatures, and all times. In no case are study and investigation of even a single individual necessary for him. But it does not follow from this, that Satan, a powerful, experienced and sagacious spirit, may not know them, to a certain extent, in consequence of his minute observation and scrutiny; nay, when we consider how they are connected with our bodily frame, and operate upon it, that he may not know them, in some cases, by a kind of direct inspection.

In order to form as accurate an idea as possible of Satan's temptations, we have only to consider how any man, distinguished for his mental power, knowledge of human nature, address, and depravity, would act, in endeavouring to render others subservient to his corrupt purposes. We may be certain that, in addition to taking advantage of their tempers, and frames, and habits, and circumstances, and employing generally the fittest instruments to effect his purposes, he would exhaust all the arts of sophistry, and false, yet specious reasoning.

That everything which is calculated to induce the young, for instance, to defer attention to religion to a future period; the careless to continue to trifle, or the proud to indulge their high imaginations; the self-righteous to build for eternity on their own works; the moral and amiable to rest satisfied with their essentially defective goodness; the impure to indulge their appetites and passions; the passionate to give way to anger and rage, and the vindictive to gratify their revenge; the infidel and atheistic to say in their hearts, "There is no God;" the rich to trust in their riches, and the poor to indulge discontent, or to murmur at the arrangements of providence; the Christian to be slothful, to conform to the world, and to omit any present duty; in short, all that can be an apparent reason, or afford a specious disguise, in the case of any individual, for the commission of any sin, or for neglecting what God requires, will be suggested and urged by him in the most forcible way; or, as has been said, that in tempting men, he will exhaust all the arts of sophistry and false logic. This he did in the case of our first parents, and of the blessed Redeemer; and in order to gain an acquaintance with the way in which he attempts to ruin us, we should carefully study these examples and exposures of his devices.

It follows from this, and from the representations of the Bible in general, that our danger from evil spirits is very great; and, perhaps, the more so, because it is impossible to distinguish, generally speaking, betwixt their suggestions, and the propensities and workings of our own hearts. The great object of Satan is, by means of these, to conceal his purposes, to keep us in ignorance of his agency and intentions, and thus to prevent us from taking the alarm, and making resistance. How necessary is it in this respect, as well as in others, to live and walk by faith, and not by sight! simply, and firmly, and practically to believe what the Scriptures state, and to act under the persuasion that it is all strictly true! Alas! how much of our security arises from our inability to see, and hear, our spiritual enemies the hosts of hell, and from the practical unbelief of which this is the occasion! But we must in this respect as well as others, " look not at the things which are seen, but at those which are not seen." And whether we believe it or not, the fact is certain, that these malignant, wretched, yet crafty and powerful spirits, are determined to ruin every one of us for ever and ever, if they possibly can; and that we must overcome them by the weapons of truth and piety, by the force of wisdom, and holy dispositions, and right principles, or else they will vanquish, and completely destroy us. There is no medium; none can avoid the conflict. They will attack us; they have attacked us. Let us beware of the extremes of either attributing to Satan everything which is sinful, or nothing; of thinking and speaking as if he were omniscient or omnipresent, or as if we forgot that his knowledge, and power, and activity, are fearfully great.

The question then, is, how are we to vanquish these infernal deadly foes? To this I answer, First—We can conquer them only through the power, and grace, and merit of the Saviour. Here, especially, "without him we can do nothing." We must be sure, then, that we are interested in him, and in the promise, "The God of peace shall bruise Satan under your feet shortly." We must be in such a state, that we can " be strong in the grace that is in Christ Jesus." Nothing can possibly be a substitute for his mediation and influence.

Secondly. We must keep our hearts with all diligence; we must be careful that they are in such a state, that, in some degree, we may be fortified against the temptations of Satan by our views, and dispositions, and habits; by knowledge, and wisdom, and self-command, and purity; in a word, by all the graces of the Holy Spirit, and thus we must "put on the whole armour of God." "He that is of God," in this respect, "keepeth himself, and the wicked one toucheth him not." "He that is born of God cannot sin, for his seed remaineth in him," even " the incorruptible seed of the word."

Thirdly. We must constantly watch over ourselves as it regards our circumstances, and everything that might give Satan the advantage over us. "Be sober, be vigilant," is the command of the great Captain of salvation, in relation to this part of our duty. We must realize the presence of God, and be careful not to "grieve the Holy Spirit."

Fourthly. We must carefully and conscientiously use all the means of grace. He that waits on God in them, has a promise that he "shall renew his strength." And the command in connexion with this subject is, "Praying always with all prayer and supplication in the Spirit." This is a part of the whole armour of God, as well as the way to call in the aid of omnipotence, and so to "be strong in the Lord, and in the power of his might."

In these Lectures our attention has been directed to subjects the most mysterious, the most awful, the most cheering and consolatory, and the most practical. First— The most mysterious: the permission of sin, and all its dreadful consequences, respecting which we must still exclaim, after all the researches of piety, and genius, and learning, "Oh the depth of the riches, both of the wisdom and knowledge of God! how unsearchable are his judgments!" And from it we may learn our own weakness, and the extent and magnificence of the plans of God. Secondly—The most awful and alarming. We have had to meditate on the complete ruin of myriads of glorious creatures, formed originally in the image of God, and on the fall, and depravity, and wretchedness of our own race, and on the lamentable victories which Satan has gained over them. Oh! what a spectacle is a whole world, is *our own world*, lying in wickedness, and in the wicked one! How perilous the circumstances of every one of us! Thirdly—The most glorious subjects: the victories and triumphs of the Son of God, and the Redeemer of the human race, gained in the most honourable way, and for the most benevolent and glorious purposes. Fourthly—To the most practical. They come home to the business and bosoms of every one of us. We cannot fully explain the way in which sin entered the universe, nor the reason why it was permitted. But we are plainly informed, how we may be delivered from it. We may easily and clearly understand how we may be made as holy as ever we were impure: how we may be as effectually justified as if we never had been guilty, and be rendered as safe as if we never had been exposed to any danger. There is much that is mysterious in the manner in which Satan tempts, and endeavours to destroy us. But we have all necessary directions respecting the way in which we may obtain the victory over him. And notwithstanding his power, and craft, and malice, and our own weakness and folly, he cannot ruin us, but in consequence of our refusing to avail ourselves of the privileges which we enjoy, and of the grace that is offered to us. Oh! let us remember, and may God cause us to feel, that we are actually, certainly, inevitably engaged in a conflict with the powers of darkness, (unless we are already vanquished by them, and are therefore wretched captives and slaves,) for our lives, and souls, and all the happiness of heaven! He that is overcome must *lose*— " he that overcometh shall *inherit* all things."

APPENDIX.

A. Page 8.

CHRYSOSTOM seems to have thought that the flame in which the rich man was tormented in hell, had banished his selfishness and apathy, and rendered him, in some degree at least, benevolent and pitiful. Αὐτὸς ἀποτυχῶν τῆς εὐεργεσίας, ἑτέροις προξενεῖ τὴν σωτηρίαν λοιπόν. Εἶδες πῶς ὠμὸς ἦν πρὸ τούτου, πῶς φιλάνθρωπος ἐγένετο μετὰ ταῦτα; πρὸ τῶν ὀφθαλμῶν κείμενον παρέτρεχε τὸν Λάζαρον ζῶν, νυνὶ δὲ καὶ ἀπόντων φροντίζει τῶν συγγενῶν· καὶ τότε μὲν ἐν περιουσία ὢν, πρὸς τὴν ἐλεεινὴν οὐκ ἐπεκάμπτετο τοῦ πτωχοῦ θέαν, νυνὶ δὲ εν ὀδύναις καὶ ἀνάγκαις ὢν απαραιτήτοις, κήδεται τῶν αὐτῷ προσηκόντων, καὶ ἀξιοῖ πεμφθῆναι τὸν ταῦτα ἀπαγγελοῦντα αὐτοῖς; ὁρᾷς πῶς φιλάνθρωπος γέγονε καὶ ἥμερος καὶσυμπαθητικός.—Chrysostom's Works, vol. ii. part 1, p. 790. 1838.

"When he could not obtain any benefit for himself, he would afterward have secured the salvation of others. Observe how cruel he was before; how benignant he had become then. When he lived on the earth, he passed by Lazarus lying before his eyes; but now he feels solicitous even for his absent relations; then, when he abounded in riches, he was not moved to pity by the affecting spectacle of a poor beggar; but now, when he was affected by endless pains and torments, he was concerned for his kindred, and prayed that one might be sent to testify to them of what he suffered. Do you see how benignant, and clement, and merciful, he had become?"

B. Page 83.

I KNOW this is questioned, or rather denied by many whose sentiments, on account of their ability, learning, and piety, are entitled to the most serious consideration. But I must beg leave respectfully, yet decidedly, to differ from them. I cannot but think that all those actions, which some would ascribe to reason, in what are *commonly*, but *erroneously*, if the hypothesis which I am controverting is correct, denominated irrational animals, may easily be accounted for from their instincts, the acuteness of their senses, and the habits which these enable them to form. For what purpose is instinct bestowed by the great Creator? Obviously, just to enable those creatures which have it, to do what *reason*,—it may be said, *perfect reason*,[1] were it possessed,—would dictate. When bees, for instance, build their cells in the form of regular hexagons, and arrange them in such a way as to give them the greatest degree of strength, this is just what they would do if they were profound mathematicians; and when they select those flowers which contain the juice most eligible for forming honey, they act just as if they were accomplished naturalists. If there are any who will maintain that they do these by ratiocination, and not by instinct, I must decline, for reasons which I shall not state, to enter into any controversy with them. Instinct, and the acuteness of their senses, enable the inferior animals to do more wonderful, more apparently intelligent things, than any which they are supposed to do by reason; and if these can enable them to effect the greater, why not also the less? The faculty of reason, I must think, forms a part of the image of God, in which *man* alone was created, and it renders him capable of the moral image of his Maker. And it was respecting him, and not the inferior animals, that God said, "Let us make man in our image," &c. The Scriptures favour, I had almost said, teach, the doctrine that brutes cannot reason.—Ps. xxxii. 9: "Be not like the horse or the mule, which have no understanding."—Job xxxv. 10: "None saith, Where is God, my Maker, who teacheth me more than the beasts of the field, and maketh me wiser than the fowls of heaven."—2 Peter ii. 12: "But these, as natural brute beasts, (ἄλογα ʹζῶα, dumb or irrational animals,) made to be taken and destroyed."—Jude, verse 10: "But what they know *naturally* as brute beasts, (ἄλογα ζῶα, *dumb or irrational animals*,) in these they corrupt themselves."

---

[1] "And reason magnify o'er instinct as you can,
In this 'tis God directs, in that 'tis man."—*Pope.*

C. Page 89.

I RETAIN the English translation of this important verse, because I am convinced that it is correct. It agrees much better with the literal meaning of the words in the original, with the Hebrew idiom and construction, and with the connexion and scope of the passage, than any other that I have seen. It is very generally translated, "Who maketh the winds his messengers, flaming fire his ministers." And I regret to find that Walford, in his very excellent translation of the Psalms, renders it so. I am glad, however, that Storr and Flatt, in their Biblical Theology, show that it cannot, with a due regard to the construction of the original, be so rendered. "עֹשֶׂה מַלְאָכָיו רוּחוֹת מְשָׁרְתָיו אֵשׁ לֹהֵט, 'He employs his angels like winds, and his ministers like flaming fire.' It is evident from grammatical considerations, that in this passage angels are meant. In the commentary in the Epistle to the Hebrews, chap. i. 7, these words are rendered thus, 'He employs his angels like winds, and his ministers like lightning.' But if the idea of the passage were intended to be this, 'He employs the winds as his messengers,' the word רוּחוֹת, *winds*, must have been before מַלְאָכָיו (his angels,) just as, in the third verse, עָבִים precedes, in the sentence, הַשָּׂם עָבִים רְכוּבוֹ, 'He uses the clouds as his chariot;' Moreover it ought to be מְשָׁרְתוֹ instead of מְשָׁרְתָיו in the hemistich, 'He maketh the flaming fire his minister or servant.' With this interpretation the context fully accords; for it was not the object of the writer of the Psalms to give a general description of the visible works of creation, and to begin with a representation of heaven. On the contrary, this psalm rather contains a delineation of the providence of God, in special relation to this earth, beginning with the 5th verse. To this description is prefixed a short song of praise and celebration of the greatness and glory (v. 1—4) of our Lord and Benefactor, just as in the 103d Psalm, an ode in commemoration of the greatness of God is appended to the description of the Divine goodness (v. 1 and 2;) but the mention of the angels is quite as appropriate in the celebration of the greatness of God, as are the contents of the second and third verses, (compare Isa. xi. 22, and Psalm lxviii. 3, &c.) Thus, also, are the angels mentioned in the descriptions of the Divine greatness in Psalm ciii. 20, 1 Kings xxii. 29, Dan. vii. 10."—Ward's Storr and Flatt's Biblical Theology. By S. S. Schmucker, D.D., p. 138.

With Storr and Flatt, as far as it regards the grammatical structure of the words, I entirely agree. The translation, "He maketh the winds his messengers, flaming fire his ministers," would never have been suggested by a simple consideration of the Hebrew text. It is not what the psalmist says, but what some commentators think he must have meant, because they imagine he could not be speaking of those beings who are usually termed angels. Thus Walford : "There is no reason to think that angels are here meant, because the psalmist is speaking of those material agents whom God employs to perform his will." I venture, however, (though it is with diffidence I differ from so accurate a scholar,) to assert that there is sufficient reason to think that the psalmist is speaking of angels, and of the creation of angels; and that it was quite consistent with his design to do so. It is true, that, as Storr and Flatt have asserted, "the psalm contains a description of the providence of God in special relation to this earth." But what could be better suited to his design, than to commence with a reference to the creation of the earth, and of the universe in general? What could be more calculated to impress the mind with the greatness and glory of God? Creation was the introduction to providence. How natural, then, to make a reference to the former, an introduction to a delineation of the latter, especially when the psalmist was about to dwell on the effects of the laws which God established when "in the beginning he made the heavens and the earth." Accordingly, this he does in the second and following verses. There is an allusion to the creation of light, and to its being diffused all abroad as a kind of covering to the heavens, the habitation and throne of God; to the stretching out of the firmament, and to its "dividing the waters from the waters," and to the formation of the clouds and winds, as well as to their being employed as the instruments of accomplishing his pleasure; and then to the creation and nature of the angels; then, to laying the foundation of the earth, and to various operations which were connected with moulding it into a suitable habitation for men; after which he proceeds to point out the continued operation, in the dispensations of providence and as instruments in the hand of God, of the laws which had been established, and of the agents which had been created. What could better illustrate the greatness and glory of God than the creation of angels, his most glorious agents and messengers, and rendering them spirits and flames of fire, and thus representing their nature and powers by language borrowed from wind, or air, and fire—the most subtile and powerful, and, according to our ideas, spiritual substances with which we are acquainted; especially when he employs the very same imagery to assist us, in forming some conceptions of his own spirituality, and power, and glory? "God is a *Spirit*"—Πνεῦμα ὁ Θεός· the Greek word, it is well known, exactly corresponds to the Hebrew רוּחַ, the plural of which is employed in the passage under consideration. "Our God is a consuming fire;" and fire was one of the indications of the Divine presence, when God appeared to the patriarchs, Exod. iii. How natural, then, I repeat it, and how accordant with what the Scriptures teach us of the nature and powers of these celestial beings, called angels, or, by way of eminence, messengers, and how consistent with the design of the psalmist to refer to the creation of angels, and to represent them as being made spirits and flaming fire, and therefore as amongst the most glorious of the works of God! I can see no occasion for rendering the passage as Storr does, "He employs his angels like winds, and his ministers like flames of fire." Indeed, this is not so much a translation as a paraphrase. There is no particle of comparison in the original. It is not what the psalmist says, but what some, influenced by their own theories, and their views of the connexion, think he must have meant; but the grammar and the construction of the Hebrew language are against them. Add to this, that the Septuagint renders the passage exactly as it is given in our version, Ὁ ποιῶν τοὺς ἀγγέλους αὐτοῦ πνεύματα, καὶ τοὺς λειτουργοὺς αὐτοῦ πῦρ φλέγον. And the inspired author of the Epistle to the Hebrews adopts, and therefore sanctions their translation, and that, when, incontrovertibly, he is speaking of the nature and dignity of angels, in order to show that, spiritual, great, and glorious as they are, they are still inferior to the Son of God. Most certainly he unequivocally asserts, that the meaning of that portion of the Old Testament which he quotes, is, that God has made his angelic ministers and messengers, spirits. Those who disbelieve the plenary inspiration of the sacred writers, and maintain that, even when writing in the name of their Lord and Master to the churches, and furnishing those records which were to be preserved for the instruction and guidance of the disciples of Christ in all ages, they were fallible, and liable to misquote and misapply passages from the Old Testament, may, in consistency with their hypothesis, maintain that the meaning of the psalmist is, "He maketh winds his messengers, and flaming fire his ministers;" but I cannot see how those who contend for the infallibility of the penmen of the New Testament, when writing to the churches in the name of God, can do so. I must think that it is unspeakably dishonourable to an inspired apostle to insinuate that, in order to show who and what angels are, he should quote and apply to them a passage from the Scriptures of the Jews, which had no relation to them, and which, therefore, could prove or illustrate nothing respecting them; nor will it be of any avail to say that the apostle quotes from the Septuagint, a translation of the Old Testament which was commonly used amongst the Jews. If that translation was erroneous, if it misrepresented the mind of the Spirit as originally communicated to the psalmist, can we suppose it would have been quoted by an inspired writer to prove or illustrate an important doctrine? Surely not. I must own that, were I to think that the translation which I am controverting is correct, I should be disposed to adopt the Socinian hypothesis, and maintain that the writers of the New Testament might err, even in their doctrinal sentiments, and in their views of the meaning of the Old Testament Scriptures. I can see no alternative. It is no valid objection to what has been advanced, that the word רוּחוֹת is in the plural in Psalm civ. 4 ; because it is used in this form when undoubtedly applied to spirits. Prov. xvi. 2: "The Lord trieth רוּחוֹת the spirits;" Zech. vi. 5: These are the four spirits (רוּחוֹת) of the heavens, which go out from standing before the Lord of the whole earth." See also Numb. xvi. 22, xxvii. 16. The importance of the subject, and of the principle connected with it, must be my apology for dwelling so long on this passage. Even if we were to adopt Storr and Flatt's interpretation, the passage would convey the idea, that angels are far superior to men in activity and power, and can move with inconceivable force and rapidity from place to place.

D. Page 93.

JONATHAN EDWARDS supposes that "Satan, before his fall, was the chief of all the angels, of the greatest natural capacity, strength, and wisdom, and the brightest of all the stars of heaven. That the king of Tyrus was but a type of Satan, Ezekiel xxviii. 12—19. Nay, that before his fall, he was the Messiah or Christ, as he was the anointed; so that, in this respect, Jesus Christ is exalted into his place in heaven; and that Lucifer, or Satan, while a holy angel, and having the excellency of all those glorious things that were about him all summed up in him, was a type of Christ." And that as he was the highest of all God's creatures, so he was the top and crown of the whole creation; he was the brightest part of the heaven of heavens, that brightest part of the whole creation. "He was the archangel, the prince of the angels, and all did obeisance unto him." "And that he had, as God's chief servant, and the grand minister of his providence, and the top of the creation, in some respect committed to him, power, principality, and dominion over the whole creation, and all the kingdoms of providence. But when it was revealed to him that, high and glorious as he was, he was to be a ministering spirit to the race of mankind which he had seen newly created, which appeared so feeble, mean, and despicable—and that he should be subject unto one of that race who was afterwards to be born; this occasioned his fall." And he thinks that, in his fallen state, "he is so much superior to the rest, that he maintains a dominion over them, and is able to govern and manage them; that they durst not raise rebellion against him; all the rest of the devils are his servants, his wretched slaves; they are spoken of as his possession, 'The devil and his angels.'"—Works, vol. ii. p. 608. Much of this, I must think, with all due respect for the piety and intellect of Edwards, is purely gratuitous assertion; much more of it is built on a very slender foundation. Still, it is evident from the Scriptures, that there is one of these spirits vastly superior to any of the others: that he rules over them, and employs them as his agents in executing his plans.

E. Page 95.

EDWARDS, in the passage which has been quoted, supposes that the first sin of Satan was refusing to act the part of a ministering spirit to man, a creature which had been recently brought into existence, and far inferior to himself; and, especially, his refusing to consent to do homage to one of his race, who was afterwards to be born, viz., the Lord Jesus Christ. There are, however, several things taken for granted here, which should have been proved; such as, that Satan did not rebel till man was created; that anything was revealed to him respecting Jesus Christ, or the plan of human redemption. We have no evidence that this was the case; and he might, for anything that we know, have sinned ages before the creation of our world. But, even if the conjecture of Edwards is correct, still the essence of his sin was towering ambition.

F. Page 163.

"THE narrator of the following story, Peter Walker, though an enthusiast, was a man of credit, and does not even affect to have seen the wonders, the reality of which he unscrupulously adopts on the testimony of others, to whose eyes he trusted rather than to his own. The conversion of the sceptical gentleman of whom he speaks is highly illustrative of popular credulity, carried away into enthusiasm, or into imposture, by the evidence of those around, and at once shows the imperfection of such a general testimony, and the ease with which it is procured, since the general excitement of the moment impels even the more cold-blooded and judicious persons present to catch up the ideas, and echo the exclamations of the majority, who from the first had considered the heavenly phenomenon as a supernatural weapon-schaw, held for the purpose of a sign and warning of civil wars to come.

"'In the year 1686, in the month of June,' says the honest chronicler, 'many yet alive can witness, that about the Crossford Boat, two miles beneath Lanark, especially at the Mains on the water of Clyde, many people gathered together for several afternoons, where there were showers of bonnets, hats, guns, and swords, which covered the trees and the ground; companies of men in arms marching in order upon the river side; companies meeting companies, going all through each other, and then all falling to the ground and disappearing; other companies immediately appeared, marching the same way. I went three afternoons together, and as I observed there were two-thirds of the people who were together saw, and a third that saw not, and *though I could see nothing*, there was such a fright and trembling on those who did see, that was discernible to all from those that saw not. There was a gentleman standing next to me, who spoke as too many other gentlemen speak, who said, 'A pack of damned witches and warlocks who have the second sight! the devil ha't do I see!' and immediately there was a discernible change in his countenance. With as much fear and trembling as any woman I saw there, he called out, 'All you that do not see, say nothing; for I persuade you it is the matter of fact, and discernible to all that is not stone blind!' And those who did see, told what works (i.e. locks) the guns had, and their length and wideness, and what handles the swords had, whether small or three-barred, or Highland guards, and the closing knots of the bonnets, black or blue; and those who did see them there, whenever they went abroad, saw a bonnet and a sword drop in the way.'

"This singular phenomenon, in which a multitude believed, though only two-thirds saw what must, if real, have been equally obvious to all, may be compared with the exploit of a humourist, who placed himself in an attitude of astonishment with his eyes riveted on the well-known bronze lion that graces the front of Northumberland House in the Strand, and, having attracted the attention of those who looked at him, by muttering, 'By heaven it wags—it wags again!' contrived, in a few minutes, to blockade the whole street with an immense crowd, some conceiving that they had absolutely seen the lion of Percy wag his tail; others expecting to witness the same phenomenon."—Scott's Demonology, pp. 13—15.

G. Page 170.

It may be expected, that some notice will be taken of the Jewish exorcists, of Simon Magus, and of the Philippian damsel, who was possessed with the spirit of divination. The first and the last of these will come, more naturally, under the case of demoniacs. And with regard to Simon Magus, all that it is necessary to notice, after what has been advanced, is, that the words ἐξιστῶν and ἐξεστακέναι, which are translated bewitched, Acts viii. 9. 11, merely mean to fascinate, or, more properly, to astonish greatly. Now, in a figurative sense, it might be said that he bewitched them, that is, by his pretences and his arts, he fascinated or charmed them, just as we sometimes say of beautiful scenery, it is quite charming, or of persons, that their manners are quite fascinating or enchanting. But there is reason to think that, as our translators were believers in witchcraft, and as the pedantic and bigoted monarch, under whose auspices, far from being of a favourable nature, the translation was made, wrote a book on that art, they used the word in the ordinary, literal sense, and perhaps it has been very generally so understood. The passage, however, ought to be rendered, "There was a certain man called Simon, who beforetime, in the same city, practised *magic* and *greatly astonished* the people of Samaria. And to him they had regard, because of long time he had greatly astonished them by his magic arts." It is quite unnecessary to prove to any Greek scholar, that this is a correct rendering of the original words, and that they never signify to bewitch according to the ideas of the believers in witchcraft. In Matt. xii. 23, we read, "All the people were amazed at his doctrine." Mark ii. 12, we are informed, that when Jesus Christ had cured the paralytic, "they were all amazed, and glorified God." Mark v. 32, when the Saviour raised the damsel to life, those who saw it, "were astonished with a great astonishment." Many other passages might be quoted, but it is unnecessary. In all those passages the same verb is used which in the case of Simon Magus is rendered "bewitch;" and what should we have thought, or what sense would there have been conveyed, if in the texts just quoted we had read, "The people were bewitched at his doctrine;" "They were all bewitched, and glorified God;" "They were bewitched with a great witchery." So far, then, the case of Simon Magus gives no countenance whatever to the modern notions respecting witchcraft. He is, indeed, said to have used sorcery, (μαγεύων.) But it ought to have been rendered "used" or "practised magic." The magicians, it is well known, were a sect of Eastern philosophers, famous for their wisdom and learning. To them those wise men who were led by a remarkable star to Bethleham, to pay their homage to the infant Saviour, belong (and are we not warranted, from this narration, to hope that there may have been other wise and good men belonging to this sect in all ages before the birth of Christ? What right have we to suppose that these were the only ones that ever existed?) So famous was this race of philosophers, that a learned man and a magian became equivalent terms. As might have been expected, the consequence of the fame they justly acquired was, that a multitude of pretenders to science, and empirics who deceived the vulgar by their arts, professed to belong to this class of philosophers. This brought discredit on their name, and the term magician was frequently taken in an unfavourable acceptation. In the bad sense in which it was understood, a magician may be defined, one who pretended to supernatural powers, and who supported his credit by an acquaintance with some facts in natural philosophy, not generally known, and by juggling tricks. From what the sacred historian then says of him, Simon may be viewed as one who pretended to supernatural power, and who gained credit, because, by an acquaintance with the secret powers of nature, he could produce effects that astonished the illiterate, or, because by his dexterity as a juggler, he imposed upon their simplicity. This is the utmost that can be deduced from what Luke says respecting him, and in this there appears no such compact with Satan, as is understood to take place in witchcraft."*

H. Page 177.

I SPEAK generally : I know some exceptions to this statement may be produced. For instance, during the witchcraft mania in New England, some respectable persons were accused and executed; a Captain Aldin was committed, but made his escape after he had been in prison fifteen months, so that he was never brought to trial. Mr. Burroughs, a minister of the Gospel, was put to death, on a charge of witchcraft: but he died protesting his innocence, and refuting the charges which had been brought against him, which he did in so solemn and pathetic a manner, as to draw tears from many of the

* Paterson on Witchcraft, p. 100.

spectators. Several of those who were executed during that melancholy period seem to have been persons of respectable characters in every sense of the word. A Mr. Philip English and his wife fled the country, rather than expose themselves, though conscious of their innocence, to the danger of a trial. They left behind them an estate worth fifteen hundred pounds, which was confiscated, and only about three hundred pounds of it was restored to them, when they found it safe to return home. But even in this case the accusers commenced with a poor Indian maid, who probably was a believer in witchcraft, as her countrymen generally were, and might talk about it to the children of Mr. Parris, a minister of Salem, in whose house she lived, and boast to them of her skill in spells and charms; and this would be sufficient to inflame their imaginations, stored as their memories doubtless were with stories respecting witches and ghosts, and cause them to suppose that they saw and heard ten thousand things which never existed. All, who, in the period of childhood and youth, have, unhappily for themselves, been accustomed to hear such accounts from their parents or others, and have been believers in even their possibility, and been terrified by them, can recollect the state of their minds and feelings on some occasions, and how easily, if their nerves had not been pretty strong, they might have believed that they saw spectres, and felt strange effects produced on their bodies. This maid servant, then, was first accused by those children, whom probably she had prepared for such a work, and presently others thought themselves bewitched, and charged different persons with being accomplices of Satan, in causing their sufferings. Even a child of four or five years old was accused and apprehended as a witch. The accusers said this child bit them, and they would show the marks of small teeth upon their arms. As many as the child cast its eye upon would complain that they were in torments; and even a dog was said to bewitch some, and cause them to fall into fits, when it looked upon them, and it was, in consequence, put to death! But at last, after a storm of sixteen months, during which, nineteen persons having been hung, and one pressed to death, and eight more condemned, and above fifty having confessed themselves witches, of whom not one was executed—above one hundred and fifty having been put in prison, and above two hundred more executed, the accusers, who commenced with an Indian slave, having become sufficiently bold to accuse of witchcraft the more respectable people amongst them, and even the justices that had prosecuted others—it was thought full time to put a stop to those practices, and accordingly soon after (April, 1693) all the accused were set at liberty, and those who had fled for their lives returned home; and it was found in this case, as in others, that when men ceased to believe in witchcraft, and to prosecute for its supposed crimes, it soon ceased to exist.

I. Page 177.

A REMARKABLE case of this kind is related in the Encyclopædia Britannica.* "Gassendi, the philosopher, found a number of people assembled together, to put a man to death for having intercourse with the devil; a crime which the poor wretch readily acknowledged. Gassendi begged of the people that they would permit him to examine the wizard before putting him to death. They did so, and Gassendi, upon examination, found that the man firmly believed himself guilty of this impossible crime. He even offered to Gassendi to introduce him to the devil. The philosopher agreed; and when midnight came the man gave him a pill, which he said it was necessary to swallow before setting off. Gassendi took the pill, but gave it to his dog. The man having swallowed his, fell into a profound sleep, during which he seemed much agitated by dreams. The dog was affected in a similar manner. When the man awoke, he congratulated Gassendi on the favourable reception he had met with from his sable highness. It was with difficulty Gassendi convinced him that the whole was a dream, the effect of soporific medicine, and that he had never stirred from one spot during the whole night."

K. Page 201.

IT has been shown only too clearly, by those who have most carefully studied this subject, that the Fathers are not entitled to the praise of even sincerity and honesty, much less of accurate discrimination, and careful sifting of evidence, in their attempts to defend the cause of religion. There appears to be too much truth in the following charges of Farmer against them. "Indeed, the Fathers so often speak from those motives" (of policy) "alone, as all must allow, that it is sometimes difficult to know when they speak according to their own inward persuasion. St. Jerome gives the following very just account of them: 'Quia interdum coguntur loqui, non quod sentiunt, sed quod necesse est, dicunt adversus ea quæ dicunt Gentiles.' Whenever they have an end to serve, no caution can be too great, in following them."† I may well add with him, "In the

* Article Spectre.   † Farmer on Demoniacs, p. 53.

case before us, they had many ends to serve." The same Jerome, speaking in another place of the different manner which writers found themselves obliged to use, in their controversial and in their dogmatical writings, intimates, that "in controversy, whose end was victory rather than truth, it was allowable to use every artifice which would best serve to conquer an adversary. In proof of which, Origen, says he, Methodius, Eusebius, Apollinaris, have written many thousands of lines against Celsus and Porphyry; consider with what arguments and what slippery problems they baffle what was contrived against them by the spirit of the devil; and because they are sometimes forced to speak, they say not what they think, but what is necessary against those who are called Gentiles. I do not mention the Latin writers, Tertullian, Cyprian, Minutius, Victorinus, &c., lest I be thought not so much to be defending myself as accusing others."* Those who are best acquainted with the writings and character of the Fathers, will be most disposed to think, that I have, in various parts of these Lectures, attached too much, rather than too little importance to their testimony respecting oracles, demoniacs, and miraculous gifts. Middleton and others have proved to a demonstration, that no true miracles were ever wrought after the time of the apostles, and that all those to which the Fathers attached so much importance are amongst those "signs, and lying wonders, and deceivableness of unrighteousness," by which the man of sin, coming after the working of Satan, was to be characterised. If not, where are those lying wonders to be found? for those miracles were intimately connected with the corruption of the doctrine, discipline, and practice of the church, and, therefore, with the rise of the man of sin, and they are "part and parcel" of the system of popish miracles, as they are performed to the present day. And there cannot be a doubt, that if Puseyism, with its pestilent heresies, destroying the very spirit of the Gospel, should make a little more progress, it will soon have its lying miracles, to subserve the schemes of the crafty, and excite the astonishment of the ignorant and superstitious. Thus it will, in two ways, most effectually answer the ends of Satan: it will counteract and neutralise, in the case of those who embrace it, the influence of the religion of Jesus Christ, and expose it to the sneers of infidels and of the profane, and furnish them with pretexts for altogether rejecting the claims of the Bible.

* Middleton's Free Inquiry, p. 138.

L. Page 203.

It does not come within the plan of these Lectures to give a history of oracles. A brief view of some of the chief of them, abridged from Rollin, must suffice.

The oracle of Dodona, a city of the Molossians, was one of the most celebrated. There Jupiter was supposed to give answers, either by vocal oaks, or doves, or by resounding basons of brass, or by the mouths of priests and priestesses.

The oracle of Trophonius, in Bœotia, was also in great repute. Those who consulted it were required, before they could obtain answers, to pass through a process which we may afterwards have occasion to describe, quite sufficient to shake the strongest nerves, and to disturb and confound the soundest reason, and to render any man the dupe of the priest by whom it was managed.

Another ancient and highly esteemed oracle was that of the Branchidæ, in the neighbourhood of Miletus. It had its name from Branchus, the supposed son of Apollo. Its temple was plundered and burnt by Xerxes, in his return from Greece, but he established the priests belonging to it in a remote part of Asia, to secure them from the vengeance of the Greeks. They were afterwards re-established at Miletus, where a temple was built that exceeded in riches and magnificence all the other temples of Greece.

There was an oracle of Apollo at Claros, a town of Ionia, in Asia Minor, where the answers were given by a man, and not by a woman, as at Delphos. This man, though unlearned, and indeed ignorant, required to know only the names and number of those who came to consult him. When he had obtained these, he returned into a cave, and having drunk of the water of a certain spring within it, he delivered answers in verse to those who came to consult him, though he was not acquainted with the laws of metrical composition. He was said to have foretold to Germanicus his sudden death, though in dark and ambiguous terms, according to the custom of oracles.

M. Page 221.

The following story taken from Plutarch, is inserted by Eusebius, in his "De Præparatione Evangelicâ," and he, apparently at least, thinks it worthy of credit, and Balbus himself does not deny that Eusebius believed it, though it was not the only ground of his faith in regard to oracles.

"There was a certain pilot of the name of Thamus, whose vessel was entirely becalmed one evening between the islands of Cephalonia and Corfu. All who were in the ship were perfectly awake, indeed the greater part of them were spending the evening in drinking together, when very suddenly they heard a voice which came from the island, and called Thamus by name. He did not regard it the first and second time, but at the third he answered. The voice commanded him, when he should have arrived at a certain place, to proclaim aloud that the great Pan was dead. All who were in the ship, whether sailors or passengers, were immediately seized with fear and terror; and the question was, whether the master of the ship should obey the voice. Thamus concluded that if, when he arrived at the specified place, he should have a favourable wind, he would proceed without taking any notice of what had happened, but that if he should be arrested by a calm, he would make the proclamation, as he had been ordered by the mysterious voice. He was surprised to find that no sooner had he reached the place mentioned by the voice than the wind ceased, and a dead calm ensued ; and consequently he cried aloud with his whole strength, 'The great Pan is dead.' No sooner had he uttered these words, than all who were in the ship heard groans and lamentations from every quarter, as of a great number of persons who were surprised and distressed by the news. All who were in the vessel were witnesses of the adventure. The report of it soon reached Rome, and the emperor Tiberius having wished to see Thamus himself, assembled a number of those who were skilled in the pagan theology, to learn from them who this great Pan was. And it was concluded amongst them that he was the son of Mercury and Penelope." This is one of the stories that we must believe if we would attach much importance to the testimonies of the Fathers respecting the cessation of the oracles. Another follows, which was taken by Eusebius from Porphyry, one of the most determined opponents that Christianity ever had. "The priestess is no longer able to utter her voice; she has been long since condemned to silence. Present always to Apollo the sacrifices which are worthy of a God." And thus the heathen oracles were believed to announce the fact, that they were silenced by the birth of Jesus Christ. Augustine, however, owns that Porphyry may have forged these oracles to deceive the Christians, and thus involve them in disgrace.

N. Page 309.

It deserves consideration, whether Satan is not called "the prince of the power of the air" for the same reason that birds are called "the fowls of the air," because they pass through it from place to place. I cannot admit the theory of spirits having no relation to place or to material objects. If the former and the latter are both realities, both substances, and if Satan is engaged in going to and fro on the earth, they must surely have some relation to each other. Satan, then, is called the prince of that infernal power, or army, which transports itself from place to place with the greatest celerity; not by moving on the earth, but by passing through the air. The fowls of the air are so denominated, not because they inhabit it properly speaking, any more than land animals do, or have power over it, but because it is the medium through which they move from one place to another. And this power, taking the words ἐξουσίας and πνεύματος as nouns of multitude, is "the spirit that worketh in the children of disobedience," the spirit that influences them and tempts them to sin. They "are entangled in the snare of the devil," and "led captive by him at his will."

O. Page 332.

I WOULD just observe here, that while the volume to which I have referred discovers great piety, and learning, and acquaintance with the human heart, and may be read with much advantage by those who know how to discriminate, it can by no means be recommended as containing a philosophical, accurate, scriptural view of the important subject of Satanic temptation. Gilpin's plan is, after ascribing to the devil all possible bad and depraved qualities, (and in this he may be allowed to be correct,) to represent him as the direct author, by his own influence, by his sophistical reasoning, and crafty devices, of all the errors that have ever been invented or embraced, and all the crimes that have ever been committed in the world, and therefore, of all the wicked inventions which men have ever found out; while it is certain that their own depraved ingenuity and corrupt passions, and various circumstances, would have led them, in many cases, to act in the specified way, even if there had been no fallen spirits in existence. It is comparatively easy to write a volume in this way. But the plan of ascribing every temptation, and error, and crime to Satan, and thus of *practically*, though not *theoretically*, representing him—at least through the instrumentality of his agent—as omnipresent, is not calculated either to make men sensible of their own guilt, or to enable them to form correct views of their danger, or of the real power of their infernal enemies.

INDEX.

Abaddon, a title of the devil, 104.
Adversary of David, Satan was, 69, 70.
Ahab and his lying prophet, 72.
Angels, a flame of fire, 351, 353.
Angels, good, 86 ; their power, 87, 88.
Angels that sinned, 17, 27; fallen, 82 ; their fall, 97, 98.
Antichristianity of Rome, from Satan, 322.
Apollo, oracle of, at Delphos, 203.
Balaam, a magician, 156, 159.
Baptismal regeneration, a delusion of Satan, 323.
Baxter, a believer in witchcraft, 131, 132; his testimony, 173, 175.
Baxter's World of Spirits, 134.
Beelzebub, the idol of Ekron, 53 ; chief of evil spirits, 54 ; heathen oracle of, 207 ; worshipped by the Phœnicians, 251, 253.
Blasphemous thoughts suggested by evil spirits, 340, 341.
Brown, Sir T., on vulgar errors, 220.
Bunyan's temptations, 340, 341.
Campbell, Dr., on pious frauds, 225.
Christ's miraculous cures, and dispossessing of devils, 46, 47 ; rebuke to the devil, 310, 311 ; victory over the world, 312.
Christ's temptations, five theories of it, 279 ; examination of them, 280, 281 ; theory of Hugh Farmer examined, 282, 292 ; conflicts during the forty days, 298, 300.
Chrysostom on hell torments, 349.
Credulity and infidelity dangerous, 2, 3.
Crœsus, his proposition to the oracle at Delphos, 215, 216.
Danger from the temptation of Satan, 344, 345.
David by Satan and evil spirits, 55, 67, 68.
Delphos, oracle of Apollo at, 203.
Demoniacs, their condition, 232, 233 ; real possessions, 234, 236.
Demons of the heathen, 5 ; celestial beings, 239.
Devils or demons, of the heathen, 237 ; natural gods, good and evil, 241 ; possession of men by, 247, 254 ; a legion enter into one, and into the swine, 260, 263.
Devil, the, tempts Christ, 296, 306 ; shows him all the kingdoms of the world, 307, 309.
Devil, what the name imports, 28, 31 ; the first tempter, 34 ; his anticipated punishment, 42, 43 ; the chief of evil spirits, 91, 104.
Diabolus, or devil, its signification, 51, 55 ; chief of the evil spirits, 96 ; "tempts, God proves," 316.

Divination, 137, 138.
Diviner, Balaam, a, a false prophet, 139.
Edwards, President, on the fall of Satan, 354.
Egyptian magicians, their impositions, 145, 156.
Endor, the witch of, 160, 161; did she raise up Samuel? 162, 167.
Eusebius believed the oracles to be the work of impostors, 219.
Evans, John, the case of, 272, 275.
Evil spirits,—their existence, 1; taught throughout the scriptures, 4, 5; probable from analogy, 6, 7; from reason and experience, 9; they are tempters, 10; dreaded, 11; deniers of the doctrine of, 12, 13; opinions of Russell Scott, 14, 16; criticisms of their denial of the doctrine, 17, 20, 36; Satan, the chief, 53, 57; tempt men, 70, 71; their power, 93, 95; their depravity and malignity, 100.
Existences, material and rational, 84, 85.
Fallen angels, 90.
Fall of man, the history of the, 62, 64.
Farmer, Hugh, on miracles, 148; on the magicians of Egypt, 149; on demoniacs, 232, 237; on possessions by devils, answered, 260, 268; his theory of Christ's temptations, examined, 281,296.
Fathers, the, their testimony regarding the heathen oracles, 222, 223; its value, 224, 226.
Frauds and impostures at Delphos, 213.
Gassendi, a story by, 360.
Gesenius, on the word Satan, 55.
Gilpin's Demonologia, 317; fascinations of Satan, 329, 331; untenable, 332.
Gloucester, the Duchess of, accused of witchcraft, 177.

God, the, of this world, Satan, 318.
Good, Dr. J. M., on the Book of Job, 73.
Gregory, Thaumaturgus, on the heathen gods, 223.
Hall, Robert, on temptation by Satan, 334, 335.
Heathen gods, 240, 241.
Heathen oracles, 202; their character, 204, 205; how delivered, 209; temples and altars the delusions of Satan, 320, 321.
Heathen priests impostors and liars, 206.
Heaton, Mr., his case of John Evans, 272, 275.
Heber, Bishop, on evil spirits, 66.
Herodotus, Hesiod, and Xenophon, on Demons, 238.
Hopkins, the witch-finder, an impostor, 180, 186.
Imagination, the power of the, in enthusiasts, 356.
Irenæus, on the continuance of miraculous gifts, 229.
Job, the tempter of, 72, 75; did Satan produce the fire to destroy his property? 119, 129.
Josephus believed the existence of evil angels, 243.
Judas, tempted by Satan, 76, 77.
Jupiter and Apollo, gods of the Greeks and Romans, 240.
Justin Martyr, his judgment, 227.
King James on demonology, 129, 130.
Lactantius, on the silencing of the heathen oracles, 192, 227.
Luther, a believer in witchcraft,131.
Magician, Balaam, a, 156, 157.
Magicians, the Egyptians, 145; impostors, 146, 147; their tricks, 148, 151.
Mather's Wonders of the Invisible World, 134.
Mexicans, their human sacrifices, 315.
Middleton, Conyers, on the fall of Adam, 60; on miraculous gifts, 229; on miracles, 361.

INDEX.   367

Ministers of Satan, infidel writers are, 328.
Miracles, none after the apostles' time, 361; when they ceased, 229.
Moses, miracles of, in Egypt, 146, 154.
Mysteries of the heathen, 210, 211.
Mystery of iniquity by Satan, 322.
Notes in Appendix, 349, 364.
Oracles. *See* heathen oracles, and Sibylline oracles.
Oracles, new ones established, 216, 218; how silenced by Christ, 230; Rollin on, 362.
Pan said to be dead, 362.
Pinnacle of the temple, Christ tempted on, 304, 305.
Pious frauds, 225.
Plott, Dr., a story by, 217.
Plutarch, on the heathen oracles, 240.
Possessions, demoniacal, 242, 245; not miraculous, 247; real cases of, 249; cases examined, 256, 260; objections against by Farmer, examined, 261, 267.
Priestley, Dr., his rash statement, 255.
Puritans, the, believed in witchcraft, 139.
Pythian oracle, 203.
Reason and instinct, 350.
Robinson and his witch-accusers impostors, 182, 184.
Rollin, on the heathen oracles, 362.
Romish idolatry, 322, 324.
Romish Inquisitors, torturing the Waldenses, 174.
Samuel, the prophet, — was he raised up? 164, 166; Samuel was not raised, 168, 170.
Satan, his delusions, 44, 45; meaning of the name, 51, 53; who intended, 55, 57; the tempter of Eve, 60; and of Cain, 61, 62; of David, 66, 68; a human adversary, 69; the chief of fallen angels, 91, 92; the author of heathenish superstition and idolatry, 126, 127; permitted to afflict Job, 129, 276; aided by a legion, 336.
Satan taking Christ upon the temple, 303.
Scott, Russell, his criticisms regarding diseases cured by Christ, 16, 46, 47.
Scott's Demonology, 176, 177.
Serpent, the, an intelligent enemy, 60.
Serpent, the old, the devil, 319.
Shore, Jane, charged with witchcraft, 177.
Sibyls, their origin, 191, 192.
Sibylline oracles, the, 191; political forgeries, 192, 193; their falsehood and destruction, 194; character of the Sibyls, 195, 196; examined, 197, 198; proofs of their being forgeries, 199, 202.
Simon Magus and his sorcery, 357.
Sorcery and witchcraft, 128; charges of, 177.
Spirits. *See* evil spirits.
Spirits have power over matter, 106, 107; objections against, considered, 110, 111; their activity, 112, 113; have a locality, 114; knowledge of, 115.
Stories of witches, 174, 175.
Temptation by Satan, 278, 314; inhuman sacrifices by the Mexicans, 315; by many evil spirits, 333; suited to the various characters of men, 337, 339.
Tempter, the, Satan, 327.
Tertullian, on the falsehood of heathen oracles, 221.
Torture to compel confessions of witchcraft, 178, 180.
Trophonius, the cave of, 211.
Unitarian expositions of testimony regarding Satan, 60, 65.
Ventriloquism, 140, 141.
Walker, Peter, history, 355.
Wardlaw, Dr., on the power of Satan, 117, 120.
Watchfulness necessary to Christians, 346.

INDEX.

Watts, Dr., some opinions of regarding angels, 106, 114.
Wilderness of Judea, 282, 298.
Witchcraft and sorcery, 127, 128; believed by Luther, Bacon, Baxter, and Hale, 131, 132; not countenanced by the Scriptures, 135; its professors knaves, 136, 137.; disappearance of, 187, 189; persecution for, 358, 359.

Witches hanged in Suffolk and Essex, 173; theories of, 174, 181.
Witches impostors, deceivers, &c., 143.
Witch, its meaning, 135, 136.
Witchfinders, 180, 186.
Wizard, a diviner, 138, 139.

THE END

www.ingramcontent.com/pod-product-compliance
Lightning Source LLC
Chambersburg PA
CBHW020827160426
43192CB00007B/558